THEORIES OF MYTHOLOGY

ANCIENT CULTURES

These enjoyable, straightforward surveys of key themes in ancient culture are ideal for anyone new to the study of the ancient world. Each book reveals the excitement of discovering the diverse lifestyles, ideals, and beliefs of ancient peoples.

PUBLISHED

Theories of Mythology
Eric Csapo

IN PREPARATION

Greek Political Thought
Ryan Balot

Medicine in the Ancient World
Markham J. Geller

The Spartans
Nigel Kennell

Sport and Spectacle in the Ancient World
Donald G. Kyle

Ethnicity and Identity in the Ancient World
Kathryn Lomas

Roman Law and Society
Thomas McGinn

Economies of the Greek and Roman World
Jeremy Paterson

The City of Rome
John Patterson

Sexuality in Greek and Roman Culture
Marilyn B. Skinner

Food in the Ancient World
John M. Wilkins and Shaun Hill

THEORIES OF MYTHOLOGY

Eric Csapo

Blackwell
Publishing

BLACKWELL PUBLISHING
350 Main Street, Malden, MA 02148-5020, USA
9600 Garsington Road, Oxford OX4 2DQ, UK
550 Swanston Street, Carlton, Victoria 3053, Australia

First published 2005 by Blackwell Publishing Ltd

2   2005

Library of Congress Cataloging-in-Publication Data

Csapo, Eric.
Theories of mythology / Eric Csapo.
    p. cm. — (Ancient cultures)
Includes bibliographical references and index.
ISBN 0-631-23247-8 (alk. paper) — ISBN 0-631-23248-6 (pbk. : alk. paper)
1. Myth—History. 2. Mythology—History. I. Title. II. Series: Ancient cultures (Malden, Mass.)

BL304.C79 2005
201'.3–dc22

                                                                2004003051

ISBN-13: 978-0-631-23247-6 (alk. paper) — ISBN-13: 978-0-631-23248-3 (pbk. : alk. paper)

A catalogue record for this title is available from the British Library.

Set in 10/12.5pt Rotation
by Graphicraft Ltd, Hong Kong
Printed and bound in the United Kingdom
by TJ International, Padstow, Cornwall

The publisher's policy is to use permanent paper from mills that operate a sustainable forestry policy, and which has been manufactured from pulp processed using acid-free and elementary chlorine-free practices. Furthermore, the publisher ensures that the text paper and cover board used have met acceptable environmental accreditation standards.

For further information on
Blackwell Publishing, visit our website:
www.blackwellpublishing.com

For my mother and father,

Marg and Steven Csapo

Contents

Figures

Preface

This book presents the major schools of mythological interpretation: their theories, their methods, their insights, and their shortcomings. Each school of thought is represented by one or two key or founding figures. Their theories are explained, placed in their social and historical contexts, and then criticized. Their methods of analysis are described, exemplified, and problematized. This is an introduction: I require nothing of the reader but an inquiring mind. Sample analyses are all taken from Greek myth or stories which are likely to be familiar to most readers, but, where necessary, the myths are told with the analyses. The majority of the sample analyses come from the theorists themselves. But I have not hesitated to add several of my own, wherever I thought I could exemplify a method with greater simplicity or clarity, or wherever I had to deal with a theorist, such as Lévi-Strauss, who worked mainly with obscure mythic material, or a theorist, such as Freud, who avoided extended analysis of myth altogether. The final chapter, for reasons which will be explained, deals not with a specific theorist, but with widespread contemporary theoretical trends. It exemplifies the method of ideological analysis which will already have an air of familiarity, having already been applied, broadly, in the criticism of the earlier theories of mythology themselves. The discovery of the shortcomings of this method I leave to the readers, the reviewers, and the future critical discourse on myth.

In pursuing so ambitious a project, I have necessarily been selective. The list of theorists who do not appear in this book is very long. Famous and important names, like Jung, receive only passing mention, and others, like Dumézil or Girard, none at all. Although this book iś, I believe, in its way, the most comprehensive general introduction to theories of myth, it is far from complete. This is partly due to reasons of practicality and cost, but has also much to do with design. I have used important figures largely to exemplify the orientation and tendencies of a whole school of thought at a given point in time. The detailed enumeration of variant opinions within a school seemed to me more likely to obscure the exposition of the general trends and to seem to most nonprofessionals as dull name-dropping. There are names and variants enough in the pages of this book, but they are mentioned mainly for the sake of illustrating a general principle. The professional reader will find much that could have been stated with more reservation, qualification, and a host of quasi-exceptions. I leave no footnotes and no regrets. The devil is too often lost in the detail. This is a book about large contours.

The most conspicuous difficulty with the selections I have made, particularly the focus on key and founding figures, is the impression it may leave that many of these approaches died when their shortcomings were discovered, or at least failed to evolve beyond them. This is true in the case of solar mythology, much less true in the case of psychoanalysis and structuralism, and certainly not true in the case of comparatism or ritualism. In most cases these schools evolved, when they did evolve, by absorbing and taking into account the criticism of the schools that followed them. Not everyone who practices the comparative method thinks like James Frazer, but comparatism is still a useful method insofar as it takes account of the criticisms that are and were leveled against him. The order of exposition, the links between the criticism of one theory and the presentation of the next, are designed to suggest a dialogue, or rather a dialectic process. Some familiarity with all of these theories is required in order to have a real understanding of any of them. Some appreciation of the relations between theories is necessary for any who will grasp the progress, if there has been any, in our understanding of myth.

Why study dead theories at all? With the exception of solar mythology there are no dead theories in this book, though there are a fair number of dead theorists. The history of the science of mythology (if we can call it that, and I will) does not resemble a revolving door. The theories we have examined were not simply canceled and replaced when their faults came to light. Most of the theories studied in this book live on in their own right. Moreover, they live on in one another. Each new theory reacted to and corrected the faults of the earlier theory. But it also incorporated a great deal of what it did not reject. By the same token, the adherents of earlier theories have reacted to and incorporated the insights and criticisms of later theories. It is partly this dialogue that has made possible the current fashion for theoretical eclecticism. Different approaches are better for producing different results, while the more fundamental incompatibilities have often been expunged.

Throughout the book I have emphasized the importance of the theorists' social and theoretical contexts. It will soon become obvious that I believe that there has been progress in the science of mythology, but that this progress has been stunted by the limited perspective and false accents created by the social ideologies of its practitioners, and also stimulated by the rational criticism of those who reacted to and exposed the limits and errors of their predecessors. The social background to theorists and theories is not just presented for the sake of human interest and local color: it is vitally important for understanding just why and how a theorist should take the peculiar and sometimes otherwise unintelligible perspectives that he does. Social background does not serve only as a negative factor in this history. Different backgrounds, different times, and different perspectives also enable other theorists to detect and demystify the mythopoeic activity of ideology, even if the rational criticism is only enabled by a different ideological perspective. I do not share the resignation of those who see nothing but one ideology replaced by another equally deleterious ideology. It is true that ideology is likely always to be present in any science, but so is rational discourse, and not in equal measure, but in inverse proportions to one another.

Translations from Greek and Latin are my own. For the Hittite texts of the succession myths I have supplemented Pritchard (1969: 120–5) with Penglase (1994) and West (1997: 278–9). For the sake of accuracy I have consulted the original texts for most theorists writing in French or German and (unless indicated otherwise) given my own translations directly from the original or standard edition (English translations are listed in the Bibliography and Further Reading). I have not burdened the page with the citation of English editions of these works: any who wish to examine wider contexts of these citations will find them easily enough, in most cases: the Bibliography gives details of the more important or more accessible English translations. In the case of Burkert's *Homo Necans* I refer generally to the standard English translation (1983), which has fuller referencing than the German original. My inability to read Russian has led to some difficulty in the case of Propp, and I have often had to sift through several translations, in English, French, German, and Italian, in order to eliminate some ambiguities and discrepancies which are frequent; I may not always have been successful.

The idea for this book arises from many years of teaching introductory courses in mythology and in theories of myth at the University of Toronto. I am most grateful to the many encouraging and enthusiastic students who taught me just how exciting and entertaining theories of myth could be. I owe thanks for information on Ukrainian folk customs to N. Kazansky, M. Mykytiuk, and B. Swystun. Thanks are also due to C. Capozzi, K. Lu, and D. Windt for directing my attention to helpful books. I am extremely grateful to Blackwell's editorial controller, Angela Cohen, the picture researcher Leanda Shrimpton, and the desk editor, Juanita Bullough, for their enduring patience, flexibility, and hard work, and I am most especially grateful to Blackwell's Classics editor, Al Bertrand, for his wisdom in seeing the value in this project and his constant support thereafter. To the Classics Faculty of Oxford University and the Fellows of New College I am most grateful for providing, during Trinity Term 2004, a stimulating atmosphere in which I engaged in the otherwise numbing task of proofreading and indexing: in particular I would like to thank Oliver Taplin, Robert Parker, Robin Lane Fox, and Peter Brown. The greatest debt of thanks I owe to Margaret Miller, Sebastiana Nervegna, and Ben Zaporozan, for reading, correcting, drawing, chasing down lost references to citations, and for giving encouragement when it was needed, which was often.

E.C.

1

Introducing "Myth"

Whenever someone discloses something, one may ask: What is this supposed to hide? From what does it divert our gaze? What prejudice is it meant to evoke? And further: How far does the subtlety of this distortion extend? And where does he go astray by it?

F. Nietzsche, Morgenröte, § 523

Definition is never the innocent first step in a process of empirical discovery that it is sometimes made to seem: it is rather always the final precipitate of an already elaborate theory. To begin with a definition is therefore in an important sense to begin at the end, and to urge acceptance of a position before presenting the arguments or the evidence. If I begin with a discussion of the problems of defining myth, it is to urge suspicion. In this chapter I look with particular care at a definition which has become standard and perhaps even represents a general common-sense consensus. I will show how it predisposes the reader to adopting a methodological perspective akin to that of comparatism, which will be studied in Chapter 2. In the end I will offer my own definition, which is no less loaded, and akin to the ideological perspective studied in Chapter 6. Since this book is about other people's theories, it is not at all necessary to accept this definition either. Awareness of my definition does, however, allow the reader to understand why this book is shaped in the way that it is. I argue, namely, that theories of myth themselves to a large degree constitute mythologies. But much depends on what we mean by "myth."

Let us begin with a couple of cautionary tales about definition. In a famous article reviewing various definitions of myth, Stith Thompson (1965) alludes to an East Indian folktale about three blind men. An elephant wandered down the road and stopped beside them. Sensing that some great beast had come into their midst, the blind men touched the elephant to discover its nature. The first blind man felt the trunk and said "It is like a water pipe." The second blind man felt the ear and said to the first "Clearly this beast is like a fan." The third felt the side of the animal and said "Idiots! You are both wrong. This beast is like a throne."

Among the many definitions of myth the most common weakness is selectivity. There are many myths in the world: privileging myths of a certain type as "real" myths will shape the material to fit many a predetermined theory. For example, Jane Harrison, who argued that myths are connected with rites, urged that "it would be convenient if the use of the word *myth* could be confined to such sequences, such stories as are involved in rites" (1963b: 331), and Joseph Fontenrose formulates a similar view (1959: 434): "It is undeniable that myths are closely attached to rituals. In fact, if a story has not been associated with cult or ritual, explicitly or implicitly, it is better not to call it myth, but legend or folktale." Such definitions tempt circularity. If the theory says that all myths are based on ritual, then the definition excludes from study everything that is not ritual. After a preliminary sorting, the mythologist is pleased to observe that what all his myths have in common is that they are based on ritual.

Second anecdote. There is an ancient story about Plato's school, which, like the later Greek philosophical schools, had a mania for defining things. Diogenes the Cynic attended one of the lectures at which Plato was applauded for defining "Man" as "an animal, biped and featherless." Diogenes left the room to return a little later, holding up a plucked chicken, announcing "Here is Plato's Man!" So Plato amended his definition, adding the words "having broad nails." If the first anecdote is a caution against saying too little, this is one against saying too much. Above all, one must beware of definitions that are mere compilations of empirical and often trivial distinctions (usually drawn, as in this case, to "pin down" a predetermined category concept). As with Plato's definition, every challenge and change in perspective will require further supplements. If Diogenes brought in a prairie dog the definition would have been expanded with "and not excessively hairy." But what if such empirical research is wrong in assuming that the objects are simply out there waiting to be collected and studied? Then such discriminations are not only trivial, they are arbitrary. At the very least, since myth is a human product, some account must be given of the attitudes and needs of the creators as well as the attitudes and needs of the observer.

It may appear that the safest solution to the problem of definition is to see how the term "myth" is actually used. But by whom? Ordinary usage would apply the term to a story that is considered false ("a purely fictitious narrative," according to the *Oxford English Dictionary*); but most experts will say that in the society for which the myth is a myth its quality as myth usually depends upon its being received as true ("myth is 'true' for those who use it," according to Leach 1982: 6). The quality of the object assumed by the observer is diametrically opposed to the quality assumed by the participant. From what has already been said, some attention will have to be paid to both of these responses.

Let us examine a classic and much-cited attempt by an anthropologist to come up with a definition of myth based on the conceptualization of myth by the mythmakers themselves. The study is by William Bascom (1965), and is based on the recorded observations of folklorists and anthropologists studying myth in nonliterate and traditional societies. From this data he concludes that myths are "[verbal] prose narratives which, in the society in which they are told, are considered to be truthful accounts of what happened in the remote past" (1965: 4). By prose narrative, Bascom meant a form of oral recitation of a tale. Myths are apparently not myths when they are written down, but only when they are told by word of mouth. Narrative also means that it has some form of a story, with a beginning, middle, and end, and some form of continuity of theme, character, or narrative purpose. Prose narratives also include legends and folktales (even jokes and anecdotes, which Bascom thinks subtypes of legends and folktales). Legends are defined as "prose narratives which, like myths, are regarded as true by the narrator and his audience, but they are set in a period considered less remote, when the world was much as it is today." In opposition to myths and legends, "folktales are prose narratives which are regarded as fiction." The main criteria for all three, then, is that they be prose and orally delivered.

	Myths	Legends	Folktales
Thought true	+	+	−
World like today	−	+	+

If thought true, then myth or legend. If thought untrue, then folktale. If true and referring to a remote time when the world was unlike it is today, then myth, but if true and referring to a less remote time when the world was more or less as it is today, then legend. This short definition is a good one, and we will make some use of it later, but I suspect it has some of the faults of the kind of partial vision which the tale of the blind men and the elephant cautions us against. Bascom himself feels this definition is too broad, and so gives a number of further more specific criteria which distinguish myth, legend, and folktale. These list a potentially unlimited series of empirical distinctions based on the observation of already predetermined categories – the sort of thing for which the anecdote about Diogenes and the chicken is a caution (Bascom 1965: 4–5):

Myths are the embodiment of dogma; they are usually sacred; and they are often associated with theology and ritual. Their main characters are not usually human beings, but they often have human attributes; they are animals, deities, or culture heroes, whose actions are set in an earlier world such as the sky or underworld. Myths account for the origin of the world, of mankind, of death, or for characteristics of birds, animals, geographical features, and the phenomena of nature. They may recount the activities of the deities, their love affairs, their family relationships, their friendships and enmities, their victories and defeats. They may purport to "explain" details of ceremonial paraphernalia or ritual, or why tabus must be observed. . . .

Legends are more often secular than sacred, and their principal characters are human. They tell of migrations, wars and victories, deeds of past heroes, chiefs, and kings, and the succession in ruling dynasties. In this they are often the counterpart in verbal tradition of written history, and they also include local tales of buried treasure, ghosts, fairies, and saints.

Folktales may be set in any time and any place, and in this sense they are almost timeless and placeless. . . . Fairies, ogres, and even deities may appear, but folktales usually recount the adventures of animal or human characters.

For brevity's sake I have edited the number of these empirical distinctions, but the style is clear.

How does Bascom arrive at these definitions? Let us take the true/false distinction which is the discriminator between myth and legend on the one hand and folktale on the other. For this Bascom points out that a very large number of cultures have the separate words "myth," "legend," and "folktale." For example, the Trobriand Islanders have *Liliu* (myths), *Libwogwo* (legends), and *Kukwanebu* (folktales). Yet even in cultures where there exist no explicit vocabulary distinctions, Bascom claims that implicit conceptual distinctions can be demonstrated by differences in the style and formal structure of the narratives. Some societies use conventional opening and closing formulae to distinguish folktales from myths, legends, and other forms of discourse. These verbal formulae may warn the listener that what is going to be said is not to be taken as truth. Ashanti narrators begin tales by saying "We do not really mean, we do not really mean . . ." and end with "This is my story, which I have related; if it be sweet, if it not be sweet; some you may take as true and the rest you may praise me for." In the same way a European folktale begins and ends with tags marking it out as fiction: "Once upon a time . . ." or "And they lived happily ever after" require the listener to receive the story as fiction.

Even extratextual associated behavior can show the distinction. The different tales may be told at different times of day. The Marshall and Trobriand Islanders, the Fulani, and the Yoruba all have taboos against telling folktales before dark, but serious stories (myths and legends) may be told at any time of day. Should they tell a folktale during the day, the Fulani believe that they risk the loss of a close relative, and the Marshalls that the narrator's and listeners' heads will swell up as "big as a house." The Yoruba only fear that telling a folktale during the day will cause the narrator to lose his way in the story. Even the time of year appropriate to the tales can mark the distinction. The Trobriand restrict the telling of folktales to the month of November, between the planting and fishing seasons; legends may be told at any time, but especially during the period of trading voyages; myths are normally told during the preparation for rituals performed at different times during the year. There are also other kinds of constraints upon the narrators and listeners which are said to mark the distinction between the categories of tale. In Hawaii no listener may pass in front of the teller of a myth. Among the Inuit a storyteller must recite myths verbatim after a canonical oral text, but is allowed to display virtuosity by introducing variations into a folktale. Families in the Trobriand Islands regard folktales as private property, and fathers teach them to their sons in the privacy of the bedroom after the rest of the family has retired, but myths and legends are public.

So what is wrong with Bascom's definition? It appears objective, based on the observation of the facts – and facts of reception: the concepts of the mythmakers and mythhearers themselves. But is it? If we consider the possibility that some of the data are distorted by the lens of the observer, by his intellectual milieu, his institutional allegiances, and his professional habits, we may be struck by a number of coincidences.

Bascom was a modern Western anthropologist of a comparatist persuasion with a professional interest in folklore. Anthropologists in the 1960s were almost exclusively interested in nonliterate and "traditional" societies. Surprisingly, or not, Bascom finds that myths are oral traditional tales. Conveniently, myths can only be found in those places where, as a professional anthropologist, Bascom is uniquely equipped to look for them. As a specialist in an ancient culture, I confess that I have serious difficulties with Bascom's insistence on orality and prose, since nearly all ancient cultures have transmitted their mythology primarily in written form, verse, and visual icons. Any definition of myth that excludes the contents of the *Iliad*, the Mesopotamian *Epic of Gilgamesh*, the Hittite *Song of Ullikummi*, or the Vedic scriptures of India to me seems unpersuasive. Notwithstanding minor discipline chauvinism, Bascom betrays his intellectual and cultural vantage point in fundamental ways.

Folklorists have habitually distinguished between myth, legend, and folktale since the time of the first collections of folklore by Jakob and Wilhelm Grimm, who began to record traditional tales in Germany, and simultaneously created the science of folklore, in the early nineteenth century. Yet it is noteworthy that neither English nor any other European language traditionally made this distinction before this time. The English term "folktale" (inspired by the Grimms' conception of *Märchen*) betrays the origin of the concept in German nationalism, with its lionization of the German *Volk*, as does the English term "folklore" (cf. folksong, folk-custom, etc.). Given the historical contingency and, indeed, the very short life span even in European tongues of this tripartite classification of oral traditional narrative genres, it would be remarkable to find that this system of classification is otherwise a human universal.

The comparatist in Bascom comes out in the style of the argument, but also the working assumptions that support that style. He introduces a proposition and backs it by listing illustrative examples from different cultural contexts. The more massive the lists and the more disparate the cultures the better, as if the argument could succeed by progressing phalanx upon phalanx and crushing the readers' resistance by the sheer weight and breadth of its examples; the diversity of the examples, as one hopscotches over history and the globe, predisposes the reader to believe that the propositions they illustrate must be universal or at least somehow normal. It is true that Bascom lists exceptions. In the matter of vocabulary distinctions, for example, he notes that the Ponapeans and Hawaiians of the Pacific, like the Dakota and Kiowa of North America, only distinguish "folktales" from "myth-legend." The Winnebago only distinguish two categories of narrative, both of which are true. Others, like the Wind River Shoshoni, have only one word for all narratives. The list of exceptions, too, is a stylistic feature of comparatist argument. It serves to give an impression of exhaustive thoroughness. Nearly always, however, the list of positive examples far exceeds the number of exceptions, and this is nearly always because the list of positive examples includes everything known to the writer and the list of exceptions includes only a few cases, selected from a potential list which could be at least as long as the first (he does not, for example, mention that Greek knows no distinction between myth, legend, and folktale). Rhetorically, exceptions are paraded, like freaks in a circus, to prove a general rule.

But one cannot begin an argument by listing all the words for myth and legend when one has set out to establish the equality of these concepts in the first place. In casting his net far and wide to produce a definition which will suit all cultures or at least all known myth-producing cultures, Bascom ends up tangled in his own cultural assumptions. In applying a wide variety of different criteria, an anthropologist may succeed in forcing the distinctions made by other cultures into familiar pigeonholes, but when one empties one of these pigeonholes and compares the contents one with another, the genre-concepts labeled "myth" differ radically from one another in shape and size. And even when you look at some of the specific criteria used, you begin to wonder whether the concepts anthropologists translate as "true" or "sacred" really mean the same thing to a Trobriand Islander, a Winnebago, and a nineteenth-century German. It is very unlikely that a mythmaker would share the modern Westerner's true/false distinction. There are cultures (e.g., the Winnebago, according to Bascom) that only know true narratives. Our own concept of false narrative depends on our concept of true account, and the opposition false/true narrative is shaped by such other oppositions as myth/science, legend/history, myth or legend/literature. Westerners invented the concepts of science, history, and literature partly to distinguish our own cultural thought and expression from that of mythmaking societies. How, then, could these distinctions be the same for us and them? Myth-producing societies are excluded from knowing these distinctions by the comparatist's own definition.

The problem of the equatability of concepts across cultures is one too rarely confronted by comparatists. In its classic formulation the method assumes that all myth-producing cultures are simple and primitive, closer to the common stock, as yet undifferentiated, and hence have a good deal in common. It is very possible, however, that all cultures, even the ones we regard as basic, have very little in common, so that in the end any definition of myth based on real consensus will be so dilute as to be uninformative, or will have to exclude some kinds of myth or the myths of some cultures in order to make more interesting statements.

Bascom's definition ends up telling us at least as much about Bascom as it does about myths. He is a comparatist and an empiricist and, as such, he displays an essentialist bias toward categorization. The essentialist assumes that categories exist in the mind because the objects placed in these categories all have a certain number of traits in common, and that the art of definition simply consists in detecting what all members of a given category share. But concept categories do not work this way; if they did, defining myth would hardly be a problem. As it is, "myth" does not lend itself to a clear definition of any sort and particularly not one based on form or content. But this claim introduces two problems which are best kept apart. One is the problem of understanding cultural categories. The other is the problem of using formal or content criteria for a definition of myth. Let us look at these separately in turn.

We could attempt to impose a rigid "scientific" definition upon "myth," listing a number of essential constitutive characteristics, such as "related to ritual" or "the main characters must be gods." Any story which did not meet these criteria could then be called "legend," "folktale," "anecdote," or whatever. But it is an arbitrary and Procrustean method of dealing with the problem. It is also out of line with much current thinking about the way verbal and conceptual categories work. A more helpful model, which has been urged for genre concepts in literary studies generally, is a looser sort of classification system which goes back to the so-called theory of family resemblances, first formulated by Ludwig Wittgenstein. As an illustration of the difficulty of linguistic definitions in general, Wittgenstein chose the concept of "games" (1958, §§ 65–77):

> What are games? These phenomena have no one thing in common which makes us use the same word for all – but they are *related* to one another in many different ways. . . . We see a complex network of similarities overlapping and criss-crossing. . . . I can think of no better expression to characterize these similarities than "family resemblances"; for the various resemblances between members of a family: build, features, colour of eyes, gait, temperament, etc., etc., overlap and criss-cross in the same way. And I shall say: "Games" form a family.

Certain activities are declared games by reason of their similarity with some other already existing member or members of the category "games." There is a certain element of the culturally arbitrary in placing new members into the category. Moreover, the category is defined by a set of dominant but ever-changing archetypes: for us video games, for our parents Monopoly, for ancient Greeks bashing quails on the head. We speak of something being a myth or legend because it reminds us in some way of stories that our culture has canonized as typical of that genre.

For this reason it is impossible to insist, for cultural products at least, if not for natural products, on essential criteria. It is in any case impossible to find universals in myths, though there is no reason why we might not find meaningful cross-cultural patterns, and even norms, in the classification of narrative genres. There is, moreover, no reason why genre distinctions should be conscious or universal in order to be useful or meaningful to us. Even if we are sure that the culture we study made very different distinctions between tale-types, our own classification of myth, legend, and folktale might be useful to us, so long as we are aware of the fact that the distinction is ours.

For all that, I think Bascom's study has positive value beyond demonstrating that the intellectual predispositions of the observer can become enshrined in an object of study by the constitutive act of definition. His observation of certain cross-cultural tendencies in the classification of narrative shows not *where* the boundaries of narrative genres are drawn, so much as *why* they are drawn, if they are drawn at all. His primary criterion stresses not content, but reception, and points to not an essentialist but a functional definition of myth.

To say that in any culture some stories are felt to be in some sense more important or more serious than others is sufficiently banal to stand as a universal proposition. Bascom's data show that when distinctions between types of tales are drawn, they are drawn because different weight is attached to the tales. Though the meaning of true and untrue, sacred and secular, divine and human, will differ vastly from one culture to the next, the distinctions are distinctions of value and, if there is need, that distinction can be expressed in the language or behavior which accompanies the narration. Myth might be more usefully defined as a narrative which is considered socially important, and is told in such a way as to allow the entire social collective to share a sense of this importance; legend is less important or important for only part of that society; folktale is even less important. But precisely where to draw the lines between myth, legend, and folktale is necessarily relative, hazy, and variable. A focus on social importance can account for the gradations of contents or contexts found in myth, legend, and folklore. The fact that some stories are meant to be received as true is only a sign of their social importance. Hence the truth criteria. Gods are normally more important than heroes, heroes more important than ordinary men, and ordinary men more important than animals. Hence the gradations of character-types in tales. More important stories are surrounded by greater ceremony and surrounded by more taboos. Hence the rules about not passing in front of the narrator, or not claiming a myth as your personal property.

But it is not just importance which lies behind the complex story-gradations described by the anthropologists. That this importance is "social" also has consequences for the different forms these tales may take. The way we know something is of social importance is through use: if it is important a story will be repeated or alluded to frequently in social discourse. Many modern definitions insist that a myth or legend must be "a traditional tale." This can lead to all kinds of problems and artificial exclusions. Popular usage allows people or events to become "legends in their own time," and this need not be just a figure of speech. There can be myths about recent events, contemporary personalities, new inventions. To insist that a myth or legend be a traditional tale is to confuse a symptom of their function of transmitting something of collective importance for part of their essence. Myth is a function of social ideology – Bruce Lincoln (1999: xii) would define it as "ideology in narrative form" – and we should not insist on certain contents and contexts but rather use these as evidence for the existence of the mythic function.

2

Comparative Approaches

From one perspective, the British may indeed have seen the peoples of their empire as alien, as other, as beneath them – to be lorded over and condescended to. But from another, they also saw them as similar, as analogous, as equal and sometimes even as better than they were themselves. . . . And this view was not just socially conservative, but politically conservative too. . . . the whole purpose of the British Empire was "to maintain traditional rulerships as a fortress of societal security in a changing world." And in that enterprise, the colour of a person's skin was less significant than their position in the local social hierarchy: "the really important category was status," and as such it was "fundamental to all other categories."

D. Cannadine, *Ornamentalism*, 123–4

He is a barbarian, and thinks that the customs of his tribe and island are the laws of nature.

G. B. Shaw, *Caesar and Cleopatra*, act 2

2.1 THE RISE OF THE COMPARATIVE METHOD

Some social conditions behind the birth of comparative mythology

Comparative mythology became a discipline during the age of European imperialism. More than coincidence links the method with its social context. Since the Renaissance, anything that might be regarded as "myth" had been only of interest to students of Greco-Roman literature, and principally because of its transformation into literature. For any other purpose "myths" were objects of revulsion and contempt. But the fortunes of myth rose gradually with the imperial enterprise, when, increasingly, it was myth in its raw, preliterary state which captured the European imagination. This is not to say that myth rose significantly in estimation. Myths were still objects of revulsion and contempt, but interesting objects, mainly for the light they supposedly shed upon the character of the mythmaker. The mythmaker, in his turn, whether non-European or ancient European, was primarily of interest as an object of comparison – a foil – for his European observer. Myth became a tool of European self-discovery.

The story of the invention of the modern science of mythology is inseparable from the story of the invention of anthropology. When Europe began to expand, first by exploration and then by trade, finally by conquest, exploitation, and colonization, Europeans came into contact with a great many races with strange customs, languages, and religions. It was useful to gain some understanding of the ways and manners of these many diverse nations, if only to learn to deal with them more effectively. But neither the ability nor the desire to describe others comes naturally. The earliest travelers' reports are surprisingly uninformative about native peoples, tending toward superficial sketches in the midst of more detailed inventories of the real estate and its mineral, botanical, and zoological riches. Even when the natives managed in some way to make an impression upon the early explorers' consciousness, the descriptions tended to be contradictory, even self-contradictory, and the contradictions tended to extremes. Tzvetan Todorov's *Conquest of America* (1984) shows that Columbus's letters describe the "discovered" populations at times as vicious beasts, and at others as "noble savages" living in a state of Edenic innocence. Indeed, he was able to reach these opposite conclusions while observing the very same traits in different contexts. The Caribbean aboriginals had no concept of private property. When they allowed him to help himself to their goods, Columbus declared them the most upright, generous, and liberal people in the world. A little later they helped themselves to Columbus's goods; he declared them vicious, perverse schemers and cut off their ears and noses. Both explanations missed the point because Columbus could only understand the actions of the Indians within his own cultural framework. Both explanations create an absolute distance between the aboriginals and Europeans. Civilization for the early European explorers meant European culture. With such a definition, the Caribbean Indians could only exist either in a subhuman or in a precivilized state. Columbus was completely unable to perceive that their system of values was simply different from his own. He mistook this difference for an absence of values. "These two elementary figures of the experience of alterity are both grounded in egocentrism, in the identification of our own values with values in general, of our *I* with the universe – in the conviction that the world is one" (39–40).

So long as Europe adhered to its traditional values with unswerving conviction, the perception of similarities and differences, whether of institutions, customs, or myths, would rarely exceed an interpretive framework which was itself explicitly mythical. For example, Diego Durán, a Dominican friar who accompanied Cortez, is one of the most acute observers of the Aztecs. He noted many similarities in their rituals to Christian rituals, but exaggerated them. They were nearly the same or "exactly" alike, and the doctrine was often treated as identical: the Aztecs "revered the Father, the Son and the Holy Ghost, and called them Tota, Topiltzin and Yolometl; these words mean Our Father, Our Son, and the Heart of Both, honoring each one separately and all three as a unity" (1967.1: 8). To explain this Durán offered two theories: that St. Thomas had come to Mexico to spread the Gospel, but it degenerated and came to be mixed "with their idolatry, bloody and abominable" (9); or that "the devil our cursed adversary forced the Indians to imitate the ceremonies of the Christian Catholic religion in his own service and cult" (3). Myths and rituals either preserve the true faith or are parodies scripted by the devil.

So long as Europeans remained confidently centered in their traditional ways and beliefs, the "other" could be observed, but the data could only be measured on a single scale, which might show the savage better or worse than the European, but never qualitatively different. European exploration and conquest do not, in themselves, explain the rise of mythology or anthropology: they provided only the experience of foreign cultures, the raw data, but not the mindset which could turn their observations into a meaningful science. This depended on fundamental changes in Europe itself, which undermined the European's confident assumption that his ways were God's. The most intense period of European expansion, from the seventeenth into the twentieth century, was also a period of rapid change, upheaval, and serious division within European society. Economically there was a change from the dominance of agriculture to the dominance of industry. Politically and socially there was a shift from a hierarchic to a more egalitarian configuration of power. These processes sufficed to install a new and very different set of values, but in the context of imperialism, they did much more: they engendered what sociologists call "a crisis in values."

In *Ideology and Utopia* (1936) Karl Mannheim explains how a process of democratization in combination with an imperial enterprise is likely to lead to a crisis in values. Democratization creates a period of high social mobility, in which people of one class change social status and learn to see their society through the eyes of another class. Imperialism brings people into contact with other nations with different ways and different values. Neither imperialism nor democratization by themselves need upset traditional values. But one source of cultural disorientation reinforces the other, and the combined impact of vertical mobility between classes and horizontal mobility between cultures is very likely to shake the belief in the eternal and universal validity of one's traditional way of thinking. Mannheim was describing, in the first instance, the ancient Greek, not the modern European "Enlightenment," though the latter was very much in his mind. With the addition of industrial capitalism this process is only intensified, since the new economic system displaced huge segments of the population from rural to urban areas, greatly increased the mobility between classes, upward and downward, by increasing the volubility of wealth, and also increased the traffic of people and goods to the colonies by integrating them within the economy of the imperial capital as sources of raw materials, sources of labor, and markets for manufactured goods.

The large-scale vertical and horizontal displacements of the modern era enabled Europeans to perceive and then to entertain different systems of values, and eventually to be more tolerant and finally more receptive to other ways of thinking and doing things. The once unified, absolute, and authoritarian code of Christian belief yielded to the pluralistic, relativistic, and (more) egalitarian discourse of today's "global culture" (which, despite its name, is thoroughly Western). In four hundred years European civilization and its offshoots passed from a state of absolute assurance that their ways were the ways of God, while the ways of other peoples were curiosities, perversions, errors, or heresies, to a belief in the artificiality and constructedness of all values. The final victim of European imperialism was Europe itself. As Terry Eagleton puts it: "it is hard to remain convinced that your way of doing things is the only possible one when you are busy trying to subjugate another society which conducts its affairs in a radically different but apparently effective way" (1991: 107). It becomes impossible, when, through the inner dynamics of one's own culture, one's values are in doubt even before confronting the other.

Comparative mythology and comparative anthropology would never have been interesting, nor really possible, unless European values were shaken both internally through rapid cultural change and externally through rapid imperial expansion. Comparative social science has no place in a world of cultural absolutism. In such a world there is only one culture and nothing to compare it to but an absence of culture. But comparatism fares little better in a world of complete cultural relativism. In such a world there are no grounds for comparison, and no evident profit in the exercise. The discipline found its ideal habitat somewhere in the middle ground between the cultural absolutism of the seventeenth century and cultural relativism of the twenty-first, when cultures were looked upon as different, and different in their own right, but not so different that they defied common measure, no matter how abstract the scale. The heyday of comparative mythology lasted from about the 1850s to the 1920s when there was still a confident belief in the superiority of European culture, but far less agreement about how precisely one defined its distinctive difference: one could still draw direct comparisons, and, not coincidentally, profit from an air of scandal whether one insisted on the sameness or difference of another culture's ways to one's own.

Mythology was an especially important figure in the discourse of self and other. It was thought to give direct access to mentality and intelligence. When, in its heyday, comparative mythology explicitly compared myths, beliefs, and cultures, it implicitly compared the mental powers of men of different races, in terms of agility, rationality, the capacity to rise above superstition, see truth, give direction, and provide leadership – at stake ultimately was the justification of European hegemony. But if much of the excitement generated by early comparatism had to do implicitly or explicitly with race and imperial relations, it was also connected implicitly or explicitly with the competing value systems within Europe itself. If the image of the savage, with all its contradictions, was essentially a foil for European self-definition, sometimes the poles of its contradictions were set by opposed value systems within European society. Savage societies, and often even highly civilized ones, were reconfigured after the image of European society, in such a way as to offset differentially the chief divisions within European ideology. We will see this double-determination at work in the comparative method, practiced by Müller, Frazer, and other myth-theorists examined in this volume.

William Jones and the discovery of Indo-European

The development of an administrative apparatus for the effective maintenance and commercial exploitation of Europe's overseas empires provided the stimulus for the earliest scientific ethnographic research. In particular, it was the administration of British India, the most complex and sophisticated of all European dominions, which supplied the immediate context for the creation of comparative linguistics and comparative mythology.

Imperial expansion eastward brought a new interest in Oriental languages to English schools. In the mid-eighteenth century the middle-class Welshman William Jones (1746–94) was able to acquire at Harrow and Oxford, in addition to the usual fare of Greek and Latin, a knowledge of Hebrew, Arabic, Persian, Turkish, and Chinese. (Sanskrit, the ancient language of India, written from about 1500 BC, first acquired a place in the curriculum of a European institution of higher learning with the foundation of a training school for the East India Company, East India College, in England in 1806.) Despite his interest in Oriental languages, Jones, by his own admission, would never have studied Sanskrit, even when appointed Justice of the High Court of Bengal in Calcutta in 1783, if not for his distrust of the pandits hired by the Court to advise him on indigenous law (which was based on the interpretation of ancient texts). He soon became an enthusiast, however, and when he founded an "Asiatic Society" in Calcutta, he delivered a number of lectures comparing Sanskrit language and mythology with others. In one of these lectures in 1786 Jones declared (1807: 34–5):

> The Sanskrit language, whatever be its antiquity, is of a wonderful structure; more perfect than the Greek, more copious than the Latin, and more exquisitely refined than either, yet bearing to both of them a stronger affinity, both in the roots of verbs and in the forms of grammar, than could possibly have been produced by accident; so strong indeed, that no philologer could examine them all three, without believing them to have sprung from some common source, which, perhaps, no longer exists: there is a similar reason, though not quite so forcible, for supposing that both the Gothick and the Celtick, though blended with a very different idiom, had the same origin with Sanskrit; and the old Persian might be added to the same family.

With these words Jones is credited with the discovery of the language family that later came to be known variously as Indo-Aryan, Indo-Germanic (so called by German scholars after 1823), or Indo-European (coined in 1813). Jones was not in fact the first to notice close similarities in the vocabulary of contemporary and classical European languages, nor the first to posit a common origin for them (nationalistic European scholars had been claiming a privileged connection between their mother tongues and Greek and Latin since Giraldus Cambrensis in the twelfth century; most influentially, Marcus Boxhorn in the seventeenth century, derived European languages from Scythian!). Though Jones's linguistic arguments showed better scientific method (nothing, after all, is known of Scythian), his success had a great deal to do with immediate ideological concerns. He was, as Lincoln says, "the right man in the right time and place: that which he said was – or was taken to be – very much the right thing" (1999: 84).

Once the primordial unity of European languages was scientifically demonstrated this "fact" could be and was invested with mythical values. A common linguistic origin was immediately taken to imply a historical, cultural, and racial unity, and once the Proto-Indo-European or "Aryan" nation became an object of imagination, whether scientific or popular, it began to accumulate characteristics, usually to the detriment of other races and cultures. The accomplishments of the highly idealized cultures of Classical Antiquity, like the art and literature of ancient India, testified to the superior talents of this prodigious race in its earliest recorded history and purest expression. This tendency was equally pronounced among those who, like Jones himself, believed that linguistic comparison vindicated the biblical account of the original unity and dispersal of all mankind (Edenic unity, the Fall, the tower of Babel, the sons of Noah). For though European theorists might posit an original unity for all mankind (not just Europeans), they tended not to treat all races as equal any more than did the biblical story, but established hierarchies among races by arranging the descendants of Shem, Ham, and Japheth in various orders of priority, and ascribing different ethical qualities to them.

Herder, Grimm, Romanticism, and comparative philology

Paradoxically Jones's "discovery" had its greatest impact on Germany, where internal turmoil and, above all, the fragmentation of the German-speaking population into numerous small and independent principalities with strong political and regional differences had prevented effective participation in the colonial enterprise so successfully pursued by European powers to the West and East. In its stead, however, the aspirations of a largely liberal and middle class for the unification of Germany within a modern nation-state created a deep need for the creation of a common German national identity. In the struggle for the political unification of Germany (which succeeded in 1871), language, literature, and folklore proved indispensable ideological tools.

In Germany the equation of language and *Volk* (common people, folk, nation) was an easy one. According to the highly influential critic and philosopher Johann Gottfried von Herder (1744–1803), language, folksong, and mythology were all the spontaneous (and true) expressions of national character. Great poetry, the highest form of cultural expression, was only possible if a language was itself poetic (and Herder's study of German syntax and phonetics demonstrated the still untapped poetic potential of German). But poetry was healthiest when a people was permitted spontaneous expression of emotion and imagination through its national language, and the best poetry was rooted in traditional folksong and folktale. By contrast, a language, and its literature, were prematurely withered by rationalism, or stunted by foreign influence. Herder argued that the vigorous development of German literature in the Middle Ages had been stunted by Enlightenment rationalism and all the foreign political, cultural, and religious influences that had seeped into Germany since the European Renaissance. Herder's ideas had an incalculable influence upon the nationalistic movements in Germany and throughout Europe. They also directly inspired two successive literary movements: *Sturm und*

Drang and Romanticism owed Herder their characteristic antirationalism, medievalism, and patriotism, their cults of spontaneity, emotion, nature, and original genius, and their pursuit of the *Volksgeist* (national spirit) through folklore and myth.

In *Thoughts on the Philosophy of Human History* (1784–91) Herder had in fact anticipated Jones in asserting the historical unity of all mankind (which he also located in Central Asia). Once the various races had dispersed from their ancestral home they developed different physical, spiritual, and moral characteristics through subgroup endogamy (i.e., marriage exclusively between members of the community), the process of adaptation to the climates and geographical features of the countries they inhabited, and, most importantly, through the development of separate languages and mythologies. The theory made the historical study of poetry, language, and folk mythology the key to the reconstruction and recovery of the national psyche in its originary and pure form.

Typical of the intellectual ferment of post-Herderian Germany was the range of activities pursued by the brothers Jakob (1785–1863) and Wilhelm Grimm (1786–1859). Among their numerous publications they produced critical editions, collections, and studies of Old German poetry, minstrelsy, epics, legends, mythology and folktales, even ancient German law. Most important, however, were Jakob Grimm's *History of the German Language* and *German Grammar*. Taking advantage of Jones's discovery of Indo-European, Grimm was able, through comparing the forms of German with other Indo-European languages, to reach much farther back into the linguistic history of the Germanic peoples than written records allowed. In his study of grammar, notably, Jakob Grimm applied a rigorous method for describing consonant shifts in Indo-European, for which many credit him, along with his compatriot Franz Bopp (1791–1867), as founder of the science of historical linguistics.

As a simple illustration of what has come to be known as "Grimm's Law," consider the following list of stop consonants (sounds made by blocking the airflow of the vocal column) and aspirates (constriction but not complete stoppage of vocal column):

	1 *Voiceless stop*	2 *Voiced stop*	3 *Voiceless aspirate*	4 *Voiced aspirate*
Labial	p	b	ph or f	bh
Dental	t	d	th	dh
Palatal	k	g	kh	gh

```
          ------------------------------------------------>
          <---------------------------
                        <------------------------------------------------
```

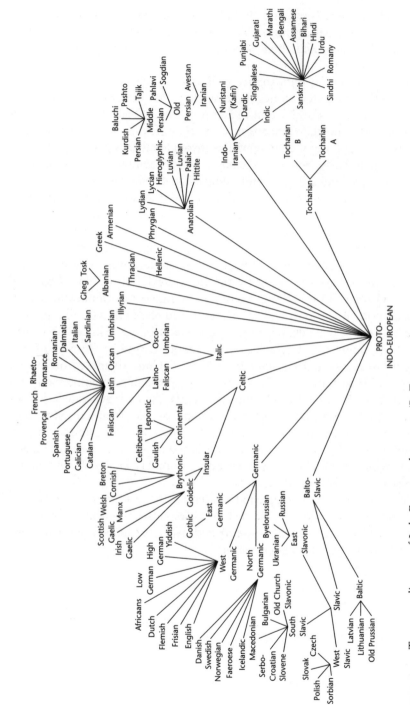

FIGURE 1   Tree-stem diagram of Indo-European languages (B. Zaporozan)

According to Grimm, the changes from Proto-Indo-European to Germanic languages (including English) could be mapped as a general shift of consonants from column 1 to column 3, from column 2 to column 1, and from column 4 to column 2. This can be demonstrated by comparing words in Germanic languages with words in Indo-European languages thought to be closer to the original form. Thus the first rule (voiceless stop to voiceless aspirate) is illustrated by English "foot" (cf. German *Fuss*) compared to Sanskrit *pat(a)*-, Greek *pod*-, Latin *ped*-. The second rule is demonstrated by English "knee" (cf. German *Knie*) compared to Greek *gonu*, and Latin *genu*. The third rule is illustrated by English "brother" (German *Bruder*) compared to Sanskrit *bhrátar*. The observation of regular patterns such as these facilitated the reconstruction of the original Proto-Indo-European vocabulary, helped to identify linguistic subfamilies (e.g., "Germanic," "Celtic," "Italic," etc.), and also held out the prospect of a historical reconstruction of the relative departure and movements of the various linguistic groups from the common Indo-European homeland (this, however, has proved more problematic). Indo-European was (and is) generally conceived as a large family, whose historical movements and groupings can be iconized in the manner of a family tree (see Figure 1).

2.2 MAX MÜLLER AND SOLAR MYTHOLOGY

Max Müller and attitudes toward British India

Friedrich Maximilian Müller (1823–1900), alias Max Müller (the more aristocratic-sounding double surname he adopted), is generally regarded as the founder of comparative mythology. A German by birth, he studied Sanskrit in Leipzig, Berlin (with Bopp), and Paris, and went to England in 1846 to edit and translate the (Sanskrit) *Rig Veda*. Upon receiving a commission for the work from the East India Company, he settled in Oxford and became a British subject. In 1868 Müller was appointed to a chair of Comparative Philology created specially for him, partly in consolation for narrowly missing an appointment as Boden Professor of Sanskrit. It seems his foreign birth and his political and religious views counted against his candidacy for the chair in Sanskrit (endowed expressly for the purpose of spreading Christianity to India by translating the Bible into Sanskrit). The bane of race theorists and assimilationists, throughout his life Müller spread admiration for India's languages, social structure, religion, and culture, emphasizing, wherever possible, not only their essential similarity, but their genetic relationship to their British equivalents. He counted it as one of the great accomplishments of nineteenth-century Orientalist research (as championed by himself) that the people of India had not only "ceased to be [regarded as] mere idolaters and niggers, they have been recognised as our brothers in language and thought" (1892: 34).

This is not to suggest that Müller's theories were generally anti-racist and anti-imperialist. They were so only with regard to India, and indeed only with regard to certain castes and regions of the Subcontinent. Müller adopted a two-race theory of the history of India. In remote antiquity the "Aryan" ("Japhetic" or "Caucasian") conquest brought the benefits of civilization to the "black" "Hamitic" races. The direct descendants of these Aryan warriors/culture heroes were, according to Müller, the upper-caste Brahmans (a priestly and scholarly caste which preserved and studied the Sanskrit texts). They were natural allies of Britain's own "civilizing mission." Indeed, Aryan and Briton played parallel roles at either end of the long history of Indian civilization: "it is curious to see," he declared, "how the descendants of the same race [i.e., the Aryan English], to which the first conquerors and masters of India belonged, returned, after having followed the northern development of the Japhetic race to their primordial soil, to accomplish the glorious work of civilization, which had been left unfinished by their Aryan brethren" (1847: 349). But he showed, through the example of India itself, that the task of civilization succeeded best where the conquerors worked through the medium of the conquered people's own language and culture. What was good for India seems pretty neatly to have coincided with what was good for Sanskrit studies: indeed, Müller knew and cared for only so much of the Indian subcontinent as was exactly coterminous with his academic discipline.

Despite Müller's triumphant claims, there were many even among Orientalists who continued to urge the inferiority of Indians in race and culture. Vigorous and widespread opposition to Müller came from two camps, described by Trautmann as "race science, which theorized the English common-sense view that the Indians, whatever the Sanskritists might say, were a separate, inferior, and *unimprovable* race"; and "a developmentalist, progressivist, liberal, and non-racial-essentialist critique of Hindu civilization in aid of a program for the improvement of India along European lines" (1997: 187–8). The latter urged a slightly less high-handed variety of coercion through assimilation, anxious to extend the benefits of science, technology, and economic progress, in sympathy with the broader spectrum of the British bourgeoisie, who were anxious to reap them. Both attitudes were doubtless common in the administrative culture of the East India Company: its East India College, typically, was founded to prepare British youths for the trials of life among "People every way dissimilar to their own" (Trautmann 1997: 115). The view that British and Indian were polar opposites allowed no hope of cultural coalescence.

Yet in the imperial administration, if not in academic circles, attitudes sympathetic to Müller's eventually prevailed. In 1858, in the wake of the Indian Mutiny, when the East India Company ceded administrative control of India to the Crown, the new imperial administration acquired a much more traditionally aristocratic character, less likely to see racial difference in "every way" than to find an appealing similarity between the hierarchical social stratification of India and Britain. Race became less interesting than pedigree, and indiscriminate claims of ethnic superiority less compelling than graded class distinctions. As David Cannadine's *Ornamentalism* amply demonstrates, British aristocrats came to regard India's culture as an idealized vision of a way of life that they as a class hoped to preserve – traditional, timeless, agrarian, intricately layered, and perfectly integrated: "it was atop this layered, Burkeian, agrarian image of Indian society that the British constructed a system of government that was simultaneously direct and indirect, authoritarian and collaborationist, but that always took for granted the reinforcement and preservation of tradition and hierarchy" (2001: 43). Viceroy, Governor, Maharajah, and Brahman were truly collaborators and brothers in the Aryan reconquest.

Adapting Aryans to a British public

In 1856 Müller published the first of many versions of a long essay on what he called "Comparative Mythology" (1867: 1–141). The work was a huge success and revolutionized contemporary thought on the origin of myths. The problem with which Müller wrestled in this and many subsequent works was not so much the "surprising coincidences in the folklore, the superstitions and customs of the most remote races" (1885: 902) as the disturbing similarity between the mythologies of "savage" races with those of the early European races. "To those who are acquainted with the history of Greece," he said (1869: 384–5),

> and have learnt to appreciate the intellectual, moral, and artistic excellencies of the Greek mind, it has often been a subject of wonderment how such a nation could have accepted, could have tolerated for a moment, such a religion. . . . But the more we admire the native genius of Hellas, the more we feel surprised at the crudities and absurdities of what is handed down to us as their religion. Their earliest philosophers knew as well as we that the Deity, in order to be Deity, must be either perfect or nothing – that it must be one, not many, and without parts and passions; yet they believed in many gods, and ascribed to all of them, and more particularly to Jupiter, almost every vice and weakness that disgraces human nature. Their poets had an instinctive aversion to everything excessive or monstrous; yet they

would relate of their gods what would make the most savage of the Red
Indians creep and shudder.

And so, Müller undertook to provide an explanation for myth which would
exonerate the ancient Greeks from the charge of savagery, which would
exonerate the study of mythology from an apparent fascination with ugly
and perverse nonsense, and which, incidentally, would raise the ancestors
of all European races well above the contemptible savages who inhabited
other corners of the globe.

Just as William Jones's study of Sanskrit and his comparison of Sanskrit
to Greek and Latin had led to the discovery of Indo-European and in-
augurated the science of comparative linguistics, so Müller thought that a
comparative study of the Vedas, the oldest Sanskrit texts, together with
Classical and other European mythologies, could serve as the foundation
of a science of comparative mythology: "The mythology of the Veda is to
comparative mythology what Sanskrit has been to comparative grammar"
(1867: 75). The Vedas, written around 1450 BC, a good seven centuries
before our earliest Greek texts, had a special quality: they represented
religious thought still in the formative stage, transparent and unsystematic. For example, the names of the gods in the Vedas have clear meanings, unlike those of most Greek gods. At the same time they have little
fixed personality, and no fixed relations, apart from the meaning of the
words. One could, therefore, determine that the name of the Vedic
supreme sky god, Dyaus, comes from the Sanskrit root *diut*, "to beam,"
and its substantive form *diu*, which means "sky" and "day." Dyaus pita,
"father Dyaus," and Zeus pater, "father Zeus," could be shown to derive
from the same Indo-European root, as could Latin Jupiter, who is also
known by the older form Diespiter, and the Nordic sky god, Tiw, who
gave his name to Tuesday. The same root gives Latin *deus* "god" and *dies*
"day." He concludes, therefore, that the Indo-Europeans had an important Sky god named Dyeus.

This is all extremely helpful and tells us something important about
Indo-European religion, but Müller does not stop here. He presents a
picture of the evolution of mythology which permits the Indo-European
etymology of the word Zeus to serve as a full explanation of the meaning of Zeus as a mythological figure. Thus Müller does not so much model
comparative mythology on comparative linguistics as incorporate the
study of mythology as a branch of linguistics.

Müller describes the early history of Indo-European speakers in essentially mythical terms. The Proto-Indo-Europeans, or Aryas, as he called
them, lived together as one big, happy family. This was a Golden Age in
which men were "noble and pure," and not savages, but "ancient poets

of language"; they had "the healthy and strong feelings of a youthful race of men, free to follow the call of their hearts – unfettered by the rules and prejudices of a refined society and controlled only by those laws which Nature and the Graces have engraved on every human heart" (1867: 127). The notion that the Aryas was a race of poets is overdetermined in his account: they were poets by nature, but they were also poets by necessity. They were poets by nature because their natural exuberance, pure in the simplicity of their pastoral life, was uncorrupted by social refinements. They were poets by necessity because they spoke a primitive language. Their language had as yet no abstract words, and, it seems, very few concrete ones. Therefore simple nouns and verbs had to carry the burden of many meanings, but at the same time one idea could be expressed through many words. Being a poet by nature, the noble Aryas felt powerfully the living presence of the world around him. He focused on the striking qualities of objects. But he expressed his huge emotions in a limited number of words inadequate to the task. Müller would have us believe that everything his Aryas said was poetic metaphor. Thus the Aryas could not say simply "the sun sets," but rather "the burning one sits down on his golden throne." These odd phrases then became somehow ossified in the language, despite increasing linguistic sophistication. At a certain point people no longer understood what these expressions really meant. No doubt the separation of various peoples from the primal horde abetted the partial loss of this cultural heritage (only partial since for some unknown reason the expressions outlasted their meanings). At that point people made up stories to explain the expressions. These were the first myths.

One of Müller's clearest examples is the myth of Endymion. Endymion was the son of Zeus and Kalyke and the King of Elis. One night he fell asleep in a cave and was seen by the goddess Selene, who fell in love with him. Selene bore him many children, but they parted when Zeus offered Endymion whatever he wished and he chose to sleep forever, remaining deathless and ageless. "We can best enter into the original meaning of a Greek myth when some of the persons who act in it have preserved names intelligible in Greek," says Müller (1867: 78). In this case Selene's name is conveniently transparent: it means "Moon." Zeus, as we have already seen, is the bright sky of daytime. "Endymion" Müller explains as coming from Greek *duo* which means originally "I dive into," and this verb can be used of the sun setting. "We may suppose, therefore, that in some Greek dialect *enduo* was used in the same sense; and that from *enduo*, *enduma* was formed to express sunset. From this was formed *endumion*, like *ouranion* from *ouranos*. Endymion, therefore means the setting sun" (1867: 79).

Now, "if *enduma* had become the commonly received name for sunset, the myth of Endymion could never have arisen," says Müller (1867: 80):

But the original meaning of Endymion being once forgotten, what was told originally of the setting sun was now told of a name, which, in order to have any meaning, had to be changed into a god or a hero. . . . In the ancient poetical and proverbial language of Elis, people said "Selene loves and watches Endymion," instead of "the sun is setting and the moon is rising"; "Selene kisses Endymion into sleep," instead of "it is night." These expressions remained long after their meaning had ceased to be understood; and as the human mind is generally as anxious for a reason as ready to invent one, a story arose by common consent, and without any personal effort, that Endymion must have been a young lad loved by a young lady, Selene. . . . Such is the growth of a legend, originally a mere word, a *mythos*, probably one of those many words which have but a local currency, and lose their value if they are taken to distant places, words useless for the daily interchange of thought, spurious coins in the hands of the many – yet not thrown away, but preserved as curiosities and ornaments and deciphered at last by the antiquarian, after the lapse of many centuries.

In like manner one can derive the myth of Apollo and Daphne from a misunderstood Proto-Indo-European phrase, "the opener of the gates of the sky pursues the burning one," which meant simply that the sun rises after dawn, but not surprisingly, the awkward expression ceased to be understood when the Greeks separated from the original horde. In this way, too, a perfectly innocent and respectable meaning can be read into the Greek myth concerning the succession of Ouranos, Kronos, and Zeus. Kronos eating his children originally signified nothing more terrible or interesting than "the heavens devoured and later released the clouds."

How to talk rubbish and influence people

One of the most conspicuous problems with Müller's interpretations was that almost every myth known in any Indo-European language was traced back to an Aryan myth about celestial phenomena. Still worse, as time went on and Müller churned out more and more interpretations of myth, the range of celestial phenomena represented by myth shrank to an exclusive concern with sunrises and sunsets: Heracles, Theseus, Odysseus, in short, everybody, represented the sun. This was an obvious point of criticism eliciting much defensive rhetoric: "'Is everything the Dawn? Is everything the Sun?' This question I had asked myself many times before it was addressed to me by others . . . but I am bound to say that my own researches lead me again and again to the dawn and the sun as the chief burden of the myths of the Aryan race" (1869: 520). "Was not the Sunrise to [the Aryas] the first wonder, the first beginning of all reflection, all

thought, all philosophy? Was it not to him the first revelation the first beginning of all trust, of all religion?" (1881: 599–600).

Given the fact that the Aryas seems to have been interested in nothing
else, it might strike us as odd that the words "sunset" and "dawn" are so
conspicuously absent from the Proto-Aryan vocabulary. But here, perhaps,
lay the great moral superiority of the Aryan race, their complete impracticality in matters of language and thought was evidence of their utterly
unbourgeois spirituality: they contrived circumlocutions for colorful
celestial events, while other truly savage races grubbed in the earth looking for a bellyful of roots and berries, and presumably spoke of nothing that
could not be eaten, and never expended their jaws on circumlocutions.

But it is precisely here that we find a less-often-noticed problem with
the theory. Müller's narrative of the origins of mythology contradicts itself.
In describing the Aryas as "poets of language" Müller, despite himself,
creates not a little confusion about just where, in his theory, poetry and
mythology break in upon the scene. According to Müller's own "history,"
what the Aryas are creating is not poetry or mythology. They are simply
attempting to record their observation of nature with a very crude and blunt
linguistic tool. Mythology only develops at a later stage, when language
gains in sophistication, and these old expressions are still remembered,
even though no longer understood. At this point the quaint old expressions,
most of which mean "the sun is rising," take on a life of their own and grow
into myths as people try to explain or make sense of the obscure phrases.

This contradiction lies at the surface of one much more deeply rooted
in the cultural discourse of nineteenth-century Europe. Britain and
Germany, the heartlands of the Industrial Revolution, were particularly
ruffled by a cross-current of reaction to the rationalistic, scientific, utili-
tarian, and materialist worldview of the increasingly dominant industrial
bourgeoisie. The Romantic movement was essentially the aesthetic arm
of the aristocratic and religious reaction to the values promoted by industrial capitalism, with its appeal to a more spiritual and chivalrous age governed by mystery, passion, high ideals, and a yearning for a vanishing
lifestyle in harmony with nature and traditional morality.

In painting his picture of the pure, simple, pastoral, and poetic life of
the Aryas, Müller seems at first to inscribe them within this framework
of romantic sensibility. The mythology of the originary poetic language
owes much to Herder (see Section 2.1), and can be found fully articulated, like the full bloom of the myth of the noble savage, as early as 1783
by Rousseau: "The first speech was all in poetry; reasoning was thought
of only long afterwards" (1968: 45). This poetic purity and innocence,
according to Herder, was lost with the growth of social organization, the
refinement of language, and the consequent growth of reason.

In fact, despite this description, both Müller and his Aryas have a good deal of the rationalism, scientism, and utilitarianism of the champions of the Industrial Revolution. Though he praises the Aryas for their metaphors, Müller has no great admiration for poetry or even myth. In poetry he delighted as one delights in the simplicity of children, while treating it with all the cordial and tolerant contempt which became a Victorian gentleman of sound reason and good education. In his view poetry emerges as the natural expression of simple minds. Myth fares much worse. It is a product of an uncomprehending rationalizing mind responding to words whose meanings have been lost in a degenerative process which Müller referred to as a "disease of language." The purpose of comparative mythology is rather to excuse the existence of myth by showing that something more innocent and reasonable once lay behind the stories that "would make the most savage of the Red Indians creep and shudder."

Here again is the great contradiction in Müller's idyll. The poets by nature who are also poets by necessity are not poets at all. If their expressions are suggestive they are suggestive only to later races. The Aryans themselves are utter bores who do nothing but discuss the weather or the time of day with the most banal kind of observations: "the sun is setting", "it is night", "it's cloudy." The conversation of the noble Aryas might have made polite palaver for the parlor – certainly more civil than the usual mythic fare of cannibalism and castration – but it was not poetry. The poetry is entirely in the succeeding generation which took these fossilized phrases and made interesting stories from them. The Aryas, indeed, seems to have no poetry, mythology, nor much religion of any sort, and his spare time is taken up entirely by the observation of natural phenomena, while his conversation obsessively tries to record these observations with all the accuracy that his blunt linguistic tools will allow. Far from being a romantic and a poet, his sympathies sooner match the practical, hard-nosed Victorian rationalist and man of science. Mythology, far from being a misguided rationalization of forgotten poetic phrases, sooner emerges as the later poetic and imaginative recasting of the Aryas's soulless meteorological data. Myth and religion were created together, by mistake, when the bland observations of the Aryas no longer made sense.

Müller, though a writer who proved very persuasive for the audience of his day, was not a very original thinker. Solar interpretations of myth are as old as the Hellenistic age, when they were just as much the product of scientific rationalism. The plague of solar interpretations was so great that in a parody Firmicius Maternus has the Sun himself complain of it (*De errore profanarum religionum* 8). Müller's theory is foreshadowed by many nearer contemporaries. Take, for example, Charles François Dupuis's remarkable *Origin of all Cults*, written in 1795. Dupuis thought all myths and religions could be traced back to Egypt, and that in origin all the Egyptian myths were about the intricate movements of the stars and other heavenly bodies, or (to anticipate Freud) the miracle of sexual reproduction. The astrological material consisted of exact scientific observations which were mysteriously concealed from the uninitiated in mythological language. The priestly allegories came in time to be misunderstood, however, and religion emerged as a result. Here again we have the interesting opposition of astronomy to religion, perhaps because astronomy represents the ultimate science (a matter of pure quantification, inert matter, and impersonal forces, as far removed as possible from the mythological conception of the planets), while at the same time the source of the greatest poetic and religious awe. And we could mention here one further leitmotif of Victorian myth-criticism. Müller's Aryas spends his days observing the movements of the heavenly bodies, seeming to spout poetry because his linguistic apparatus is weak; Dupuis allows his primitive counterpart to pursue science more explicitly. Both Müller and Dupuis, however, allow a fundamentally anticlerical reading: it is when society and the human character became complex and lose their innocence that these early pursuits become, through misunderstanding, corrupted into religion.

Müller's comparative method struck a deep chord in Victorian England and Europe. He was a sensation at a time when people like Dupuis were completely ignored. The Victorians gobbled up solar myths with insatiable appetites. Patronized by royalty, adored and imitated by some of the most distinguished intellectuals and men of letters, adulated by the reading public, Müller is an outstanding testament to the power of saying the right thing at the right time. Throughout his life newsstands were filled with imitations of his solar interpretations, and by authors as distinguished as Wilhelm Grimm, Michel Bréal, and even William Gladstone. In 1909 Otto Rank could still complain that scholarship on myth was monopolized by the question of whether divine and heroic myths were about "the young sun rising from the waters, first confronted by lowering clouds, but finally triumphing over all obstacles," or whether these myths were really about the moon doing the same thing (1964: 7). When Müller died in 1900 his funeral was attended by the Crown Prince of Siam; his widow received telegrams of condolence from royalty throughout the world, including Queen Victoria; the Queen of Romania complained of a sleepless night spent in grief.

Part of the art of saying the right thing, it seems, is to tell everybody, or at least everyone who counts, precisely what they want to hear, which often means expressing many and contradictory opinions. Müller distinguished the ancestors of all Europeans with a mentality that ennobled them above other savages, despite the similarities one could find between

Aryan and other myths. The character with which he endowed the Aryas, too, had a very broad appeal to European tastes, mixing normally opposed features of both Romanticism and science. And even while appealing to the hard rationalist, insofar as he implicitly discredits religion as originating in philological error, he nonetheless retained a strong appeal for conservative Christians. The Aryas, namely, is presented as practicing a distinctly Christian sort of monotheism. All myths were eventually about the dawn precisely because Müller would not suffer his Aryas to be anything less than a proto-monotheist. His comparative philology had proven that Europeans, Persians, and Indians once "invoked the Giver of Light and Life in heaven by the same name which you may still hear in the temples of Benares, in the basilicas of Rome, and in our own churches and cathedrals" (1881: 220). In an essay on "Greek Mythology" Müller describes the true "divine character" of Zeus, which is shared by the supreme god of all other Aryan mythologies, in unmistakably Christian terms (1876: 146–7):

> When we ascend . . . to the most distant heights of Greek history the idea of God, as the supreme Being, stands before us as a simple fact. Next to this adoration of one God, the father of heaven, the father of men, we find in Greece a worship of nature. The powers of nature, originally worshipped as such, were afterwards changed into a family of gods of which Zeus became the king and father.

The Aryas, unlike the savage, arrived at his disgusting myths innocently, and, moreover, even when myths were created to satisfy idle curiosity, the better intellects never really took them seriously: "their earliest philosophers knew as well as we that the Deity, in order to be Deity, must be either perfect or nothing – that it must be one, not many, and without parts and passions." The national spirit of Europe had indeed never been so much like it was in its origin: Christian, romantic, and precociously interested in observing the powers of nature. They had most emphatically never been savages.

Müller eventually succumbed to the temptation to extend his solar interpretation to some myths of non-Aryan races (1885). But it was the theory which distinguished and privileged white savages which took hold of the Victorian imagination and was vigorously developed by others. Most ambitious perhaps was a two-volume extravaganza by the clergyman George William Cox, called *The Mythology of the Aryan Nations* (1870), which translates seriatim every Aryan myth into a story of the sun, represented by the hero, with his rays, represented by the hero's arrows and lances, smashing through the forces of darkness, represented by the doomed monsters and villains. The exercise, he tells us, "raised and strengthened my faith in the goodness of God," while it justified "His wisdom which has chosen to educate mankind through impressions produced by the phenomena of the outward world" (1870: x). Sunrise is here a God-sent revelation of the true nature of the divine. Sunrise impressed upon the Aryan nations (332) "the genuine belief in one almighty Being who is at once our Father, our Teacher, and our Judge." Indeed, Cox contends that the Aryas never really departed from the spirit of monotheism, despite the development of mythology, which as a purely rationalizing and intellectual exercise had no real impact on spiritual beliefs. It had no connection with that "loathsome and degrading fetishism" practiced by most of mankind, but "rejected by every portion of the great Aryan family of nations" (97). St. George became a kind of archetype for myth, with the light of the sun becoming a convenient symbol not just of the light of the true faith, but of reason and science, the cultural basis of the advanced Western nations, smashing through the darkness of the superstitions of the more primitive nations on earth and freeing mankind from its misery. Says Cox (168): "The story of the sun starting in weakness and ending in victory, waging a long warfare against darkness, clouds and storms, and scattering them all in the end, is the story of all patient self-sacrifice, of all Christian devotion."

In Section 2.1 we noted the contradiction whereby Europeans regarded the same primitives at once as "noble savage" and subhuman. Much depended upon the European's attitude to developments in his own society, and particularly whether he thought the trends of recent history degenerative or progressive. To this extent Müller's theory had a more fundamentally deteriorationist appeal in sympathy with religious orthodoxy and aristocratic distemper in an age of growing materialism and bourgeois hegemony. His attitudes are echoed in their way by the interests of the church and the aristocracy: to borrow but two examples from Robert Fraser, Bishop Whately, who interpreted Genesis as a parable of "decline from a state of Stone Age virtue," and Lord Monboddo, for example, whose zoological theories granted hominids little progress from their orangutan ancestor who is "a pattern of gentility" (1990: 13). Müller's theories largely represented one mainstream ideological tendency in Victorian Britain which collided (and even sometimes merged) ever-more forcefully (or awkwardly) with another in the last half of the nineteenth century. Müller's "noble Aryas" sits at an opposite end of the Victorian imaginary from James Frazer's savage: the childish romantic and dreamy Aryas, whose very impracticality is a protest against utilitarianism and economic determinism, could hardly be more different, as he stares gooey-eyed at the sunrise like Dickens's Sissy Jupe at a circus, from Frazer's hardheaded

Gradgrindian savage who is interested in nothing but reason, economic productivity, and applied science.

2.3   JAMES FRAZER

The rise of comparative anthropology

Even today James Frazer (1854–1941) is the most widely read exponent of the "comparative method" in the study of myth. Frazer's comparative method could not have been more different from Müller's. The latter was a direct borrowing from comparative linguistics. Müller subordinated anthropological interpretations to linguistic etymologies: his crude equations (e.g., Zeus = Dyaus) were based chiefly on linguistic arguments. Frazer's method was more purely anthropological. Having no interest in linguistics, he compared myths with myths and rites with rites.

Anthropology only gradually came unto its own as a formal discipline in the nineteenth century. Despite some initial impetus from linguistics and comparative philology at the beginning of the century, anthropology's chief sources of inspiration lay elsewhere. The first was the gradual increase (in quantity and quality) of available ethnographic data. Much of this was in the form of government reports or government-sponsored research. The nineteenth century produced the first serious studies of the indigenous cultures of Africa, the South Pacific, and Australia. Significantly, most of these cultures were simple societies based on tribal units.

Further stimulus came from the neighboring disciplines of geology and archaeology. Until about 1860 European scholars generally accepted a short chronology for human (and world) history: most influential was the chronology of Archbishop James Ussher who, in the 1650s, calculated, on the basis of a close reading of the Bible, that Creation began in 4004 BC. Charles Lyell, in *Principles of Geology* (1830–3), demonstrated that the geological features of the earth were to be explained as the result of processes that continue to operate. Moreover, he was able to show the great antiquity of life-forms through fossils contained in geological strata, and even the possibility of dating human remains, through stratigraphic analysis, to a much remoter antiquity than previously imagined. Lyell's lesson in chronology was slow to penetrate scholarly consciousness and only finally struck home a quarter-century later, when an only remotely related archaeological discovery captured the popular imagination. In 1858 quarrymen at Brixham in southwest England discovered a sealed cavern. A select committee of eminent geologists probed the cavern floor and found stone tools in a mix of mammoth, rhinoceros, and cave-bear bones. For the scientifically minded, philologically based theories, like Müller's, now barely a year out of press, lost some of their éclat. The "Aryan family," which, on the traditional chronology, was close to Eden in time and place, lost some of its pristine and originary glamor, when it acquired, almost overnight, a two-million-year prehistory, which threatened to compromise its putative racial purity and, with it, its biological uniqueness.

Archaeology, with the aid of geological chronology, not only gave human prehistory greater depth, but it also suggested a new field in which European science could engage the other. At the same time as the ethnographic material was flooding in with reports of distant races of men, differently shaped, living in the most elementary tribal societies, and using stone tools, amateur archaeologists, closer to home, were digging up bones and artifacts which showed that European ancestors once lived in comparable simplicity, with primitive technology and measurably smaller and thicker skulls. The irresistible temptation was to equate the European distant past with the conditions of life in the ethnographic present in Africa, Australia, and the South Seas. All that was needed was the formulation of an evolutionary stage theory to justify the use of data drawn from the observation of contemporary savages for the reconstruction of European prehistory. Darwin's *Origin of the Species,* published within a year of the discovery of the Brixham Cave, only acted to confirm the plausibility of the evolutionary model. As human history was now to be measured in what seemed geological ages, rather than a few millennia, it was not difficult to transfer the image of layered stratigraphy from geology and archaeology to history.

John Lubbock, banker, politician, naturalist, archaeologist, was also first president of the Royal Anthropological Institute, "whose founding in 1871 was effectively the beginning of British anthropology as we know it" (Trautmann 1997: 166). Inspired by Darwin, Lubbock pioneered just the kind of evolutionary cultural stratigraphy that could bring archaeology and ethnography together within a single science (he notably coined the terms "paleolithic" and "neolithic"). Lubbock's *Pre-Historic Times, as Illustrated by Ancient Remains and the Manners and Customs of Modern Savages,* published in 1865, is one of the first attempts to distill history from a mishmash of archaeological and ethnographical data. He justifies his approach with a direct appeal to Lyell's geology (1865: 416):

> the archaeologist is free to follow the methods which have been so successfully pursued in geology – the rude bone and stone implements of bygone ages being to the one what the remains of extinct animals are to the other. The analogy may be pursued even further than this. Many mammalia which are

extinct in Europe have representatives still living in other countries. Our
fossil pachyderms, for instance, would be almost unintelligible but for the
species which still inhabit some parts of Asia and Africa; the secondary
marsupials are illustrated by their existing representatives in Australia and
South America; and in the same manner, if we wish clearly to understand
the antiquities of Europe, we must compare them with the rude implements
and weapons still, or until lately, used by the savage races in other parts
of the world. In fact, the Van Diemaner and South American are to the anti-
quary what the opossum and the sloth are to the geologist.

The image of the fossilized pachyderm evokes *in ovo* a second key concept for anthropological comparatism. Not only do evolutionary stages exist
which permit the direct comparison of stone-age Europeans and modern
savages, but there is yet a third source of evidence which links later with
earlier stages of evolution, a kind of cultural "fossil" or "survival." A
cultural "survival" is a custom or belief which arises in one stage of social
development but lingers on in further stages of social development
despite the loss of much of its original function, meaning, or importance.
Thus certain beliefs or practices at home in savage societies were seen to
survive in later ages up to the present, like the sloths Lubbock assigned
to glacial times, or the ossified and forgotten Indo-European expressions
which, Müller supposed, gave rise to myth. The notion of the survival is
"an integral part of the comparative method" and "in one form or
another it came into use more or less simultaneously in the writings of
the great evolutionists" (Harris 1968: 165). But Edward Tylor's *Primitive
Culture* (1871) was the first to use the term "survival" and give it explicit
definition: "These are processes, customs, opinions, and so forth which
have been carried on by force of habit into a new state of society different from that in which they had their original home, and they thus remain
as proofs and examples of an older condition of culture out of which a
newer has been evolved." Survivals might be such things as magicians'
rattles, which are powerful instruments in primitive culture but lived on
in Victorian Europe as children's toys. Survivals might also be ritual acts
which in later cultures appear as actions in myths or fairytales, long after
the ritual is forgotten. As Tylor's words indicate, survivals are not just
the corollary of theories of cultural evolution, but the proof.

Among survivals, the most useful for the anthropologist and the most
exciting for his readers are those which Tylor identifies as "worn out, worthless, or even bad with downright harmful folly," preserved by "stupidity,
unpractical conservatism and dogged superstition" which a more "practical
utilitarianism would have remorselessly swept away" (1958: 156). It is
these conspicuously irrational traits that stand out, at least in the modern
world, as ill-fitting, absurd, or contradictory.

Frazer's comparative method

Frazer's comparative method could be described as an easy four-step process. The first step is to find a particular problem: a rite, myth, or institution which seems odd or self-contradictory, or simply one that evades rational comprehension: chances are that the oddity is a survival from a previous stage of cultural development. The second step consists in gathering as many examples of this particular rite, myth, or institution from as many cultures as one can find. The third step is to find a generalizing explanation for the phenomenon. This will often emerge from some of the specific examples collected, since some are likely to be closer to the "origin" of the phenomenon than others. The correct explanation will be the one which has the power to account for all of the collected examples with the least degree of complexity and special pleading. The fourth step is simply to wrap up by reapplying the general explanation to the original problem.

An easy example is Frazer's treatment of the story of Cain and Abel from the Old Testament. The biblical text reads as follows (Genesis 4):

> Now Adam knew Eve his wife, and she conceived and bore Cain, saying, "I have gotten a man with the help of the Lord." And again, she bore his brother Abel. Now Abel was a keeper of sheep, and Cain a tiller of the ground. In the course of time Cain brought to the Lord an offering of the fruit of the ground, and Abel brought of the firstlings of his flock and of their fat portions. And the Lord had regard for Abel and his offering, but for Cain and his offering he had no regard. So Cain was very angry, and his countenance fell. The Lord said to Cain, "Why are you angry, and why has your countenance fallen? If you do well, will you not be accepted? And if you do not do well, sin is crouching at the door; its desire is for you, but you must master it." Cain said to Abel his brother, "Let us go into the field." And when they were in the field, Cain rose up against his brother Abel, and killed him. Then the Lord said to Cain, "Where is Abel your brother?" He said, "I do not know; am I my brother's keeper?" And the Lord said, "What have you done? The voice of your brother's blood is crying to me from the ground. And now you are cursed from the ground, which has opened its mouth to receive your brother's blood from your hand. When you till the ground, it shall no longer yield to you its strength; you shall be a fugitive and a great wanderer on the earth." Cain said to the Lord, "My punishment is greater than I can bear. Behold, thou has driven me this day away from the ground; and from thy face I shall be hidden; and I shall be a fugitive and a wanderer on the earth and whoever finds me will slay me." Then the Lord said to him, "Not so! If anyone slays Cain, vengeance shall be taken on him sevenfold." And the Lord put a mark on Cain, lest any who

came upon him should kill him. Then Cain went away from the presence
of the Lord, and dwelt in the land of Nod, east of Eden.

In *Folklore in the Old Testament* (1918.1: 78–103) Frazer problematizes
this mark that God puts on Cain. On the usual interpretation the mark
served to protect Cain from human assailants. But there are as yet no
other human assailants (no one yet lives on earth, according to Frazer's
reading of the Bible, except the murderer and his parents). Moreover, the
biblical passage makes Abel's blood and the ground itself, which will become
barren, the agents of Cain's exile. Frazer compares this to the widespread
belief in blood pollution causing infection or crop failure. Many cultures,
therefore, preserve the custom of driving murderers into exile or tempor-
ary seclusion for fear of famine or contagion. These parallels suggest that
the mark of Cain was a warning to others to avoid contact with him. But
other examples show that revenge was sought not by the blood of the
murdered man, but by his ghost. Frazer gives many examples of rituals
performed to appease the ghost of a murdered man. The examples, however, do not become immediately relevant until Frazer discusses the use
of marks and disguises to protect a murderer from the ghost of his victim.
Of the twenty-two selected examples we need take only three of the shorter
ones – the style is already familiar from Chapter 1 (1918.1: 92–7):

> Among the Ba-Yaka . . . "a man who has been killed in battle is supposed
> to send his soul to avenge his death on the person of the man who killed
> him; the latter, however, can escape the vengeance of the dead by wearing
> the red tail-feathers of the parrot in his hair, and painting his forehead red."
> . . . Among the Borana Gallas, when a war-party has returned to the village,
> the victors who have slain a foe are washed by the women with a mixture
> of fat and butter, and their faces are painted red and white. Among the
> Southern Massim . . . a warrior who has slain a man remains secluded in his
> house for six days. During the first three days he may eat only roasted food
> and must cook it for himself. Then he bathes and blackens his face for the
> remaining three days.

"Thus," Frazer concludes, "the mark of Cain may have been a mode of
disguising a homicide, or of rendering him so repulsive or formidable in
appearance that his victim's ghost would either not know him or at least
give him a wide berth" (1918.1: 98–9).

The essay moves from the discovery of the problem, to the collection
of evidence of similar beliefs and practices, to a generalizing explanation.
But the example also shows that the process may be a little less straightforward than the four-step description allowed. In practice, step one at
least sometimes presupposes step two: i.e., the "problem" often emerges

(or is constructed) only after the comparative material has already been gathered and sifted. Also, step two must to some extent presuppose step three: just what constitutes "examples of this particular rite, myth, or institution" can generally only be determined once one has decided where the original logic lay. In the present example, it is only with the help of the anthropological parallels that the "mark" or "sign" seems problematic: it seems to be an indication that Cain was under God's special protection and not a disguise of any sort. Nor would anyone begin to solve this problem, supposing it was noticed in the first place, by collecting passages relating to the protection of murderers from ghosts. This is not just a similar example of the practice, since there is no mention of ghosts of any sort in the biblical passage: both the identification of the initial "problem" and the selection of relevant comparanda depend on the decision that the mark is a disguise against ghosts.

Frazer defends his generalizing explanation on the grounds that it has "the advantage of relieving the Biblical narrative from a manifest absurdity" (1918.1: 100–1):

> For on the usual interpretation God affixed the mark of Cain in order to save him from human assailants, apparently forgetting that there was nobody to assail him, since the earth was as yet inhabited only by the murderer himself and his parents. Hence by assuming that the foe of whom the first murderer went in fear was a ghost instead of a living man, we avoid the irreverence of imputing to the deity a grave lapse of memory little in keeping with the divine omniscience. Here again, therefore, the comparative method approves itself a powerful *advocatus Dei*.

But the conclusion, far from protecting God from a lapse of memory, calls attention to a hitherto unnoticed absurdity in the biblical passage (for neither God's nor Cain's "anyone" can really refer to the world's first ghost), and it compounds the absurdity by supposing God to threaten punishment to a ghost. Frazer's dry sense of humor (so arid that many doubt its existence) will not allow us to decide whether he really hopes some fundamentalist Christian reader will accept his interpretation as a defense of the literalness of the Bible, or whether he is just having more fun at the expense of those who insist on the literal truth of this text. (Immediately before this passage he wonders whether God "decorated Cain with red, black, or white paint, or perhaps with a tasteful combination of these colours" or just painted him red like a Fijian, white like a Ngoni, black like an Arunta, or half-red and half-white like the Masai and the Nanadi, "or he may have plastered his head with mud, like the Pimas, or his whole body with cow's dung, like the Kavirondo.") The real moral of the story appears in the essay's final paragraph (1918.1: 103):

The venerable framework of society rests on many pillars, of which the most solid are nature, reason, and justice; yet at certain stages of its slow and laborious construction it could ill have dispensed with the frail prop of super- stition. If the day should ever come when the great edifice has been carried to completion and reposes in simple majesty on adamantine foundations, it will be possible, without risk to its stability, to cut away and destroy the rotten timbers that shored it up in the process of building.

So much for Frazer's defense of scripture.

Frazer's Golden Bough

Frazer's magnum opus, *The Golden Bough,* is one of the truly great works of modern anthropology, a professional as well as a popular classic. For over a century it has adorned the shelves of more home libraries than any anthropological work written before or since. It was originally pub- lished in two volumes in 1890, expanded to three in the second edition of 1900, to twelve in a third edition of 1911–15, and acquired a further supplement volume in 1936. In 1922 a 714-page abridgment of the work was made, largely by Frazer's wife; Frazer himself "was constitutionally incapable of abridging anything" (Fraser in Frazer 1994: xl). Much is said about Frazer's style when we note that the abridgment reduced the bulk of the work by a whopping 84 percent, mainly by eliminating the notes and thousands of superfluous examples. Another abridgment by Gaster (1959) reduces the work by a further 30 percent, only to make up for it in endnotes. The best abridgment is by Robert Fraser (1994), but the 1922 version is better known, and is therefore cited here wherever possible.

Any attempt to summarize this enormous work undercuts its persua- sive eloquence and the compelling weight of its widely researched and sometimes detailed examples. Frazer's impulse to expand, rather than con- tract, was well-founded: when the liopleurodon is stripped to its bare bones, robbed of the intimidating bulk of its scholarship and the narcotic splen- dor of its poetry, one finds a fairly thin line of argument with sometimes very loose and awkward joins. This in itself makes the exercise worth- while; though it can only be done at the cost of obscuring typical features of argumentation which make the work rhetorically persuasive despite the tenuous logical links. Conspicuous features of Frazer's style of argument (and that of most of his contemporary comparatists) are: (1) the looseness of the equations; (2) the reliance on suggestive and circumstantial detail; (3) the tendency to persuade by suggesting a large number of alternat- ives, all tending in the same direction, as if exhausting the possibilities, and cumulatively overdetermining the desired connection; (4) the disparate quality of the sources of evidence; and (5) the tendency to list all positive examples, but either no or few negative ones. Feature 1 arises from the assumptions behind Frazer's use of the comparative method. Convinced that human society everywhere goes through the same stages, then "if some behaviour has been observed in, say, the jungles of the Amazon but, unfortunately, not in the jungles of the Congo . . . then it is perfectly in order to use data from the Amazon to make a point about the Congo" (Ackerman 1987: 47). The logical "knight's move" may be observed also in the reliance on circumstantial detail (feature 2). Not all the examples given in Frazer's lists include the details relevant to the point he is making, but are included because they resemble relevant examples in other circumstantial details, and so allow the missing links to be inferred. This feature also appears at more important junctures in the argument of the *Golden Bough*: note, for example, Frazer's argument which connects mistletoe to the fire of the sun. Frazer can find no example of a direct link, but he can make a direct link between fern-seed and the sun; as there are many similarities in the cultivation and treatment of mistletoe and fern-seed (both are collected in midsummer and midwinter and used in divining rods), it only stands to reason that the recorded folktale which makes fern-seed the blood of the sun uncovers a primitive logic which must assert the same of mistletoe. Features 4 and 5 have to some extent been discussed in relation to Bascom in Chapter 1, though in relation to the former it is worth noting that the early part of *The Golden Bough* relies most heavily on ethnographic data from contemporary savages, the central section on Greco-Roman and Near Eastern myth, and the last section on modern European folklore.

The Golden Bough opens with a skillfully drawn landscape with figures. A few miles south of Rome in the Alban hills of Latium there is a small volcanic basin which contains a lake, surrounded, in antiquity, by a dark oak forest. This forest was sacred to Diana, and in it she had a temple. The priest of the temple was selected by a bizarre rite. Only a runaway slave could accede to the priesthood by finding his way into the grove, plucking a branch (called "the golden bough") from a sacred tree, and then killing the former priest in single combat. In his turn, the new priest would spend his days and nights vigilantly guarding the tree, and waiting for the ineluctable appearance of his own assassin and successor. The priest was called the "King of the Wood."

True to his method, Frazer begins immediately by identifying this rite as a "survival": "No one will probably deny that such a custom savours of a barbarous age, and, surviving into imperial times, stands out in striking isolation from the polished Italian society of the day, like a primaeval rock

rising from a smooth-shaven lawn" (1922: 2). But an explanation is possible, thanks to the very rudeness of the custom (2):

> For recent researches into the early history of man have revealed the essen-
> tial similarity with which, under many superficial differences, the human mind
> has elaborated its first crude philosophy of life. Accordingly, if we can show
> that a barbarous custom, like that of the priesthood of Nemi, has existed
> elsewhere; if we can detect the motives which led to its institution; if we
> can prove that these motives have operated widely, perhaps universally, in
> human society, producing in varied circumstances a variety of institutions
> specifically different but generically alike; if we can show, lastly, that these
> very motives, with some of their derivative institutions were actually at work
> in classical antiquity; then we may fairly infer that at a remoter age the same
> motives gave birth to the priesthood of Nemi.

Frazer begins by drawing attention to Diana's character as a goddess
of fertility and as a keeper of sacred fire. The cult was initiated when Orestes
brought the image of Artemis (= Diana) to the grove, from Taurus, where
she notoriously demanded human sacrifice. In myth Diana's young lover
Hippolytus was said to have been brought back to life, transported to Nemi,
and given as a consort to the nymph Egeria. Frazer finds parallels to the
relationship between the goddess and the king in the relationship of other
goddesses to short-lived mortal consorts, such as Aphrodite and Adonis or
Cybele and Attis. The grove of Nemi is also the place where Numa, the
Roman king, consorted with Egeria. The overture ends with many hanging
questions: Why is this priest a "King of the Wood?" What is his relation
to Diana? What is their relation to Numa and Egeria? Why is he sacrificed?
What is the "King's" relation to the sacred fire? What is his relation to
the golden bough?

Frazer then elaborates a three-stage scheme for the history of human
culture upon which the answers to these questions will depend. An Age
of Magic, surviving still among the Australian aborigines, is followed by
an Age of Religion, and then by an Age of Science, known so far only in
the West. Magic is a straightforward attempt to manipulate nature on the
basis of an erroneous theory of natural causality, whereas religion is an
attempt to control nature through the propitiation of spirits or gods. Magic
is paradoxically more scientific than religion: it is a false science based
upon a spurious system of natural law. Of magic, there are two types.
The first Frazer calls "imitative" (or "homeopathic") magic, which operates through a law of similarity. This is the belief that by acting on something which resembles another object, you act upon that object iself, as,
for example, when you put pins into a voodoo doll with the intention of
harming the person in whose image the doll is made. The second type is

"contagious" magic, which operates through a law of contact, so that acting upon a part of something is supposed to affect the whole, as, for example, when a witch sticks a knife in a person's footprint in the hope of laming that person. Religion arises when the belief that nature is governed by "immutable laws acting mechanically" is abandoned for a belief that the course of nature is determined "by the passions or caprice of personal beings"; religion is thus defined as "a propitiation or conciliation of powers superior to man which are believed to direct and control the course of nature and of human life" (50–1). The Age of Magic shades into the Age of Religion through stages as magical powers become increasingly concentrated. At first magic was practiced communally, then concentrated in the hands of a caste of medicine men, and finally in the hands of a single all-powerful "priest king." Later, when greater magical powers are ascribed to a particular individual, somewhere "midway between the age of magic and the age of religion" (162), there are "divine kings." The Age of Religion properly begins when divinity is finally abstracted from the person of the king. In the age of divine kings, though there is a notion of divinity, nature can still be manipulated, through contagious magic, by acting upon the person of the king.

Turning his attention now to the priest of Diana, who was also styled "King of the Wood," Frazer examines the plentiful evidence for belief in tree-spirits. The progress from animism to polytheism is demonstrated by the replacement of the belief that the tree embodies a spirit by the belief that the spirit only occasionally inhabits the tree. Tree-spirits come to be thought of as having human or animal form. Male and female tree-spirits are sometimes represented as bridegroom and bride, sometimes also as king and queen. Frazer infers from European spring festivals (deemed "remnants") that "our rude forefathers personified the powers of vegetation as male and female, and attempted, on the principle of homeopathic or imitative magic, to quicken the growth of trees and plants by representing the marriage of the sylvan deities in the persons of the King and Queen of May" (135). Ancient sacred marriages also served to promote fertility. Thus, Frazer concludes, the King of the Wood and Diana formed a sacred couple for fertility magic. The same divinities appear in the marriage of Numa, the Roman king, with Egeria, another name for the goddess of the grove. The Roman kings represented themselves as Jupiter at times, and Jupiter must have been the divine embodiment of the early Roman kings. Jupiter was god of the oak and of lightning. The early kings must have represented themselves as oak-spirits with the power to control the lightning and the rain. Early Rome, like many early societies, was matrilineal – the kingship was handed down by marriage with the princess, who was won in a contest, held annually. The King of the Wood was none other than Dianus (or Janus, a form of Jupiter), the Aryan god of the thunder and the oak. His consort was Diana (a form of Juno), goddess of the oak (Egeria was a dryad, an oak nymph) and the sacred fire. In Aryan religion the communal, perpetual (Vestal) fire was fed with oak-wood. Nemi was an oak grove. So the fire and the oak were identical.

After demonstrating that the King of the Wood was originally a "divine king," Frazer turns his attention to the manner of his ritual killing. The comparanda show, he argues, that divine kings are normally sacrificed and replaced, at first when their powers begin to wane (so as not to allow a sympathetic withering of the crops), in order to renew nature, ensure fertility, and secure the food supply. The memory of this sacrifice is preserved in the myths of the death and rebirth of the god/mortal lover of the goddess (e.g., Adonis, Attis, Osiris, Dionysus). Later, the dying god is thought of as a vegetation spirit (tree-spirit, corn-spirit). Hence the sacrifice, earlier linked to the life of the king, is synchronized with the agrarian cycle and becomes an annual sacrifice to guarantee the renewal of spring. Sacrifice evolved from the periodic sacrifice of the divine king to the sacrifice of a substitute, then to the sacrifice of a human victim only in times of emergency, and finally to animal sacrifice. Scapegoat rituals are explained in terms of the primitive belief that evil could be transferred to inanimate objects, then to sacrificial victims. Since the king (or his substitute) was being sacrificed anyway, it was convenient to transfer sins to him so that he could take them away.

Having dealt with the sacrificial combat of the divine King of the Wood, Frazer probes further into his relationship to the sacred fire kept in Diana's temple. In Europe, since the Middle Ages, at certain times of year fire ceremonies take place which show traces of human sacrifice: usually an effigy of Winter, Old Age, or Death is burnt or one of the company is selected for mock-immolation (in some cases dressed up in green leaves), while the peasants dance around the fire or leap over it, which they do for fertility and purification (cf. divine king and scapegoat). These customs, he urges, originate in the burning of the vegetation-spirit: in addition to renewal through replacing the old spirit, the fire imitates the light and heat of the sun, necessary to the growth of crops, and so is a form of sympathetic magic. Sacrifice by burning the victim alive has wider cosmological implications than simple blood-sacrifice, since it renews not only the fertility of nature but also the light of the sun. Later, Frazer surmises that the King of the Wood originally met his end in a fire-sacrifice.

The final sections of The Golden Bough are taken up in a search for the rationale behind the requirement that the challenger of the King of the Wood pluck a branch from the sacred oak. In the Norse myth of Balder,

Balder is invulnerable to everything but the mistletoe, by which he is slain, and thereafter he is consumed by a great fire. Ancient Aryans attributed great powers to the mistletoe which they thought sent from heaven, notably by lightning falling upon oak trees. In Nordic countries mistletoe is collected on Midsummer's Eve at the time of bonfires called "Balder's balefires." "In other words, we may assume with some degree of probability that the myth of Balder's death was not merely a myth, that is, a description of physical phenomena in imagery borrowed from human life, but that it was at the same time the story which people told to explain why they annually burned a human representative of the god and cut the mistletoe with solemn ceremony" (664). In view of the importance of the oak to Aryan mythology and the use of oak in the fire festivals, Frazer concludes Balder was the tree-spirit of the oak. The myth of Balder is to be explained by a belief that the seat of life of the oak was the mistletoe which grows evergreen upon the deciduous tree, and that in order to take the life of the tree-spirit, one had first to remove the mistletoe. The mistletoe was apparently thought to be indestructible and communicated its indestructibility to the oak so long as it was attached.

If the mistletoe had to be removed before killing the tree or the tree-spirit, this does not quite explain why a branch of the oak had to be removed before killing the tree- or vegetation-spirit behind the King of the Wood. To explain the plucking of the golden bough, Frazer has recourse to a large number of modern folktales (Punchkin) in Indo-European languages which show a belief in an "external soul," i.e., an inanimate object, animal, or plant in which a person deposits his soul or life for safekeeping (and for the apparent Aryan belief in the external soul, Frazer can find ample comparanda in the totemistic practices of various non-Aryans). Balder's life, he concludes, was deposited in the mistletoe just as the life of the oak. The same must have been true of the King of the Wood and the golden bough. Conveniently, a passage of Virgil's *Aeneid* compares the golden bough growing in the holm oak to a mistletoe. "The inference is almost inevitable that the Golden Bough was nothing but the mistletoe seen through the haze of poetry or of popular superstition" (703). Hence the life or external soul of the King of the Wood (= oak-spirit) was deposited in the golden bough (= mistletoe), and this is why the bough had to be plucked before he could be killed in combat. "And to complete the parallel," Frazer adds (703–4),

> it is only necessary to suppose that the King of the Wood was formerly burned, dead or alive, at the midsummer fire festival which, as we have seen, was annually celebrated in the Arician grove. The perpetual fire which burned in the grove, like the perpetual fire which burned in the temple of Vesta at

Rome and under the oak at Romove, was probably fed with the sacred oak-wood; and thus it would be in a great fire of oak that the King of the Wood formerly met his end. At a late time, as I have suggested, his annual tenure of office was lengthened or shortened, as the case might be, by the rule which allowed him to live so long as he could prove his divine right by the strong hand. But he only escaped the fire to fall by the sword. . . . The rite was probably an essential feature in the ancient Aryan worship of the oak.

But why is the bough "golden" when mistletoe is in fact white, or at best a yellowish-white? To answer this question Frazer invokes the analogy of the fern-seed, said in a German fairytale to be the blood of the sun, and also collected by peasants throughout Europe at the time of the summer and winter solstice (like mistletoe). Contemporary European peasants used it, like the mistletoe, as a charm against fire (homeopathic magic), and also as a divining rod for finding gold. Mistletoe is therefore conceived as an emanation of the golden fire of the sun. Now the reason for the midsummer bonfires, according to Frazer, is to "feed" the sun at the time of the solstice; hence it was also thought that the sun's fire was an emanation of the mistletoe, as the seed of this fire, or as the soul of the oak which fed the fire. One last flourish: the Aryans connected the oak with lightning because, among trees, it is the most likely to be struck. The Druids thought that the mistletoe descended from heaven, and in Aargau mistletoe is called "thunder-besom." This shows that the old Aryans believed the mistletoe to be celestial fire descended from heaven by lightning on Midsummer's Eve. The oak is struck by lightning more often than other trees and so was thought to be the sacred terrestrial repository of the sky-god's soul. Mistletoe is thought to be golden because the fire from heaven remains smoldering inside.

The priest at Nemi was therefore a degenerate survival of a divine king/vegetation-spirit, later turned sky-god. The rule of succession through combat is the survival of a time when divine kings were sacrificed (first by fire and then by the sword) and replaced in order to ensure the reinvigoration of the crops. The particular requirement that the golden bough be plucked was a survival of the time when the sky-god/tree-spirit's soul was thought to be deposited in the mistletoe. Various aspects of the sky-god/tree-spirit's cult were transferred to his consort, Diana, originally Queen of Heaven: in particular she remained the guardian of forests and animal life, and the guardian of the sacred flame.

Lurking in the shadows behind the priest of Nemi is another divine king: Jesus Christ is in an important sense the real subject of the book. Frazer's full revised edition has seven parts (some with two volumes), of which the sixth is devoted to discussion of the scapegoat. This section of the work is barely mentioned in my summary because totally irrelevant to the explanation of the priesthood at Nemi. It has, however, a great deal to do with the impact and success of the *Golden Bough*. Implicitly in the first edition, then explicitly in the second, Frazer characterized Jesus Christ as a typical Near Eastern dying-god figure, a fertility spirit, rooted in primeval magic, whose death and resurrection were designed to promote agriculture. But Christ also took away men's sins, and so Frazer's sixth section, the climax of the whole work, ends with an extended comparison of Christ with typically barbaric rites of human sacrifice. Christianity is reduced to just another example of the murky confusion of savage thought. As if in fear the point might be lost to subtlety, Frazer's great peroration in the last paragraph of the twelfth volume describes the traveler/reader returning on the Appian Way in language that insists that Christ and the Christian martyrs descend in a direct lineage from the runaway slave burned in the wood at Nemi: "glimpsing the sky aflame with sunset, its golden glory resting like the aureole of a dying saint over Rome and touching with a crest of fire the dome of St. Peter's," and as he looks back at the unchanging grove of Diana, he hears borne on the wind (at an impossible distance) the church bells of Rome ringing the Angelus. "Sweet and solemn they chime out from the distant city and die lingeringly away across the wide Campagnan marshes. *Le roi est mort, vive le roi! Ave Maria!*" (714). The Golden Bough really does argue "the essential similarity with which, under many superficial differences, the human mind has elaborated its first crude philosophy of life." Christianity was just one of those superficial differences and Christian morality could no longer be reckoned among the features that distinguished the European from the savage. Only science could.

Despite all the delicious scandal aroused by this treatment of Christianity and the notoriety and success it guaranteed for his work, Frazer was cowed by the criticism it provoked. In his third edition the section dealing with the crucifixion of Christ was relegated to an appendix. In Frazer's abridgment it was deleted altogether, along with several other sections implicitly relevant to Christian beliefs (Fraser's 1994 abridgment reinserts it in its proper place). Robert Graves suggested that Frazer muffled his iconoclasm in order to keep his nice office at Trinity College. But this is surely too cynical: by all accounts Frazer was a shy and retiring man, sensitive to criticism, and indeed a regular churchgoer, able, in the name of social respectability, like many of the great Victorian atheists, to separate science and religion in practice as easily as they did in thought. We have seen the care Frazer took, in *Folklore in the Old Testament*, to characterize his method and scholarship as an *advocatus dei*, however hollow or subtly ironic the claim.

2.4   THE WORLD ACCORDING TO FRAZER:
PROBLEMS AND PRESUPPOSITIONS

A principle of sameness and difference

A promiscuous comparative method, like Frazer's, which freely gathers data from any culture and historical epoch, needs to articulate some way in which all societies are alike – some principle of sameness which will permit meaningful comparison. Frazer in fact required a very strong principle of sameness, since his method posited that cultures throughout the globe and throughout time, even cultures that had apparently never been in contact, nonetheless somehow produced myths that were not just similar, but in some sense "the same." For Frazer the primary universal is human need and desire. Frazer speaks of "the essential similarity of man's chief wants everywhere and at all times" (1922: 711) and we are to suppose that the quest to satisfy this basic need everywhere gave rise to similar ways of thinking and acting: "recent researches into the early history of man have revealed the essential similarity with which, under many superficial differences, the human mind has elaborated its first crude philosophy of life" (2).

Frazer's man is primarily a thinking stomach. He needs to secure his food supply and he wants to do so by controlling and dominating nature. Upon the indigent savage Frazer (like most early comparatists) projected the Victorian bourgeois gentleman's obsession with material accumulation. He flattered his readers with the notion that their own preoccupations with economic growth and the progress of science and technology were both natural and universal objects of desire, but also objects of their own unique attainment.

Once it was decided that all human thought and activity were directed to the same ultimate ends – ends which in themselves were perfectly sensible and reasonable – then it seemed to follow that, if the thoughts, practices, and narratives of other cultures seemed so much nonsense and absurdity, this was because of some deficiency in the mental processes expended to attaining these ends. For Frazer this deficiency consisted in logical errors which characterized the thinking of the earlier stages of cultural development and the superstitious ignorance compounded by these errors. Reason and knowledge, therefore, provided comparatism with the great principle of difference, which it needed in order to make cultural comparison transcendently interesting and meaningful.

Reason and true knowledge provided the necessary principle of difference. Cultural difference was the outward manifestation of mental disparity. Like most later Victorian anthropologists Frazer measured this difference in terms of evolution (some races and cultures developed more quickly than others). With this principle of difference over time, Frazer could sort whole cultures and isolated practices within cultures into different stages according to their manner of thought, whether magical, religious, or scientific, and distribute them over the evolutionary timeline. So variable was the rate of progress, that Frazer's contemporary world contained representatives of every stage: the Australian aborigines still lived in the Age of Magic, and only Europeans had yet attained the Age of Science.

Armed with this kind of anthropology, Western Europeans could flatter themselves that they were intellectually (and, since reason brings self-control, also morally) superior to other cultures in a way which appeared not to conflict with the Christian and liberal notions that all human beings are somehow equal before God and the Charter of Rights. All societies might in time reach their age of (true) reason, and attain the science and technology for which they were striving, but they would reach it even sooner with the aid of more advanced nations. In this way the relationship between Britain and her colonies was assimilated to an adult/child relationship. The adult's superior power of reason justifies the exertion of a benevolent control over the child. Comparative anthropology offered a theoretical and scientific basis to the imperialist ideology which turned colonial exploitation into an expression of Christian charity or enlightened humanism, a "white man's burden" to protect savages and semi-savages from their irrational fears and the self-inflicted sufferings caused by superstition. And if at times the savages appeared ungrateful, it was like the ingratitude of a child: one day they will thank you for the punishment they receive today at your hands. Time became the great mediator of Victorian ideology. As in Christian ideology, it was time that would set wrongs right, but with the added advantage that present wrongs may only be apparent wrongs which time will vindicate as rights.

In comparatism's dialectic of sameness and difference, the savage, through his difference, became a walking advertisement of the cultural, moral, and intellectual superiority of Europeans, but still more, through his sameness to the more traditional manifestations of European culture, he became a guarantor of the superiority of a particular type of European, the elite, highly educated progressive European who placed his faith in reason, science, and technology. None of these ideas or attitudes are peculiar to Frazer, though he embodied them exceedingly well. The following paragraphs will sketch the degree of Frazer's integration within the currents of Victorian anthropology and examine some of the assumptions they shared.

Evolution and evolutionary stages

Anthropology was much inspired by Darwin's *Origin of the Species* (1859), and especially by its call for the application of evolutionary theory to the history of civilization in its concluding pages: "In the distant future I see open fields for far more important researches. Psychology will be based on a new foundation, that of the necessary acquirement of each mental power and capacity by gradation. Light will be thrown on the origin of man and his history" (1968: 458). But evolutionary theory in anthropology does not begin with Darwin. The very words quoted strangely echo the brief mention of Herbert Spencer (1820–1903) at the other end of the book (60: "[Spencer] has also treated Psychology on the principle of the necessary acquirement of each mental power and capacity by gradation"). It was in fact Spencer who first intoned the leitmotifs of so-called "Social Darwinism." In a series of essays dating back to the 1840s Spencer laid out a theory of social evolution based on increasing intelligence (to which Darwin's theories added little refinement). He spoke of primitive men as smaller, less intelligent, and more emotional than civilized men. But size, intelligence, and self-control increased as a result of "adaptation," and human "progress" was characterized as a "struggle of the fittest" – this phrase was first used by Spencer, though later adopted by Darwin as an alternative to "natural selection," and it points to the more fiercely competitive aspect of Spencer's evolutionism in which superior individuals and races generally succeed by killing off the inferior. Others would develop this "eat or be eaten" ethic; to his credit, Spencer was a pacifist and thought ruthless extermination of the weak injurious to the moral development of more advanced societies.

As a universal law governing all development, Spencer laid down that "evolution is definable as a change from an incoherent homogeneity to a coherent heterogeneity" (1862: 291). The inspiration for this view came from two sources. One was continental biology, especially the theories of K. E. von Baer, who saw in "differentiation" the principle of growth both in individual organisms and in the evolution in species: in fact one mirrored the other, or as the German biologist Ernst Haeckel put it, "ontogeny recapitulates phylogeny" (= "recapitulationism," i.e., the development of embryos from single cells to whole organisms replayed the stages of the development of life-forms from simple to complex). The other source was Adam Smith's economic theory that the division of labor (= heterogeneity) increases productivity and adaptability. Differentiation was, in other words, the very process of adaptation which made some organisms, individuals, species, or races better fit for the struggle for survival than others. The weak and ill-adapted will perish, indeed must be allowed to do so, if evolution, the improvement of the species, and the progress toward perfection are not to be arrested. Nature favored imperialism and laissez-faire capitalism. The laws of nature became indistinguishable from the laws of political economy.

In *The Principles of Psychology* (1855) Spencer adapted von Baer's differentiation to human evolution: all primitive human societies are simple and uniform; only advanced nations show any real individuality. The same principle governed the growth of human beings from childhood to adulthood, and, according to the principles of recapitulation, by exactly the same stages. Thus light could be thrown on the mentality of savages by the study of children in civilized societies (or on children by studying ethnographic studies of savages – so the American "genetic psychologist" G. Stanley Hall)! Spencer's ideas enjoyed a huge general success among Victorian anthropologists. The belief that savages were all alike justified the general practice of using evidence from Patagonia in order to make a point about the Congo. The belief that the mind and temperament of savages were those of a child greatly eased acceptance of the belief that cultures, like children, gradually attain an "Age of Reason."

Despite the talk of gradations, Spencer elaborated no evolutionary stage theory based on mental capacity. This was left to anthropologists like E. B. Tylor, L. E. Morgan, Frazer, and a host of others. Each anthropologist had different nomenclature and distinguishing criteria for the various ages of mankind. Tylor's "savagery," "barbarism," and "civilization" became the default. Closer to Frazer was August Comte, who distinguished evolutionary stages by their characteristic style of thought: the animistic or mythological, the religious, and the scientific. Frazer is most pretertypically Victorian in his rationalism and scientism: he distinguishes the stages of human development by the logical premise underlying their theory of natural causality: an "Age of Magic" (based on the false premise that nature is governed by laws of similarity and connection), an "Age of Religion" (based on the false premise that nature is governed by the will of superior beings), and an "Age of Science" (based on the true premise that nature is governed by general laws of causality).

Reason and purpose

From the 1860s through the 1890s, in the wake of the Church's reaction to Darwin's *Origin of the Species*, anticlerical sentiment ran high among progressive, scientifically minded British intellectuals. During these decades Frazer studied, wrote, and published the first *Golden Bough*, and became famous overnight owing to the excitement it generated among his Victorian readers. Despite his wry and understated style, Frazer's assault on traditional religion could not have failed to make a vivid impression: he exposed the simple-minded error underlying religion, the barbarous practice underlying the story of Christ, and the savage origins behind Catholic and Anglican rituals.

In a less polarized atmosphere, where religion and science have both receded from the fray, it is easier to see that everything Frazer discovered of the savage origins of Christian myth and ritual might be true without leaving much of a dent upon Christianity. Origins, after all, do not leave an indelible stamp on complex social institutions. But the evolutionary framework of Victorian social anthropology generally urged a strong connection between antecedent and subsequent beliefs and practices, or, in their vocabulary, "origins" and "survivals," and in Frazer's system the link was particularly strong. For Frazer the process of reasoning that gave rise to the invention of a belief or practice necessarily also characterized its perpetuation. Given that the end of the thought and practices studied by Frazer was always ultimately the manipulation of nature, beliefs were simply correct or incorrect, and practices either worked or did not work. Magic and religion were incorrect and dysfunctional. Those who perpetuated doctrines and rituals formed during these ages despite the advent of the Age of Science revealed a mental inflexibility worse than that of the savage, and far more dangerous, since it was not the survival of savage societies in the world, but the existence, at the very heart of civilized society, of those who stubbornly adhered to the products of primitive thought which threatened to arrest if not reverse the progress of civilization.

Those who do not share Frazer's rationalism and scientism may doubt that the mental processes and goals Frazer attributes to the origin of a myth or ritual have any bearing on the survival of that myth or ritual. Few Christian readers will readily acknowledge the technological and economic motives ascribed to their beliefs and practices, and fewer will be persuaded to give up the faith, simply because Frazer demonstrates that it was badly thought-out and unlikely to yield the results to which, in theory, it aims. Christian ritual is not really "explained" when Frazer says that a condemned criminal served as a substitute divine king/scapegoat and that the roasted flesh of a murdered human retainer of the soul of a fertility god was the chief entrée of a communal meal. None of this prevented Frazer's regular attendance in church.

If we grant, for the sake of argument, that magicians and priests aim their rituals and myths toward the control of nature either directly or through the propitiation of higher powers, could this constitute a full and adequate explanation of what myths and rituals do? Frazer says that an important

motive for moving from one evolutionary stage to another is the discovery that the previous technology did not really work. Perhaps it took
500,000 years to discover that magic did not work because it was largely
a matter of indifference whether or not it affected the natural environment. There is a strong possibility that the real function of myths and
rituals is beyond the explanatory powers even of their practitioners and
something for which an expressed technological motive might serve only
as a rationalization or a pretext. The reasons for the origin of a myth or
rite may be quite different from the reasons for their survival. Even if we
accept that in origin myths and rituals had technological and economic
intentions, we have no cause to infer the continuance of these original
motives, even for a short period.

But not all rituals are like rain dances, and most rituals, let alone myths,
are far less susceptible to the easy inference of some pragmatic intent.
In most cases Frazer is simply blind to nonrational and noneconomic motives.
Rituals and myths could, for example, satisfy emotional or psychological
needs. Wittgenstein argued that if Frazer saw you kissing the photograph
of a loved one he would think it an example of homeopathic magic
(1979: 4e): "Burning in effigy. Kissing the picture of a loved one. This is
obviously *not* based on a belief that it will have a definite effect upon the
object which the picture represents. It aims at some satisfaction and it
achieves it. Or rather, it does not *aim* at anything; we act in this way and
then feel satisfied." Jane Harrison made essentially the same criticism
(1963b: 83):

> You get a letter that hurts you, you tear it up instantly. You do this not
> because you think you are tearing up the writer, but just because you are
> hurt, and hurt nerves seek muscular discharge. . . . The simplest case of all
> is Mr. Marett's famous bull [1909: 44]. A man escapes from an enraged bull
> leaving his coat, the bull goes on goring the coat. Of course, as Mr. Marett
> prudently observes, "it is very hard to know what is going on in the bull's
> mind," but one may guess that the bull does not act in obedience to a
> mistaken application of the laws of association; he is simply letting loose
> his rage on something that happens to be goreable.

Even behind a rain dance there may be psychological, social, or historical
causes which make the rain dancer's declared or implicit intentions of
limited explanatory value. Frazer and his colleagues would ignore the very
real effects of consolation, release of anxiety, or reaffirmation of social
bonds, etc., which may belong to a myth or rite, while focusing upon the
(almost always inferred) intentions of the practitioners or narrators, and
then further reducing that intent to a supposed universal profit-motive.

Origins and survivals

But if the inferred reason and intent behind myths and rituals are problematic, the logic that links "origins" and "survivals" is still more so. It sits ill even with the basic premises of Frazer's anthropology. A survival is an object, practice, symbol, or idea, which continues to exist, like a fossil or empty shell, in an age informed by a different and more advanced mentality, and despite the fact that there is no longer any understanding of the purpose of the object, practice, symbol, or idea. But Frazer's system is so squarely constructed on the assumption that myth and ritual are directed to rational and practical purposes that it scarcely allows for the repetition of gestures that have become meaningless. The reasoning and motives assigned by Frazer are no longer applicable the moment Frazer's savage forgets that a ritual is designed to promote the fertility of the crops, or the moment he forgets just how the ritual produces the desired effect. If the rite continues with no awareness of the original means and ends, then it must be for some reason other than the pragmatic intention originally attributed to it. If it continues into an age governed by a new theory of natural causality, then it will be thrown back into the ever-present forge of pragmatic goal-directed reason, and fully reconfigured to suit the new mentality; if it is not, then the retention of forms marked by an earlier mentality must be attributed to some cause which escapes the rational pragmatic intentionality Frazer ascribes to all myths and rituals. Neither possibility seems to allow for empty shells: if beliefs and practices really have the rational basis Frazer ascribes to them, and if they really are directed to pragmatic ends, then they will fully conform to the level of reasoning achieved by the theorist or practitioner. If myths and rituals have reasons and ends other than those Frazer ascribes, then there is no common denominator permitting comparison, and nothing which could allow us to match them with an evolutionary history of human mentality. It would appear, on the surface of it, that the theory of survivals is incompatible with Frazer's theory of the evolution.

Yet the theory of "survivals" is a practical necessity for the comparatist enterprise of writing the history of human evolution. Without "survivals," one could only rely on texts and anthropological reports, which would not permit Frazer to reach very far back into human prehistory: on the one hand, all literary remains are from relatively advanced societies; on the other hand, there are only a limited number of societies described in the ethnographic literature which even Frazer could call truly primitive. In fact, for the initial and longest stage of human intellectual development, the stage of magic, Frazer could name only one living representative, the Australian aborigines. Without an elaborate theory of survivals of magical thought into later ages, Frazer could hardly have garnered enough evidence to construct "magic" as a universal stage in human development. "Survivals" of course also played a big part in marketing comparative anthropology to the Victorian public. How else could these interminably long-winded and highly documented anthropological studies become bestsellers? By unveiling raw savagery just beneath the surface of European civilization, a skillful author like Frazer, no matter how dispassionate, slow, and methodical in style, could fill his pages with drama, revelation, a delicious sense of scandal, and even flattery. Revealing religion as a barbarous relic was only part of the appeal: as we will see, early comparatist theory combined a recipe for justifying Western hegemony abroad with a justification of bourgeois hegemony at home.

Savages and social class

It is partially in order to avoid the theoretical problems posed by "survivals" – to allow himself the theory of ever-purposive and practical aims without thereby sacrificing his meaningless cultural fossils – that Frazer constructs an image of society which essentially maps the hierarchy of mental and moral development, extracted from the evolutionary timeline, onto each and every society. Society, it seems, never moves forward together in step, but one has to distinguish a progressive and regressive sector in every culture. There is a cultural elite, which is the repository of conscious and purposive thought, and there is the ignorant mass, which is the repository of primitive ideas, which would even readily revert to the savagery of a previous age if it were not firmly controlled by the cultural elite. Indeed, the masses do periodically in times of stress reverse the direction of human progress. Evolution and progress might be arrested and reversed even in Western society, if the regressive element is not strictly contained (1922: 712): "It is probably not too much to say that the hope of progress – moral and intellectual as well as material – in the future is bound up with the fortunes of science, and that every obstacle placed in the way of scientific discovery is a wrong to humanity." This regressive element still carries about in its collective head the fossils of past theories and practices, without really needing, within their dim collective intellect, to entertain any consciousness of their original meaning and function. Here is Victorian anthropology's internal other, the social counterpart of the savage, whose existence, as we saw in Section 2.1, is necessary to the whole enterprise of comparative self-definition.

The regressive element in Frazer's own society is not just the clergy, or Christians in general. These at least generally reside in the Age of Religion. Far more dangerous and regressive are most of Europe's peasantry, who still firmly reside in the Age of Magic – and a good thing, too, since most of Frazer's key evidence for primitive human mentality comes from contemporary European folk-customs. Regressive, too (as we will see), are the uneducated and undereducated, which must mean chiefly the urban proletariat of Europe's industrial nations. To take Frazer at his word one would have to believe that the majority of the population of Britain in his day were still living at the most savage stage of cultural evolution, clutching at atavistic ideas tens of thousands of years out of date.

The racist implications of evolutionary comparatism have often been noticed. Much less attention has been paid to the comparatists' elitist and class sentiments. Yet Frazer, who only feels the curiosity value of the savage without, writes openly and explicitly of the threat to civilization posed by the savage within. His fear and loathing of the peasantry and working classes appear most vividly in a discussion on material and technological progress (which he typically confuses with intellectual and social progress). It is worth quoting at length (55–6):

> But if in the most backward state of human society now known to us [i.e., Australia] we find magic thus conspicuously present and religion conspicuously absent, may we not reasonably conjecture that the civilised races of the world have also at some period of their history passed through a similar intellectual phase . . . in short that . . . on the intellectual side there has everywhere been an Age of Magic? There are reasons for answering this question in the affirmative. When we survey the existing races of mankind from Greenland to Tierra del Fuego, or from Scotland to Singapore, we observe that they are distinguished one from the other by a great variety of religions and that these distinctions are not, so to speak, merely coterminous with the broad distinctions of race, but descend into the minuter subdivisions of the states and commonwealths. . . . Yet when we have penetrated through these differences, which affect mainly the intelligent and thoughtful stratum of the community, we shall find underlying them all a solid stratum of intellectual agreement among the dull, the weak, the ignorant and the superstitious, who constitute, unfortunately, the vast majority of mankind. One of the great achievements of the nineteenth century was to run shafts down into this low mental stratum in many parts of the world, and thus to discover its substantial identity everywhere. It is beneath our feet – and not very far beneath them – here in Europe in the present day. . . . It is not our business here to consider what bearing the permanent existence of such a solid layer of savagery beneath the surface of society, and unaffected by the superficial changes of religion and culture, has upon the future of humanity. The dispassionate observer, whose studies have led

him to plumb its depths, can hardly regard it otherwise than as a standing menace to civilisation. We seem to move on a thin crust which may at any moment be rent by the subterranean forces slumbering below. From time to time a hollow murmur underground or a sudden spurt of flame into the air tells of what is going on beneath our feet. . . . But whether the influences that make for further progress, or those that threaten to undo what has already been accomplished, will ultimately prevail; whether the impulsive energy of the minority or the dead weight of the majority of mankind will prove the stronger force to carry us up to higher heights or to sink us into lower depths, are questions rather for the sage, the moralist and the statesman, whose eagle vision scans the future, than for the humble student of the present and the past. Here we are only concerned to ask how far the uniformity, the universality, and the permanence of a belief in magic, compared with the endless variety and the shifting character of religious creeds, raises a presumption that the former represents a ruder and earlier phase of the human mind, through which all the races of mankind have passed or are passing on their way to religion and science.

Against incredulity one has to force oneself to recognize that Frazer, with the allegory of Typhon about to burst out of Tartaros and ravage all civilized order, is describing his own domestic servants, his tradesmen, certainly all undereducated working men, but also perhaps to a much lesser degree his neighbors, his college chaplain, his wife, and most Cambridge undergraduates. The very same mechanism by which Victorian comparatism justified European imperialism also justified ruling-class domination, indeed laid upon them an obligation to exercise the same sort of paternal hegemony toward the working classes as toward the colonies, to save them both from the consequences of their own abject minds.

This fundamental classist dichotomy of all societies into progressive and regressive elements allowed evolution to coexist with survival. The intelligent, thinking elites of every culture, pushing at the frontiers of progress, are all conceived of as individual, free thinkers, who somehow through the exercise of their mental powers are able to break free of the superstitions that weigh upon the dull brains of the masses around them. Frazer found this neat dichotomy so appealing that he gave it a central place in his account of mental and social evolution at the cost of some serious internal contradictions.

The intelligentsia, whom Frazer always equates with the governing elite (an easier error to make in his day, perhaps, than ours), are at times characterized as lovers of truth, committed only to science, reason, and progress, and alone entirely responsible for the evolutionary progress of the human species. Elite individuals observe the evidence and apply their reason in defiance of the reflexes conditioned by the dull creeds of the vast majority of their fellows. New explanations catch on because they are immediately recognized as superior by the elite as a whole, because they are proto-scientists and scientists dedicated to truth. It would not matter to them if they lost their jobs or priesthoods, so long as truth prevailed. For Frazer human evolution is barely distinguishable from the progress of academic scholarship. He seems often to forget that his scheme gave supremacy to the economic motive. Or else perhaps he is so confident of the bond between science, industry, and politics that he cannot imagine a conflict of interest between these spheres.

Within such a scheme it comes as a surprise to find the servants of truth and progress acting with something less than pure motives at our very first encounter with them in *The Golden Bough*. The magicians and priests were the first to discover that their magic and religion did not work, he says, but they kept up a hypocritical pretense for the sake of prestige and gain. "Thus the ablest members of the profession must tend to be more or less conscious deceivers; and it is just these men who in virtue of their superior ability will generally come to the top and win for themselves positions of the highest dignity and the most commanding authority" (46). In other words, the elite, as well as having always been to some extent scientists and lovers of truth, have also to some extent always been manipulators and hypocrites.

A similar contradiction appears in the characterization of the masses whom Frazer sees as inert, changeless, and immovable. Indeed, Frazer writes as if ignorance were a sufficient (or even a necessary?) condition for the transmission of cultural heritage over thousands, even hundreds of thousands of years, allowing the masses to accomplish without effort what the elite can scarcely achieve with twenty years of schooling. (Doubtless Frazer would have defended his view by saying that magic is simple and science complex – but the mythic associations Frazer describes are anything but simple; thirteen volumes do not suffice fully to describe them.) Even the character of Frazer's masses changes with the needs of his argument. When he needs survivals, they are all die-hard conservatives. When he needs to explain progress, they are the sheepish followers of the elite.

History and progress

The Victorian anthropologists had little interest in history. The attitude is typified by Spencer: "My position, stated briefly, is that until you have got a true theory of humanity, you cannot interpret history; and when you have got a true theory of humanity *you do not want history*"

(Duncan 1908: 62). One begins with a philosophical conception of the laws governing human development. Historical "facts" are only required as examples to illustrate the general conception, not as evidence to prove the point. Phenomena that fit the general scheme are treated as essential; the value of those that offer counterevidence are undercut by being treated as merely incidental. As Peel puts it: "where it is believed that a uniform evolutionary law runs through history, and has been determined, detailed data of all kinds are dispensable: for either they fit the law, in which case they are superfluous, or they do not, in which case they are incidental" (1971: 163).

Likewise Frazer acquired his insight into the structure of human history from David Hume's *Treatise of Human Nature* (1739–40) in which Hume examined the "association of ideas" that gives rise to beliefs. Credulous beliefs arose from associations formed by contiguity or resemblance, whereas true beliefs came from the associations formed by an observation of cause and effect. From this Frazer was able to derive the distinction between the scientific and magico-religious mentality that is the fundamental division of his evolutionary scheme. "It is highly significant," notes (Robert) Fraser, "that the lion's share of the examples Hume cites of such credulity are taken from the realm of religion, and more especially of Catholic ceremonial" (1990: 19).

There are of course many more divisions in the structure of Frazer's edifice, but one does not have to be a particularly careful reader to see that the regular alternation between grand philosophical speculations and long lists of anthropological exempla corresponds exactly to the establishment of each level and division within the evolutionary scheme and the mere decoration of its spaces. It is perhaps no surprise then, that when Frazer needs to inject a little history into the story, namely when he needs to explain how humanity moves from one level to another and one space to another, he cannot do it with any plausibility. His attempts to explain the critical moments in cultural history, especially the great transition points from one age to another, are too often absurd and contradictory. As Ackerman puts it: "[Frazer] cared hardly at all for history and complaisantly replaced it with logic, as he offered speculative reconstructions of blanks in evolutionary sequences, based on what he regarded as the likeliest line of development" (1987: 47). "Likeliest" in this case meant Frazer imagining what he would think or do if he found himself in the circumstance of a savage. It is this habit that Radcliffe-Brown ridiculed as the "if-I-were-a-horse" fallacy: "This refers to a story of a Middle West farmer whose horse strayed out of its paddock. The farmer went into the middle of the paddock, chewed some grass, and asked himself: 'Now if I were a horse, where would I go?' " (Gluckman 1965: 2).

The result is a Flintstone vision of history in which the savage has all the individualism, rationalism, utilitarianism, and scientific instincts of Frazer himself, lacking only the vital mental technology of a true theory of causality. In attempting to account for the origin of totemism through a false application of the law of association, Frazer imagines that a pregnant woman, when walking in the bush one day, may have seen a kangaroo cross her path, and then, when she later gave birth, falsely associated the kangaroo with the pregnancy, and declared the kangaroo to be the father of her child (1910.4: 57). Unfortunately for Frazer, it is obvious to anyone who does not believe in the omnipotence of the rationally gifted individual that the savage, despite her commitment to false causality, could not have made this association unless she previously had a concept of "paternity," and if she had a concept of paternity she would hardly have made the association. The same absurd logic is employed to explain the discovery of the concept of "cornspirit" (1922: 463–4). Frazer supposes that threshers saw a pig running out of the cornfield, and falsely assumed that the pig was the corn-spirit. But Frazer's experiment in savage thought fails, once again, because the existence of the concept "cornspirit" was prerequisite to the selection of the right candidate to fit the job, not its result. Frazer speaks as if this happened the other way around, because his own commitment to empirical science requires that observation precede deduction (elsewhere in the same book [712] this procedure is said to distinguish science from magic). That the mind could simply create new categories of thought out of chance observation, and that these categories were immediately accepted by entire cultures, seemed to require no argument.

The omnipotence of individual, rational, pragmatic thought is nowhere so well attested as in his description of the progress from dying god to scapegoat (576–8):

> He was killed, not originally to take away sin, but to save the divine life from the degeneracy of old age; but, since he had to be killed at any rate, people may have thought that they might as well seize the opportunity to lay upon him the burden of their sufferings and sins, in order that he might bear it away with him to the unknown world beyond the grave.

It is as easy as if you asked someone who was going to the corner to take along a letter to post. But earlier societies may not give efficiency and expedience the same priority as Frazer's. Even in our pragmatic and opportunistic society it seems unlikely that the Catholic Church could easily be persuaded to substitute an egg McMuffin for the holy wafer simply because you pointed out that one "might as well" have a quick breakfast while taking communion.

It is difficult enough to understand how totemism and the worship of corn-spirits can be the result of a failed scientific enterprise, but it is far more difficult to see how the supposed errors of association were replicated throughout the globe and throughout history as any given society was ready to emerge from one stage to another. Even if we grant that there is only one correct scientific explanation for a natural phenomenon and one appropriate technology for controlling it, there can be no doubt that the pathways of error are multiple, and in ages which are based entirely on error, it is quite impossible to fathom the regular and unilinear development posited by Frazer. What is the theoretical justification for supposing that the same error of observation is so universal that one culture's errors can be elucidated by reference to another's? And how, since only scientific explanations are actually correct by this scheme, does one false explanation come to be seen as better than another, or one technology that does not work come to be accepted as better than another technology that does not work, not just in one culture, but in all? As there are no real advances until the time of science, and no explanations that are truer than the previous, progress, it seems, is measured by some other yardstick than truth and reason. Perhaps the grand evolutionary scheme should have been based not on the growth of human reason, but rather on the growth of convenience, as in the "progress" from sacrificing kings to scapegoat rituals – but then explaining history in terms of the convenience of a social elite is quite a different thing from explaining it in terms of the evolution of the human mind.

2.5   THE URMYTH: A STUDY IN AND OF COMPARISON

In the thirteenth appendix to his edition of the great ancient compendium of Greek myths, *The Library* of Apollodorus (1921: 404–55), Frazer prints thirty-six tales recorded from various parts of Europe and Asia from the twelfth to the nineteenth centuries AD. All bear a strong resemblance to the tale of Odysseus's encounter with Polyphemus in Homer's *Odyssey*. Many other comparable tales are known (Hackmann 1904 collects 221 "Cyclops stories"). We will confine ourselves to Frazer's corpus of thirty-six tales in illustrating typical characteristics of a "classical" comparative analysis. Let us begin by selecting two of the longer stories.

Here is a tale (Frazer's no. 2) told by a blind fiddler from the isle of Islay:

> A certain man called Conall Cra Bhuidhe undertook with the help of his
> sons to steal the brown horse of the King of Lochlann; but in the attempt

they were caught by the king, who would have hanged them, if Conall had not saved their lives by telling the story of his adventures. . . . "I was there as a young lad," said Conall, "and I went out hunting, and my father's land was beside the sea, and it was rough with rocks and caves and chasms. When I was going on the shore, I saw a smoke curling up between two rocks, and while I was looking at it, I fell; but the place was so full of manure that neither skin nor bone was broken. Then I heard a great clattering, and what was there but a great giant and two dozen of goats with him, and a buck at their head? And when the giant had tied the goats, he came up and said to me, "Ho, Conall, it's long since my knife is rusting in my pouch waiting for thy tender flesh." "Och," said I, "it's not much thou wilt be bettered by me, though thou shouldst tear me asunder; I will make but one meal for thee. But I see thou art one-eyed. I am a good leech, and I will give thee the sight of thy other eye." The giant went and he drew the great cauldron on the site of the fire. I told him how to heat the water so that I should give its sight to the other eye. I got heather, and I made a rubber of it, and I set him upright in the cauldron. I began at the eye that was well, pretending to him that I would give its sight to the other one, till I left them as bad as each other; and surely it was easier to spoil the one that was well than to give sight to the other.

When he saw that he could not see at all, and when I myself said to him that I would get out in spite of him, he gave a spring out of the water and stood at the mouth of the cave, and he said that he would have revenge for the sight of his eye. I had to stay there crouched all night, holding my breath that he might not feel where I was. Then he heard the birds calling in the morning, and knew that it was day, he said, "Art thou sleeping? Awake and let out my goats." I killed the buck. He cried, "I will not believe that thou art killing my buck." "I am not," said I, "But the ropes are so tight that I take long to loose them." I let out one of the goats, and he caressed her, and he said to her, "There thou art, thou shaggy white goat, and thou seest me, but I see thee not." I let them out one by one, as I flayed the buck, and before the last one was out I had flayed him bag-wise. Then I put my legs in place of his legs, and my hands in place of his fore legs, and my head in place of his head, and the horns on top of my head, so that the brute might think that it was the buck. I went out. When I was going out, the giant laid his hand on me, and he said, "There thou art, my pretty buck; thou seest me, but I see thee not." When I myself got out, and I saw the world about me, surely, oh King! joy was on me.

When I was out and had shaken the skin off me, I said to the brute, "I am out now in spite of thee." "Aha!" said he, "hast thou done this to me? Since thou wert so stalwart that thou hast got out, I will give thee a ring that I have here, and keep the ring, and it will do thee good." "I will not take the ring from thee," said I, "But throw it, and I will take it with me." He threw the ring on the flat ground, I went myself and I lifted the ring, and I put it on my finger. Then, he said, "Does the ring fit thee?" I said to him, "It does." He said, "Where art thou, ring?" And the ring said, "I am here." The brute came towards where the ring was speaking, and now I saw that I was in a harder case than ever I was. I drew a dirk. I cut off my finger, and I threw it from me as far as I could on the loch, and the place was very deep. He shouted, "Where art thou, ring?" And the ring said, "I am here," though it was at the bottom of the ocean. He gave a leap after the ring, and down he went in the sea. I was pleased when I saw him drowning, and when he was drowned I went in, and I took with me all he had of gold and silver, and I went home, and surely great joy was on my people when I arrived. And as a sign for thee, look thou, the finger is off me."

The Mongolian tale (Frazer's no. 36) of Depé Ghoz (= Eye-Head) is taken from a history of the Oghuz, a Turkic people, dating from the thirteenth or fourteenth century AD:

An Oghuzian herdsman surprised and caught at a spring a fairy of the Swan Maiden type, and had by her a semi-divine son named Depé Ghoz, who had the form of a man, except that he possessed only a single eye on the crown of his head. His birth was attended with prodigies, and as his fairy mother flew away she prophesied that he would be the bane of the Oghuz. The prediction was unhappily fulfilled. The monster began a long career of villainy by killing the nurse who gave him the breast, and he soon began to carry off and devour his own people, the Oghuz. It was in vain that they sent troops against him, for he was invulnerable; his fairy mother had put a ring on his finger, saying, "No arrow shall pierce thee, and no sword shall wound thy body." So no man could stand before him, and he put his foes to flight with great slaughter. Therefore they were forced to send envoys to negotiate a peace. Depé Ghoz at first, pitching his pretensions in a rather high key, stipulated for a daily ration of twelve men to be consumed by him; but the envoys pointing out to him with much force that at such a rate of consumption the population would soon be exhausted, the Ogre consented to accept the more reasonable ration of two men and five hundred sheep a day. On this basis he made shift to subsist until a distressed mother appealed to the heroic Bissat to save her second son, who was doomed to follow his elder brother into the maw of the monster. Touched by her story, and burning to avenge his own brother, who had been one of the giant's victims, the gallant Bissat declared his resolve to beard [i.e., cut the throat of] the Ogre in his den and to rid society of a public nuisance. It was in vain that the princess endeavored to deter him from the dangerous enterprise. He listened to none of them, but stuck a handful of arrows in his belt, slung his bow over his shoulder, girt his sword on his thigh, and bidding farewell to his father and mother set out for the giant's home.

He came to the rock where Depé Ghoz devoured his human victims. The giant was sitting there with his back to the sun. Bissat drew an arrow from his belt and shot it at the giant's breast, but the shaft shivered at contact with his invulnerable body. A second arrow fared no better; the monster only observed, "A fly has bothered me." A third shaft likewise shivered, and a piece of it fell before the giant. He started up. "The Oghuz are waylaying me again," said he to his servants. Then he walked leisurely up to Bissat, gripped him by the throat, and carried him to his abode. There he stuck him in his own ox-hide boot, saying to the servants, "I'll roast him on a spit for supper." So saying he went to sleep. But Bissat had a knife, and he slit the ox-hide and stepped out of the boot. He asked the servants how he could kill the giant. "We know not," said they, "there is no flesh on his body except his eye." Bissat went up to the sleeper's head, and lifting his eyelid saw that the eye was indeed of flesh. He ordered the servants to heat the butcher's knife in the fire. When the knife was red-hot, Bissat thrust it into the giant's eye, destroying it entirely. Depé Ghoz bellowed so that the mountains and rocks rang again. But Bissat sprang away and fell into the cave among the sheep.

The giant perceived that his foe was in the cave. So he took his stand in the doorway, setting a foot on each side of it and calling out, "Come, little rams, one after the other." As each came up, he laid his hand on its head. Meantime Bissat had killed a ram and skinned it, leaving the head and tail attached to the skin. Now he put on the skin and so arrayed drew to the giant. But the giant knew him and said, "You know how to rob me of my sight, but I will dash you against the wall." Bissat gave him the ram's head into his hand, and when the giant gripped one of the horns and lifted it up, the skin parted from it, and Bissat leaped out between the giant's legs. Depé Ghoz cast the horn on the ground and asked, "Are you freed?" Bissat answered, "My God has set me free." Then the giant handed him a ring and said, "Put it on your finger. Then neither arrow nor sword can harm you." Bissat put the ring on his finger. The giant attacked him and would have wounded him with a knife. Bissat leaped away and noticed that the ring again lay under the giant's feet. The giant again asked, "Are you freed?" and Bissat again replied, "My God has set me free." Finally, the hero contrived to slay the monster by cutting off his head with a sword.

We might begin our analysis by noting that the ring-motif in the Mongolian tale seems confused and pointless. Why does Depé Ghoz give Bissat a ring? The "problem" of the ring-motif is easily solved by reference to the tale of Conall, where the function of the ring is explicit and well integrated into the logic of the narrative. The ring-motif is also recognizable in about a third of the stories in Frazer's corpus. Frazer's own comments on these texts are minimal. On the story of Depé Ghoz he notes: "in this Mongolian or Turkish version the giant's offer of a ring to his escaped prisoner recalls the incident of the ring in some of the other versions already noticed; but here the ring does not talk and thereby betray its wearer's presence to his vengeful enemy."

The Urmyth

Frazer's remark illustrates some of the basic assumptions of the comparative method. The most basic is that all these stories are in an important sense "the same story," hence they are called "versions" or "variants." A further assumption is that there is an original version of a myth or folktale or a given motif from myth or folktale in which the narrative logic is explicit and clear. Later versions are more or less degenerate versions of this original tale. Frazer would say that this is because the stories were first created by individuals with a particular gift for narrative, but survived because retold by the populace at large which had no particular skill, and freely introduced errors and changes which destroyed the coherence of the original.

This does not necessarily mean that comparatists are wedded to the idea of a single origin for all "versions" of a tale, a difficult claim to make in cases where the "versions" belong to cultures which appear to have had little or no contact with one another. However, Frazer and other comparatists made certain further assumptions which allowed them to believe that several different originals could exist for the same story, and that these different originals all shared the same story-logic. They assumed, namely, that cultures all shared a certain pattern for potential growth, and differed mainly in the stage of development that they had attained. This potential growth or evolutionary scheme is universal, but the rates at which cultures evolve is different. At each stage people tend to think in the same ways and therefore tell the same kinds of stories, even indeed *the same story*. If we can believe this, then we are free to speak of what we might call the "Urmyth," behind all variants, whether the Urmyth is represented by a single original or multiple originals around the globe. Since it is unlikely that the Urmyth will be preserved in its pure form, the task for the comparatist is to reassemble the original tale from the clues found in the surviving variants.

Note how important the model of comparative linguistics still is. Despite the fact that linguistic arguments are far less important to the analysis than for Müller, it is still very much like reconstructing the Indo-European word for "brother" *bhrater* from the variants *brodthor* (Old English), *bruodar* (Old High German), *frater* (Latin), *bhratr* (Sanskrit), etc. The linguist may be able to devise rules by which the "corruption" of the original sounds occurred. The mythologist, by this theory, can draw upon reason, in the expectation that the Urmyth is a coherent whole, in a way that none of the variants are likely to be. Even the addition of local coloring or the updating of a tale by the substitution of a spit or a pistol for the wooden stake used to blind the Cyclops can affect the original logic and vitiate the narrative by weakening the plot logic or making the altered detail pointless or even nonsensical.

I would like to examine Frazer's corpus of "Cyclops stories" using these assumptions. But let us admit from the beginning that there is much that is questionable about them. To take but a single example, we could doubt that stories necessarily degenerate in telling or that myths and folktales have an origin in the head of an individual who might be identified as the "author." But even if this were so, it is hardly guaranteed that his way of telling the story was best, whether from an aesthetic or a logical point of view; it is at least possible that in some cases stories improve through collective "authorship," and that their plots become more elaborate and better integrated through popular transmission.

In search of the original Cyclops

Frazer would say that the logic of the ring-motif in Conall is closer to the original story than its use in Depé Ghoz. But this part of the story of Depé Ghoz, unsatisfactory in itself, can be rendered perfectly intelligible once we "discover" the original logic behind it; once we suppose, namely, that the ring was intended to produce a sound which allowed the giant to locate the hero despite his blindness. In Frazer's no. 8 we have another apparent absurdity: a blinded giant throws the escaped hero a ring as a keepsake. The hero puts it on, but

> no sooner had he done so than his finger was turned to marble, and he could not budge from the spot. In vain did he tug at the ring; he could not stir it from his finger. And now the giant was all but up with him. In despair the fugitive drew a knife, which he had in his pocket, and cut off his finger. Then he could move again, and away he tore.

If we choose to be critical of the tale's logic we will be troubled to find a marble finger rooting the wearer to the spot. Marble is heavy, but a finger's-worth is not enough to immobilize the average hero. Also it is very hard to cut marble with a knife, especially when one is in a hurry. Here is another absurdity which we can elucidate by comparing it to the parallel motif in the story of Conall. One could also find fault with Frazer's no. 10, where the hero escapes and is pursued by the giant, but in the woods finds a golden ax stuck to a tree, grabs it, sticks to it, and has to hack off his entire hand (with a knife, not the ax). This is much less satisfactory, since it is more time-consuming than finger chopping, and, if we really insist on canons of plausibility, the whole operation is likely to be fatal, given the conditions of its performance. As we will see, there are even some reasons to think that in the Urmyth the finger is not cut but bitten off, as happens in a few of the tales of the corpus.

If we pay attention to the function of the ring-motif in Conall we find that it is much better integrated into the narrative than most other uses of the motif. In Conall's version, it has a nice reversal: the giant tries to outwit Conall, but in the end, by throwing the finger and ring into the sea, Conall outwits the giant and kills him by drowning, bringing the story to a neat close. In another "variant" (no. 1), the ring is simply thrown away without consequence. In another (no. 9), the hero has cut off his finger which sticks to a shepherd's crook; the giant then gives chase, but being blind, falls into a stream and drowns. An odd version of the tale (no. 7) has the hero cut off his finger with the ring and throw it in the giant's face, whereupon the giant eats the finger and says "At least I have tasted of you." Two other tales in the corpus (nos. 5 and 6) use the ring to lure the Cyclops to a watery grave, and the conclusion that this is the original version seems compelling.

One version of the ring-motif is particularly enlightening (no. 1). As the hero reports: "I took the proffered ring and put it on my finger, and at once I was bewitched by some devilry or other and began to shout 'Here I am! Here I am!' " Though the ring-motif does not appear in Homer's version of the tale, there are two curious details which suddenly begin to make sense in light of this motif. When Odysseus gets out of the cave and into his ship, he starts to abuse the Cyclops (*Od.* 9.475ff). This helps the Cyclops aim a mountaintop at Odysseus, which just misses the prow of his ship, and the splash drives Odysseus and his companions back to the Cyclops's island. Odysseus, with uncharacteristic stupidity, again starts taunting the Cyclops once they are back out at sea, even though his men beg him to shut up. The Cyclops again follows the sound of Odysseus's voice to aim an even bigger missile. Before throwing it, however, the Cyclops invites Odysseus to return and receive some gifts. We see here precisely the same motifs as in the ring story: an invitation to take a gift, an impulse to cry out which guides the blinded giant toward his enemy, and a tossing of objects into the sea. There is no question that with the help of Frazer's corpus we can re-create an Urmyth which makes better sense and is more integral than even Homer's tale. Considerations such as the above no doubt led Frazer to conclude (1921: 404) that "the resemblance between the various versions of the tale [is so close] that they must all apparently be derived from a common original, whether that original was the narrative in the *Odyssey*, or, more probably, a still older folktale which Homer incorporated in his epic."

Economies of reason

One can go through the corpus of tales motif by motif and find multiple avenues of approach. Virtually every story has something which seems "odd, self-contradictory or simply evades rational comprehension." It is clear, for example, that in the Urmyth the Cyclops is a primitive who lives in a cave together with his sheep and, as a primitive, is considered to be godless, on remote terms with his neighbors, if he has any, and a cannibal. If the Cyclops does not live in a cave there can be no motive for blinding him rather than killing him outright, since the logic of blinding him as expressly stated in the *Odyssey* is that he is the only one who can shift the rock from the entrance of the cave and let the hero out. Yet a great many of the tales place the giant in a hovel, house, castle, palace, or some other nondescript building. In some of these, the heroes blind their respective giants and then simply walk out the door, yet there are plenty of opportunities for walking out the door without risking an assault on the giant. In no. 30 the blinded giant just runs howling out the house door and is followed by his prisoners. No. 17 occurs in an unspecified place, but the heroes simply run away after blinding the giant in his sleep. Nos. 14 and 31 do take place in caves, but after blinding their respective giants the heroes, after a chase, simply chop off the giants' heads. There is no hint at any particular difficulty in leaving.

The blinding clearly works best if the hero only has one eye. In some versions where the giant has two eyes, two spits are used simultaneously to good effect. But credulity is definitely strained in no. 27, where there are two prisoners and two giants, and each giant has two eyes in front and two eyes in back of his head, and, as if this were not enough, the giants sleep with their eyes open. The prisoners sneak up on them wearing sheepskins, each armed with two hot pokers, and the giants obligingly sleep (open-eyed) through the first application. The eye-motif seems to have been particularly susceptible to corruption. Several stories make the giant blind in one eye and the prisoner pretend to be a doctor, as in Conall. In others the giant is only persuaded that he has eye trouble. But in no. 14, the giant is blind to begin with, though this does not spare the hero the trouble of sticking a hot poker into his eye. In no. 25 the giant is blind but can smell human flesh, yet this does not prevent the hero from using the sheepskin trick to make his escape. No. 31 is particularly bizarre: it is the giant who blinds his prisoners by giving them enchanted milk to drink. In several versions the hero is a smith who pretends to forge eyes for the monster (nos. 10 and 11). In one case the prisoner really does heal the giant's eyes and the grateful monster adopts him as a son (no. 29).

It is fairly clear that the hero must not be too well armed. In this respect very few versions are really consistent. In the *Odyssey,* for example, Odysseus is about to kill Polyphemus with his sword, but (as mentioned) only thinks better of it when he considers the difficulty of removing the slab of rock closing the mouth of the cave. It is not clear, however, why the sword is not used to blind Polyphemus, and why such effort is put into cutting and hardening a stake to do this job. In no. 18 the prisoner puts his knife in the giant's eye with no further ado. In several versions, after blinding the giant with a coal or spit, the prisoners then pull out knives to skin the sheep or to cut off their ringfingers. In no. 19 the hero blinds the giant by shooting him with his pistol, but the gun is later forgotten when the hero uses the sheepskin trick to get past the giant as he stands in the entrance of his hut. It would seem that cold pokers would do as well as hot. If we are to insist on logic and realism in this regard, then we must assume that in the Urmyth neither the giant nor the prisoner had any weapon more sophisticated than a stick and that the burning of the end of the stick in the fire was for the purpose of hardening its point. Burkert (1979: 34) in fact seizes upon the production of this very primitive spear in arguing for a paleolithic origin for the Cyclops tale, though the reference to its glowing in the fire already shows corruption by a later metallurgical bias.

The logic of the situation requires the trick of the escape by hanging onto the underside of the sheep, as in the *Odyssey.* Since the hero should not be armed in the Urmyth, all versions in which the hero skins a sheep and crawls out under its pelt are in violation of strict story logic, especially those in which the hero is detected but nevertheless throws off the sheepskin and escapes by running out between the giant's legs (nos. 4 and 21). Still more corrupt would be the version in which the prisoner gets out by wearing a dogskin (no. 18). Clearly derivative would be the version in which the prisoner wears the sheepskin blanket which the good giant provided for his bedding (no. 10), and decadent the version in which the hero puts on a sheepskin to infiltrate the giant's cave and steal his parrot (no. 20). Wholly inadequate, by this logic, is the tale in which we are told that the hero happened to be armed with a paring knife and an awl, only to find the hero hanging onto the underside of the sheep and sticking the awl into its stomach to spur it on (no. 28).

Some problems with the method

In this way one can examine each motif and separate an originary logical form from corrupt and derivative forms. But in most cases the perception of weak or absent logic appears only after the study of the comparative material. If one does not begin with the assumption that a given corpus is a variant of a single tale, one can often find a logic specific to any given story. In the story of Depé Ghoz, for example, there is a suggestion that the function of the ring is to lure Bissat close to the giant. We are told that after the first attack "the ring again lay under the giant's feet." The ring-motif thus functions to reveal Bissat's physical and mental dexterity in facing new perils and temptations: the giant attempts to outwit him, but he outwits the giant and gains a treasure. We are not likely to problematize the narrative unless we have already seen a large number of other tales where a ring speaks. In Depé Ghoz there is also a specific logic to the removal of the giant's ring that does not appear in other tales; we are told, namely, that this is what makes his flesh (apart from his eye) invulnerable, and its removal appears to facilitate the eventual slaying of the giant.

In *Odyssey* 9 Odysseus's decision to stay at the cave to see if he can get some gifts may seem implausible because we have already been told that the primitive oaf owns nothing but goats and cheese. A comparison with other tales in Frazer's collection shows that some heroes are caught while raiding the giant's premises (in Conall, for example, there are allusions to gold and silver hidden in the cave). Other heroes come to the giant's premises because they are destitute and need a handout. The comparative material would encourage one to think that in the Urmyth the hero came to the giant's cave for food and shelter and was caught there upon the giant's return. But if we assume that this is the real story of which Homer's episode is a decadent reflection, we lose sight of those aspects of the tale which are specific to Homer: for example, Odysseus's heroic thirst for honor, glory, and trophies, the theme of gift-giving, guest-friendship, the Cyclops's violation of Zeus Xenios (Patron of Strangers, Guests, Hosts), and so on. Do the comparisons help us explain a myth or tempt us to incorporate extraneous motifs that we like or understand better? Who really corrupts the logic of the myth, the ignorant Oghuzian narrator, or the comparatist? Are we substituting a different tale? Odysseus's taunting of the giant might have been explained in a different way, if the corpus were a little smaller. In no. 34, for example, the giant is taunted and dies of vexation. Earlier in that story the same giant gives proof of a low frustration-threshold when he is so enraged at being blinded that he bites off his own finger.

Frazer argued on the basis of such motifs as the singing ring, which occurs in the majority of variants, but has no equivalent in the *Odyssey* story, that this ring-motif was probably part of the original story, and that therefore the encounter between Odysseus and the Cyclops in *Odyssey*

9 is just another variant on a much older folktale. But maybe the ring was a later addition, even a later improvement. Or maybe we are misguided in thinking that these tales are somehow the "same" rather than similar but different, that they derive from a common source, or that in their inconcinnities they reveal the corruption of some original tale logic.

2.6 COMPARISON OF THE GREEK AND HITTITE MYTHS OF THE DIVINE SUCCESSION

Despite the cautions and reservations expressed in the last section, there are instances in which the comparative method yields unmistakable connections between tales with truly illuminating results. A famous example are the Greek and Hittite myths of divine succession, which we will examine in detail in order both to reveal the virtues of the comparative method and raise some interesting questions about the nature and meaning of comparanda.

Greek myths of divine succession

The Greek myth of the first divine kings of the firmament is well known from Hesiod (c.700 BC). According to his *Theogony* Earth gave birth to Sky (Ouranos or Uranus), her "equal," so that he might "cover her entirely and be a secure platform for the blessed gods" (126–7). They then had a large number of children, most of whom were powerful, monstrous, and unruly. These included the Titans, the Cyclopes, and the Hundredhanders. Sky hated his children and "hid his children in Earth's depths as soon as they were born and would not let them into the light" (156–9). This appears to mean that the children were kept inside Earth's womb by Sky's "unremitting embrace." Earth was not pleased with this state of affairs: "she groaned within and devised a crafty and evil scheme" (159–60). She fashioned a great sickle from grey flint, and gave it to her son Kronos to avenge the "shameful actions" of his father (166, 172). Kronos is described as "the youngest of all [the Titans], wily and most terrible, who hated his lusty father" (137–8).

When night came Sky descended upon Earth and began to copulate with her (despite the contradiction this implies in the story-logic of Sky's unremitting embrace). From within Earth's womb, Kronos seized Sky's genitals as he penetrated Earth, chopped them off and threw them away. The genitals fell upon Earth, further impregnating her. From the blood were born the Erinyes, the Giants, and the Melian Nymphs, and from the sperm which oozed out of the severed member as it fell upon the sea there arose Aphrodite. At this point Sky largely drops out of the story, but before he does so he warns Kronos that he, in turn, is fated to be overthrown by one of his own children (463–5). Kronos then chooses his sister Rhea as wife and becomes king.

Kronos and Rhea then beget the Olympian gods, but Kronos proves himself a chip off the old block, except that instead of locking his children up in their mother's body, he locks them in his own. As each child is born, he swallows it, keeping in mind his father's prophecy.

Hesiod continues (467–73):

> A deep and lasting grief took hold of Rhea, and when she was about to bring forth Zeus . . . she entreated her own parents, Earth and Sky, to advise her how she might bring forth her child in secret and how the avenging fury (Erinys) of her father, Sky, and of her children whom great Kronos of the crooked counsel swallowed, might exact vengeance. And they readily heard their dear daughter and were persuaded, and they counseled her about all that was destined to happen.

They advised Rhea to withdraw to Crete and give birth to Zeus. Earth then hid the child. To Kronos Rhea gave a stone disguised as a child and he swallowed it.

Zeus quickly grew to manhood and Kronos was forced by some trick of Earth and by the strength of Zeus to vomit up his brothers and sisters in reverse order of consumption, beginning with the stone which substituted for Zeus (and was deposited at Delphi to serve as a cult object). Hesiod does not say how Kronos was overpowered. The version of Apollodorus has the Titan Metis give Kronos a drug (1.2.1) and an Orphic source claims that, on Night's suggestion, Kronos is drugged with honey, tied up, and castrated with the same sickle with which he castrated Sky. With the help of his brothers and sisters Zeus wins the war ("Titanomachy") against Kronos's brothers and sisters, the Titans, whom Zeus packed off to Tartaros, deep inside Earth. Zeus then marries Metis and becomes king of the gods.

Zeus's reign is permanent, but he is not left unchallenged. Threats come from several different quarters and the chronology of these threats is variable or uncertain. Several of these replicate the story patterns of the earlier events in the succession myth. According to Hesiod's *Theogony* (886–900), Earth and Sky warn Zeus that his queen, Metis, will bear powerful children, first a daughter who will have strength and wisdom equal to her father, and then a son who would replace Zeus as king of gods and men. To prevent this unwanted birth Zeus swallows Metis, but he does this at a time when Metis is already pregnant with Athena. In this way Zeus assumes responsibility for giving birth to the child. When the pregnancy comes to term, Athena springs fully armed from Zeus's head. The birth canal is opened with the help of Hephaestus, who splits Zeus's skull open with an ax. This female birth proves no threat to Zeus; Athena is generally a loyal supporter of her father's cause, but the son who would have replaced Zeus is never conceived.

Other threats come from Earth and her progeny. First Earth, angered with the Olympians, either because of their treatment of the Titans, or for some other reason, stirred up her children, the Giants, to wage war on the Olympians, a battle ("Gigantomachy") in which the Giants were wiped out by the Olympian gods. Earth then begot a child named Typhon (or Typhoeus), by whom she intended to get her revenge upon Zeus and the Olympians. The paternity of Typhon is variously given as Tartaros and Kronos. The fullest and most interesting version of the tale is told by Apollodorus (1.6.3, Frazer's translation with minor changes):

When the gods had overcome the Giants, Earth, still more enraged, had intercourse with Tartaros and brought forth Typhon in Cilicia, a hybrid between man and beast. In size and strength he surpassed all the offspring of Earth. As far as the thighs he was of human shape and of such prodigious bulk that he out-topped all the mountains, and his head often brushed the stars. One of his hands reached out to the West and the other to the East, and from them projected a hundred dragon's heads. From the thighs downward he had huge coils of vipers, which when drawn out, reached to his very head and emitted a loud hissing. His body was all feathery; unkempt hair streamed on the wind from his head and cheeks; and fire flashed from his eyes. Such and so great was Typhon when, hurling kindled rocks, he made for the very heaven with hissings and shouts, spouting a great jet of fire from his mouth. But when the gods saw him rushing at heaven, they made for Egypt in flight, and being pursued they changed their forms into those of animals. However, Zeus pelted Typhon at a distance with thunderbolts, and at close quarters struck him down with an adamantine sickle, and as he fled pursued him closely as far as Mount Casius, which overhangs Syria. There, seeing the monster sore wounded, he grappled with him. But Typhon twined about him and gripped him in his coils, and wresting the sickle from him severed the sinews of his hands and feet, and lifting him on his shoulders carried him through the sea to Cilicia and deposited him on arrival in the Corycian cave. Likewise he put away the sinews there also, hidden in a bearskin, and he set to guard them the she-dragon, Delphyne, who was a half-bestial maiden. But Hermes and Aegipan stole the sinews and fitted them unobserved to Zeus. And having recovered his strength Zeus suddenly from heaven, riding in a chariot of winged horses, pelted Typhon

with thunderbolts and pursued him to the mountain called Nysa, where the
Fates tricked the fugitive; for he tasted of the ephemeral fruits after he was
persuaded that he would be strengthened by them. So being again pursued
he came to Thrace, and in fighting at Mount Haemus he heaved whole mountains. But when these recoiled on him through the force of the thunderbolt,
a stream of blood gushed out on the mountain, and they say that from
that circumstance the mountain was called Haemus [*haima* = Greek for
"blood"]. And when he started to flee through the Sicilian sea, Zeus cast
Mount Etna in Sicily upon him. That is a huge mountain, from which down
to this day they say that the blasts of fire issue from the thunderbolts that
were thrown.

The Hittite myth of divine succession

Almost all of our variants for the myth of Typhon locate the place of his
birth in Cilicia (in southern Turkey, at the northeast corner of the
Mediterranean Sea). This is at the extreme eastern limit of Greek settle-
ment in the Archaic period. Important events in the story take place at
Mount Casius, which is well beyond Greek territory and close to the mouth
of the Orontes. One might have suspected, therefore, that elements of this
myth were generated in the Near East, and this was conclusively proven
by the discovery and decipherment, early in the last century, of some
cuneiform tablets in the Hittite language. The Hittites were the dominant
power in Asia Minor in the last part of the Late Bronze Age (LBA III,
c.1460–1200 BC). At their greatest extent they controlled nearly all of
modern Turkey and Syria (including the territory of Cilicia and Mount
Casius). The Hittite language is Indo-European (see Figure 1), and as these
tales are as old as the Vedas, one might have expected – indeed, sharing
the assumptions of the early comparatists, would have expected – that
their contents would take us closer to the original myths of the Indo-
Europeans. But, unlike the Vedic deities, the names of the Hittite gods
are semitic and evidently taken from the Hurrian and Syrian people whom
they conquered. It does not necessarily follow that the stories are also
pre-Hittite, although this conclusion is urged by many (and denied by
others) on the basis of their content. Of particular interest are three poems,
the *Myth of the Kingdom of Heaven*, *The Song of Ullikummi*, and *The
Myth of Illuyanka*. They cover the early history of the gods, just like
Hesiod's *Theogony*. The main characters of this story are Alalu, his son
Anu (Sumerian "An" and Akkadian/Babylonian "Anu" mean "sky"),
Kumarbi, Teshub, who is the Storm-god, and Ullikummi, whose name means
"destroyer of Kummiya," which is the city of Teshub.
   This is the story told by the *Myth of the Kingdom of Heaven*.

Once long ago Alalu was king in Heaven. As long as Alalu was seated on his throne, the mighty Anu, first among the gods, stood before him. He would sink at his feet and set the drinking cup in his hand.

For nine years [or ages] Alalu was king in heaven. In the ninth year Anu gave battle to Alalu and he defeated Alalu. Alalu fled before him and went down to the dark earth, and Anu took his seat upon the throne. As long as Anu sat upon the throne, the mighty Kumarbi gave him his food. He would sink at his feet and set the drinking cup in his hand.

For nine years Anu was king in Heaven. In the ninth year Anu gave battle to Kumarbi and, like Alalu, Kumarbi gave battle to Anu. When Anu could no longer withstand Kumarbi's eyes, he fought his way out of Kumarbi's grip and fled. Like a bird he moved in the sky. Kumarbi rushed after him, seized him by his feet and dragged him down from the sky.

Kumarbi bit Anu's "knees" [what others translate as "hips" or "loins" is clearly a euphemism for "genitals"] and his manhood went down into Kumarbi's inside. When it lodged there, and when Kumarbi had swallowed Anu's manhood, he rejoiced and laughed. Anu turned back to him and said: "You rejoice over your inside, because you have swallowed my manhood. Do not rejoice over your inside! In your inside I have planted a heavy burden. First, I have impregnated you with the noble Storm-god. Secondly I have impregnated you with the River Tigris, which cannot be withstood. Thirdly I have impregnated you with the noble Tasmishu [this is a minion of the Storm-god]. Three dreadful gods have I planted in your belly as seed. You will go and kill yourself by banging your head against the rocks of your own mountain."

With these words Anu flew up to the sky and disappeared from sight. But Kumarbi, "the wise king," began spitting. He spat out Anu's sperm and as it hit the earth it produced various mountains, rivers, and gods. The tablet has multiple breaks at this point but apparently Kumarbi is unable to spit out the seed of the Storm-god, and some others, and has to give birth to them himself.

Here follows an amusing episode. Kumarbi is faced with a serious problem. He is male and he is pregnant. He is pregnant, moreover, with the offspring of the god Anu, whom he has just deposed, and this offspring is apparently destined to usurp his power and avenge his father. Kumarbi starts having dizzy spells and goes to Aya to seek advice. This Aya corresponds to the Akkadian/Babylonian Ea or Sumerian Enki, who is the lord of Sweet Water and a trickster figure – like water, he is able to get around barriers – and the god of arts and crafts. He seems an appropriate god to deal with difficult problems like male pregnancies. Unfortunately the tablet is badly broken at an intriguing passage: "As Kumarbi walked along and took his place before Aya, he became dizzy and collapsed." There seems to follow some discussion of how to give birth.

Finally a god named Kazal comes out of what might be his head. The text continues: "Kumarbi began to speak to Aya: 'Give me my son, I want to devour my son! Which wife of mine(?) . . . What . . . the Storm-god to me, I will eat: I will crush him like a brittle reed.' " It is not easy to make much sense of the fragmentary text that follows, but it seems that Kumarbi gets something hard to eat and it hurts his mouth. Arguably it is a stone. It seems someone says to him "Let them call it the . . . stone, and let it be placed in. . . ." Kumarbi puts the stone in the place indicated and says, apparently to the stone: "Let them go and call you . . . , and let rich men and warrior lords slaughter for you cattle and sheep; let poor men sacrifice meal to you." It appears then that Kumarbi has given birth to a son, has been given a stone to eat, presumably in place of the son which he intended to eat, and has spit it out and placed it somewhere to serve as a cult object.

After this, Aya, like a good doctor, refers Kumarbi to specialists, oddly called "the poor," who mend his head, or whatever was split, and seem to put him on a diet of porridge. Meanwhile Kumarbi is still trying to find some means of ridding himself of the Storm-god. The foetus of the Storm-god inside Kumarbi's body is in communication with his father Anu on another difficult matter. Since Kumarbi is male, he has no natural birth canal and so one has to be created. The Storm-god consults with Anu on how best to force his way out of Kumarbi's body. Anu lists at least three possibilities: he can come out of Kumarbi's mouth, out of his *tarnassas* (the word probably means anus), or out of "the good place" (probably a euphemism for "penis"). The Storm-god is not happy with any of these, but finally votes to split open Kumarbi's *tarnassas*. Anu, however, wants him to come out of "the good place." In the end the Storm-god has to follow Anu's advice, because Kumarbi's assistants have "made his *tarnassas* secure." Unfortunately the details of this operation are lost or not given. The last details of the remains of this poem make it clear that the Storm-god succeeds in emerging from Kumarbi. There is then a conversation between the Storm-god and possibly his bull Sheri. The Storm-god's interlocutor seems to report the hostile words of Kumarbi. The Storm-god is confident that he has sufficiently weakened his enemy. He is warned against overconfidence. His words are reported to Aya, who is angry. The rest of the tablet is destroyed, except for an indication that Earth becomes pregnant by Apsu (the Subterranean realm) with two children and Aya is happy with the news.

We can pick up the Hittite theogony again in the *Song of Ullikummi*. When this poem begins the Storm-god, Teshub, is in power and Kumarbi wants revenge. Kumarbi plans to sire a mighty rebel who will defeat the Storm-god and destroy his city. To do this he finds a big rock, a sexy one, which roused his desire, and apparently also the narrator's – the text breaks off as it builds up to a rhetorical climax: "five times he took her, ten times he took her." In another tablet we have a description of the birth of the child delivered by the Good-women and Mother-goddesses and how he is placed on Kumarbi's knee and he fondles him and lets him dance up and down. He decides to give him the name Ullikummi, signifying destroyer of the Storm-god's city. Then he becomes afraid lest the Sun-god or any of the other gods should see his son and "crush him like a reed in the brake." So he sends for some remote female deities, the Irsirra deities, and asks them to take his son "down to the dark earth" and care for him. The child is made of diorite stone. The deities take him and place him on the shoulder of an Atlas-like god, Ubelluri, who carries the world on his shoulders. From Ubelluri's shoulder the child grows "like a shaft" at an ever-accelerating rate. On his fifteenth day he has grown so big that the sea only reaches up to his waist. On that day the Sun-god notices him and reports him to the Storm-god. The Storm-god and his minion Tasmishu go to the top of Mount Casius and are joined by Ishtar (the goddess of sex and war). They look down at the diorite man emerging from the sea and the Storm-god decides to attack. By this time we are told that Ullikummi is 9,000 leagues high and 9,000 leagues wide, and his head rises above the gates of the city of the gods.

Things go badly for the Storm-god and his allies at first and the gods are driven out of their city. The Storm-god then goes to Aya for advice. Aya in turn interrogates Ubelluri:

"Ubelluri, don't you know? Did no one bring you the news? Don't you know the vigorous god whom Kumarbi has created to oppose the gods? Don't you know the frightful death which Kumarbi is plotting for the Storm-god? He is making a rival for him who thrives in the sea in the form of a diorite stone. Don't you know him? He rises like a tower and has blocked off heaven, the holy houses of the gods, and Hebat [wife of the Storm-god]). Is it because you are far away from the dark earth, Ubelluri, that you don't know of this vigorous god?" Ubelluri [who obviously has more muscle than brains] answered Aya: "When they built heaven and earth upon me I did not know anything. When they came and severed the heaven from the earth with a cleaver, I did not know that either. Now my right shoulder is a little sore. But I do not know who that god is." When Aya heard these words he turned Ubelluri's shoulder. The diorite man stood upon Ubelluri's right shoulder like a shaft.

At that moment a solution occurs to Aya. He advises the gods to open the ancient storehouses of their forefathers and find the "old copper knife with which they severed heaven from earth." They use it to cut through the

feet of Ullikummi, and this seems to destroy his power and the Storm-god
is able to defeat him. Possibly it is the act of severing his connection with
the earth that is significant here, as in the tale of Heracles' defeat of Antaeus
or the Giant Alcyoneus.

This is not the end of the Storm-god's troubles. In the *Myth of Illuyanka*
a dragon Illuyanka next challenges him, actually defeats him, and takes
away his heart and his eyes. The Storm-god goes away and marries a poor
man's daughter, has a son, and when this son grows up he marries the
daughter of the dragon Illuyanka. The Storm-god then instructs his son
to ask his father-in-law for his heart and eyes. He asks and they are freely
given. After they are restored, the goddess Inara helps defeat Illuyanka
by inviting him to a feast. There he overindulges and, when too bloated
to return to his lair, is tied up by the hero Hupasiya and then killed by
the Storm-god. As he is about to kill Illuyanka, the Storm-god's son intervenes on Illuyanka's behalf, so the Storm-god kills them both.

The main parallels between the Greek and Hittite succession myths could
be summarized by the following table:

Greek (mainly told by Hesiod, c.700 BC)	*Hittite/Hurrian (recorded c.1200 BC)*
Triadic succession of gods: Uranus (Sky), Kronos (Corn-god?), Zeus (Storm-god).	Triadic succession of gods: Anu (= Sky), Kumarbi (Corn-god), Teshub (Storm-god).
Conversation of unborn god (Kronos) in womb with external advisor, Earth (= Gaea).	*Conversation of unborn god (Storm-god) in womb with external advisor (Anu).*
Uranus is castrated by Kronos from within Earth's womb. Gives warning to Titans.	Anu is castrated by Kumarbi as he flees up to the sky. Gives warning to Kumarbi.
Kronos swallows his children as they are born from Rhea; has children locked in his belly. *Cf. myth of birth of Athena: Zeus swallows Metis and gives birth to her fetus.*	Kumarbi swallows Anu's genitals, is made pregnant, has embryos in his belly.
Blood and seed from Uranus's member impregnates Earth, who bears various gods.	Kumarbi spits out Anu's seed and impregnates Earth, who bears various gods.
Parent (Rhea) gives infant god (Zeus) to remote deities to be raised concealed in cave.	*Parent (Kumarbi) gives infant god (Ullikummi) to remote deities to be raised concealed in earth.*
Kronos swallows a stone instead of Zeus. The stone is set up in Delphi.	Kumarbi wants to devour his son (?) but eats something hard (a stone?). Sets up as cult object.

Kronos vomits up children through his mouth. *Cf. Athena is born from Zeus's head.*	Storm-god is born from the "good place." Another god is possibly born from Kumarbi's skull.
Zeus rules. Kronos goes to Tartaros.	Storm-god rules. Kumarbi is displaced.
Kronos (or Tartaros) unites with Earth to beget Typhon, who rebels against Zeus.	First Earth bears twins by Apsu, who challenge the Storm-god, then Kumarbi unites with rock to beget Ullikummi, who rebels against Storm-god.
Mount Casius in eastern Asia Minor is site of a battle between Typhon and Zeus.	Mount Casius is site of an assembly of the gods in emergency session to deliberate about Ullikummi's attack on the Storm-god.
The sickle used to castrate Uranus is reused by Typhon to cut Zeus's sinews.	The Storm-god reuses the knife which divided heaven and earth to defeat Ullikummi.
Zeus's son Hermes steals back his sinews.	The Storm-god's son tricks Illuyanka into returning his father's heart and eyes.
The Fates trick Typhon into eating the ephemeral fruit which prepares for his defeat at the hands of Zeus.	Inara tricks Illuyanka into overindulging at a feast which prepares for his defeat at the hands of the Storm-god.

* events which are out of sequence in the narrative appear in italics.

Since the discovery of the Hittite tablets scholars have recognized more than a casual connection between the Hittite and Greek succession myths recorded by Hesiod. Strong confirmation came with the discovery in 1962 of a papyrus book beside a tomb in the Derveni Pass in northern Greece. Largely because of the difficulty of reading this carbonized remnant, a full text has only recently been made available. Written about 350 BC, it is a copy of a commentary on a mystic *Theogony* probably composed sometime in the sixth century BC and ascribed to the mythical poet Orpheus. The poem gives a version of the creation myth we find in Hesiod, but it differs from Hesiod in a number of ways. Most significantly, it reproduces the most striking episode of the Hittite theogony, namely, Kumarbi's swallowing of Anu's genitals. In the Orphic text Zeus "swallowed the genitals of the god who first ejaculated the brilliance of the sky." These are presumably the genitals of Sky (if so, oddly, we skip a generation; we would expect Kronos, not Zeus, to swallow Sky's genitals). Through this act Zeus gets pregnant: "and on him grew all the immortals, blessed gods and goddesses, the rivers, lovely springs and all the rest, all that had then been born."

Models of divergence and convergence

That there exists some connection between the Greek and Hittite myths, there can be little doubt. But just what kind of connection is less clear. Most scholars argue for a single archetype for both the Greek and Hittite theogonies. The Hittite text antedates Hesiod by 500 years, and itself records a probably much older epic poem. Yet the differences between the two are also significant. The myth we find in Hesiod is not a recent borrowing. Hence Kirk (1970), for example, would place the time of the Greek borrowing sometime around 1500 BC.

In this way the relationship between the poems is usually conceived in terms of a genetic or tree-stem model which derives each variant from an archetype. According to this model, influences only work vertically, from original to copy. As we saw, comparative mythology inherited this model from comparative linguistics' first exercises in tracing European and Sanskrit words back to their Indo-European originals (see Figure 1). But this is not the only possible model for explaining comparable myths, or even the comparable vocabulary and syntax of Indo-European languages. In a famous essay, published in 1939, the Prague structuralist N. S. Trubetzkoy offered an alternative model. It is an observable linguistic phenomenon that distinct linguistic groups in contact over long periods of time borrow vocabulary and forms from one another. Though this was traditionally treated as an exceptional or marginal phenomenon, Trubetzkoy proposed to see this as a norm and explained the similarities in Indo-European languages as the result of mutual influences extending over many generations. Through various forms of cultural contact language A influenced a change in language B and language B influenced language C, which came also to absorb influences from language A. A was in turn influenced by language B and came also to absorb forms from language C, and so on. In this way the similarities of the Indo-European languages could be explained through *convergence* and not, as usual, through divergence from an Ur-language. The advantage of the convergence over the divergence model is that it has the power to explain differences as well as similarities. The models need not be exclusive, however: in principle, the Indo-European language group may have been created by a long process involving both divergence and convergence.

If we were to try to explain the compelling resemblances between the Greek and Hittite myths of succession on the divergence model alone, we would find discomfort at some equally compelling discrepancies. The divergence model can account for these only as a result of corruption. But the corruption is so great as to put at risk the very assumption that we are dealing with variants of the same tale. Certain character types and motifs recur in both myths: we have a succession of divine kings who correspond functionally, and monstrous challengers; we have recurrent motifs like preventing the birth of children, castrating gods, male pregnancy caused by swallowing sperm, and the creation of other gods by spitting or splitting. But when we examine the myths in detail, more often than not we find that the parallel motifs are attached to different characters in the set. We also find that motifs which occur only once or twice in the Hittite myth are replicated with variations for many characters or episodes in the Greek succession myths. The male pregnancy motif, vividly portrayed in the episode of Kumarbi, reappears not only in the parallel Kronos episode, but also in the myths of the birth of Athena, of the Orphic Zeus, and arguably also in the usual tale of Dionysus's birth from Zeus's thigh. The castration motif, vividly portrayed in the battle of Anu and Kumarbi, in Greek sources is replicated to include castrations of Kronos as well as Sky, while the removal of Zeus's sinews by Typhon, performed with the same sickle used to castrate Sky, is more suggestive of castration than the Hittite parallel where Teshub uses the "copper knife" to cut under the feet of Ullikummi. We might add that despite its allegedly derivative nature, the Hesiodic myth is sometimes closer to the presumptive Urlogic than the Hittite. In Hesiod the castration is cosmogonically connected with the separation of Earth and Sky, but Earth receives no mention in the *Myth of the Kingship of Heaven*. The inference, urged by comparison with the Greek myth, that the castration explains the original separation of Earth and Sky is confirmed by the reference to the "old copper knife with which they severed heaven from earth" in the *Song of Ullikummi*.

But explanations based on a divergence model become even more convoluted when we examine (non-Indo-European) Near Eastern traditions. An Egyptian myth also seems to explain the separation of Earth (Geb) and Sky (Nut) as the result of an act of castration putting an end to an unremitting coital embrace. But in this case, the roles are reversed: it is Sky who is female, and she also eats her children, which is the cause of the initial discord between her and Earth. Phoenician mythology also displays a bewildering mixture of the familiar and the incongruous. Here, the divine couple Sky (Shamem) and Earth have a falling-out because of Earth's jealousy of Sky's other lovers. There is a period of separation during which Sky occasionally visits Earth, forces his attentions upon her, and then leaves. But when their son El grows to manhood he prepares a sickle and a spear and wages war on Sky and deposes him. There follow thirty-two years of intrigue and warfare, El finally ambushes his father and castrates him, and "the blood from his genitals dripped into the springs and the waters of the rivers" (Philo of Byblos, *FGrH* 790 F 2).

Still more uncanny is the reappearance of the male pregnancy motif, the castration motif, and the *in utero* dialogue motif, all in the context of a battle for divine succession, which we find in the Egyptian tale of the battle of Horus and Seth (whom Greeks and Egyptians equated with Zeus and Typhon). When Horus and Seth dispute the divine kingship, Seth seeks to trick Horus by having intercourse with him while he sleeps. But Horus is not really asleep and puts his hands between his legs to gather up Seth's seed. When Horus's mother Isis finds out about this, she cuts off his hands with a copper knife and throws them into the river. She then plays a trick on Seth by smearing Horus's semen on a lettuce leaf and giving the lettuce to Seth to eat. At an assembly of the gods Seth lays claim to the kingship on the grounds that he has humiliated Horus. Seth's semen is called to testify. It answers from the marsh. Then Thoth calls upon Horus's semen. It answers from Seth's stomach (Simpson 1973: 121)

> "Come out, you semen of Horus." Then it said to him: "Where shall I come out from?" Thoth said to it: "Come out from his ear." Thereupon it said to him: "Is it from his ear that I should issue forth, seeing that I am divine seed?" Then Thoth said to it: "Come out from the top of his head." And it emerged as a golden solar disc upon Seth's head.

A variant still closer to the theogonic uses of the male pregnancy motif is known from the temple of Min at Edfu, beside a relief showing the King offering Min some lettuce (trans. Griffiths 1960: 45): "Offering lettuces. For recitation. The beautiful plants, the herbage from the district, rejoice thou at seeing it. Cause thy seed to enter the body of the enemy, that he may be pregnant, and that thy son may come forth from his forehead."

Though the Hittite and Greek myths of divine succession are particularly close, Robert Mondi (1990) shows a vast number of similarities which they share with the myths of contiguous cultures, including Babylon, Phoenicia, Egypt, and even India. He argues strongly against any simple transmission and corruption of either an Indo-European or semitic archetype. Mondi views the similarities between the Greek and Hittite myths as evidence of a much looser commonwealth of motifs and ideas which exist not only at a "source" for all variants, but which result from long and continuous intercultural contacts. He argues that the recurring characters and motifs were not, as a rule, transmitted as a fully embodied narrative, from which they were somehow shaken loose by the hazards of transmission, but rather that they were transmitted as already somewhat loose clusters of characters, motifs, themes, and functions; we are dealing, for the most part, with the creative redeployment of common, and evolving, clusters of mythical ideas.

A divergence model encourages scholars to take differences for granted, appealing only to the organic metaphor of disintegration and degeneration over time. But the differences in these tales are so great that we can hardly be content only to regard them as "variants" of the same tale, or to consider them interesting or meaningful only in relation to a lost original. If the similarities between tales may sometimes be likened to branches emerging from a common tree trunk, they are sometimes also the result of lateral contacts between branches of the tree at any moment. Indeed, the need for recognizing horizontal as well as vertical causality shows the tree-stem icon to be profoundly inadequate and limiting. We need to supplement it with the image of a network, but one that is constantly changing shape. Better still, we might dispense with visual icons and attempt to conceive of the relations between these tales as something more like a gene pool, which in relatively isolated communities will retain distinctive characteristics over a long period of time, but where, with the constant alteration of the genetic code, its members will frequently, perhaps normally, bear as close or closer relations to one another at any point of time than to any particular ancestor.

Psychology

"Reality" is a fantasy-construction which enables us to mask the real of our desire.

S. Zizek, *The Sublime Object of Ideology*, 45

3.1 FREUD AND THE DISCOVERY OF THE UNCONSCIOUS

Freud, Charcot, and Breuer

Sigmund Freud (1856–1939) is responsible for what is probably the single most important contribution to the interpretation of myth: the first serious exploration of the unconscious life of the mind and the earliest articulation of its importance to consciousness. And yet Freud himself, unlike many of his students, paid relatively little attention to myth in developing his psychoanalytic theories. Freud's description of the relation between the conscious and unconscious mind, particularly as it affects the process of symbolization, lies behind all modern psychoanalytic approaches to myth, but it also exerted an important influence on most subsequent theories, including ritualism, structuralism, and ideological analysis.

Freud studied medicine in Vienna and decided to specialize in the pioneering field of nervous diseases. Vienna, soon to be the Mecca for such studies, was still backward: "it was a time when even the great experts in Vienna used to diagnose neurasthenia as a brain tumor" (Freud 1940–68.14: 37). Like many others in the field, Freud was drawn to Paris, where in 1885 he attended the "Tuesday lectures" of the great neurologist, Jean Martin Charcot (1825–93). He remained in Paris for only four months, but Charcot's lectures proved one of the most important formative experiences of his life.

A century earlier, Franz Mesmer had successfully used hypnosis to treat psychiatric patients in Freud's native Vienna. But his explanation, that his own personal "animal magnetism" possessed the patient, long guaranteed a poor repute for hypnosis among physicians. In Vienna hypnosis was still considered the property of mystics, mountebanks, and popular entertainers. Even Charcot appreciated its theatrical potential. Indeed, he had a flair for the histrionic. André Brouillet's famous painting of Charcot's *Leçon clinique* shows us a young woman, swooning backwards like some chesty Andromeda (echoed by a swooning female in a painting on the opposite wall); beside her stands the wild-eyed Charcot; and in front the audience start from their seats in palpable amazement. Freud kept a copy of Brouillet's painting in his consulting-room. It reminded him of the "magic" of Charcot's lectures, each "a little work of art" (1940–68.1: 26, 28). But he also noticed, like Brouillet, the erotically charged atmosphere in the interaction between doctor and patient: the normally young and female patients frequently displayed what Charcot's student Janet called a "magnetic passion" for the hypnotist (1911: 132–5).

Charcot used hypnosis to treat hysteria, a disease which, since antiquity, had been ascribed to a purely physiological cause (it means irritation of the womb and hence was thought peculiar to women). Charcot demonstrated that hysteria was a nervous disorder and that it could affect men as well as women. The symptoms of traumatic hysteria (i.e., hysterias consequent upon a traumatic event) frequently corresponded to ordinary concepts of the body: a hysteric, for example, could suffer paralysis of the leg, meaning the limb extending from the toe to the hip, which is not a neurophysiological grouping. This indicated that the disease was ideogenetic (produced by mental ideas about the body), and not directly attributable to any physiological damage. Charcot proved the point by using hypnotic suggestion to produce the symptoms of hysteria in healthy individuals, or to modify or alleviate the symptoms of hysterics.

The other great formative influence upon Freud was a patient treated by his Viennese colleague and mentor, Josef Breuer (1842–1925). In 1880, 21-year-old Bertha Pappenheim, "the founding patient of psychoanalysis," came under Breuer's care for a year and a half. Learning of the case some months after Breuer finished his treatment, Freud took a deep interest, but it was not until the 1890s, at Freud's urging, that he and Breuer published an account of it ("Preliminary Communications," 1893, and *Studies in Hysteria*, 1895). Breuer describes Anna O. (the publication's pseudonym for Bertha Pappenheim) as "consistently healthy," "markedly intelligent," with "great poetic and imaginative gifts," but suffering from "an extremely monotonous existence in her puritanically-minded family";

at the same time "the element of sexuality was astonishingly undeveloped in her;" she "had never been in love," but "was passionately fond" of her father (Freud 1953–74.2: 21–2). She was a systematic daydreamer, and regularly escaped from the austerity of her family life into what she called her "private theatre"; "while everyone thought she was attending, she was living through fairy tales in her imagination" (22).

In 1880 Anna's father suffered a long illness and subsequently died of an abscess. Nursing him continuously for several months, she herself fell ill and became bedridden. Among several other symptoms she experienced rigid paralysis on her right side, a severe nervous cough, an aversion to food and drink (she ate only fruit), a periodic inability to communicate, especially in her native German (when she was forced to use English, French, and Italian instead), headaches, a squint, and visual problems. Throughout her illness she also experienced self-induced hypnotic states. For a long time her shifts in consciousness followed a regular pattern. During the day she would often be abusive and refractory, and frequently became disconnected with the people and world around her, lapsing into a condition she called an "absence." In this condition she would often experience terrifying hallucinations and sometimes muttered as if enacting a dialog. In the afternoon she generally fell into a "somnolent state," and then, after sunset, into a deep hypnotic state which she called a "cloud." At night her mind was perfectly lucid, provided Breuer pursued a certain treatment. She did not go to bed until around 4 A.M. Her waking nights and sleeping afternoons imitated the rhythm she had adopted while nursing her father.

The treatment, apparently discovered by Anna herself, was what she called, in English, a "talking cure" (or sometimes "chimney sweeping"). One day, between visits from Breuer, someone repeated to Anna words she had muttered during an "absence." Anna responded by telling a story, and after she emerged from her "absence" she felt much better. After this Breuer would visit her during her evening "cloud," and listen to her tell stories, at first mostly fairytales, sad ones, normally beginning with a girl anxiously watching over a sickbed, but later, a series of frightening hallucinations. The treatment made her calm and agreeable, though if omitted for some reason, she grew moody and contrary.

A year after she became ill, she began to relive the previous year in her hypnotic states, as if thrown back in time. On its anniversary, she spontaneously described an incident and one of her symptoms disappeared. The symptom, her inability to eat or drink, disappeared when she recalled the disgust she had felt upon seeing her English roommate's dog drink out of a glass. Hoping to replicate this result, Breuer began to hypnotize her each morning, question her about one of her symptoms, then in the evening, with the help of his notes, prompt her to give a full account. One by one each symptom was traced to specific events or imaginings she had experienced at the time she nursed her father, and one by one, as they were described, the symptoms disappeared. The recollections bore interesting similarities to her symptoms. For example, the paralysis of her right side and her periodic inability to speak German were traced to a hallucination in which she saw a snake approaching her father's bed, but was unable to react because her right arm, draped over the back of a chair, had gone to sleep, and as she tried to pray, she could think of nothing but some children's verses in English.

The case of Anna O. gave empirical proof of the existence of an unconscious life of the mind which could have a profound effect on conscious life. Charcot's observation that hysteria could be triggered by painful events did not go quite far enough. The case of Anna O. demonstrated that hysterical symptoms are not caused by a traumatic event, but by the memory of a traumatic event which is not permitted to fade ("abreacted") in the normal fashion. In trying to forget the painful experience, the hysteric represses the memory, but this only acts to preserve it by forcing the emotions connected with the trauma to attach themselves to related memories which are accessible to the conscious mind. In Anna's case the hysterical symptoms were physical re-enactments of memories related to the traumatic event. The traumatic event was the illness and death of Anna's father. The associated memory was a hallucination and the sight of a dog drinking from a glass. The physical re-enactment was partial paralysis and a revulsion toward food and drink.

Despite the claims made in Freud and Breuer's publications, Anna O. was only partially cured. The hysterical symptoms were "talked away," but not the hysteria itself. The real outcome of the case, suppressed in order to save Breuer personal embarrassment, is recounted in a letter Freud sent to Stephan Zweig in 1932. Freud records that Breuer dropped the case in sudden panic on the very evening of the day that all Anna's symptoms had been brought under control. Breuer had been called back for a second visit only to find her writhing on the floor with abdominal cramps. Asked what was the matter, she replied "Here comes Dr. B.'s child." To Freud's mind, Breuer held "the key in his hand . . . [but] in conventional horror he took to flight and left the patient to a colleague" (cited by Gay 1988: 67). Anna was sent safely out of the way to a Swiss sanatorium. The French Charcot made theater of the erotic charge behind the doctor–patient dynamic; the Viennese Breuer hid its slightest trace even from the light of science, to Freud's very great frustration.

Psychoanalysis

In 1886 Freud set up a private practice for the treatment of nervous diseases. At first he relied heavily upon hypnosis, but found that patients
did not all respond equally well. He experimented with other methods of
reaching into their subconscious minds. Two proved even more effective
than hypnosis: "free association" and dream analysis. Like hypnosis, they
permitted the release of mental phenomena with minimal resistance. In
free association patients were encouraged to talk about their symptoms
in a relaxed way. Freud set it down as a "fundamental rule" that the patient
report everything that came into his mind, however frivolous and senseless. Freud repeatedly encountered renewed resistance in the course of
tracing the unconscious associations that linked a patient's symptoms
with painful events, but especially when he attempted to reach behind
the trauma to search out the cause of the excessive repression which
prevented normal abreaction of the memory of traumatic events. For this
reason it was necessary to listen not only to what the patient said, but
also to the patient's silences. Freud, unlike Breuer, was not a passive
listener, but an active investigator with an ear trained to detect evasions
and omissions, always urging his patients unto paths they would rather
not take. Even in cases where the patient was able to give a full account
of the associated event, they could not, without the analyst's help, find
the cause of the excessive repression which had forced their hurts to seek
such indirect expression.

Freud's account of the treatment of an obsessional neurotic demonstrates
the process (1940–68.11: 268–71). Unlike traumatic hysteria, in which a
traumatic experience translates itself into a physical disorder (the repression of action), an obsessional neurosis translates a traumatic experience
into a "ritual" (an action compulsion).

A lady of nearly thirty years of age suffered from the severest obsessional
symptoms. . . . In the course of a day she would perform the following
peculiar obsessive act, among others, several times over. She ran out of her
room into an adjoining one. There she took up a certain position at the table
in the centre of the room, rang for her chambermaid, gave her a trivial order
or sent her away without, and then ran back again. . . . Every time I asked
the patient, "Why do you do this? What does it mean?" she answered,
"I don't know." But one day, after I had succeeded in overcoming a great
hesitation involving a matter of principle, she suddenly knew and accounted
for the contents of this obsessive act. More than ten years previously she
had married a man very much older than herself, who had proved impotent on the wedding-night. Innumerable times on that night he had run out

of his room into hers to repeat the attempt, each time without success. In the morning he said angrily: "It's enough to disgrace one in the eyes of the chambermaid when she makes the bed," and seizing a bottle of red ink which happened to be in the room he poured it on the bedsheet, but not exactly in a place where such a mark should be. At first I did not understand what connection this recollection was supposed to have with the obsessive act in question; for I could see no correspondence between the two situations, apart from the running from one room into the other, and perhaps also the appearance of the chambermaid. The patient then led me to the table in the second room and brought to my attention a great stain on the tablecloth. She also explained that she stood by the table in such a way that the maid, when summoned, could not miss seeing the stain. After this, I had no doubt of an intimate connection between the current obsessive act and the scene following the wedding-night, but there were still a few more things to learn.

It is clear, first of all, that the patient identified herself with her husband; indeed she played his part insofar as she imitated his running from one room into another. To maintain the equation we must also assume that she substituted the table and tablecloth for the bed and sheet. This might seem arbitrary [but it was evidently chosen as a symbol because of a psychic connection between them]. In dreams a table is very often found to represent a bed. "Table and bed" together mean marriage, so that the one easily stands for the other [in German *Trennung von Tisch und Bett* means "divorce"].

In this case the same relation exists between the trauma and the bed-sheet as existed between Anna O.'s trauma and the glass from which the dog drank. Both are memories merely associated with the trauma which have come to symbolize the trauma (which itself is repressed). But the repressed trauma re-enacts itself in the one case through the aversion to food and drink and in the other through the ritual of the stained tablecloth.

Trauma	Illness of father	Unconsummated marriage
Associated event	drinking dog	ink-stained sheet
Symbol	drinking water	stained tablecloth
Enactment	avoidance of drink	ritual of calling maid

In the case of this obsessional neurotic, however, the analyst has to take the further step of explaining why the ritual is perpetuated through continued repression of the trauma (270):

We have already given the proof that the obsessive act is meaningful; it seems to be a representation, a repetition of that all-important scene. But we do not need to stop our investigation with semblances; if we look more closely into the relation between the two acts we can probably learn something more significant, the purpose of the obsessive act. The crucial component is evidently the summoning of the chambermaid, to whom she displays the stain, in contrast to her husband's observation: "It's enough to disgrace one before the maid." In this way he, whose part she is playing, is not ashamed before the maid, the stain in her representation is where it ought to be. We see therefore that she did not simply repeat the scene, but extended and corrected it, transforming it into what it ought to have been. In this way she also corrects that other problem that made the night so distressing and the red ink necessary: namely, the impotence. The obsessive act thus says: "No, it's not true, he was not disgraced before the chambermaid, he was not impotent."

In other words, the re-enactment of the trauma is an attempt to wish it away. The husband's attempt at correcting appearances offered itself to the woman as a ritual in which she corrected the unhappy reality. In this particular case, Freud relates, the woman still loved her husband very deeply, but she had been separated from him for many years and was trying to make up her mind whether to sue for divorce. This re-enactment was therefore both a wish that their relations were normal and a wish to defend her husband against the charge of inadequacy – both for his impotence and his absence – and to talk herself out of the more reasonable course of suing for divorce.

Dreams

Freud's other technique, dream interpretation, he considered "the Royal Road to the unconscious." For the development of psychoanalytic theory dream interpretation was particularly valuable, not only because it provided Freud with his most important insights into the structure of the unconscious mind – largely through self-analysis and the interpretation of his own dreams – but because dream interpretation provided the medium by which he was able to convince the public that discoveries made in the treatment of hysterics and neurotics revealed *general* truths about the psyche which were valid for all humanity: even the healthiest people experience dreams. For the psychoanalytic interpretation of myth, dream analysis provides a more fruitful model, since the myth-analyst can normally neither hypnotize nor question the mythmaker.

In 1900 Freud published *The Interpretation of Dreams*, which he later deemed his most important work. In it he defines a dream as "a (disguised) fulfillment of a (suppressed or repressed) wish." The satisfaction of a wish does not always entail the satisfaction of the wisher. There are two chambers of the mind, the conscious and the unconscious, whose desires are frequently at variance. When a desire is the same in both, then "a dream is a fulfillment of a wish" *tout court*. But when unconscious desires are opposed to those of the conscious mind, then "a dream is a disguised fulfillment of a suppressed or repressed wish" (1940–68.2/3: 562).

The most restful sleep is that in which the mind is least active. The function of dreams is to buffer consciousness and preserve sleep (hence repressive from the outset). As a schoolboy I was more than once able to block out the noise of my alarm clock (in those days alarm clocks had bells) by dreaming myself to be lying in a sunny meadow on a Swiss mountainside, restfully lulled by the distant sound of cowbells. As the alarm persisted, however, I sometimes dreamt that I had shut it off, got myself dressed, and was making my way to school. Dreams not only act as a buffer between consciousness and external stimuli, they also buffer consciousness from internal mental stimuli. In the first dream, the alarm clock was an external stimulus. In the second, the dream buffered sleep against an internal stimulus, a (not terribly strong) sense of duty. But in both cases the dreams directly fulfilled a wish: that the alarm would not disturb my sleep, or that I could do a day's work without getting out of bed.

When the desires of the two chambers of the mind are at variance, things are more complicated. In this case the repressive mechanism of the dream transforms the unconscious desire. For this process Freud has an interesting simile, likening psychological repression to an encounter with Austria's imperial bureaucracy (1940–68.11: 305–6).

I compare the unconscious system to a large antechamber in which the various mental excitations bustle about like individual beings. Adjoining this room is a second, smaller one, a sort of waiting-room, in which consciousness resides. But the threshold between the two is controlled by an official doorkeeper who scrutinizes the individual mental excitations, censors them, and denies them entry into the waiting-room if they arouse his disapproval. You will see at once that it makes little difference if the doorkeeper turns any impulse back immediately at the threshold, or directs it back out once it has entered the waiting-room; that is merely a matter of the degree of his vigilance and perspicacity. With this image in mind we can further develop our terminology. The excitations in the antechamber of the unconscious are removed from the gaze of consciousness, which is of course in the other room, so to begin with they remain unconscious. When they have pressed forward to the threshold and been turned back by the doorkeeper, they are incapable of becoming conscious; we call them then *repressed*. But even those excitations which the doorkeeper allowed over the threshold do not thereby necessarily become conscious. They can become so only if they succeed in catching the attention of consciousness. With good reason then we refer to this second room as *the preconscious system*. In this way the process of becoming conscious retains its purely descriptive sense. For any single impulse, repression means not being permitted by the doorkeeper to pass out of the unconscious into the preconscious system.

But some of these repressed elements prove persistent and find ways of getting by the doorkeeper, despite his vigilance. Unpleasant wishes may disguise themselves as admissible thoughts, or attach themselves to admissible thoughts by hiding in their baggage, or they may transmit messages through these admissible thoughts. When the doorkeeper or the "censor" (as it is usually called) is at work, then the dream that steals through looks different from the original wish. In this case one has to distinguish between "manifest contents" (what appears in the dream) and "latent contents" (the undisguised unconscious wishes that generated the dream).

The activity of the dream-censorship (or "dreamwork") can be illustrated by Freud's analysis of the dream of "a young woman, but already married for many years." She dreamt (1940–68.11: 120):

> She sits in the theatre with her husband, and one side of the stalls is quite empty. Her husband tells her that Elise L. and her fiancé also wanted to come, but could only get bad seats, three for a florin and a half, and of course they could not take those. According to her it was certainly no misfortune.

The analysis could only proceed with free association. Freud first questioned the woman about the occasion of the dream. Most of it was composed of memories of recent activities (what Freud calls the "residue"). The woman's husband really had told her the day before that Elise L., an acquaintance of her own age, had become engaged to be married. A week earlier she had also gone to the theater with her husband and, indeed, one side of the stalls in the theatre had been empty. This was significant, she explained, because she had been anxious and booked tickets so early that she had to pay extra for them and it became clear that she could easily have waited till the day of the performance. Her husband had in fact teased her for being in too great a hurry. The dreamer also traced the detail that the seats cost a florin and a half to another event of the previous day. Her sister-in-law had been given a gift of 150 florins and "had nothing more pressing to do, the silly goose, than run to the jeweller's and exchange it for a piece of jewelry." But she could make little of the absurd detail that Elise was offered three tickets for two people, except that Elise was only three months younger than herself.

This was sufficient information for Freud (121–2):

> With her few associations she provided us with so much material that it is possible to discover the latent dream-thoughts. We cannot but notice that in her statements about the dream there are references to time at several

points, and these lend a basic coherence to the diverse subject matter. She booked the theatre tickets *too soon*, picked them up in *too great a hurry*, so that she had to pay extra for them; her sister-in-law was similarly *in a hurry* to take her money to the jeweller's to buy an ornament with her money, as though she might *miss something*. If the strongly emphasized points: "*too early*," "*too great a hurry*," are connected with the occasion for the dream (namely, the news that her friend, only three months *younger* than herself, had now found a good husband after all) and with the criticism expressed in her gripe about her sister-in-law, that it was *senseless* to be in so great a rush, then, as if spontaneously, we are confronted by the following construction of the latent dream-thoughts for which the manifest dream is a severely distorted substitute: "It was truly senseless of me to be in such a hurry to marry! By Elise's example I see that I too could have found a husband later on."

Assuming that Freud's analysis is correct (the patient denied that she held her husband in low esteem), we have here a good illustration of what, according to Freud, are the four activities of dreamwork: condensation, displacement, representation, and secondary revision. It is important to dream analysis to understand the precise nature of the dreamwork's distortions of the latent thought, since the act of interpretation is precisely to reverse these activities and reach the latent thought by systematically unraveling the dreamwork's distortions.

Condensation is the "substitution of a part for the whole" with the result that "the content of the manifest dream has less content than the latent thoughts" (1940–68.11: 174). When its function is most vigorous, condensation may involve the omission of certain latent elements altogether. In this example all references to being "in too great a hurry," indeed all references to time, are eliminated altogether. This vital element only emerged in the free associations attached to the empty stalls and tickets. Usually, however, condensation selects a subset of a larger set of associated thoughts ("of many complexes in the latent dream only a fragment passes into the manifest content"). In this dream the observation that "one side of the stalls was quite empty" stands in abbreviated form for her embarrassment at having unnecessarily been in too great a hurry to purchase tickets. A third product of condensation is the blending of several "latent elements sharing some common characteristics . . . into a single whole" in the manifest dream. In this case "florin and a half" groups together several ideas at once: that her sister-in-law was a silly goose to spend 150 florins in a hurry; that the dreamer could have done a hundred times better with the money; that her sister-in-law purchased a worthless ornament out of haste; that getting married is like going to the theater; that the dreamer was in a hurry to get a husband with her dowry; that it was absurd (three tickets for two people) to behave as she did. This kind of condensation is most common in slips of the tongue, as when one refers e.g., to "futility rites" (= "fertility rites are futile").

Displacement is a process by which "a latent element is replaced, not by a part of itself, but by something more remote, by an allusion." In this case, "going to the theatre" and "buying an ornament" stand for "acquiring a husband." It might be noted that the particular items of substitution are often suggested by vernacular expressions or other sources of language or public discourse. Freud determined that the displacement of marriage with going to the theater was something quite personal to the dreamer (infantile scoptophilia). But the link between buying an ornament and acquiring a husband may be due not only to popular conceptions of the function of the dowry and its importance in the formation of marriage alliances among the Viennese bourgeoisie, but may (I hazard) have something to do with the meanings of *Schmuck* in Yiddish, which includes "jewel," "worthless male," and "penis head." As another product of displacement, "the *accent* may be transferred from an important element to another which is unimportant." In this case we can see that the accent was moved from the significant element "husband" in the subconscious onto the element "hurry," even though the latter element only remained under the surface of the manifest dream. An extreme form of displacement is total inversion, i.e., replacing something with its opposite (e.g., clothing symbolizes nakedness). This, we are told, totally dumbfounds the dream-censor.

Representation is the process by which abstract thoughts are manifested concretely or graphically. In this dream the thought "it was absurd" to marry so early is represented by the introduction into the manifest dream of an absurd element, namely, "buying three tickets for two people" (this is also expressed by the feeling that one and a half florins was an absurd price to pay). The final activity of dreamwork, "secondary revision," is simply the combination of the immediate results of the earlier dreamwork into a single and reasonably coherent narrative.

Finally, we should note that the images produced by the dreamwork are generally referred to as symbols and that these are of two types: private and universal. The private symbols are those for which only the dreamer can give an account; universal symbols, by contrast, may be total mysteries to the dreamer, though they are transparent to the experienced psychoanalyst. We will examine universal symbols in Section 3.2. At present suffice it to say that the number 3 represents the male, male genitals, or in this case, the husband. The purchase of three tickets means the purchase of the husband (by a dowry).

Freud's conception of the working of censorship is essentially rhetorical. Hence his appeal to later structuralists who saw the mind as essentially a construct of language. The structuralist/Freudian Jacques Lacan, indeed, equated condensation and displacement with the two great rhetorical tropes of metonymy (association by contiguity) and metaphor (association by analogy). Freud's distinction is not so rigorous or consistent, but the structuralists have amply shown that the processes that Freud identified with repression and the activity of the unconscious are really something fundamental to the creative activity of the mind, whether conscious or unconscious.

3.2 PSYCHOANALYSIS TO MYTH ANALYSIS

The origin of the psychic dynamic

The discovery of the unconscious helped Freud explain psychological abnormalities as a result of a conflict between the unconscious and the conscious mind. In normal healthy individuals this conflict is less acute because infantile desires in the process of maturation are not only repressed but in large part transformed into socially acceptable desires. But those who suffer from psychological ailments do so, according to Freud, because of an abnormally powerful antagonism between unconscious and conscious desires. In these cases, usually because of some early childhood trauma, the normal process of socialization and maturation is stunted and desires abhorrent to the conscious mind remain in the unconscious. The result is excessive repression of the unconscious. But unconscious energy is like a flowing stream. Blocked one way, it will surface in another. Because of the work of the censor it emerges in a distorted form, attaching itself to loosely associated acts and ideas, but often forcing its way with such energy as to create hallucinations or ritual compulsions.

Maturation depends on learning to manage the mechanisms of repression and to channel repressed energy toward ends that are mutually acceptable to both the conscious and unconscious mind. At the center of Freud's discussion of how children learn to control their impulses and master the "pleasure principle" is the Oedipus complex. Freud rejected the polite Victorian view that children were innocent little angels who knew no evil (apparently acquired through acculturation), and nothing of sexuality (apparently one of the corrupting appetites). His analyses of neurotics and dreams forced him to conclude that human sexuality is present in earliest infancy. He defined four principal stages of the process of normal maturation.

1 *Autoeroticism*. This stage is governed by the "pleasure principle." The infant is largely self-sufficient and barely conscious of the existence

of others. It finds the centers of pleasure in its own body. It knows no repression and its desires can be described as polymorphously perverse. At this stage the child is dominated by the part of the mind, labeled the "id," which seeks immediate gratification of its impulses.

2   *Oedipal stage*. Around the ages of three to seven the child chooses the mother as an erotic object. He wants his mother exclusively to himself and this brings him into direct conflict with his father. Because of desire for the mother and hostility to the father, the child imagines himself threatened by the father, and this threat is somehow represented in his mind as a threat of castration. But the child also loves the father and the fear of the father is accompanied by fear for the father in the face of the child's own hostility. The Oedipal experience thus mobilizes the two sources of internal repression, fear and guilt. Neurotics do not succeed in fully outgrowing the Oedipal stage.

3   *Latency*. The advent of the "castration complex" marks the end of the Oedipal stage. The ambivalence of his feelings cause the child to suppress his sexuality altogether. This internal repression, which is reinforced by the perceived external threat from the father, is managed by the formation of the "superego," the part of the mind responsible for taming and socializing the animal impulses of the id. The superego functions according to the "reality principle," just as the id is driven by the pleasure principle. (The ego, which is basically the controlling, deliberative, and rational part of the mind – the part with which we most readily identify – is not always well differentiated from the superego in Freud's writings. For the sake of simplicity, we might think of the superego as the repository of ethical ideals, while the ego is the practical negotiator between the often conflicting demands of id and superego.)

4   *Maturity*. Latency ends with the onset of puberty. The child detaches himself from his mother, reconciles himself with his father, and tries to find a love object similar to, but not identical with, his mother.

Freud's theories of childhood development are notoriously male-oriented (we will examine this problem in Section 3.4).

Universal symbolism and myth

Provided we admit certain analogies between the development of the individual and the development of whole societies, it is possible to transfer the concepts and tools of psychoanalysis to the explication of myths. The reconciliation of dream analysis (which has to do with the individual unconscious) and myth analysis (which must reflect a collective social unconscious) is facilitated by the observation that the individual learns to repress desires through the process of socialization, so that the maturation of the individual is itself a product of social repression. The norms of public activity and public behavior are internalized as the reality principle. But the degree of social repression even in healthy individuals would be intolerably high, if some activities were not left free from its dominion. It is above all in fantasy and daydreams that ordinary individuals find relief from the constraints of the reality principle, and this creative activity of the mind often finds social expression in art and literature, which, though subject to censorship, are normally far less regulated than other public actions. In short, repression is an agency of culture and committed to the reality principle; fantasy is an individual expression of allegiance to the pleasure principle. Myths – and art generally – belong to the realm of collective fantasy mediating between the two.

But Freud argues for an even stronger tie between myth and the fantasy-life of the individual unconscious. If we characterize the connection just established as a "metonymic" connection (that is, one of contiguity, since repression in the individual psyche is merely an extension of repression in society at large), the further connection Freud makes between myth and the unconscious is a "metaphoric" one, based on an analogy between the maturation of the individual and the evolution of the species from the savage to the civilized state. In the next section we will explore this analogy in greater depth. For the moment, suffice it to say that Freud believed that civilization was gained at the cost of repression. Savages thus resemble children in their freedom from inhibition. In *The Relation of the Poet to Day Dreaming* (1908) Freud described myths as "the distorted vestiges of the wish fantasies of whole nations – the age-long dreams of young humanity" (1940–68.7: 222). He supposed that myths, as the product of savage fantasy, aimed at wish-fulfillment, as do dreams, and he noted that they most resemble the dreams of children: their content is largely symbolic but shows relatively little distortion and elaboration by the "dreamwork," so that one could discover the latent thoughts behind them with comparative ease. There is, therefore, something of a double-determination behind the equation of myth and dream. Insofar as myths are products of fantasy they are, like dreams, products of relaxed repression. Insofar as myths are products of primitive cultures, they are also products of relatively unrepressed minds. Myths are therefore a privileged source of information about the unconscious.

For this reason psychoanalysis is indispensable to myth analysis, but myth analysis is also of great importance to psychoanalysis. Myths throw light on a large number of symbols which would otherwise be unintelligible. According to Freud's model, as children our mental life is all more or less the same since it consists of biologically determined instincts and drives. It is with the development of the mechanisms of repression that we become individuals with distinct personalities. Similarly, Freud posits for the species a moment when all cultures were the same, but grew apart with the development of different organs of social repression and control. From his analysis of dreams and neurotic fantasies Freud discovered that, despite much that was peculiar to the individual author of the dream or fantasy, there were also what he called "typical contents," usually symbols, which pointed back to the same or similar latent thoughts. These universal contents were mainly derived from the experiences of earliest childhood, usually the pre-Oedipal or Oedipal stages, before the individuation of the mind. Similarly it had been shown by comparative anthropologists, such as Frazer, that the myths and beliefs of "savage societies" had a great deal in common, no matter where they were individually located in time and space. Freud, therefore, felt free to explain the apparent universality of myths and symbols across cultures in the same way he explained the universality of dream symbols: all are products of universal psychic activities. He did not hesitate, therefore, to compare typical dream symbols with myth symbols. Frazer, to justify the comparison of the thought and practice of his own culture with that of "savages," had recourse to the superstitious peasantry and lower classes, dressing them up as an internal savage within the heart of civilization. Freud went one better, planting the internal savage in the very heads of all his civilized compatriots with no deference to their class, education, or professed beliefs. Beneath the patina of civilization the modern human psyche differed little from the most ancient and primitive. In particular, the psychic dynamic that gave rise to ancient myths survived only too unremittingly in the modern mind. Not coincidently, Freud frequently labeled many of the traumas, impulses, and aberrations of his Viennese contemporaries with the names of characters from Greek myth: Oedipus, Narcissus, Eros, Thanatos.

If we adopt this belief in a universal human psyche, we find ourselves in a very good position to analyze myths as one would analyze dreams. Though there is no opportunity to interrogate the mythmaker as one can the dreamer, this disadvantage is more than compensated for by the assurance that the mythmaker is probably less repressed than the dreamer (and his latent thoughts therefore less distorted). Thus, with the aid of "folktales and myths, jokes and witticisms, from folklore, i.e., from the study of the manners and customs, sayings, and songs of different peoples, and from poetic and colloquial usage of language" Freud was able to compose, almost in glossary form, a list of "universal" symbols, which can help the psychoanalyst crack any psychic code when other approaches prove impossible or no longer profitable (1940–68.11: 154–60).

Typical symbols for *family members* are kings and queens, who represent father and mother, especially in fairytales, and little animals, who represent children. A disproportionate number of symbols represent the human body, and in particular, quite predictably, the genitals. The *female body* is especially symbolized by enclosed spaces like houses, towns, citadels, castles, and fortresses. The gates, doors, windows, and other openings symbolize female genitals. So do ovens, hearths, vessels, containers of almost any sort, hats, shoes, gloves, and, by a somewhat different logic, earth, landscapes, horseshoes, diamond-shaped objects, and linen. By a formal analogy, often systematically linked with the above, *male genitals* are symbolized by just about any oblong object, but especially tools and implements, plows, fire, heads, feet, hands, fingers, tongues, trees, snakes, birds, swords, knives, guns, cannons, and the number 3. Eyes refer specifically to the *testicles*. Falling into water or emerging from water is a symbol for *birth*. *Death* is symbolized by a journey. *Nakedness* (through the logic of inversion) is symbolized by uniforms or clothes generally. Symbols for *sexual intercourse* are climbing stairs or ladders, steep places, sweeping chimneys, flying, and riding horses. *Evil impulses or passions* appear as wild animals and monsters. *Masturbation* is symbolized by playing games, or musical instruments, sliding, gliding, or pulling off a branch. *Castration as an imagined punishment for masturbation* is represented by the knocking out of a tooth.

Though they are not specifically recognized by Freud, we should probably acknowledge the existence of a type of symbol intermediate between the personal and the universal. We might label these broadly "cultural symbols," i.e., symbols fairly universal within the confines of a specific culture. These are normally closely related to the universal symbols listed above, but include objects or ideas which are not by any means universal. In this group we would have to include products of modern technology. For example, cars, cigars, joysticks, and antiballistic missiles could easily be read by the psychoanalyst as typical phallic symbols of modern global culture.

Prometheus and the bringing of fire

Having shown the way, it is somewhat surprising to note that Freud left us only two (or, if we include Oedipus, three) analyses of myth. This is probably because he had always been uneasy with the mechanical translation of dream symbols without proper consideration of their context in the dream or the psychic economy of the dreamer. In particular, he grew increasingly uncomfortable with the practices of Carl Jung and other students of psychoanalysis who trusted too much in a belief in universals, both in the analysis of dreams and in the analysis of myths. Freud thought them insensitive to the particulars of individual psychological and social contexts.

The only extended analysis of a myth is that of Prometheus and the theft of fire (1940–68.16: 3–9). In some ways it is predictable. Fire is a libido symbol. The fennel stock in which Prometheus stole the fire is a phallic symbol. The eating of Prometheus's liver by the eagle of father Zeus is a castration symbol. But it gets odder and more interesting when Freud asks why primitive men imagined so cruel a punishment for the culture hero who brought them fire and civilization. Fire could only be preserved, says Freud, once the natural male instinct to urinate on fire (apparently confirmed by psychoanalytic investigation) was repressed. Behind Prometheus stands a lawgiver who forbade urination on the fire. His subjects were grateful for the ensuing benefits of fire, but also resentful for the repression of their libido, and so imagined his punishment. The symbolism contains an inversion of fire and water. Prometheus is credited with giving fire, but he forbade watering. The fennel stock contained fire, but the penis it symbolizes contains water.

The inversion is itself inverted in the related myth of Heracles, who releases Prometheus from his punishment and kills the eagle. Heracles kills a monster called the Hydra, a watersnake, but one that has multiple raging heads, like fire (see Euphronios's Hydra, Figure 2). Like fire it is a libido symbol, and like Prometheus's liver, the severed heads of the Hydra regenerate. But this watersnake is finally extinguished by fire, since Heracles, or his companion Iolaus, is forced to cauterize the snake's heads to keep them from regenerating. This water extinguished by fire symbolizes both the fire that was extinguished by water, and the libido that was repressed when Prometheus curbed man's impulse to pass his water on fire. Oddly, Freud supposes that real people and real events stand behind the myths. Prometheus was a lawgiver who forbade urinating on fire, but Heracles was a lawbreaker who "redeemed" Prometheus, by using his water, like Gulliver in Lilliput, to extinguish a fire that had grown dangerous. Thus the ambivalent deed of the first culture-hero was compensated for by the unambiguously good deed of the second. The analysis might be more convincing had the "natural impulse" to urinate on fire survived with sufficient vigor to extinguish our doubts as well, but the interpretation has, for Freud, the virtue of making civilization's first step an act of repression.

FIGURE 2   Detail of Attic red-figure neck amphora by Euphronios, *c*.510 BC.
Hermitage, inv. B.2351 (B 610)

The Medusa

The second analysis of myth attempted by Freud amounts to no more than
a series of jottings on the subject of the Gorgon head which were not published until after his death (1940–68.17: 47–8):

> I have not often attempted the interpretation of individual mythological images.
> An interpretation suggests itself for the terrifying, severed head of Medusa.
>   Cutting off the head = castration. The terror inspired by Medusa is
> therefore the terror of castration, which is linked to something seen. From

numerous analyses we know the occasion: it happens when a boy, who formerly refused to believe in the threat, sees female genitals. Probably adult genitals, surrounded by pubic hair, in principle the mother's.

If the hair of the Medusa's head is so often represented in art as snakes, this also arises from the castration complex, and surprisingly, as frightful as they are, they actually serve to modify the horror, for they replace the penis, whose absence causes such horror. A technical rule [called "compensation"] is here confirmed: the multiplication of penis symbols means castration.

The sight of the Medusa's head makes one rigid with fear, turns the viewer into stone. The same source in the castration complex and the same emotional reaction! Growing rigid means erection, and so in the original situation it is the consolation of the viewer. He still has a penis, and confirms it through getting an erection.

Athena, the virgin goddess, carries this symbol of horror on her clothes. Rightly, since by it she becomes an unapproachable woman who wards off all sexual advances. She therefore displays the fearful genitals of the mother. This depiction of woman threatening man with his own castration is only to be expected of the thoroughly homosexual Greeks.

This is short, but highly suggestive, and accounts for much more of the myth and its associated imagery than Freud indicates. A Lakonian plastic vase of the late seventh century BC shows Medusa squatting in such a way as to reveal her genitals (see Figure 3). The connection between the severed head of Medusa and maternal genitals also might seem to be insisted upon by the fact that children are born from Medusa's severed neck. Freud himself noted the function of the Medusa head as an apotropaic symbol used on shields and armor to strike terror into the hearts of the enemy (see the ancient breastplate, Figure 4). Other features of Medusa condense the threat of castration with compensatory phallic imagery: note the canine teeth, the boar's tusks, and the fact that the Gorgon normally sticks out her tongue. According to Apollodorus the Gorgon has bronze arms and golden feathers: the metals in either case offering both reassurance in their rigidity and a threat, since metal is the material of offensive weaponry. But the element of compensation, through the flourish of phallic symbolism, is most apparent in the children who are born from the truncated body of Medusa. Chrysaor, in Greek "he of the Golden Sword," may be taken as a reassuring self-projection of the subject of these infantile fears, since the sword is an obvious phallic symbol, particularly in a context where a female has been wounded, and its goldenness suggests not only its brilliance but a reassurance of its imperishability. From the neck of Medusa also sprang the flying horse Pegasus, who condenses two images of sexual activity, the horse, and flying. The name "Pegasus" is formed from the Greek verb *pegazo*, which means "to gush forth," and

FIGURE 3   Laconian plastic vase, late seventh century BC. Antikenmuseum Basel und Sammlung Ludwig, inv. LU 89. *Photo*: Claire Niggli

alludes to an important episode in the life of this beast when, with his foot, he struck the rock of Mount Helicon and caused the "Horse-fountain," *Hippokrene*, to gush forth. Yet a third birth, the poisonous snakes of the North African desert, both phallic and threatening, were said to have been born from the blood dripping from the head of Medusa as Perseus flew overhead.

FIGURE 4   Bronze breastplate from Scythian grave near Kuban, fourth century BC.
Hermitage

Perseus

If Freud is right about the meaning of the Medusa head, then the myth
of Perseus and Medusa must also be primarily an expression of Oedipal
fear and desire. (Apollodorus's version of the myth of Perseus is given
in Section 5.2, pp. 195–7.) Caldwell notices a remarkable symmetry in
the character set in this tale, one which illustrates a process of imaginative thought, called "decomposition," and which is parallel to the process
of symbolization (1990: 353). Whereas symbolization usually entails the
condensation of several latent thoughts into a single image, decomposition
is the splitting of a single latent personality into several different characters.
The principle male and female characters in the myth, with whom Perseus
interacts, are divided into groups of three. On the female side, there is a

stark parallelism between Danae and Andromeda. Each was pursued by a paternal uncle (Proetus and Phineus) and each woman was put into isolation by the actions of her father. Each is also saved by Perseus from an unwanted marriage. If these figures represent the mother, we must assume that the figure of the mother is split in two because of the child's emotional ambivalence, caught between filial love and sexual desire, symbolized by the maternal Danae and the erotic Andromeda. There is, of course, a third figure, the threatening mother in the form of Medusa. Freud had already associated the Gorgon symbol with a castration threat related to the mother. Medusa could then represent the feelings of terror which induce the child to withdraw his attentions from the mother. We notice that Medusa is closely connected with Athena. Medusa is as threatening and malignant as Athena is untouchable and benign. Medusa symbolizes the fear of the discovery of the child's erotic intentions; Athena symbolizes the security of detachment. There is perhaps also a cross-reference between the names *Med*usa (Ruler) and Andro*meda* (Man-ruler).

The splitting of the father-figure has a still more impressive symmetry. There are three pairs of twin brothers, Acrisius and Proetus, Polydectes and Dictys, Phineus and Cepheus. Each pair is marked by mutual hostility, and each pair contains a benign father-figure and a malignant, threatening one. Perseus ends up killing the malignant father-figure in each of these pairs. Freud might have argued that each is killed by a symbolic castration, a turning of the threat against the threatener. Phineus and Polydectes are both victims of the Medusa head, and Acrisius is killed when struck in the foot by a quoit thrown by Perseus. Thus two are turned to stone and the third killed by a stone. We may note, moreover, that though wounds in the foot are not normally fatal, they often are in myth, arguably because the foot symbolizes male genitals

The organization of the characters into groups of three might suggest a preoccupation with the relations of the nuclear family: child, mother, and father. In fact, we find a further three sets of three sisters, each set marking a stage of Perseus's quest. Oedipal desire and fear are most evident in these encounters. The Graiae are sisters of the Gorgons, grey and old. Between them they share a tooth and an eye. We recall that the removal of a tooth is one of Freud's universal symbols for castration, as is the removal of an eye, since the eyes symbolize the testicles. Perseus gains access to the nymphs by depriving them of their eye and tooth. Judging from their name, the "nymphs" are presumably the opposite, young and attractive, and they freely give Perseus three gifts: winged sandals, a cap which makes him invisible, and a leather bag. All of these appear in Freud's list of symbols for female genitals. We have already seen that the three Gorgon sisters are symbols of castration. We learn that of the three only one, Medusa,

is vulnerable. Each set of three sisters thus seems to have a special relation with one member of the nuclear family. The Graiae with the father,
since they are old and grey, and have names that evoke terror: Enyo (=
"Shrieker"), Pemphredo (= "Droner"), and Deino (= "Terrible"). Perseus
threatens them with castration. The nymphs presumably represent the erotic
desire for the mother, and the Graiae, when threatened, yield access to
them. The horror of the Gorgons is, of course, evoked by the child's fear
for himself, and the latent thought behind the detail that only one of them
is vulnerable is presumably the belief that of the three members of the
nuclear family, it is the child himself who is the vulnerable one.

One further detail of the story seems to confirm the interpretation of the
myth as one of Oedipal fear. From Hermes Perseus receives a sickle, not
a weapon used by Greeks, though it often appears as a weapon in myth.
It is the instrument that Earth forged and gave to Kronos to castrate Ouranos.
It is the same instrument which was used by Typhon to remove Zeus's sinews
and render him impotent. In the last chapter we saw that the sickle was used
in the Hurrian tradition both to separate Earth and Sky, to remove the
heart and eyes of the Storm God, and to cut the feet of Ullikummi. Egyptian
myth offers a significant variation. During his battle with Hor, Seth, who
is identified with Typhon, is said to have had his sinews removed by Thoth,
who is identified with Hermes. But other variants of the tale claim that
it was his testicles which were removed. A sickle is frequently used to cut
the heads off of the Hydra (see Iolaus in Figure 5). Greek ritual employs
a sickle to castrate sacrificial victims (Burkert 1983: 68).

There is much, then, in the tale of Perseus and the Gorgon to confirm
a central preoccupation with the castration complex. But one could also
read the tale more broadly against Freud's stage theory of childhood development. The earliest part of the narrative shows the infantile imagination's
re-creation of pre-Oedipal felicity, marked by perfect union with the mother,
since together they are locked into a womblike, bronze, underground chamber, or set awash in the sea locked together in a chest. This stage is also
characterized by denial of the father, represented by Acrisius's refusal to
believe in the paternity of Zeus, and by his rejection of Danae and Perseus.
Once Perseus is perceived as a threat by Polydectes, the Oedipal relation
between father and son is relived. The hostility is marked by the killing
of the three malign father-figures. The name Polydectes itself expresses
jealousy and resentment: "the man who receives a lot." Because of
Polydectes's demands Perseus is isolated from his home and his mother
and sent to confront the fear of castration in the form of the Gorgon. The
onset of latency is itself expressed in the conversion of the mother into the
untouchable virgin goddess, Athena. The final reconciliation with the parents might be read into the return journey where Perseus finds a substitute

FIGURE 5   Corinthian aryballos, *c*.590 BC. Antikenmuseum Basel und Sammlung
Ludwig, inv. BS 425. *Photo*: Claire Niggli

for his erotic attentions in Andromeda, a woman like, but not identical
to, his mother, and the subsequent settlements with the benign father-figures
Cepheus and Dictys.

Oedipus

Oedipus is the figure of myth whom Freud made famous, but he has
only the sketchiest of references to this ancient tale and indeed, it is not

the myth but the tragedy by Sophocles which is the object of his only extended discussion in *The Interpretation of Dreams*. What attracted Freud most to Sophocles's play was the manner in which, in spite of great internal resistance, the hero of the play relentlessly pursues a quest of self-discovery, piecing together dribs and drabs of information, until finally, reaching back to the trauma of his earliest childhood, he discovers that his true relation to his father and his mother are at extreme odds with what social morality deems acceptable. The whole procedure, says Freud, is "comparable to a work of psychoanalysis" (1940–68.2/3: 268).

In the context of a discussion of typical dreams (i.e., dreams shared by almost everyone), Freud asks why Sophocles's play continues to fascinate and horrify audiences, where modern tragedies of fate leave us cold. "There must be a voice inside of us, which is ready to acknowledge the compelling power of destiny in Oedipus, while we are able to dismiss as arbitrary the devices in the *Ancestress* [by Grillparzer] or in other tragedies of fate." His answer is that (269):

> [Oedipus's] fate takes hold of us only because it could have been our own, because the oracle hung the same curse over us before our birth as over him. It was perhaps allotted to us all to direct our first sexual impulse towards our mother and our first hatred and violent ambitions against our father; our dreams convince us that this is so.

Indeed, Freud implies that Sophocles himself may have intuited the Oedipus complex through his knowledge of myths and dreams, for he has Jocasta say to Oedipus (lines 980–3): "As to your mother's marriage bed, – don't fear it! Before this, in dreams too, as well as oracles, many a man has lain with his own mother. But he to whom such things are nothing bears his life most easily." This is the key to the tragedy, says Freud. The Oedipus story is the reaction of fantasy to two typical dreams: the dream of murdering one's father and the dream of marrying one's mother. Since these dreams are accompanied by feelings of revulsion, the story of Oedipus too must end in horror, self-punishment, and exile. All the rest of the tragedy Freud dismisses as "mere secondary revision which misses the point and seeks to make it serviceable to a theologizing moral" (271). It is the universal psychological contents that make this tragedy exceptional, while the elements that make it a tragedy, namely, "the attempt to unite divine omnipotence with human responsibility, is naturally destined to failure here as everywhere else" (271).

Oedipus was incorporated not only into the mythological armature of psychoanalysis, but into the myth of Freud himself. He, like Oedipus, was after all the relentless pursuer of truth against powerful resistance, from

FIGURE 6   Attic cup, Vitticio Painter, School of Douris, *c.*470 BC. Museo Gregoriano
Etrusco 16541, Vatican. *Photo*: Alinari/Art Resource, New York

both within and without, and the solver of the riddle of his own origins
and of the human psyche. On his fiftieth birthday, Freud's students and
admirers presented him with a medallion showing his portrait on one
side, and on the other an image, based on a painting on an Attic vase (see
Figure 6), of Oedipus solving the riddle of the Sphinx and inscribed with
the words of Sophocles: "He divined the famous riddle and was a most
mighty man." Freud's students had in fact only picked up on the imagery
with which Freud surrounded himself: his study contained a copy of Ingres's
painting of Oedipus interrogating the Sphinx (see Figure 7) and a glass
cabinet of antiquities which also included a picture of the Sphinx at Giza,
as well as numerous books on Oedipus, particularly a well-thumbed copy
of Ludwig Laistner's *Riddle of the Sphinx* (1889).

FIGURE 7   J.A.D. Ingres *Oedipus and the Sphinx* (1864). Walters Art Museum,
Baltimore, MD

It is little wonder that Oedipus and the Sphinx became powerful personal symbols for Freud, given the nature of his practice and the orientation of his thought. What is more surprising is that Freud, despite his
sphingomania, never elaborated an interpretation of the myth. This
should probably be seen as a strong index of his reluctance to engage in
the analysis of myth, though he often makes free use of myth for the casual
illustration of his psychoanalytic arguments. The genealogy of the Sphinx
offers abundant confirmation of Freud's observations on the image of
the Medusa. As we saw above, Freud interpreted the rampant phallic

symbolism surrounding the Medusa as a form of "compensation" for the fear of castration which the Medusa symbolized. This symbolism, we argued, could also be extended to the children of Medusa. It is satisfying to see a high degree of consistency in the monstrosities which continue Medusa's lineage. All of them are threatening monsters and all of them are surrounded by phallic symbolism. Chrysaor, who sprang from Medusa's decapitated body, begot Geryon and Echidna. The former is a represented as triplets from the waist up, all sprouting from the same lower body. The latter was a half-woman, half-snake, who married Typhon (the enemy and, as we saw, "castrator" of Zeus), who is described by Hesiod as a creature of a hundred snake heads with darting tongues and fiery eyes. Echidna and Typhon gave birth to Cerberus, the dog of Hades, which had from three to fifty heads, a dragon for a tail, and rings of snakes wriggling at the back of each neck. Echidna and Typhon also bore: the two-headed dog of Geryon, the dragon with a hundred heads which guarded the apples of the Hesperides; the eagle that ate out Prometheus's regenerative liver; the Lernaean Hydra, which had one immortal and eight regenerative heads, the latter cut off by the sickle of Heracles; the Chimaera, a composite of lion, goat, and snake; the invulnerable Nemean lion; and the Sphinx.

These creatures, some many-headed, most snaky, and some tripartite, all have the phallic nature which Freud's analysis of the Medusa identified as compensation for the castration threat she embodied. The Sphinx is a special member of this set, however, since she is not only represented as threatening, but often has a certain sexy allure, nicely caught by Ingres's painting (see Figure 7) in which Oedipus fixes his eyes on the nipples of her full and shapely breasts which are illuminated as if by a spotlight, while all her monstrous features remain in a penumbra. Freud's fascination for the painting surely had something to do with its deeply ambivalent expression of erotic desire combined with fear and loathing. In Greek art the Sphinx is depicted as an often voluptuous woman lunging at young men in their prime and raping them as she shreds them apart (see Figure 8). But there is another aspect of the Sphinx which may have appealed to Freud's personal symbolary.

The Sphinx has a tripartite nature: a woman's face with a lion's body endowed with the wings of a bird. The Sphinx's nature thus expresses her mythological function – to ask riddles – but she herself is a riddle. Her riddle also refers to a tripartite and paradoxical creature: "What creature has four legs in the morning, two in the afternoon, three in the evening and is weakest when it has most legs?" The answer is, of course, "man," and this is also the answer the Freudian seeks in the riddle posed by the Sphinx's nature. For the bestial body of the Sphinx combined with the

FIGURE 8   Attic red-figure lekythos, *c*.470 BC. Antikensammlung, Kunsthalle zu Kiel, inv. B 553

human head has been read as an allegory: the lower animal parts are the passions, not only the crude bestial passions, which threaten civilization, represented by the lion's posterior, but also those divine winged creative passions, the erotic sublime (or sublimated eros). Both represent the life of the libido trapped in the unconscious but released in fantasy and art. To them is added the superego, symbolized by the human head, since it is the superego which makes humanity distinct from other beasts. The word "Sphinx" itself in Greek means the "strangler" and could be translated as the "repressor." Thus, the Sphinx shows man in his maturity, control-ling his animal nature, but fighting an unequal battle, since he is two parts animal to one part human. This interpretation of the tripartite creature is, in fact, already foreshadowed in Plato's discussion of the tripartite soul of man: one part is bodily appetites, one part emotions, and one part con-trolling intelligence. In *Republic* 9 (588c) Plato compares this tripartite soul to the Sphinx's siblings, Chimaera, Scylla, and Cerberus (but oddly omits the Sphinx, a symbol much better suited, it would seem, to his purpose).

Freud, like Oedipus, found the answer to the riddle of the Sphinx. But, unlike Freud, Oedipus killed the Sphinx, an action Freud interpreted as a symbol of denial: unlike Freud, Oedipus denied the Sphinx's animal nature as he denied his repressed desires for his mother and hostility to his father, and this final act of repression returned to destroy him. But insofar as Oedipus also kills the human part of the Sphinx (the "repressor"), we might think of him as the man without repression. His very name, "swollen foot," is highly suggestive of uninhibited masculine sexuality. Throughout Sophocles' tragedy there are in fact a great many references to feet – feet are central to the Sphinx's riddle; Oedipus got his name from the fact that his feet were pierced by his father, who abandoned him on a mountain-side in order to escape fulfillment of the oracle that he would die by his son's hand. More specifically, it was his ankles which were pierced, and these stand in a homologous relation to the foot as the testicles to the penis. It is easy to see here a symbol of the threat of castration by the father: according to Freud, limping or crippling commonly occurs as a castration symbol in dreams. In myth one thinks, for example, of Hephaestus, crippled when thrown from heaven by his father Zeus (for taking his mother's part in a quarrel about sex), or, in inverted form, Indra in the *Rig Veda* (4.18.12), who kills his father by grabbing and crushing his foot just as Perseus crushes the foot of Acrisius with a discus. Even the names of Oedipus's father and grandfather play upon this symbolism: "Laius," or "Lefty" in Greek, suggests the uneven strength of the cripple, and "Labdacus" means the man with one shortened foot, or "Limper" (the letter lambda, or labda, was first written in the form of an inverted "V" with one long and one short descending stroke). Other castration symbolism recurs in later events, the encounter of Oedipus and Laius at the meeting of three roads, for example, where each strikes the other's head with a scepter (Laius gives Oedipus a "twin jab" in *Oedipus the King*, 809). In Euripides's account, the fight begins when Laius's horses step on Oedipus's ankles! But most of all, castration appears in Oedipus's self-punishment, where he strikes his eyes with pins, just as his ankles were struck with pins by his father (Sophocles uses the same Greek words in each case for both the pins and for the organs that are pierced: *arthra* meaning "joints," "sockets," or "limbs" is used for both ankles and eye-sockets at lines 717–18, 1032, and 1270; the word is also used elsewhere of genitals). This equation of blinding with castration has been widely studied by Freud's students and was acknowledged by Freud (e.g., 1940–68.9: 158: "In Oedipus as in the castration complex the father plays the same role, namely that of the terrifying opponent of the child's sexual interests. Castration and its substitute through blinding is the punishment he threatens").

By bringing together the progeny of Medusa, the supreme symbol of the castration threat, with the lineage of the limping Labdacids, the victims of this threat par excellence; by bringing together the "Repressor" and the "man without inhibitions," the tale of Oedipus, particularly in the context of an introspective investigation as told by Sophocles, is for Freud the most powerful and universal tragedy of all because it is the story of our own calamities, our own life story. *Mutato nomine de te fabula narratur!*

3.3   FREUD AND ANTHROPOLOGY

Freud's critics complain of "pansexualism"– the perception that everything ultimately has to do with sex. In Freud's defense, we can say that if the theory of repression is correct, and if the unconscious really is distinguished from consciousness by the inclusion of drives and desires which are repressed from consciousness, then it follows that sex plays a large role. Other basic human needs tend to be irrepressible or repressible to a very limited degree: the need for food, water, or shelter. By contrast, the desire for sex is highly repressible, and, in some cases, has proven infinitely so. Not only is the sex drive repressible, society manifestly dedicates a lot of energy to policing it.

But it is also not true that *everything* is sex in the Freudian unconscious. There is also a lot of violence. Freud's theory endows every individual's unconscious with a liberal helping of hostility and hatred (even if, in many cases, it can ultimately be traced to sexual jealousy, frustration, or resentment). Violence can and must be repressed, every bit as much as sexual desire, if individuals are to mature or humanity to progress. In the individual, the initial formation of the basic mechanism of repression, the superego, requires, or at least benefits from, the ability to play one drive against the other, love against hatred, or fear against desire. The superego is forged by the ambivalent feelings released during the Oedipal crisis when hostility is tempered by love for the father, and desire for the mother is tempered by fear and revulsion. A strictly analogous process is, in Freud's view, responsible for humanity's progress from savagery to civilization.

Ambivalence

Ambivalence, contradictory feelings, especially of love and hatred, coexist in most individuals, though the individual, in deference to social morality, usually represses one pole of the contradiction within his unconscious. Ambivalence characterizes the most important human relationships, and especially early childhood relationships, which are formed before we learn how to sift and direct these energies in less self-defeating ways. But within the forge of ambivalence there are several settings, depending on the degree of repression exercised by the censor.

In the *Interpretation of Dreams* Freud relates the case of a young girl who suffered from a female Oedipal complex (1940–68.2/3: 265–6). The illness had three stages. In the first, when her illness began, she expressed, in a confused rage, violent hatred for her mother. As soon as her mother drew near she began to beat her and verbally abuse her. At the same time she showed great tenderness for a much older sister. The second stage was marked by general clarity, mixed with apathy and a very restless sleep. A great many of her dreams dealt with the imagined death of her mother in more or less concealed fashion. She dreamt, for example, that she attended the funeral of an old woman, or that she saw herself and her sister dressed in mourning and sitting alone at the table. In the third stage, the illness progressed to hysterical phobia. Her most pressing fear was that something had happened to her mother. Wherever she was when it came upon her, she had to run home and reassure herself that her mother was allright.

The case showed "as if in multilingual translation the different ways in which the psyche could react to the same stimulus." In the first phase the girl's conscious mind was overwhelmed by the power of her unconscious emotions. In the second phase the rule of the censor was restored but her hatred found an outlet in the dreamwish for her mother's death. In the third phase the repressive mechanism was fully restored and created an exaggerated concern for the mother as a kind of hysterical defensive reaction against the unconscious hostility.

In this case the censor, faced with ambivalent feelings, filtered out the hostile feelings, but, at a certain stage, overcompensated as if to drown them out by a protest of exaggerated devotion and concern. A similar pattern exists where the feeling that needs to be filtered is desire. We could schematize the dynamics as follows:

Repression	Off	Low	High	Very High
Hostility	violence	symbolic satisfaction	guilt	fear for or avoidance
Desire	erotic pursuit	symbolic satisfaction	shame	rejection or avoidance

In the case of the Oedipal girl the phobia was a "fear for" the object of hostility. The censor can, however, disguise unacceptable feelings through displacement. Freud recounts a case in which a woman transfers her "fear for" her husband to an object (1940–68.9: 117–18):

> One day she heard her husband order the servants to take his dull razor to a specific shop to be sharpened. Driven by a peculiar anxiety she herself went to this shop and after her return she ordered her husband to do away with this razor because she discovered that beside the shop he had mentioned there was a warehouse full of coffins and funerary equipment. The razor developed a strong connection with the idea of death. It is clear that the connection between the razor and death was made before the woman went to the shop to find a rationalization for her phobia in the discovery of the warehouse. Subsequent analysis showed that the taboo of the razor sprang from an unconscious desire that her husband would cut his own throat while shaving and the guilty feelings aroused by the suppression of this desire.

Not only can either hostility or desire be transferred to an object, but the whole complex of ambivalent feelings can be displaced in this way, as happened in the remarkable case of the Chickenman, reported by Sándor Ferenczi (1913). Here is Freud's summary (1940–68.9: 158–9):

> Little Árpád was two and a half years old when during a summer holiday in the country he tried to urinate in the henhouse. This incited a chicken to bite or snap at his member. When he returned to the same spot a year later, he himself became a chicken, and took an interest in nothing other than the henhouse and everything that went on there. He gave up human communication for clucking and crowing. By the time he came under psychiatric observation (five years old) he was speaking again, but in his conversation he was entirely preoccupied with chickens and other fowl. He had no other toys, and only sang songs in which there were lyrics about birds. His behaviour toward chickens was exquisitely ambivalent, excessive hate and

love. His favorite game was slaughtering toy chickens. This was altogether a festival for him. He was capable of dancing for hours around the chicken corpses. But then he kissed and caressed the slaughtered images of chickens to which he had done violence.

Little Árpád himself took care to reveal the meaning of his unusual behaviour. He translated his wishes from totemistic expression back into ordinary speech. "My father is the rooster," he said once. "Now I'm small, now I'm a little chick. When I get bigger, I'll be a chicken. When I get still bigger, I'll be the rooster." On another occasion he suddenly wished to eat "mother in a pot" (on the analogy of "chicken in a pot"). He was very generous with castration threats to others, as he himself had experienced as a result of his onanistic activities.

In this case the whole complex of ambivalent feelings was transferred from the father to chickens through an association created when a chicken threatened his genitals in much the same way he imagined his father did.

Totemism

Armed with such observations about the mental life of children and neurotics, Freud felt able to give his own explanation for what comparatists regarded as "the essential similarity of myths and rituals in primitive societies throughout the globe." The belief that the thought of savages resembled that of children and neurotics constitutes the point of departure for Freud's most important anthropological work, *Totem and Taboo* (1913). Savages, children, and neurotics all shared underdeveloped organs of repression; their thought is characterized by relatively direct and free expression of unconscious wants and needs. On the strength of this belief Freud drew an equation between the stages of psychological development in individuals ("ontogenetic") and the stages in the evolution of the psyche of the human species as a whole ("phylogenetic"). Though never worked out fully or explicitly, *Totem and Taboo* posits a symbiotic and mutually causative relationship between the development of internal organs of repression and the development of social organs of repression (e.g., religion, morality, law, or political organization). This gave psychoanalysis a uniquely qualified position from which to provide a causal explanation of cultural evolution.

Like many others of his day, Freud believed that an account of the origin of civilization would go a long way toward explaining its entire trajectory. He focused therefore on totemism, which comparative anthropology had declared to be the most elementary form of human civilization. Freud relied on the highly (and conveniently) schematic account of totemism given in Frazer's *Totemism and Exogamy* and Smith's *Lectures on the Religion of the Semites.* Much of what they had to say about the distinguishing features of totemism was questionable, even in their day, but we are not concerned here with the accuracy of the account.

A "totem" is properly an edible animal, or, less often, a plant or a natural element like rain. The word may also be used of the totemic band, a social group united through common identification with a particular totem. Membership in the totem is usually inherited through the mother. It is not simply a matter of blood ties (and is regarded as stronger than blood ties), nor is it bound to any given locality, since members of different totems normally cohabit a village. Totemic bands regard their totem as father of their group and also as a helper and protective spirit. They share a common cult, meet periodically for common festivals, and share common taboos. By the strictest taboo, members of the totem must not kill the totem animal or eat its flesh. Occasionally, however, totem members get together for a festival where they sacrifice and eat the totem animal. In this way, as in the case of the Chickenman, the savage displays ambivalent feelings toward his totem.

In totemic societies relationships are not defined in terms of individuals, but in terms of generational divisions. Everyone old enough to be one's father or mother is called "father" or "mother," while everyone of the same generation within the totem is called "brother" or "sister." As a consequence, a strict taboo against incest extends to all totem members, even though actual blood relationship may be remote. The exaggerated fear of incest in totem societies is reinforced by no less exaggerated ritual "avoidances." On Lepers Island, one of the New Hebrides, boys leave home at the age of initiation and take up lodgings at the Men's House. For the rest of his life, though he may visit his home and take meals there, a Lepers Islander cannot do so, if his sister is at home, or must leave, if she returns. When brother and sister encounter each other in the open, they run away or hide themselves in the bushes. A boy never speaks his sister's name, or says any word which incorporates a part of her name. Though in Lepers Island only natural sibling relations are governed in this way, exaggerated avoidance rules are, in other societies, extended to all totem siblings, as in Fiji, or they may be extended to all family relations to govern also social contacts between parents and children, as in Sumatra. Such avoidances are comparable to the exaggerated avoidance displayed by neurotics.

Taboo

Ambivalence is attested not only by the taboos governing relations with the totem animal or relations between totem members; it is attested by the very nature of "taboo" itself. Anthropologists regarded taboo as the most primitive form of human law. It differs from law in more developed societies by the nature of its authority and by the manner of its enforcement. These are not derived from any external source, unlike religious laws which rely upon the power of god, or civil laws which rely upon parliaments, police, courts, and prisons. In totem societies taboos are regarded as natural, self-evident, and self-reinforcing. Indeed they *are* so, to any who believe in their power.

Direct taboos attach themselves to specific persons, places, or things within the community. They are a form of sacred avoidance affecting authority figures such as chiefs and priests, but also such things as corpses, births, initiations, marriages, sexual activity, menstruating women, warriors before and after battle, certain foods, etc. It is as if these persons, places, or things exuded a form of supernatural power ("mana") against which ordinary people need to shield themselves and the community. One might think of this power as something resembling an electrical charge which runs easily through the chief, but will destroy an ordinary person whose circuitry is designed to operate at a lower voltage. Certain rituals can protect one against these sources of mana, as, for example, the court ceremonial of the Nuba, who bare their left shoulder when entering the chief's hut, until it is touched by the chief, as if thereby grounding and defusing his dangerous charge.

Like an electrical charge, mana can also be transferred by contact or contagion to other objects. Such objects are then governed by indirect taboos, as in the case reported by a traveler to New Zealand, where a young and perfectly healthy slave discovered some food on the roadside, ate it, and then went into convulsions and died as soon as he was informed by a horrified onlooker that the lunch had been left by a Maori chief. Because of the fear of contagion, the community will act to remove the threat posed by a violator of a taboo, for example, by excommunicating him or driving him into exile.

Taboos display the same characteristics as the objects of neurotic phobias. The excessive concern with avoiding or protecting certain persons, especially authority figures, betrays the overcompensation of the neurotic toward the object of his hostility or desire. In the same way, these suppressed feelings are easily transferred to associated objects or places, as in the case of the neurotic who placed a taboo on her husband's razor, or as in the case of Anna O. who avoided drinking water. As we saw in Section 3.1, the ambivalent feelings of a neurotic can also express themselves in the form of ritual obsessions. Primitive people, like neurotics, give unconscious expression to repressed hostility and repressed desire through irrational prohibitions and rituals. Savages, like neurotics, presumably need these prohibitions and rituals in order to alleviate tension caused by excessive repression. Though the objects of taboos, or the contents of ritual actions, are inherited by savages from their forefathers, the efficacy of these avoidances and rituals presupposes the survival of those feelings of hostility or desire which originally produced the avoidances and rituals.

The original sin

Why, asks Freud, are the two consistent features of totemism the exaggerated incest taboo and the taboo against killing (or eating) the totem animal? Freud begins his explanation by looking back at the shape of human society in its natural state, before the dawn of civilization, and before totemism. Conveniently Darwin's *Descent of Man* (1871) had already constructed, from his (excessively limited) observation of higher apes, the protohuman condition in the form of the "primal horde," a small family group composed of one dominant male and several females. In it, the dominant male jealously kept all the women for himself. When a male child grew up, his father drove him away, or was himself killed in the fight. This patriarchal band could be set in stark opposition to totemism, which Freud characterizes as bands of men enjoying equal rights with one another, but all equally enjoying none of the women. The very polarity of this reversal, from the rule of might to the rule of rights, from uninhibited sexual dominance to complete repression, suggested that no gradual evolutionary process, but a powerful and sudden explosion was needed to set nature so completely on its head.

Totemic society itself offers psychoanalysis two essential clues. First, in all totemic societies the members of the totem regard the totem animal as the original father of the group. Secondly, totemism shows the same feelings of ambivalence toward the totem animal as children and neurotics show toward their fathers. Freud drew upon Smith's lurid (and purely hypothetical) account of totem feasts. At periodic (usually annual) feasts, the clan members dress up in imitation of their totem animal, imitate it with songs and dances to demonstrate their identity with it, and then, all together, they ceremoniously kill an animal of the same species and eat it raw, "blood, flesh, even bones" (1940–68.9: 169)! Afterwards they weep over the murdered animal, and then break into a joyous riot characterized by a release from all inhibitions (incestuous orgies are hinted at). "The carnival atmosphere," Freud suggests, "is created by the liberation of drives that are otherwise repressed" (170).

These clues are enough to permit psychoanalysis to apply to prehistory lessons learned about the father complex of modern children. The transition

from primal horde to totemic band was effected by the actual performance of a crime about which modern children and neurotics only dream
(172–3).

> One day [back in the time of the primal horde] the repressed and exiled
> sons formed a conspiracy, beat their father to death and ate him and so put
> an end to the patriarchal horde. United they dared and accomplished what
> they could not have done individually. (Perhaps some advance in culture,
> the handling of a new weapon, gave them the feel of superiority.) It is
> self-evident in the case of cannibalistic savages that they also ate the mur-
> dered man. The powerful primal father was certainly the envied and feared
> role-model for each member of the group of brothers. Now in the act of
> consuming his flesh they confirmed their identification with him, and each
> appropriated a bit of his strength. The totem meal, perhaps the first human
> festival, would have been a repetition and commemoration of this memor-
> able, criminal act, in which so much found its origin: social organization,
> customary restraints, and religion.
>
> Starting from this hypothesis, to find these conclusions credible, it is only
> necessary to suppose that the conspiring brothers were governed by the same
> contradictory feelings toward their father that we can prove to be the con-
> tent of the ambivalence of the father-complex in every one of our children
> and neurotics. They hated their father, who stood so powerfully in the way
> of their own needs for power and sex, but they also loved and admired him.
> After they had done away with him and satisfied their hatred, they also needed
> to give way to their overpowering feelings of tenderness. This took the form
> of repentance, and a feeling of guilt arose, which here coalesced with the
> repentance they shared. The dead man now became more powerful than he
> had ever been in life; we see all of this today in the lives of common human-
> ity. That which he had forbidden them by his existence, they now forbade
> themselves in the mental condition so well known to psychoanalysis,
> "belated obedience." They tried to expiate their crime insofar as they pro-
> hibited the killing of the father's substitute, the totem animal, and insofar
> as they renounced their claims on the fruit of their crime, the women of the
> horde who had now been made accessible to them. In this way, the guilty
> conscience of the sons created the two fundamental taboos of totemism –
> and for this reason they coincide with the two repressed wishes of the Oedipal
> complex.

By this psychoanalytic tour de force the Oedipal complex is shown to
inaugurate human civilization just as it inaugurates the mental development of each human individual. The brothers' renunciation of their primal
father's egotism is the origin of the superego as well as the social order.
Their Oedipal guilt, and the compulsive need for a commemorative ritual
enactment of their crime, also create cult, and by implication, religion, art,
and culture.

From savagery to religion

Freud argued that all religions stem from this yearning for the father. Indeed, the chief god in most religions is called "the father." Moreover, surviving traces of the identification of the totem animal with the father could be found in historical religious systems. In most ancient religions, typically, each god had his holy animal, which was sacrificed to him "in certain especially holy sacrifices, the mysteries" (178). Often divinity was worshiped in the form of an animal, and in myth the gods frequently turn themselves into animals, especially their special sacred animal.

This yearning, however, was not without ambivalence. The evolution of society and religion are marked, above all, by variation in the mixture of love and hate directed toward the father-figure, and in particular by the reduction of hostility in favor of love and admiration. On the onto-genetic plane, Oedipal guilt, shame, and fear engender the superego, which initiates the latency phase, and which, as it grows in vigor gradually suppresses or redirects libido. So, on the phylogenetic plane, the guilt and shame consequent upon the murder of the father, mixed with fear that one of the brothers would merely replace the father, created the order characteristic of totemism. But as time passed, the hostility toward the father lessened, and gave way to admiration and imitation. Society was allowed to become more patriarchal and more hierarchical, as individuals strove and a few succeeded in manifesting his idealized qualities. Freud allows the egalitarian totemic brotherhood to develop into something bearing a close resemblance to Frazer's age of magic, in which shamans, priests, and priest-kings associated themselves increasingly with the power of the god. As their power increased, the totem animal/god became more human, remade in their and the original father's likeness. Religion became less of a collective enterprise and rather a form of submission and personal obeisance to a more human father-figure. Somehow the worshipers and subjects of the priest-kings and god-kings took advantage of their new relations to alleviate the burden of guilt even further by imagining that the god himself demanded sacrifice (it is in this phase that we find myths which show the gods themselves killing their holy animals). The description of the process offers analogies with the maturing individual's preparation for an eventual psychological reconciliation with the father. But ambivalence was not by any means extinguished: this was, after all, the phase of Frazer's dying gods and god-kings, whom the people worshiped, but also sacrificed and sometimes ate.

Eventually the religion of guilt and yearning for the father was complemented by the development of a form of mother cult. Freud attempted to find a correspondence between the onset of puberty, which ends latency, and the agricultural revolution of the neolithic. Ontogenetically the onset of the sex drive at puberty reawakens the repressed desire for the mother and brings the adolescent once again into conflict with the father (though in the individual this leads to the eventual substitution of the mother with an eligible female and the final resolution of the Oedipal complex). Phylogenetically, the agricultural revolution introduced huge changes in human society and culture. But the agricultural revolution was not without a purely psychological dimension. "With the advance of agriculture, the working of mother earth, the incestuous libido of the son received a new stimulus" (183). The awakened libido of adolescent humanity gave rise to the worship of the mother-goddess. It is in fact true that the archaeological remains of the neolithic in Europe and Asia are dominated by the ubiquitous "Venus statuettes," large-busted, big-buttocked, naked birth-goddesses. Remnants of the mother-goddess cults are easily seen in the historical religions of Greece, Asia Minor, and the Middle East. They are characterized by the worship of a mother-goddess and a divine son. "The son's striving to put himself in the place of the father god emerges with ever greater clarity" (185).

If the mythic remnants of earlier tribal times resembled guilty nightmares fixated on the father, those of the neolithic are erotic fantasies fixated on the mother. The great goddess figures (Inanna, Isis, Venus, Cybele) all had their mortal lovers (Dumuzi, Osiris, Adonis, Attis), whom Frazer had shown to appear throughout the world as youthful vegetation-spirits. These youthful lovers now emerge as ego-figures for young peasants in surexcitation from long hours behind the plow. Though Freud almost certainly overstates the joy of agriculture, some of these myths offer impressive support to his claim that the imagined satisfaction of desire for the mother elicits guilt feelings, and is usually spoiled by imagined punishment. The youthful lovers of the mother-goddess invariably come to a bad end, and in the classic instances of Osiris, Attis, and Adonis, do so explicitly by castration. In the case of Adonis, the operation is performed by Aphrodite's own sacred beast, the wild boar, which in one version is said to be Ares, Aphrodite's jealous husband, the father-figure, in disguise.

The shift of focus from father to son (from rival to ego-figure) in religious thought can also be exemplified by the myth of Zagreus. Zagreus was in fact later identified with the "father" gods, Zeus and Dionysus, but in the myth promulgated by the Orphic mysteries he was a young child when he was torn apart by Titans and eaten raw. Despite the displacement of father by child, the tale is ridden with guilt and remorse. Zeus (who appears in his own right in the myth handed down to us) fried the Titans with a thunderbolt in punishment. Prometheus then mixed the ashes of the Titans with the clay from which he made humankind, explaining man's fallen, "Titanic" nature. Part divine, unlike other beasts, but also part Titan, humanity was condemned, by this original sin, to expiate the crime of the Titans by enduring earthly existence, repeatedly through a cycle of rebirth. The savage murder of Zagreus replicates a motif common in Dionysiac myth, and has long been thought to mirror actual sacrifice performed on animals in certain mystery cults (hence the importance Freud gave to sacrifices in *mystery* religions, above).

The correspondence between ontogenetic and phylogenetic psychic development could be represented schematically as follows:

Ontogenetic

	Castration complex		Puberty		
Autoeroticism	Oedipal ↓ Latency		↓ Adolescence	:	Maturity
Primal horde	↑ Totemism/magic	↑ Religion		:	Science
	Killing father	Agriculture			

Phylogenetic

Needless to say, there is no religion which corresponds to "maturity" on the ontogenetic plane. Throughout his life Freud was a proud and militant atheist. Already in 1907 he had devoted an essay to the exploration of the relationship between "Obsessive Actions and Religious Practices," which he summed up with the suggestion that neurosis was "an individual religion," and religion was "a universal obsessional neurosis" (1940–68.7: 139). In *Totem and Taboo*, he joyfully manhandled religion, exposing its origin in the most heinous and barbarous crime imaginable and attributing its survival to the seething incest and revenge fantasies of oppressed millions. Like Frazer, Freud felt religion to be a dangerous illusion, which had to be replaced by reason and science. But with far less hypocrisy than Frazer, Freud was frank and open in debunking Christian and especially Catholic ritual and doctrine. No religion exemplified the yearnings of the id with less concealment. Christian myth spoke of the inherited guilt of mankind as a sin against God the Father. "If Christ sacrificed his life to free mankind from the burden of inherited guilt, this forces us to the conclusion that the sin was a murder . . . self-sacrifice [in primitive cultures] points to bloodguilt. And if this sacrifice of Christ's own life is compensation for God the Father, then the crime could only have been murder of the father" (1940–68.9: 185). Most sensationally, the Christian Eucharist is a direct reminiscence of the totem sacrifice in the symbolic eating of the flesh and blood of the sacrificed son/father/lamb/god.

3.4   FREUD IN HIS SOCIAL AND
THEORETICAL CONTEXT

The internal savage

Victorian science had two dominant responses to the question of how it is that so many disparate cultures share the same myths and mythical motifs. One of these, which may be exemplified by Müller (Section 2.2), was devolutionary and conservative, idealizing the distant past with its noble and Christian ideals. The other, exemplified by Frazer (Section 2.3), was evolutionary and liberal and put its faith in progress and the capacity of reason and science to rescue mankind from the savagery of religious and social tradition. The opposition between these views concealed a more fundamental agreement, that the West was the world's most advanced civilization and could only benefit the rest of the world through its colonial enterprise. The comparatist theory of social evolution also introduced, with clearer outlines than ever before, but still hidden in the shadow of the savage, the "other" of the elite Victorian theorist: clergy, peasantry, and working classes, whom I have referred to as the "internal savage" and who served to justify the hegemony of elite Europeans domestically, by the same logic that justified the hegemony of European nations internationally. Freud never questioned the evolutionary framework which he adopted from the comparatists. With Freud, however, our gaze shifts inward. The savage is brought home, not only into the slums, but into the very heads of otherwise respectable citizens. Whereas Frazer's internal savage served mainly to give evidence against the external, in Freud cavemen and totems are mainly of interest for the light they throw upon the mentality of contemporary European psychology and culture. Freud's interests were, after all, not anthropological, and besides, Austria had no overseas empire, though, like Britain, it had plenty of internal unrest.

The thematics of comparatist evolution fit easily into Freud's psychoanalytic history: in outline, at least, Freud reproduces a typical comparatist stage theory of progressive mental development, but he goes far beyond the comparatists' equation of the mentality of savages and children to elaborate a perfect parallelism between phylogenesis and ontogenesis. In doing so he drew less on Frazer's belief that the savage mind was governed by reason, however fallacious, than on the more usual thesis advanced by Frazer's colleagues that the savage barely had any rational faculties, and made little use of those he had, but was governed by instincts, emotions, and impulses, and only acquired the use of reason when well advanced toward the civilized state. In adapting this scheme Freud laid much more stress on reason as a mechanism of self-control than as an instrument of cognition. Reason is in fact downgraded to a secondary role in Freud's evolutionary narrative. The true protagonists were the libido and the ego-instincts (or in later terminology, the id and ego), and the pleasure principle and reality principle to which they were each respectively wedded. The ego, learning the lessons of its "teacher," harsh "Necessity," tames the libido by imposing obstacles to the gratification of its impulses. Though the ego employs reason in determining how to bring the libido into conformity to reality, this reason is only rarely, as in Frazer, abstract and scientific in spirit, but more generally committed to the emotional satisfaction of the individual. Indeed, the ego is ultimately as committed to pleasure as the libido: its commitment to reason extends only to a desire to avoid the frustration or pain which would result if the libido, which knows or cares nothing for reality, were to have its way.

Libidinal energy is at first polymorphous and anarchic. Maturation implies the control and management of libido by ego. In this unequal task the ego is assisted not only by Necessity, in the character of the harsh realities of the external real world, but also by deterrents that emerge from the internal imaginary world. Just such an internal phantasm is the Oedipal fear of castration, which, as we have seen, is responsible for the establishment of the earliest submission of the individual to the rule of repression. This Oedipal fear is almost always totally a product of imagination. Yet Freud felt it necessary to give it a foundation in historical reality: it is probable, he says, "that the inner impediments are derived from real obstacles in the earlier history of human evolution" (1940–68.11: 363).

For this odd belief Freud found ready support in Spencer's contention that the life-experiences of previous generations were passed on genetically to subsequent generations (this theory is generally referred to as Lamarckism, from the fourth law of Jean Baptiste Lamarck's *Natural History of Invertebrates* [1815]: "All which has been acquired, laid down, or changed in the organization of individuals in the course of their life is conserved by generation and transmitted to the new individuals which proceed from those which have undergone those changes"). The idea of a genetic transference of experience was more than just an excuse for pursuing Freud's archaeological hobbyhorse. It explained, namely, how it was that all humans, regardless of factors of culture or education, came to have knowledge of the universal symbols found both in myths and dreams. More importantly for Freud's purposes, if not for ours, it explained how certain products of the imagination, discovered mainly in the wild fantasies of Viennese neurotics, could be identical with the contents of human minds everywhere and at all times: the theory of the genetic transfer of experience provided a ground for such imaginary constructs as the fear of castration, the basic dynamism of the Oedipal complex, that played such a large role in the stages of childhood development, as well as a host of other "primal fantasies" *(Urphantasien)*, which contribute to the breakdown of normal development and "continually recur in the story of a neurotic's childhood, and seem hardly ever absent," but which cannot have occurred as often as reported (1940–68.11: 383–6):

> I believe these primal fantasies . . . are phylogenetic property. In them the individual reaches back beyond his own personal experience into the experience of past ages, whenever his own experience proves inadequate. It seems to me quite probable that everything which the analyst today hears as fantasy, the childhood seductions, the awakening to sexual excitement upon witnessing parental intercourse, the threats of castration – or rather the actual *castration* – was in the prehistoric age of the human family once reality. The fantasizing child simply filled the gaps in his true individual experience with prehistoric truth. We are repeatedly led to suspect that the psychology of neuroses has preserved more relics of human evolution than all other sources.

Indeed, neurotics provided a kind of royal road to human prehistory. In most people this inherited knowledge is buried in the unconscious after early childhood, but neurotics either preserve these traces or reactivate them: the libido tended to fixate upon objects in childhood, from which the ego was subsequently never able to disengage it, or the ego actually "regressed," as if moving back in ontogenetic development, to infantile stages in pursuit of lost gratification. This process of moving backward in ontogenetic time was also a move backward in phylogenetic time. In an unfinished essay of 1915 Freud even speculates that modern neuroses, if placed in the order of the typical age of the patients who suffer from them, could reproduce the sequence of psychic trauma in human prehistory (Freud 1985 [1987]). We have already encountered the urge to ground collective fantasy in the material reality of a speculative primal history with Freud's insistence on the historical actuality of Prometheus and Heracles (Section 2.2) or the historical reality of the murder of the Urfather (Section 2.3). The Lamarckian hypothesis, despite the obsolescence of such ideas after Darwin, proved an irresistible prop to Freud's ambitious, totalizing system: it provided psychoanalysis with essential links between present and past, individual and collective unconscious, and ultimately enlarged its domain to include anthropology and sociology.

Freud's savage is quite literally "internal": throbbing and threatening just beneath the cortex of every European brain is the savage brain, complete with its archaic contents, and, but for the blessing of repression, in

perfect working order. Moreover, this was an internal savage with a difference: unlike Frazer's savage, he could not simply be assimilated by force,
or exorcised by a good education. There were limits to the degree to which
the savage part of the mind could be repressed or ignored. The id, still
more than ego, made a vital contribution to civilized life. Though the id
might be full of repulsive desires, it was also the power source of psychic
energy. The ego, powerless except for the energy it diverts from the id,
at best merely functions to control this energy, and direct it in a way consistent with its own aims. In *The Ego and the Id* Freud compares the ego
to "the rider who is supposed to rein in the superior strength of the horse,
with the difference that the rider does this with his own, the ego with
borrowed strength" (1940–68.13: 253). Not just the progress, but the immediate survival of civilization depended upon diverting the energy of this
"internal savage" into productive labor.

If Freud's social theories have something in common with Frazer's
evolutionism, they also have something in common with Müller's linguistic
theory of the origin of myths (Section 2.2). Humanity's "phylogenetic inheritance" constituted a primitive language, in fact the most primitive human
language, nothing less than the symbolic "language" of the first humanoid
primates. Genetically transmitted, this language remained in the unconscious after the separation of the mind into conscious and unconscious
had taken place, and after the human animal acquired language as we
know it. But although it was buried in the unconscious, it was never
lost; every human child thinks in this primitive language before acquiring
spoken language, and every human reverts to this primitive language both
every day in his fantasies and every night in his dreams.

The universal symbols of dreams and myths were, however, not the only
survivals of primitive language. Freud was much taken with the theories
of the linguist Karl Abel (*Contradictory Meanings of Primitive Words*, 1884),
who surveyed a large number of words in ancient and modern languages
which, in his view, embraced contradictory meanings. He identified these
as survivals of primitive languages on the assumption that any language
which violates the most fundamental law of logic, namely the law of non-
contradiction, must necessarily hail from the period before humanity
acquired its faculty of reason. Most of Abel's examples are in fact based
on false etymology (e.g., Old English *bat* meaning "good, better" he connects with modern English "bad," though they are from different roots),
while the "contradictory meanings" of others appear only in translation
(Latin *altus*, for example, can be translated as "high" or "low," but in
Latin quite consistently refers to a distance measured from bottom to top,
whether it is a tree or a well that is described). Abel confirmed Freud's
notion that dream symbols were remnants of the Urlanguage of young

humanity, because dream symbols characteristically exhibit precisely the same property: they "show a marked preference for joining and representing opposites in a single object" or "freely represent a given element by its opposite, so that one cannot at first know whether to give a positive or negative interpretation to a dream symbol which is susceptible to contradictory meaning" (1940–68.2/3: 323). Freud's explanation of the contradictory meanings had, however, less to do with reason than the internal "conflict of the mind" in which the wishes of the unconscious mind were opposed and transformed by the repressive mechanism of a conscious mind, but a repressive mechanism not yet sufficiently vigorous to erase the opposition altogether. Later, with the invigoration of the ego, the censor more effectively squelched contradiction and so words had the more decided and univocal meanings that we normally ascribe to language.

One basic assumption is that all language and thought is initiated by the libido: "Thought is nothing other than a substitute for a hallucinatory wish . . . nothing other than a wish could set our mental faculty to work" (1940–68.2/3: 572). Another basic assumption is that language at the most primitive level expresses nothing but libidinous desire, but, with both ontogenetic and phylogenetic growth and with the development of the repressive ego and superego functions, the expression of desire is increasingly filtered away, so that at the highest level of thought and language, the exercise of logical argument, and the practice of scientific discourse, the wish-fulfillment element is reduced to a minimum. This is why science remains humanity's great hope in coming to grips with reality and Necessity, while religion is purely a wish-fulfilling fantasy. Symbol and reason thus find themselves at opposite ends of the evolutionary scale, as the linguistic correlative of the familiar antinomy between savage thought and science.

Abel's primitive language, with its contradictory meanings, already implies the existence of a healthy if still rudimentary repressive mechanism, since the contradiction arises from the opposition of conscious to unconscious mind. A still more primitive (because less repressed) stage of linguistic development was indicated by another feature of dream symbols, namely the fact that almost all dream symbols refer either to the genitals or the sex act. To explain this Freud had recourse to the theory of another historical linguist, Hans Sperber (1912). Sperber was impressed by the many words in many languages which could refer to sex or sexual organs in slang or double-entendre. The reason, he opined, was that the earliest human language developed out of mating calls, like the language of birds. Originally all words would have referred unambiguously to sex or sexual organs. Later, however, when, succumbing to Necessity, early humanity turned its attention to work, and primitive man performed his labor communally to a chorus of rhythmically repeated utterances (all of which meant "sex," since all utterances meant "sex"). "In this way a sexual interest was transferred to the work; early man made his work agreeable, by treating it as an equivalent of and a substitute for sexual activities" (Freud 1940–68.11: 169–70). For a while the same words stood for work and sex, but gradually the sexual meaning became detached and the words referred only to the work or the tools. Freud found this account irresistible: it suited his notion of a primitive universal language; it explained why all dream symbols, as remnants of the Urlanguage, referred to sex or genitals; it offered the analogy of birdsong as a language which was (then regarded as completely) innate, but best of all, this wild history of language provided an elegant first step for Freud's scheme of phylo-genetic social evolution, and also something of a solution to a theoretical problem. According to Freud's scheme humanity knew little repression at the earliest moments of civilization, yet civilization obviously cannot proceed without productive labor. But in Freud's theory, libido and labor should lie far apart: the libido, on the one hand, demands immediate gratification, is entirely egoistic, and is entirely given to the pleasure principle; productive labor, on the other hand, requires the complete deferral of gratification, the redirection of libidinous energy, and is in some sense social and altruistic and entirely a product of the reality principle. Sperber's theory closed the evolutionary gap by allowing for a concept of "libidinous labor," an ideal coalescence of libidinous sensuality and disciplined self-denial, as if there were scarcely a noticeable difference between this original grunt work and the sex act itself. The theory also provided, with the growth of consciousness and language, for the submersion of the sexual meanings of words, but not their loss, for they were only driven into the unconscious, and indeed they remained conscious in many words which, in common slang, are still used to refer to sexual intercourse ("bang," "screw," "nail," etc.). The theory of the forgotten primal language bears a striking resemblance to Müller's, replacing only the noble Aryas, blubbering about the sunset, with an equally one-tracked savage inter-minably spewing smut.

The working class

Not least attractive was the nice fit Sperber's theory made with the socio-logical side of Freud's theory. Civilization began with the renunciation of libido gratification and most of all with renunciation for the sake of productive work. The process by which libidinal energy is converted into productive work, "the deflection of sexual instinctual forces to higher

cultural aims," Freud refers to as *sublimation*: "It consists in the abandonment by the sexual impulse of the goal of gratification incidental to
reproduction or any gratification which is a component of reproductive
activity and adopting another, which has a genetic connection with the
abandoned goal, but which must now sooner be called social than sexual"
(1940–68.7: 156, 11: 358). But not all people have an equal capacity for
sublimation. Just as the ability of the civilized man to renounce gratification is vastly superior to that of the savage, so too "only a minority attain
mastery through sublimation" (1940–68.7: 156), and this minority is not
evenly distributed through society. At the high end stands the artist who
"transfers all his interest, and all his libido too, to the creation of his
fantasies" (1940–60.11: 390), though the artist is indeed too close to the
high end, and likely to suffer from neurosis due to extreme repression.
Near, but at a healthy distance behind him, stands the man of science,
whose contributions are aligned more with reason and the reality principle than the artist (Freud seems to have taken some pride in his own
sexual abstinence). Below them, but still at the higher end of the scale of
capacity for sublimation, were the middle classes, whose class culture was
characterized by far more self-denial and internal repression (providing
Freud and his colleagues with almost all of their neurotic patients). Those
on the social scale least capable of sublimation are of course the uneducated and least civilized lower classes. The logic of Freud's ontogenetic and
phylogenetic scheme, governed as it is by a class logic, seemed to require
this. And yet it was not an easy thing to theorize the complete incap-
acity for sublimation of the very class that manifestly provided almost all
of the productive labor in Europe. One solution to this impasse was to be
very chary with the word "sublimation" except when referring to the more
sublime "high culture" – a tactic Freud sometimes adopted, but only as
an avoidance tactic, since the definition fit. A second solution was to deny
that the productive labor of the working classes was really the result of
internal discipline rather than external force. In justifying the repression
of the working class Freud reasons that "one cannot dispense with the
domination of the masses by the minority any more than one can dispense
with the application of external compulsion for productive labor, for
the masses are lazy and unendowed with reason, they do not like to give
up their drives, cannot be persuaded by argument of the necessity, and
individually encourage each other not to give up their anarchic ways"
(1940–68.14: 328). But this theory also challenged empirical verification,
since whips and cudgels were no longer standard equipment, even in
Viennese sweatshops. Sperber's theory had the benefit of explaining the
worker's internal motivation without direct recourse to any notion of internal discipline and rational submission to Necessity, which might muddy

the forced clarity of Freud's equation: manual labor, the collective and rhythmic grunt work of society (the description fits industrial better than primitive labor), is a form of "libidinous" labor and so does not require much repression, nor much civilization, from the virtual savages who produce it.

Freud had no doubt of the necessity of repression. Without it civilization would slip quickly into savagery and anarchy. And since most members even of the most civilized society had only a minimal capacity to sustain internal repression, Freud had no doubt about the necessity of external repression. Society, too, had a superego in the form of its laws, institutions, and coercive mechanisms: the police, courts, and prisons. So systematic a thinker as Freud could hardly avoid drawing an analogy between the psychic and social hierarchy: the upper and lower class were like ego and id, the one holding civilization together with its powers of repression, the other sustaining it with its energy: and the synergy of the two yielding productive labor. It is only a bit of an exaggeration to say "Freud's conception of the conscious ego constantly under threat from an anarchic id approximates to bourgeois fears of civilisation being swept away by working-class radicalism. . . . It is as if, during the course of the nineteenth century, class conflict is gradually internalised as a conflict between different parts of the self" (Day 2001: 141–2). But Freud's commitment to repression had its limits: he knew too well the dangers of excessive repression. The threat of savagery came from above as well as below. Excess repression brought cultural neuroses threatening such total collapse of the structure of civilization as World War I and the Bolshevik Revolution. Oddly, it was the lesson that repression had its cost, that there would be an explosive "return of the repressed" which attracted leftist social theorists to Freudian psychology in the twentieth century: the list, beginning with Walter Benjamin and the "Frankfurt School," is long (a notable example is Herbert Marcuse's notion, in *Eros and Civilization* (1955), that capitalism generates, with surplus capital, a "surplus-repression"). Freudian psychology seemed to herald the revolution of the working classes. Paradoxically, however, the theorists of the "Freudian Left" reversed Freud's natural sympathies: they identified with the id against the ego. On the right, too, the unconscious might also be valorized at the expense of consciousness: as a source of creativity and vital energy, but also of tradition and spiritual wisdom: from this direction Jung played Müller to Freud's Frazer. It seems the ego came to represent the status quo of the military-industrial complex, an alienating and coercive force gone out of control, which threatened to rob humanity of all sources of gratification and happiness, leading to neuroses and self-destruction.

Women

The most serious problem with Freud's psychological theories is that they are phallocentric in the most literal sense. Freud assumed that male child-hood development could serve as a model for the female experience; yet just how remained a dilemma. At first he thought that female experience corresponded exactly with the male, only with father substituted for mother. Later, however, he opted for a more complex development with an initial choice of the mother as erotic object, later substituted by the father. But as late as 1928 he was forced to admit in a letter to Ernest Jones that "everything we know of female early development appears to me unsatisfactory and uncertain" (Gay 1988: 501).

Most problematic is imagining the occasion for the development of the female Oedipal complex. In a paper of 1925 entitled "Some Psychic Consequences of the Anatomical Distinction between the Sexes," the development of male and female children is treated as identical until about the age of three; in fact, both have characteristics which Freud describes as bisexual. At three the presence of the father begins to make an impact on the child's psyche, leading to the Oedipal complex in boys, which develops when the inherited trace-memory of castration is awakened, most often when boys first see female genitalia and infer the threat of castration. Castration fear is what brings on the latency stage and triggers the normal development of the repressive mechanism necessary for psychological maturation. Females, however, are unlikely to feel a threat of castration, archaic remnants notwithstanding. Instead, Freud surmises that when girls become aware of male genitals, they somehow assume that this is a norm, and become envious of brothers and male friends. This is the onset of a sense of inferiority and the development of feelings of jealousy, notoriously labeled "penis envy." Why little girls should envy males for their penises is a bit of a mystery upon which Freud throws little light: either Freud just never believed anyone could seriously doubt the superiority of the penis, or he chose to evade the problem with only a glancing reference to the penis's more impressive urination power in the hope that the "technological" appeal of superior trajectory would suffice to banish doubt. In any case, the humiliation at her mutilated condition causes the girl to blame her mother for her inadequacy, and consequently to reject her as the primary love-object, either because she thinks her mother responsible for this birth-defect, or because she thinks her mother has in fact castrated her. Both alternatives have problems which Freud also avoids: the first assumes knowledge of the facts of birth of which Freud elsewhere claims children to be ignorant, and the second is simply arbitrary – why the mother, and why not, as in the case of boys, the father, who is the most recent "intruder" in the child's consciousness? But, to resume, once the girl has rejected her mother, she transfers her feelings to her father and replaces her wish for a penis with a wish for a baby.

At this point Freud's rather crude attempt to create a symmetrical development for females only results in the creation of a greater disparity. "While the Oedipus complex of the boy is destroyed by the castration complex, that of the girl is made possible and introduced by the castration complex" (1940–68.14: 28). This means that while males develop superegos, females remain at a libidinal stage. There is something of a latency period for females, which comes as a result of fears of being rejected by the parents, but this is a force which is obviously less sudden and less urgent than castration fear for a boy. Moreover, it adds no fears which could not be supposed to be added to castration fear in normal male development. In females, therefore, the fears responsible for the development of the repressive mechanisms necessary for maturation are both belated and less intense, and hence the female psyche is less developed. Freud writes (29–30):

> One hesitates to say it out loud, but cannot resist the idea, that the level of the ethically normal is different. Her superego is never so relentless, so impersonal, and so independent of its emotional origins, as we claim it to be in a man. The modified theory of the formation of the superego here worked out would give ample justification for the character traits that critics have long ascribed to women: that she has less sense of justice than a man, that she has less inclination to submit herself to the great necessities of life, that she allows herself more often to be led in her decisions by tender or hostile emotions.

So women are less repressed, hence less mature, more emotional, in effect less rational and less civilized than men. Here we find Freud's woman serving as a kind of ideological appendix to his theory of normal (= male) psychological development, and one he would rather have cut out (it is indeed women, not men, who are threatened with castration by Freud's theory): Freud's women are the primitive side of modern society.

Freud's theory may perhaps have been an unconscious response to the threat posed to male domination by the growth of the women's movement in Europe. Certainly, it was received in that context, and served reaction by establishing a "scientific" foundation for sexual inequality. Its role in the broader discourse of self-definition was to adapt the comparatist myth of the savage to the challenges posed by the women's movement (as Freud had for the challenges posed by the labor movement). Few, even among psychoanalysts, would now defend Freud's theories of female development: they are nothing but myths and should be analyzed as such.

Ontogenesis every bit as much as phylogenesis was a value scale, centered upon Europeans as far as affected other cultures and races, centered upon the bourgeoisie as far as affected other classes, and centered upon the phallus as far as women were concerned. Little wonder that females measured up inadequately. Indeed, in "Some Psychic Consequences of the Anatomical Distinction between the Sexes" we see Freud literally measuring female genitalia against the male "norm" with the predictable outcome that they are described, first, in terms of a simple absence of the penis and, secondly, in terms of analogy and inferiority. There is, namely, a curious redoubling of the transference motif in adolescence: just as a girl has to reject penis envy for a desire for a child, she must also during adolescence reject the clitoris (considered by Freud to be an inferior substitute for the penis) as the dominant erotogenous zone in favour of the vagina. In both cases maturity results from the rejection of the desire to compete with the male in matters where he has obvious genital superiority and to accept a noncompetitive and passive role as a receptacle for his superior endowments.

It is a sad irony that Freud based his description of universal human nature upon trends that were obsolescent even in his own day. The exaggerated sexual repression of Victorian bourgeois society is now a historical curiosity. Gone too are the repressive patriarchs Freud had known in his youth. Fifteen years after Freud's death Marcuse declared the Oedipus complex obsolete, and a few years after that sociopsychologists were writing books with titles like *On the Way to a Society without the Father* (Mitscherlich 1963), a prognosis apparently already realized, seven years later, with the English translation, entitled simply *Society without the Father*. Things changed so quickly that many of us have ceased to believe in human nature or universals. But repressive fathers were never universal; during Freud's own lifetime Malinowski pointed out that in societies where the uncle is responsible for a boy's upbringing, he is also the recipient of repressed hostility, while relations with the father were warm and friendly (see Sections 4.1 and 5.4). Repression still remained, of course, as it did in the West, but even here the various forms of social repression grew more diffuse and subtle. What remains relevant is not so much the theory of sexuality as the account of the dynamics of the psyche. Modern readings of Freud tend to convert "castration complex" into pure "power relations," and the psychic dynamic into "energy flow," without reference to "healthy" and "unhealthy," "mature" and "immature," or "male" and "female."

4

Ritual Theories

[In the nineteenth century] "Self-help" was a favorite motto with leading and characteristic men of all classes. In the twentieth century, on the other hand, self-discipline and self-reliance are somewhat less in evidence, and a quasi-religious demand for social salvation through state action has taken the place of older and more personal creeds.

G. M. Trevelyan, *English Social History*, 523

4.1 SOCIAL ANTHROPOLOGY

Myth and society

Two major advances at the turn of the twentieth century altered our under-standing of myth fundamentally and irrevocably. One was the discovery of the unconscious by Freud and his colleagues. The other was the asser-tion that myth had a fundamentally social nature. Both discoveries would eventually undermine Victorian anthropology's confident belief in cultural evolution.

The theory of cultural evolution had obvious benefits for Europe's imperial mercantile and industrial interests. It generated an image of the savage which grounded Victorian rationalism and economism in human nature. Moreover, it guaranteed a universal human nature without sacrificing European claims to an advanced position in the pursuit of what everyone supposedly wanted, namely science, technology, and economic expansion. The belief that other nations differed from Europeans not in their wants, but only in their capacity to satisfy them, actively promoted the economic development of the colonies by European interests, since by virtue of this myth colonial exploitation appeared to be a form of international development and foreign aid, as if European enterprise was largely a matter of sharing the science and technology which would save savages from their eternal balance on the brink of starvation. And since philosophy grows out of a full stomach, all other cultural benefits, especially reason, morality, and good government, would soon follow.

In this economism and scientism the savage most resembled his creators' rugged individualism. If Victorian science identified hunger as the universal motive, as opposed, say, to sex, greed, envy, or the will to power, it was partly because hunger can be experienced and dealt with by an individual, alone, in Robinson-Crusoe fashion, without reference to any other individuals or to society at large. According to its canons of rational plausibility, it was the individual, not society, which proved the intelligent, creative, and dynamic force behind the material and spiritual progress of the species. The social group, as a whole, was, on the contrary, stupid, repressive, and inert. This individualistic bias repeatedly led Frazer to adopt the most absurd explanations for the invention of new concepts. We saw, for example, how Frazer attributed the origin of totemism to an error committed by a woman who discovered she was pregnant after an animal crossed her path, although the explanation presupposes the existence of the category whose origin it purports to explain (Section 2.4). The same circular logic can be found in Freud's explanation of the origin of totemism and human culture. The myth of the primal sons murdering the primal father cannot be the origin of guilt and remorse and hence the creation of the superego. The guilt and remorse could never have arisen unless the mechanisms of internal repression were already in place. But why do Frazer and Freud tell these tales as if the logic ran backwards? It is because they were committed to explaining historical developments through the experience of individual consciousness.

Categories of thought are not the products of individual consciousness processing new information. Totemism and religion are not created when distinguished intellectuals spot kangaroos and pigs. The formulation of such categories is the product of social, not individual, thought. The mind is never a *tabula rasa* before scientific observation and deduction. At best, the mind is a *tabula rasa* only, if ever, before the acquisition of language, and through it, social thought. If individual minds become aware of new categories and combinations, it is only because language has prepared them in advance and social discourse has provided the motive for their formulation.

But even if we were to allow that certain individuals are responsible for the creation of totemism or religion, the explanations offered are hardly sufficient. Totemism and religion are manifestly social phenomena and any adequate explanation must show how new ideas are transferred from the mind of the individual to society at large (let alone from the individual to all societies at a parallel stage of development). Frazer was content to refer to the sheepishness of the masses, who follow wherever gifted individuals may lead. But he never attempted to verify or demonstrate his elitist theory of mass behavior and was even content to contradict it, whenever it suited his theories. The peasant and urban masses of Europe in Frazer's own day were notably so conservative and unmoved by the progressive thinking of their scientific elite that they lived in a state of virtual savagery, practiced magic, and would, if they were not properly policed, revert to human sacrifice and cannibalism.

It is doubtful whether the thought processes of the individual *qua* individual are of any relevance to the study of myth. A narrative is not a myth the first time it is told, but only a story or an account. What makes a story a myth is the fact that it is received by a given society and that a given society participates in its transmission. There are obviously difficulties involved in determining just when any story becomes a myth, but it is perfectly clear that, by almost any currently acceptable definition, a narrative is not a myth when it is first told. It may be, of course, that the intentions of the first narrator and the umpteenth narrator are the same, but this still does not give any special status to the creator of a myth. It is far more important to realize that the intentions of a given society in transmitting a narrative may have nothing to do with the purposes of its author. Thus both in theory and in practice we can never identify any individual creator of a myth. So long as myth is a collective narrative by definition, the only relevant consideration are the mentality and purposes of the society for which the myth is a myth.

Émile Durkheim

Émile Durkheim (1858–1917) articulated the first significant theoretical and methodological departure from the individualistic, economistic, and materialist bias of Victorian anthropology. He replaced all of them with a new concept of "society." Durkheim's writings assert the primacy of society in history and in the development of individual consciousness. He was a founder of the modern science of Sociology and an important figure in the development of the French Socialist Party.

Durkheim was an idealist in the philosophical, as well as the political sense. Unlike most of his contemporaries he refused to take the individual as a starting point. "Society is not a mere sum of individuals; rather the system formed by their association represents a specific reality which has its own characteristics" (1938: 103). One of the chief characteristics of this specific reality, namely society, is a form of consciousness, which he calls the "collective consciousness." The collective consciousness of a social group is distinct from the consciousness of its members. It has its own objective existence which is perceptible through the effects it produces on the individual consciousness of the members of a social group. It is not the contributions of individual minds that create society and culture, but culture and society which create the contents and capacities of individual minds.

Division of Labour in Society (1893) is perhaps Durkheim's most effective assault on the Victorian trinity of individualism, rationalism, and economism. The work outlines a theory of social evolution which stands Victorian economic determinism on its head and it does so in the very realm where the economic seems most secure, namely, the division of labor.

Anthropologists like Spencer explained the division of labor as the direct result of the pursuit for happiness which, no one could doubt, was universal to all humanity. But in this case "happiness" means the accumulation of material wealth, which specialized labor increases because of its greater efficiency and productivity. Pushing this flawed logic to its limit, one might even argue that it was the need for specialized production which gave rise to the exchange of goods which, in turn, created the need for social structure which ultimately produced human civilization. For Durkheim this kind of argument mistook cause and effect. Greater productivity, he argued, is an incidental consequence of the division of labor, not the cause. "If we specialize, it is not to produce more, rather it is to make it possible to live when new conditions of existence present themselves" (1986: 259). Durkheim's explanation begins with society (without which specialization is inconceivable) and also ends with society: ultimately the "new conditions" prove to be the need to preserve society itself.

Primitive man, so he argues, cannot simply be assumed to desire material abundance. Where the conditions of life are simple, needs are few and easily satisfied. There is little technological development, little division of labor, and hence little social differentiation. Moreover, primitive societies have what Durkheim calls a "mechanical solidarity." Since one savage is as like another as two peas in a pod, they all bear the same mental stamp and common interests. The savage and his social group think and act as one. This situation only begins to change with social growth (the real prime mover in human history). As time goes on successful societies get larger, their populations grow more concentrated (what Durkheim calls "social condensation"), and they begin to break apart. The division of labor is not, says Durkheim, the cause of this breaking-up, but a result of it. Society responds to the breakup of mechanical solidarity by replacing it with an "organic solidarity" through the division of labor. The division of labor permits greater heterogeneity in the social system, but it also creates economic bonds of interdependence.

Advanced societies are the ultimate product of this process of social growth. The larger the social group, the farther the division of labor advances, until the interests and life-experiences of different members of the group grow highly variable. The collective consciousness grows weaker, and individual consciousness stronger. Only then can one talk of "true individuals" existing within (and apart from) the social group. Along with this relative independence from the collective consciousness comes the possibility of greater objectivity, the development of stronger powers of reason, and so on. Durkheim's new narrative of the evolution of human civilization effects a complete transvaluation of the dominant Victorian values. In particular: (1) it puts social change before economic change – indeed, social change causes economic change; (2) it puts the social before the individual – indeed, the social calls the individual into being, both in the sense that in primitive society each member of the tribe is a replica of the group personality, and in the sense that it is change in the social dynamic which calls into being "true individuals" in advanced and complex societies; and (3) it makes "reason" itself a recent arrival in human history, and consequently denies it any role in social evolution, and indeed, once again, the social is ultimately responsible for the evolution of reason, if only, in a sense, through its absence.

Though he makes wholesome havoc with Victorian science, Durkheim unfortunately does it in a way that is uncomfortably reminiscent of the usual Victorian teleology. We still see the evolution toward reason, science, and superior technological and economic development, which puts the European in a position of uncontested superiority over all other societies (contemporary as well as historical). It should, however, be noted that despite the general optimism this theory displays toward the division of labor, Durkheim was far less confident than most of his contemporaries that science and technology brought progress. The centrifugal forces unleashed by technological advancement, and the further social differentiation encouraged by the bourgeois-industrial cult of greedy individualism, threatened a complete breakdown of ethical and social norms. He further explored these themes in a book, *Suicide* (1897), in which he showed that suicide (and human unhappiness generally) was far less frequent in societies where the individual was better integrated into his culture.

The primary function of the collective consciousness is to bind the social group. Culture is therefore both infra-individual insofar as it takes its origin in the collective consciousness, and ultra-individual in that it aims at preserving the collective. Within this scheme, individualism can have only a negative and a passive role. The collective consciousness integrates the individual through its "collective representations" which embrace most of what we mean by culture. This is nowhere truer than in the realm of religion. Durkheim's *Elementary Forms of Religious Life* (1912) argued that the idea of society is the origin and "soul of religion" – and just about everything else, since "nearly all the great social institutions have been born in religion" (1991: 697).

The object of the book is not only to explain the origin and evolution of human culture, but to give an account of the origin and nature of the collective consciousness. In urging the primacy of sociology among human sciences, Durkheim felt it necessary to assert the autonomy of the collective consciousness and of collective representations. They could in no way be reducible to the material conditions of society, and still less could they merely amount to the sum of the individual consciousnesses that comprised them. Collective consciousness had to have a life and will of its own. Durkheim speaks of a synthesis of particular consciousnesses which (1991: 704–5):

> has the effect of disengaging a whole world of sentiments, ideas and images which, once born, obey laws all their own. They attract each other, repel each other, unite, divide themselves and multiply though these combinations are not commended and necessitated by the condition of the underlying reality. The life thus bought into being even enjoys so great an independence that it sometimes indulges in manifestations with no purpose or utility of any sort, for the mere pleasure of affirming itself.

"This," he concludes, "is often precisely the case with ritual activity and mythological thought."

The collective consciousness here emerges as autonomous, systemic, and rule-governed. Little wonder that Durkheim is often credited, alongside Saussure, with fathering structuralism (see Section 5.1). The autonomy, systematicity, and ruliness of collective representation is nicely exemplified by the discussion of the distinction between sacred and profane with which Durkheim begins *The Elementary Forms of Religious Life*. All religious systems presuppose a classification of all things, real or ideal, into two opposed categories, one designated by the term "profane," the other by the term "sacred." They depend on no natural cause, yet human thought offers no two categories so distinct, so absolute, and so opposed. The phenomenon of religion is misunderstood if it does not observe this distinction. "Sacred things" are isolated and protected by powerful interdictions; "profane things" are kept separate from the sacred by these same interdictions. Now magic differs from religion in that religion is a system of beliefs held in common by a community or practices performed in common by a community which serve to bind the community together; magic (which does not precede religion, but coexists with it) is practiced by individuals and practiced for private ends.

Because the comparatists fail to recognize the crucial distinction between sacred and profane, they suppose that the observation of empirical data led to the formation of religious concepts. Thus Tylor, Spencer, and the animists supposed that individuals seeing persons or animals in dreams give rise to the notion of free-ranging personal spirits; Max Müller and the nature school thought that individuals contemplating the power and splendor of natural phenomena came to anthropomorphize and ascribe godlike powers to them; Frazer, Boas, and others supposed that individuals observed natural phenomena and mistook the laws of natural causation. But the facts of common experience cannot give us a concept of something whose most fundamental characteristic is to be outside the world of common experience. Since neither human beings nor nature have the character of the sacred in themselves, this experience must have come from elsewhere, somewhere outside of nature and outside of the individual.

Durkheim searched for the answer in the most elementary form of religious life, the aboriginal societies of Australia. He correctly observed that they are not prereligious, as Frazer had claimed, but primordially religious. He also rejected the promiscuous comparisons of people like Frazer. You cannot compare the expressions of two different societies just because the expressions seem similar. To be comparable two societies must also bear each other a structural resemblance. He therefore confines himself to the close study of totem groups in Australia, though he allows some comparison with American Indian beliefs and practices, because, though more advanced societies, they express the totemistic concepts more clearly than the less advanced Australians who have only a primitive means of self-expression.

Durkheim begins his analysis by observing the centrality of the social element. Totemism is not just a belief system, it is a clan system, a form of social organization. The idea of the sacred embraces not only the totem animal or plant but also the members of the clan who *participate* in the totem. And even though the rest of the universe also participates, it is a notable fact that all other plants and animals are organized into clans and phratries no less than the members of the tribe. The principle of social organization is projected onto the cosmos. The natural world is sacred insofar as it participates in the totem emblem.

Frazer and others were wrong to think that religion necessarily involves personified or theriomorphic gods. It is true, says Durkheim, that the aborigines have no gods, but they do recognize higher concentrations of power. Within the realm of the sacred, differences are quantitative not qualitative. Impersonal forces, which different totemistic societies call *mana*, *wakan*, or *orenda*, are immanent in the world and diffused among its various material objects. The belief is not rooted in any ordinary experience and not connected with any empirical observation of the power or majesty of nature. Totem animals tend to be things like grubs, caterpillars, or frogs, not the most powerful or awe-inspiring of creatures. Yet they inspire the most intense religious emotions and are credited with supernatural power. The reason is that they are symbols which stand for another source of power. That source of power is nothing other than the power of the clan in its collectivity which they symbolize. It is, of course, society itself which stands at the root of the religious experience. Both physically and morally superior to the individual, the power and authority of the collective are the source of the individual's experience of fear and respect.

Having explained the social origin of the idea of the sacred, Durkheim feels it necessary to explain how it arose, and to continue his narrative with an account of its growth into "more advanced" forms of religion. He finds the origin of the idea of the sacred in the periodic clan gatherings designed to maintain the solidarity of the clan. These gatherings replaced normal periods of dispersed individualistic economic activities, and were characterized by moments of intensified emotion and "collective effervescence." When transported from profane to sacred existence at these gatherings, the clan sought an explanation for their altered and elevated state. The gathering of the clan is the real cause, but too complex for the primitive mind to comprehend. So the clansman looks about and sees the symbols of the clan surrounding him and assigns the cause for his altered state to these objects. He supposes that the mana flows from the graven image of the clan totem, rather than from the collectivity of the clan itself.

Eventually, and by a similar process, there developed the idea of the "soul." Australian Aborigines believe that the old souls of dead ancestors of the clan enter into the bodies of newborn children and are reincarnated. Soul is "individualized mana," an individualized representation of the clan. Belief in the immortality of the soul represents the notion that society continues to live after its individual members die.

Once there developed a belief in the existence of "souls," primitives could posit the previous existence of original souls from which the others are derived. Through this logical process the primitive deduced the belief in spirits or original ancestors at the beginning of time. The same logical process was then replicated in a number of larger arenas: when the tribes came together for their ceremonies, the primitive sought an explanation for the homogeneity and generality of the rites of the clans, and hence assumed the existence of a "civilizing hero" of the entire tribe.

Gradually the concept of divinity was abstracted from that of mana. The catalyst was the growth in social complexity, which resulted in the separation of social groups, the consequent privileging of some groups over others, and the eventual development of social hierarchies, which ascribed to some members of society higher concentrations of mana than to others. This caused the feeling of intensified group emotion to be concentrated on an individual representative, a priest or king. With the growth in social complexity and the consequent growth of communications between groups, larger social entities were formed, hence higher concentrations of mana, and the figureheads of these groups came to be regarded as gods.

One can see, in this brief account, just how much, and how little, Durkheim's vision differs from Frazer's. Frazer's economism has been completely replaced by "society" as a motive force driving evolution. But despite his effort to distance himself from the rationalism and individualism of men like Frazer, Durkheim still lingers under their spell. Notwithstanding the social origin of thought and culture, each evolutionary stage in his scheme is still played out in the heads of individuals trying to find causes for their feelings, individuals who are still inventing new concepts through observation and rational deduction. Moreover, religious concepts, if not the rituals, are still explained in terms of erroneous applications of the law of causality in the minds of these individuals.

Durkheim's theory, and in particular his demonstration of the social origin and social function of cultural forms, especially ritual, myth, and religion, had a profound effect upon the later development of ritualism and structuralism. It is, however, the approach that came to be known as functionalism that owes Durkheim the greatest debt. Functionalism came to dominate British and American anthropology for several decades. Its main exponents were Bronislaw Malinowski (1884–1942) and A. R. Radcliffe-Brown (1881–1955). Though they had very different notions of what constituted "functionalism," their essential orientation, which they owed mainly to Durkheim, was the same: they were mainly interested in myth (or rites, customs, and institutions) in their relation to a particular society (as opposed to a supposed absolute or universal context); they viewed myth in relation to the contemporary society that employs it and had no interest in myths as relics; they were interested in myth's social effect or social function; they treated cultures as systemic wholes in which cultural activities or products function in concert to reinforce and perpetuate the social system.

Bronislaw Malinowski

Malinowski was a young student at Cracow (then in Austro-Hungary), destined to be a scientist or a chemical engineer, when (according to his own account), during a period of convalescence, he read Frazer's *Golden*

Bough (then only three volumes), which changed his life. From Frazer he probably took his sense of the primacy of economic and practical activity. More decisive was undoubtedly the fact that World War I found him in the South Pacific, in enemy territory (Australia) and on an enemy research grant (British), limiting his movements and obliging him to extend his stay to include two full years in the Trobriand Islands, northeast of New Guinea, between 1916 and 1918. These years proved a happy mischance for the development and expression of this theory and method.

Malinowki's classic statement of the function of myth is a very short book, published in 1926, called *Myth in Primitive Psychology*. It begins with the claim that "an intimate connection exists between the word, the mythos, the sacred tales of a tribe, on the one hand, and their ritual acts, their moral deeds, their social organization, and even their practical activities, on the other" (1954: 96). Indeed, much more emphasis is put on the "practical" than his "even" implies. Practicality and hard work are leitmotifs which come to characterize both the savage and his myth: "myth, in fact, is not an idle rhapsody, not an aimless outpouring of vain imaginings, but a hard-working, extremely important cultural force"; elsewhere myth is an "hardworked active force," "a narrative told in satisfaction of . . . practical requirements," which "contains practical rules for the guidance of man"; it is "a vital ingredient of practical relation to the environment" (97, 101, 147). If Frazer's savage sometimes wore a lab coat, Malinowski's has a consistent preference for the hard hat.

Hard work and practicality are indeed the qualities that distinguish the man and his method. To find out how and how much a savage or his myths can labor, one has to be there beside him. These qualities mark the great difference between Malinowski and the earlier generation of armchair theorists. Even those who did practice in the field in his day he characterizes dismissively as conducting their interviews from a "comfortable position on the veranda of the missionary compound, Government station, or planter's bungalow . . . armed with pencil and notebook and at times with whisky and soda" (146–7). But Malinowski had not spent two years with the Trobrianders for nothing. He insists on the importance of a method of fieldwork that has since become standard among anthropologists. The researcher (147):

> must go out into the villages and see the natives at work in gardens, on the beach, in the jungle; he must sail with them to distant sandbanks and to foreign tribes, and observe them fishing, trading, and ceremonial overseas expeditions. Information must come to him full-flavored from his own observations of native life, and not be squeezed out of reluctant informants as a trickle of talk.

After all the anthropologist has (100):

> the unique advantage of being able to step back behind the savage when-
> ever he feels that his theories become involved and the flow of his argu-
> mentative eloquence runs dry . . . [he] has the myth-maker at his elbow. Not
> only can he take down as full a text as exists, with all its variations, and
> control it over and over; he has also a host of authentic commentators to
> draw upon; still more he has the fullness of life itself from which the myth
> has been born . . . in this live context there is as much to be learned about
> the myth as in the narrative itself.

True, it was easy for Malinowski to adopt a superior posture about fieldwork, now that the era of turbine-driven steamships had arrived, but there
is more to it than that. Malinowski's "practical" method presupposes the
importance of social context and contemporary reality, things for which
theorists like Frazer had little time.

Myth does indeed do hard practical work in Malinowski's book. It justifies
the social order, its institutions, practices, customs, and moral codes. It
"comes into play when rite, ceremony, or a social or moral rule demands
justification, warrant of antiquity, reality and sanctity" (107). It provides
"a statement of the primeval, greater, and more relevant reality by which
the present life, fates, and activities of mankind are determined" (108).
In other words, myths are the very expression and means of propagation
of the collective consciousness. They justify and perpetuate the pattern of
thought and behavior which makes up the particular mentality of a given
social group, and serve as a foundation and warrant for its customs and
institutions. They "establish a sociological charter" for individual components of the social system: "the function of myth, briefly, is to strengthen
tradition and endow it with a greater value and prestige by tracing it back
to a higher, better, more supernatural reality of initial event" (144, 146).
For future reference we should notice the special connection Malinowski
establishes between myths and rites (85):

> There is no important magic, no ceremony, no ritual without belief; and the
> belief is spun out into accounts of concrete precedent. The union is very
> intimate, for myth is not only looked upon as a commentary or additional
> information, but is a warrant, a charter, and often even a practical guide to
> the activities with which it is connected.

It is from Malinowski that we get the term "charter myth." The term is
used by later anthropologists to describe myths that behave in precisely
the manner that Malinowski describes. Needless to say there are few who
agree with Malinowski that this is how all myths function.

The most obvious kind of charter myth is a myth of origin. In many societies, including our own, origins are not simply meaningless historical events, but they are treated, quite irrationally (mythically), as having a special significance. They are reflections not so much of how things came to be, but of how they should be, or how they should remain. Insofar as they are not meaningless facts of history, "origins" are commonly retrojections of present-day cultural values. One need only think of the way the Victorian rationalists projected their own mentality upon the savage. The origin of myth in a failed act of scientific observation and deduction is a charter myth for Western science and rationality, as well as a functional affirmation of the benefits to subject nations of the imperial system.

Malinowski examines the following tale of the Trobriand Islanders (112):

> There are a number of special spots – grottoes, clumps of trees, stone heaps, coral outcrops, springs, heads of creeks – called "holes" or "houses" by the natives. . . . From one special hole, near the village of Laba'i . . . there emerged representatives of the four main clans one after the other. . . . First there came an . . . Iguana, which scratched its way through the earth as iguanas do, then climbed a tree, and remained there as a mere onlooker, following subsequent events. Soon there came out a Dog. . . . As the third came a Pig. . . . Last came a Crocodile. . . . The Dog and Pig ran round, and the Dog, seeing the fruit of the *noku* plant, nosed it, and then ate it. Said the Pig: "Thou eatest *noku*, thou eatest dirt; thou art a low-bred, a commoner; the chief, the *guya'u*, shall be I."

In order to understand this myth, one must know that each of these animals is the totem animal of a particular clan and that each of these clans is incorporated into a social caste system, in which the pig clan is supreme. Next comes the dog clan, and then the iguana and crocodile. It is also necessary to know the connection in Trobriand society between food and rank. Each clan has its own particular food taboos, as well as foods that are particularly cultivated. Hence to the pig clan, *noku*, the food of the dog people is particularly disgusting. Further, a correlation exists between the status of one's food and one's personal dignity, since you are what you eat. It is also important to know that in some parts of the territory the pig clan is still in the process of asserting its dominance. There the myth is very much "an active force." (The other clans' animals which are simply onlookers in the events are probably aboriginal people who were conquered by the dog and pig people.) Further, it is significant that the heaps of stones or "holes" are important landmarks of the community: often the chief locates his house beside them and identifies the spot as the place where *his* ancestors emerged to found the village. These few bits of contextual information suffice to make clear the close correlation between social structure and the contents of the myth.

In contrast to his predecessors, Malinowski was interested not in what made all myths alike, but in what made all myths unique and different. To the functionalist, the comparatist or psychoanalytic approach to myth was absurd insofar as it brought together motifs and symbols from the myths of totally unrelated societies. It was a bit like trying to decipher Chinese by comparing its sound patterns to English words. Once it is established that myths are social, not individual, phenomena, this kind of promiscuity is not easy to justify. With the social origin of thought the common hardware shared by all humans is at best very basic, while all of the mental software is culturally determined, and integrally connected with a unique system of feeling and thought.

Though some theorists in rejecting evolutionary and diffusionist models also rejected cross-cultural comparison outright, most functionalists allow the possibility of comparative functionalism. One can acknowledge what is unique in a given society, without blinding oneself to the possibility of finding types of societies or social structures, or types of myths which may be compared in form and function (if not necessarily, as for the comparatists, in contents). One could, for example, compare with the Trobriand myth, just examined, the story of Noah's sons in Genesis 9 of the Old Testament. After the great flood, we are told that:

> The sons of Noah who went forth from the ark were Shem, Ham and Japheth. Ham was the father of Canaan. These three were the sons of Noah; and from these the whole earth was peopled. Noah was the first tiller of the soil. He planted a vineyard; and he drank of the wine and became drunk, and lay uncovered in his tent. And Ham, the father of Canaan, saw the nakedness of his father, and told his two brothers outside. Then Shem and Japheth took a garment, laid it upon their shoulders and walked backward and covered the nakedness of their father; their faces turned away, and they did not see their father's nakedness. When Noah awoke from his wine and knew what his youngest son had done to him, he said, "Cursed be Canaan; a slave of slaves shall he be to his brothers." He also said, "Blessed by the Lord my God be Shem; and let Canaan be his slave. God enlarge Japheth, and let him dwell in the tents of Shem; and let Canaan be his slave."

Here we have a myth of origin, of the emergence of a new order. As in the case of the clan animals of the Trobriand myth, we must know that Shem, Ham, and Japheth are figures representing the ancestors of all the races of the earth: Shem is the father of the Semites, who include the Jews; Ham is the father of the Hamitic people, the ancient Phoenicians (through Canaan, hence they are called Canaanites), the Egyptians, and the black races. To appreciate Ham's offense one has to know about ancient Jewish taboos against nakedness. The offense is comparable to the eating of *noku* by the Trobriand dog, since it constitutes an infraction which justifies a racial caste system which sets the Jews at the top of the hierarchy and makes slaves of the despised Hamitic races.

4.2   JANE HARRISON AND RITUALISM

Themis

The label "ritualist" can be applied to any theory of myth which puts myth as a general category into a significant relationship with ritual (either a specific ritual or ritual in general). In its more extreme forms ritualism insists that all myths are derived from or related to rituals. In a more moderate form a ritualist theory may characterize myth and ritual as parallel responses to an external stimulus. Normally, however, a ritualist theory will privilege ritual over myth, either as the origin of myth, or as lying somehow closer than myth to the point of their common origin. The distinguishing feature of a ritualist analysis is that it explains the meaning or function of a myth by relating it to a ritual.

Jane Harrison (1850–1928) is generally regarded as the chief exponent and founder of the ritual theory of myth. She was at the hub of a group of Classical scholars, retrospectively, and somewhat misleadingly, united under the label "Cambridge Ritualists." Frazer provided a main source of inspiration for this group, and is sometimes regarded as a "fellow-traveler." But the ritualists adhered to very different values from Frazer. The group included such socially and politically engaged and progressive figures as Gilbert Murray, an activist and "radical liberal" champion of such causes as women's suffrage and pacifism, and Francis Cornford, a Fabian socialist, who campaigned for women's and working men's rights, against imperialism, and against the role of the Church in education. More decisive than Frazer for the new orientation was the sociological theory of Durkheim. If myths could be thought to be the product of individual thought, rituals were more obviously and concretely social.

It may seem a bit odd, therefore, that another of Harrison's chief sources of inspiration was the very antisocial Friedrich Nietzsche's *Birth of Tragedy* (1872), a work fairly characterized as "also the birth of the ritual theory" (Friedrich 1983: 161), though Nietzsche's contribution would have been slight without Harrison's subsequent elaboration. Nietzsche drew a strong contrast between two general forces in Greek culture: the collective, primitive, emotional, and ritual Dionysian element, on the one hand,

and the individualistic, refined, intellectual, artistic, and aesthetic Apollinian element, on the other. It was the Apollinian which was responsible for the Homeric vision of the Olympian gods, and which eventually prevailed in Classical Greece, but Nietzsche's sympathy lay with the wild, creative, and dynamic Dionysian impulse. A self-styled "disciple of Nietzsche" (1963b: viii), Harrison, in *Prolegomena to the Study of Greek Religion* (first edition 1903), described Classical Greek religion in terms of decadence. For Harrison the worship of the Olympian gods could not properly be termed a religion: to her mind the Olympians were largely the products of art and literature. The Olympians were but the decadent remnants of the true religion, which lay much further back in prehistory. True religion meant not stories, art, theology, and the refinements of intellectual reflection on nature or the human condition, but was a matter of intense feeling and excited activity. Ultimately, as we will see, this distinction between mere art and true religion, intellect and feeling, reflection and activity, will boil down to a distinction between myth and ritual. Ritual is primary and authentic, but destined to be paired, and ultimately betrayed, by myth.

Harrison took up the task of elaborating her evolutionary theory of Greek religion in *Themis* (1912). Her ritual approach is nicely illustrated by the discussion of the myths of the infancy of Zeus and Zagreus in the very first chapter of the book. We have already had occasion to refer to the myth of Zeus's infancy: how Rhea hid the infant Zeus from Kronos, who wanted to swallow him (see Section 2.6); and how Rhea gave the infant to the Kouretes, a band of young men, who hid him in a cave on Mount Dicte (sometimes Mount Ida), and danced in armor to the pipes, beating their feet and clashing their shields, to cover up the sound of his wailing. According to the standard "Olympian" version of this myth, the ruse is successful: Zeus quickly grows to manhood, forces Kronos to vomit up the other children he has swallowed, banishes him, and by assigning duties, honors, and privileges to his newly "reborn" siblings, establishes the Olympian order.

Clearly related to this myth is another which survived into the Classical period in Crete, and in the "Orphic" mystery religion. In it Zagreus, the Cretan Dionysus, is called a son of Zeus and Persephone. Zagreus was also deposited with the Kouretes, but he was killed by the Titans, Zeus's enemies (cf. Section 3.3). They waited until the Kouretes slept, and at midnight they lured Zagreus away by offering him toys. The Titans tore him apart and ate his flesh raw. But Athena managed to save his heart and revive him by putting it into a gypsum body. Zeus blasted the Titans with his thunderbolt. The fact that Cretan myth spoke of the burial of Zeus by the Kouretes, and that Cretans even worshiped at Zeus's grave near Knossos, suggests that Zagreus lies behind the Cretan Zeus as well as the Cretan Dionysus.

Harrison's explanation of these myths was inspired by an inscription found in 1904 in Palaikastro in Eastern Crete. It contained the words of a hymn copied in Roman times, but preserving much earlier material. Harrison translates (1963: 7–8):

> Io, Kouros most Great, I give thee hail, Kronian [i.e., Son of Kronos], Lord of all that is wet and gleaming, thou art come at the head of thy Daimones. To Dikte for the Year, Oh, march, and rejoice in the dance and song,
>   That we make to thee with harps and pipes mingled together, and sing as we come to a stand at thy well-fenced altar.
>   Io, etc.
>   For here the shielded Nurturers took thee, a child immortal, from Rhea, and with noise of beating feet hid thee away.
>   Io, etc.
>
>   .   .   .   .
>   .   .   .   . of fair dawn?
>   Io, etc.
>   And the Horai [seasons] began to be fruitful year by year (?) and Dike to possess mankind, and all wild living things were held about by wealth-loving Peace.
>   Io, etc.
>   To us also leap for full jars, and leap for fleecy flocks, and leap for fields of fruit, and for hives to bring increase.
>   Io, etc.
>   Leap for our Cities, and leap for our sea-borne ships, and leap for our young citizens and for goodly Themis.

Since the hymn was found in a sanctuary of Dictean Zeus, it is assumed to be the record of a ritual regularly performed there. The singers of the hymn describe themselves as dancing, then taking a stand around the altar, and singing to the music of harps and pipes. They invoke "the Greatest Kouros" to come to Dicte leading his throng of Daimones, who also dance, with magical effect for the prosperity of crops and men. A "kouros" is a young man at the age of initiation to manhood. (The word comes from the Greek *keiro*, which means to cut hair, referring to the ceremony by which young men cut off their boyhood locks to join the ranks of adult males.) Daimones are roughly "spirits," or "divinities," including many far more mysterious and less anthropomorphic than the Olympians. The Greatest Kouros is called son of Kronos and the hymn goes on to tell the myth of Rhea's hiding the infant Zeus with the Kouretes, referred to as the "shielded Nurturers" [the Greek is "shield-bearing child-rearers"], who are also dancers and presumably doubles of the dancing Daimones who will accompany Zeus. The hymn ends with a reference to "goodly Themis." *Themis* means "law" or "custom," but

Harrison will show that originally *Themis* was the projection of the social order itself: society will emerge as both beginning and end of the dance, of the hymn, and of religion itself.

Though the Greatest Kouros is identified here with Zeus, Harrison argues that he is older than Zeus. The Kouros shares something of the character of Dionysus/Zagreus insofar as Dionysus is always figured at the head of a troupe of other normally dancing divinities, usually satyrs, to whom ancient sources sometimes compare the Kouretes. The general confusion of these deities on Crete allows Harrison to conclude, probably correctly, that an older Cretan deity lies behind the cluster of deities (Zeus, Zagreus, and Dionysus), with overlapping myths known from Classical times. She identifies this older deity with the Kouros of the hymn.

Harrison began to study this inscription only a few years after the beginning of systematic excavations at Knossos by Sir Arthur Evans, and was much influenced by the mounting evidence for a flourishing Bronze Age civilization in Crete. If the Kouros was older than either Zeus or Dionysus, Harrison reasoned, the hymn from Palaikastro contained survivals of the pre-Greek, pre-Olympian religion of Crete. The survival was the cultic ritual implicit in the hymn. The reference to the son of Kronos and the position of the inscribed stone in a sanctuary of Dictean Zeus shows the degree to which the Kouros had been appropriated by Olympian religion. To make any progress, however, one had to look behind the "shifting manifold character of the myth" and fix upon the "comparatively permanent element of ritual" (16). This is the first major premise of ritualism. The myths speak of Zagreus, Zeus, Dionysus, or the Greatest Kouros, but, Harrison claims, one ritual unites them all.

The great problem for Harrison is that, apart from a reference to worshipers dancing and then singing a hymn while standing at an altar, there is no evidence for a ritual. To make any progress, therefore, Harrison articulates the second major premise of ritualism: myths are (more or less uncomprehending) explanations of ritual (i.e., myths are etiologies for rituals). "The worshippers say they invoke the Kouros because of the myth," because it was here that the Kouretes concealed the presence of the child by the noise of their dance, but "we may of course safely invert the order of things, the myth arose out of or rather together with the ritual, not the ritual out of the myth" (13). Relying on these two premises, Harrison can reconstruct the Minoan ritual *out of the myths that are derived from the ritual*. She begins by discovering what motifs all the myths have in common, i.e., reconstructing an Urritual (which, like the comparatist Urmyth, will then be used to explain the myths from which it was constructed).

The "cardinal elements" underlying the myths of Zeus, Dionysus, Zagreus, and the Kouros are (15):

1   A child is taken from his mother and carefully tended by men called Kouretes. To guard him they dance over him an armed dance. . . .
2   The child is hidden, made away with, killed, dismembered by men sometimes called Titans. . . .
3   The child reappears, is brought to life again. Sometimes this is effected by the [Titans]. . . .

Note that the death and rebirth motifs appear, properly speaking, only in the myth of Zagreus. Kronos's swallowing and vomiting up Zeus's siblings is treated as a distorted version of the same motif. To these main points Harrison adds some minor details: for example, she is convinced that the ritual involved a pretence of eating a child raw.

While the myths provide an outline for the ritual, the common motifs in the myths do not in themselves constitute either a complete or a convincing ritual. At this point she invokes the aid of Frazer's comparative anthropology. The comparative material allows her to reconstruct the ritual of the Kouretes as an initiation rite. Initiations most typically enact the death of a child, and his or her rebirth as a man or a woman. Frazer himself obligingly provided the decisive parallel. An initiation ceremony of the aborigines of New South Wales involved boys covered with blankets sitting by a roaring fire, while the elders swung bullroarers. An accompanying myth spoke of Dhuramoolan, a spirit (like Zeus) whose voice sounded like thunder, and whose office it was to kill the boys, cut them up, burn them to ash, and then remold them into human shape before taking them off to the bush to instruct them in the laws, traditions, and customs of the tribe. The name "Titans" had in fact since antiquity been connected to the Greek *titanos*, meaning "gypsum," and parallels could be found for elders disguising themselves as ghosts or demons to frighten groups of boys huddled together in terror as they awaited dismemberment. In this way the child experiences a second birth, this time a cultural birth, to emerge as a full member of the tribe. "Henceforth he belongs to something bigger, more potent, more lasting, than his own individual existence, he is part of the stream of the totemic life, one with the generations before and yet to come" (19). Comparable rituals thus show that the Kouretes are the young men of the tribe who perform the initiation rites, steal the young boys from their mothers, hide them, end their former existence in a symbolic death, and bring them back as fully socialized members of the tribe. Here, then, is a third common assumption of ritualism: that the rituals of the world are all more or less alike in important ways, and much more alike than myths – indeed, one no longer has to believe in the similarities of myths to be an effective comparatist, since they are all linked to ritual, a *tertium comparationis* which suffices to legitimate all broad-based comparisons.

Harrison's theory of evolution

The ritual explanation of this particular myth is just the beginning of *Themis*. Harrison goes on to explain: the origin of fertility magic in the rites of the Kouretes; their role in the development of dithyramb, the Dionysiac dance; the evolution of Dionysus and other Greek gods from an annual spirit, called the Year Spirit or Eniautos Daimon (who owes much to Frazer's corn-spirit and dying god); the evolution of Olympian deities from the Year Spirit; ultimately also (with the help of an "excursus" contributed by Gilbert Murray) the evolution of tragedy from dithyramb. Most important for our purposes are the generalizing and speculative intervals, scattered throughout the work: the assumption of the comparability of all ritual, or at least all ritual at different evolutionary stages, allowed Harrison to present her ideas about the development of Greek religion as a universal theory of the origin and evolution in human culture of ritual, of the idea of god, of myth, of religion, of art, and of conceptual thought.

Harrison's evolutionary scheme, when assembled from her often widely scattered comments and examples, would appear more or less as follows. In the beginning was a group of savages. Primitive man, Harrison assures us, is the slave of his emotions which he expresses physically. While together, little stimulus is required to start them hopping together with excitement. Very soon this frenetic collective movement becomes rhythmic and regularized as dance. The dances are mimetic, it seems, from the start. They begin with excited representation of real-life activities. Harrison gives the example of hunters returning to their village, still tense with the emotions aroused by the hunt. They release their pent-up emotions by dancing out the story of the hunt for the women and children of the tribe. These spontaneous, proto-ritual performances may include vocalizations: "the dancers dancing together utter their conjoint desire, their delight, their terror . . . in cries of fear or joy or lamentation, in shrieks of war" (45). Harrison fancifully suggests that perhaps "the first *muthos* was simply the interjectional utterance *mu*" (330). These proto-ritual utterances she regarded as a sort of proto-myth.

The next distinct stage is abstraction from the enactment of particular events to the performance of a generic dance which could be used for all hunts. As always, the collective dance created heightened emotion. But with the abstraction from particular to general, the mind, it would seem, was free to receive "emotional ideas," or images. It was in this stage that group emotion created a "feeling" of the sacred, in the form of supernatural, high-energy, mana, projected from the dancers' heightened emotions toward the world at large, and distributed evenly and indifferently throughout: since the savage feels at one with his group, the feeling of unity was extended without limits.

A third stage is reached when the dance is reenacted before an event (e.g., hunt or battle) to release anticipatory tension. The dance can express the desired outcome. The dancers conceive the notion that mana can be managed. Since the mana of the world is continuous, to affect a part of the continuum that one can control is thought to have a sympathetic effect on another part that one cannot. Thus, by imitating rain with rattles or victory in battle with triumphant leaps, one can bring rain or victory. This is a crucial stage in the evolution of religion: it marks the dividing line between the merely passive reaction to emotion and the active manipulation of events. It is the beginning of magic; "first and foremost magic is . . . a thing predone," but Harrison still insists on the directness of its connection with emotion: "the oneness of desire and deed . . . comes out very clearly in the simplest forms of magic" (82–3).

At a later stage, when the original group has broken into smaller ones, a sense of differentiation begins to dawn. The savage begins to distinguish his group from other human groups, and the natural world fragments along with it, not dividing human from animal, but creating divisions that run vertically across the species boundary. For some unexplained reason having to do with diet, a particular animal is selected as continuous with the human group. This is the beginning of totemism. At this stage the dance involves vocalizations which express the same general idea as the dance. Harrison gives the example of the Grizzly Bear Dance of "North American Indians" who "shuffle and shamble about like a bear in his cave" and at the same time chant "I begin to grow restless in the spring/I take my robe/My robe is sacred/I wander in summer." This is not an explanation of the dance; rather the dancer "only utters with his mouth what he enacts with his shambling, shuffling feet, the emotions and sensations he feels in relation to the . . . Bear" (329–30). The totem group dance in imitation of their totem in magical fertility rites which cause their totem (animal and tribe) to multiply.

In a fifth crucial stage a gifted dancer stands out from the group. He becomes the center of attention at the cost of the collectivity. The strong emotion of the collective dance is concentrated upon the chorus leader and the dancers call him "spirit" or "god" – "primitive gods are to a large extent collective enthusiasms, uttered, formulated" (46). Thus the Greatest Kouros and his band of spirits are originally nothing more than the dancers and their leader uplifted and sanctified by their heightened emotion. Afterwards "gradually the chorus loses all sense that the god is themselves, he is utterly projected, no longer chief daemon, but unique and aloof, a perfected [god]" (46). The projected being acquires a life-history, because of "the story-telling instinct," but the "sufferings" of the god are still at first projections of the "sufferings" of the worshipers (47). The final stage is reached when the ritual ceases to be a community performance and loses its original importance and effect, or ceases to exist. At this stage myth becomes etiological (it provides a reason for the performance of a ritual).

Society and emotion

Much in Harrison's account of the origin of religion comes straight from Durkheim. *Themis*'s subtitle, *A Study in the Social Origins of Greek Religion*, advertises the premium it places upon "the social fact." As with Durkheim, religion begins with tribal ritual which gives rise to a collective effervescence and creates the first feeling of the sacred. Society, always in the form of collective ritual, indeed normally in the form of collective dance, then goes on to produce all important religious concepts (28): "We are face to face with the fact, startling enough, that these religious figures arise, not from any 'religious instinct,' not from any innate tendency to prayer and praise, but straight out of social custom. Themis and Dike, invoked by the Kouretes, lie at the undifferentiated beginnings of things when social spelt religious." She might just as well have said "when religious spelt social:" "it was the social life of the group rather than the individual that became the object of religious representation" (47). Themis, which Harrison takes as "social order," is the mother of Dike, which Harrison takes to mean "natural order."

There are, however, important departures from Durkheim, some of which, remarkably, anticipate key themes in Freudian anthropology (she did not read Freud until much later). "Emotion" and, above all, "desire" play a larger role in Harrison's version of tribal religion than in Durkheim's. Durkheim's excessively rigid separation of "sacred" from "profane" obliged him to presuppose the existence of ritual, even in his attempt to account for its origin. True, he supposed that the collective effervescence of group gatherings gave rise to movements and shouts which "tended spontaneously towards the rhythmicisation and regularization which created song and dance" (1991: 380). But it was precisely to perform rituals that the clans gathered in the first place.

Harrison's causal explanation is more satisfying. Emotional discharge through dance is a facet of the savage's ordinary life-experience (which has little regard for maintaining the borders between sacred and profane). Durkheim gives the impression that when savages are not on holiday, they are mostly on their own and life is "monotonous, languorous, and dull"

(1991: 379); but with Harrison, savages are almost never alone, and there is almost never a dull moment. The "secular" activities of savages are full of tense, terrifying events, like thunderstorms, the hunt, or war. Pent-up emotions constantly erupt into activity. Even when the dance begins to be performed before the hunt: "the drama or dromenon here is a sort of anticipated desire, a discharge of pent-up emotions" (1963b: 45). Even when ritual dance is magical Harrison insists that it springs from desire: "*le désir c'est la père de la sorcellerie*" (83). Unlike Freud, Harrison makes the social group indispensable to the ritual discharge of emotion, just as the ritual discharge of emotion is indispensable to the social group; ultimately it works to shape and unify the emotional life of the tribe, and to "socialize" emotion (43):

> A high emotional tension is best caused and maintained by a thing felt socially. The individual in a savage tribe has but a thin and meagre personality. If he dances alone he will not dance long; but if his whole tribe dances together he will dance the live-long night and his emotion will mount to passion, to ecstasy. . . . Emotion socialized, felt collectively, is emotion intensified and rendered permanent. Intellectually the group is weak. . . . Emotionally the group is strong.

Like Freud, Harrison treats the history of religion as an archaeology of the mind. The stages of religious evolution advance in tandem with the development of the mental faculties. But while Freud's anthropology advances from domination by the id to domination by the superego, Harrison's advances from emotion to intellect. This is the overarching anthropological lesson of *Themis*: each age produced a god reflecting its own capacities. Harrison contrasts Greek and Minoan, as modern to primitive psyche: "it might almost be said that the Olympians stand for articulate consciousness, the Eniautos-Daimon for the sub-conscious" (xxi). There is some analogy, too, in the character of the catalyst. For Freud the growth of repression was the main motive force behind human evolution, and particularly cultural evolution, since repression creates the symbolic satisfactions of art and religion. For Harrison it is something that intervenes between impulse and action. In *Mythology* she makes it the distinguishing feature of the human character (1963a: xi–xii):

> In most animals, who act from what we call instinct, action follows on perception mechanically with almost chemical swiftness and certainty. In man the nervous system is more complicated, perception is not instantly transformed into reaction, there seems to be an interval for choice. It is just in this momentary pause between perception and reaction that our images, i.e., our imaginations, our ideas, in fact our whole mental life, is built up.

We do not immediately react, i.e., we do not immediately get what we want, so we figure the want to ourselves, we create an image. If reaction were instant we should have no image, no representation, no art, no theology.

In *Themis* this pause that represses is "deferral" (1963: 44):

> Psychologists tell us that representations, ideas, imaginations, all the intellectual, conceptual factors in our life are mainly due to deferred reactions. If an impulse finds instantly its appropriate satisfaction, there is no representation. It is out of delay, just the space between the impulse and the reaction, that all our mental life, our images, ideas, our consciousness, our will, most of all our religion, arise. If we were utterly, instantly satisfied, if we were a mass of well contrived instincts, we should have no representations, no memory, no *mimesis*, no *dromena*, no drama. Art and religion alike spring from unsatisfied desire.

But there was relatively little deferral in the beginning. The primordial savage did not think, properly speaking. He acted – on impulse, without knowing why he acted, without design, but by nature. The "undifferentiated beginnings of things" was a reign of pure emotion. Little matter, then, what actually went on in the savage's head. Why does the totemistic savage affirm persistently that he is a kangaroo, or an opossum, or a witchetty grub "when he quite well knows that he is not?" He does it "because to know is one thing, to feel is another" (121):

> Because to know is first and foremost to distinguish, to note differences, to discern qualities, and thereby to classify. Above all things it is to realize the distinction between *me* and *not-me*. . . . Man in the totemistic stage rarely sets himself as individual over against his tribe; he rarely sets himself as man over against the world around him. He has not yet fully captured his individual or his human soul, not yet drawn a circle round his separate self. It is not that he confuses between himself and a kangaroo; it is that he has not yet drawn the clear-cut outline that defines the conception kangaroo from that of man and eternally separates them. His mental life is as yet mainly emotional, one of felt *relations*.

Indeed, Harrison maintains that the emotional conviction of the unity of the tribe actually obstructs the development of clear, individual, or rational thought (126):

> The totem-group when it performs its rites of multiplication has indeed some dawning sense of differentiation, but its main emotion and conviction is of unity, emotional unity with its totem, a unity which it emphasizes and enhances and reintegrates by its ceremonies of sympathy. The whole human group acts and reacts on the whole plant or animal group, the *mana* of the human

and the animal group is *felt* as continuous. This is the first stage. But as intelligence advances and as actual individual observation tends to take the place of collective suggestion the sense of unity is obscured. Little by little the attention is focused on distinctions. Man, though he is dressed up as an emu, becomes more and more conscious that he *is not* an emu, but that he is *imitating* an emu, a thing in some respects alien to himself, a thing possessed of much *mana* but whose *mana* is separate, a thing to be acted on, controlled, rather than sympathetically reinforced.

Indeed, as with Durkheim, the history of the human race is a gradual movement from this confused unity toward clarity, individuality, and reason. But neither Harrison nor Durkheim is able to give a very satisfactory account of what ultimately motivates this pattern of change. Indeed, both simply assume evolutionary change, rather than argue it. For Durkheim, as we saw, there is always a movement toward growth, "social condensation," which makes things bigger and more complex. For Harrison, the real motor behind history is the growth of the human mental apparatus, as if one could simply rely on Darwin's proof that we started as animals and our brains got bigger and better, and that this overall pattern could explain differences between moderns and Minoans, or Europeans and Africans. For Harrison the key feature of the evolutionary growth of the human mental faculties lay in a supposed development of thought from the particular to the general and from the concrete to the abstract (68):

> The savage, like the child, passes from the particular to the general; the mature and civilized mind well supplied with ready-made abstractions is apt to start from generalities. To the savage this stone or tree or yam has *mana* or *orenda*, that is what concerns him; but gradually . . . from the multitude of things that have *mana*, there arises the notion of a sort of *continuum of mana*, a world of unseen power lying behind the visible universe. . . . This *continuum* . . . is perhaps primitive man's first effort at generalization.

It went without saying that humans would become more human. What argument there is, is expended to establish the proposition that, becoming more human, humans distanced themselves from emotion, from the feeling of unity with the world, and from the social group, to become more rational, individual, and self-centered.

Myth and ritual

The relationship of ritual and myth had long been a celebrated chicken and egg story, and Harrison came under fire for her clear affirmation, sharply stated in her earlier books, *Mythology and Monuments of Athens* and *Prolegomena to the Study of Greek Religion*, that rituals always precede myth. In *Themis* the relationship is stated more cautiously and ambiguously (16):

> In the study of Greek religion it is all important that the clear distinction should be realized between the comparatively permanent element of the ritual and the shifting manifold character of the myth. In the case before us we have a uniform ritual, the elements of which we have disentangled – the armed dance over the child, the mimic death and rebirth; but the myth shifts; it is told variously of Zagreus, Dionysos, Zeus, and there is every variety of detail as to how the child is mimetically killed and how the resurrection is effected. To understand the religious intent of the whole complex it is all important to seize on the permanent ritual factors.
>
> This does not, however, imply, as is sometimes supposed that ritual is prior to myth; they probably arose together. Ritual is the utterance of an emotion, a thing felt, in *action*, myth in words or thoughts. They arise *pari passu* [viz., at an equal pace, or "hand in hand"]. The myth is not at first *aetiological*, it does not arise to give a reason; it is representative, another form of utterance, of expression. When the emotion that started the ritual has died down and the ritual though hallowed by tradition seems unmeaning, a reason is sought in the myth and it is regarded as aetiological.

Yet despite Harrison, *Themis* makes the distinction between ritual and myth anything but clear. This passage declares the theoretical priority of ritual (it is the constant and original Urform that clarifies the meaning of the disparate and confused myths that attend it), even while it ambivalently denies ritual any temporal or causal priority. But, despite the protest that they arise *pari passu*, the grand evolutionary scheme that Harrison constructs in *Themis* gives priority to ritual and ritual alone, whether that priority relates to explanation, cause, or temporal sequence. Harrison's importance to ritual theory depends on this clearly granted priority, even if it is obscured by statements like the above that do not carry the courage of her convictions.

I suspect that Harrison wavered in her explicit formulation of the relationship between myth and ritual because she sensed a problem, indeed a deep contradiction, between the simple outlines of her theory and the empirical evidence she used to support it – a contradiction she could not bring herself to confront head-on. Harrison's evolutionary scheme is simple and elegant. It involves a progress from the animal, the physical, the emotional, and the social towards the human, the mental, the rational, and the individual. This was ingrained in the common prejudice of her day and needed little exposition. Her original contribution, however, was to draw a strong link between ritual and the qualities on the left-hand side of her evolutionary line, and between myth and the qualities on the right-hand side.

Action and ritual are not exactly the same thing. Action, even representational action, can be the direct or spontaneous discharge of emotion, as when the hunters release tension by re-enacting the event in dance. But "ritual" must always already involve some degree of abstraction and stereotypification beyond mere emotional reaction; it must always already contain mental imagery and symbolism; arguably it should always already require an intention to sway nature or the divine will; and normally it includes words and ideas as well as actions. All of these considerations threaten the neat distinction between impulse, action, doing, and ritual, on the one hand, and reflection, conceptualization, speech, and myth on the other. Indeed, the difference between ritual and myth is too often reduced, in Harrison's writings, to the difference between doing and thinking, as it is in *Mythology* (just before the distinction between animal and human cited above, 1963a: ix): "Each and every religion contains two elements, Ritual and Mythology. We have first what a man *does* in relation to his religion, i.e., his Ritual; then what he *thinks* or *imagines*, i.e., his Mythology." But words, images, and symbols, all the stuff that Harrison wanted to put on the side of myth, are arguably as integral to ritual as are actions.

Furthermore, ritual has not necessarily the direct connection with emotional impulse that Harrison posits, nor is it easy to maintain that mental imaging and conceptualization are at a further remove. Had Harrison read Freud she may have found her distinction between ritual and myth even more problematic. To say that strong emotions trigger excited movement is one thing, but quite another to say that rituals (let alone representational action) spring directly and spontaneously out of emotional impulse. Far from the direct release of natural emotional impulses, Freud conceived of ritual as the symbolic expression of *severely repressed* emotions, and analogous to the rituals of neurotics. Freud would have said that if any form of expression is close to its originary impulse, it is myth, which is given to the pleasure principle, both as a product of fantasy, and as a product of the relatively unrepressed savage mind. Actions are likely to be more repressed than idle words, precisely because actions *can give satisfaction* to the wishes that are the objects of repression, whereas words, thoughts, and images could only do so in a relatively harmless symbolic fashion.

However much it inspired the ritual school, Harrison's opposition between myth and ritual is awkwardly sustained. It requires all of her genius for argumentative rhetoric to keep it from collapse. The problems with the opposition between myth and ritual are frequently elided and the opposition itself scrambled to avoid detection as simplistic and unworkable. For example, Harrison frequently uses Greek terms, or, more subtly, uses the English equivalents in the Greek sense, to do work that she cannot do in plain English. The Greek terms *dromenon* and *drama* are continuously used, in preference to "ritual," because they can make the connection between action and ritual seem much simpler and more direct. The root meanings of these words in Greek is simply "doings"; but they are useful precisely because they imply the cultural activities that evolve, according to Harrison, from these "doings," specifically religious rituals (*dromena*) and secular representation in the form of theater. In this way even these very sophisticated forms can be made to seem to belong on the side of emotion and action, in opposition to myth, speech, images, and thought (1963: 42–3): "[emotional] tension finds release in excited movement; you dance and leap for fear, for joy, for sheer psychological relief. It is this excited doing, this dancing, that is the very kernel of both drama and *dromenon*." To the *dromenon* (the thing done) Harrison opposes the *legomenon* or the *mythos* (the thing said). And, as with her use of Greek terms for action, the Greek terms for speech allow her to bring speech, thought, and myth together, as if they were variant forms of the same thing. Harrison knows, of course, that utterances are frequently part of ritual, but she is able to separate out this speech-component as if it were evolving proto-myth. The Greek terms *legomenon* and *mythos* mean "what is said," but they can also mean or imply "myth." After explaining the Greek meaning of *mythos*, she is then able to speak of "the other factor in a rite, the myth" (1963: 330), though she is really referring to the words spoken in a ritual. The Greek conveniently allows utterance to be part of ritual, since the plain fact is that utterances are very much part of ritual, but the Greek term also allows speech to be seen as something alien to and opposed to ritual.

The problem is more than merely rhetorical, however. In the above-cited passage Harrison puts myth on a par with ritual only so long as myth remains "an utterance of an emotion . . . in words or thoughts," so long as it does not give reasons, or ascribe motives. In other words, so long as myth is just emotional images it has the same status as emotional actions, but the moment myth partakes of the logical and intellectual, it ceases to have the same authenticity. The more myth becomes unlike ritual, the more it ceases to be a mental *reaction*, the more it evolves into its own element of logic and narrative, the more abstracted myth becomes from its emotional roots. The kind of myths Harrison would allow to be on a par with ritual, the "utterance of an emotion . . . in words or thoughts," is not myth at all by any definition that makes myth a narrative. Harrison creates a new category of non-narrative mental images, which she identifies as a kind of proto-myth in order to save the oversimple distinctions that sustain her evolutionary scheme. The result is a more recondite, nonexplicit affirmation of the priority of ritual over myth.

If myth and ritual were truly equal, Harrison's theory of the evolution of religion would fall apart. As a theoretical construct, as a myth, it was beautifully shaped. This history presents us not just with the birth of religious thought. From the "undifferentiated beginnings of things," from the primordial chaos, everything suddenly began with a big bang (every bit as totalizing as Freud's Oedipal crime). The crucial moment for Harrison was a change in the dance ritual itself. The chorus chooses a leader, a gifted dancer, who more and more becomes the center of attention at the cost of the collective chorus itself. Then there comes a Durkheimian moment, a time when the group is experiencing the strong emotion of the collective dance and feels that this emotion is stronger than any individual experience. At that critical moment the consciousness of Harrison's savages, unlike Durkheim's, are focused on the chorus leader (45): "Strong emotion collectively experienced begets this illusion of objective reality; each worshipper is conscious of something in his emotion not himself, stronger than himself. He does not know it is the force of collective suggestion, he calls it god."

Harrison here takes a page out of Aristotle, who claims that tragedy developed from the *exarchos* of the dithyramb, Dionysus's quintessential dance-song. (The *exarchos* is one who improvises verse and prompts the choral refrain, and who is, in Dionysiac myth, frequently projected as the god himself.) By working the *exarchos* into her history, Harrison is able to condense, into a single nuclear moment: the fission of the erstwhile solid collective (leader vs. chorus), the origin of all social organization (hierarchy), the beginning of mental discrimination, the beginning of religion (concept of divinity), and the beginning of art (as the group separated into spectators and actor). All this happened under the aegis of the god Dionysus, the god of collective effervescence par excellence. It is here that Harrison's name for the ritual, *dromenon*, pays off, allowing *drama* to stand as a symbol for all the greatest achievements of "high culture," while retaining something of the emotional power of its origin in collective ritual.

But the most important product of this big bang is the human intellect itself. It begins with the creation of the first distinct idea, which is also the first truly "mythic idea." The evolution of the mythic or protomythic element is logically and chronologically posterior to the ritual action. And while ritual is more or less an immediate response to a collective emotion, the mythic idea is created by sensations first experienced in the ritual, and, so far from being an immediate response, the formation of the mythic idea presupposes a process of abstraction and symbolization, distancing it still further from the originary collective emotion and even from the ritual itself.

It is this privileging and prioritizing of ritual over myth that makes Jane Harrison a "ritualist." But this is not entirely original with her. In this she simply followed many of the comparatists: Smith, for example, argued that "in almost every case the myth was derived from the ritual, and not the ritual from the myth; for the ritual was fixed and the myth was variable, the ritual was obligatory and faith in the myth was at the discretion of the worshipper" (1887: 18), or that actions, not ideas, formed the earliest religions and that the ideas were later additions and rationalizations of actions (1894: 18–22); and passages can be found in Frazer, too, which betray the same assumption (1922: 477):

> The myth that he [Hippolytus/Virbius] had been killed by horses was probably invented to explain certain features of his worship, amongst others the custom of excluding horses from his sacred grove. For myth changes while men remain constant, men continue to do what their fathers did before them, though the reasons for which their fathers acted have long been forgotten. The history of religion is a long attempt to reconcile old custom with new reason, to find a sound theory for an absurd practice.

However, passages and letters of Frazer can also be found in which he vigorously repudiates the belief that ritual always or normally preceded myth. That "myth" in the loose sense of theory or dogma preceded ritual was indeed required by the general tendency of his views on magic and religion: insofar as ritual action had in his view a rational purpose, it presupposed a theory of natural causation or a theology. But this left a lot of room for equivocation about the nature of myth proper, which are not ideas, but narratives. What is entirely new in Harrison is not only the exclusive and near-absolute statement of the dependence of myth upon ritual, whatever meaning is applied to "myth" – indeed, she would not give the name "myth" or at least "myth proper" to anything but "such stories as are involved in rites" (1963b: 331) – but the full, careful, and relatively consistent theoretical elaboration of their relationship.

More important is the very different context in which ritual, and, in its train, myth, is conceived. Harrison shares with most twentieth-century theories a tendency to affirm the social, the emotional, and the precognitive, in reaction to the individualism and rationalism of the nineteenth century. But Harrison is still too close to the rational and the individual for most modern theorists. In Harrison one can still find the trace of the Victorian belief that all rational and creative thought must necessarily take place in the heads of individuals. Ritual could represent a pre-rational, even pre-cognitive stage. But myth involved thinking about the world, and was, for Harrison, almost as much as for Frazer, the product of individuals exercising their fledgling rational faculties. It is true that she described a form of protomythical thought, which was very nearly contemporaneous with ritual action, and which, like ritual, emerged from the symbol-making capacity of the subconscious under the influence of emotion, and group emotion sooner than individual emotion. But there was still a huge gap between these mental images and the assignment of motives and reasons which she regarded as the essential function of myth, once fully developed.

The struggle to liberate theory from rationalistic and individualistic thought was a gradual one. Many theorists tried to find something deeper and more primitive than "ideas" to help mediate this process. Some spoke of "experiences," and "deep perceptions." But the problem persists so long as myth is considered to be an attempt by a confused savage to provide a rational explanation for the existence of ritual, or its emotional impact, or its particular forms. From this perspective, all myths are basically etiological, and all necessarily rationalizations.

The problem is largely avoided if we avoid the arbitrary equations of ritual to action, myth to thought, and the consequent ranking of ritual with the precognitive, and myth with the rational. Ritual is not just action; it is a communication. It is a communication through actions and symbols, just as myth is a communication through language and symbols. Ritual and myth, when related, are not related as practice to theory. They are related as two different ways of communicating a message.

4.3 WALTER BURKERT AND SOCIOBIOLOGY

Biological determinism and constructivism

In Section 4.1 we drew a contrast between the Victorian tendency to explain myth in terms of individual experience and modern approaches which stress myth's social functions. Modern definitions generally insist upon myth's character as a "traditional" tale. Once the implications of "traditional" are grasped the Victorian theories begin to look naive and irrelevant. The errors of Frazer's wannabe scientist savage merely occasioned an origin for a tale, but for a tale to become traditional it must be received by a social group and handed down as part of the group's cultural heritage: what needs to be explained is the reception, not the conception, of the tale.

The same fault stands behind all other etiological myths about myth. Origins do not explain why any particular event or experience was considered significant enough to merit so many retellings. What has to be explained is not the event behind the myth, but the criteria of social selection, and not the moment of conception, but the process of preservation. Thus, when Müller explained myth by an original fascination with natural phenomena which was later forgotten, this forgetting voided the theory of any explanatory power. Once a culture has forgotten its rapturous fascination with sunsets, sunsets can no longer explain why the myths are told. One cannot simply assume that cultural inertia will ensure a story's survival. There is a considerable amount of collective labor involved in making and preserving a myth. Social selection is an active force. At any moment a myth might be discarded and lost. Each moment of its survival depends upon its *continuing* importance to the society that transmits it.

For this reason modern theories are preoccupied with explaining the social meaning and function of myth. But there is one minor school that bucks this trend. This is what we might call the "biological school." The biological school continues in a line of descent from Julian Huxley (1887–1975, son of the great T. H. Huxley, "Darwin's bulldog") and perpetuates many of the attitudes of Victorian comparatism. This school sees the importance of myth in relation to basic human biology and explains myths primarily in terms of universal human needs and instincts. Its origin in the social application of Darwin's thought has also given it a particular focus on individual aggression and the satisfaction of the individual's "need" for power in the struggle for survival. Advocates of this approach generally cling to some conception of human nature which is more or less constant, though they may also, in somewhat contradictory fashion, maintain that different social formations are more attuned than others to the satisfaction of this nature. This approach still tends to privilege the individual over society, but not in exactly the same way as the Victorian theorists. The biological school sees individuals as species animals, and opposed to the larger collective mainly in a quantitative, not a qualitative sense. But this difference does not prevent the lessons of biological analysis from being employed to promote rugged individualism and to combat socialism. Biologism has a particular appeal for libertarians who view most government regulation as attempts at "social engineering," denounce them as impingements upon basic biological needs, and condemn them as dangerous experiments doomed to failure (e.g., Lionel Tiger [especially 1970, 1999]). Indeed, this does not prevent other biological determinists, who think social change has gone too far, from advocating a (reverse) social engineering of their own (e.g., Morris 1967). More often than not the "human nature" which cannot be tampered with shows a marked preference for selfish aggression over social co-operation, as if Nature herself endorsed laissez-faire cowboy capitalism.

Most opposed to the biologism is the "constructivist" approach, currently the most dominant, fully articulated, and extreme of the sociological schools. It regards individuals entirely as products of their social environments. This does not mean, of course, that humans are not born with some sort of basic biological hardware, which imposes certain physical needs and limitations. Rather, the constructivists regard anything that really is universal as too basic and obvious to be of much interest. A constructivist would maintain that the animal is human only insofar as it is *re-created* socially. The biological machine is too much like an empty computer disk, useless and dysfunctional until it is filled with various cultural software, of which perhaps the most important are language and mythology. This cultural software is vital to just about every function of human society, but constructivists tend to take a particular interest in the way language and social myths define and maintain the social group. Thus, a very large proportion of recent work on myth focuses upon myth's social-engineering and policing functions. According to this view myth is an active ingredient in the construction of the needs, behavioral reflexes, desires, feelings, perceptions, ideas, and aspirations of every member of the social group. As such, myth can have little interest in anything permanent and unalterable in the human machine, i.e., precisely those universal and permanent biological instincts and drives which interest the biological school.

For the constructivist, myth constructs the citizen by promoting certain patterns of behavior and certain values precisely where other patterns and values are possible. The meaning of a myth is therefore always to a very large extent culture-specific. The constructivist is most happy when he can show that desires and instincts and whatever is deepest in the physical being are not "biological" at all, but no less socially constructed than mental attitudes and ideas. Since constructivism is largely a reaction against all notions of both biological determination and cultural universals, it rejects any universal criterion by which one culture can be compared qualitatively with any other, and certainly rejects any notion that cultures can be lined up and compared on an evolutionary scale. Cultures are simply different: the representative of the genus *homo sapiens* is little more than Promethean mud; it is only cultural cooking which makes the individual human. In this way the constructivist approach, like the biological, neatly disposes of anything the individual might call his own. Constructivism is most evident in contemporary postmodern, neo-Marxist, and many current feminist approaches.

Naturally, there is plenty of middle ground between biologism and constructivism. The sociobiological school of myth and ritual is best illustrated by the work of Walter Burkert (1931–). As the name implies, the sociobiological approach aims at a position close to the midpoint between these extremes. Burkert's theoretical points of departure are from biological ethology (a branch of the biologist approach), ritualism, and syntagmatic structuralism (examined in Chapter 5). He attempts to reconcile the biologistic, evolutionary, and comparative approaches with a later-twentieth-century focus on the social element in myth and ritual. As such, he provides an excellent illustration of modern biological approaches while providing a critical commentary on theories of raw biological determinism, which will prepare us for the more exclusively social orientation of structuralism and later theories.

Learning from animals

In *Structure and History in Greek Mythology and Ritual* Burkert argues that we can learn something about human ritual (and myth) by studying animal behavior (1979: 35–58). We are too ready to assume that a wide gulf separates human and beast, as if we lived entirely in the mind, while animals lived simply by drives and instincts. But a study of animal behavior would force us to modify our assumptions that human behavior is learnt while animal behavior is innate, or that human communication is symbolic, while animal communication is rude and functional. Indeed, Western ideology has elaborated a series of differentiae between humans and animals which are exaggerated and misleading:

Culture	Nature
human	animal
psychology	biology
spiritual	mechanical
learned behavior	innate behavior
symbolic communication	functional communication

Biological studies show that animals have purely symbolic rituals. Greylag geese regularly perform a triumph ceremony in which they show common aggression toward a nonexistent interloper. Their aggressive gestures are accompanied by triumphant cries in a way that is both symbolic and functional, since by doing this the geese not only rehearse for the eventual repulsion of an invader, but also, in the meantime, assure each other of their friendship and solidarity. The ritual, says Burkert, is based on a natural program of action (chasing away an enemy), but is at least partially redirected for the purpose of demonstration. It is action separated from the practical sphere and attached to the symbolic.

Both humans and animals manifest innate behavior which has a secondary purpose of demonstration. Weeping, smiling, and laughing are innate but important forms of social communication. Apes also weep and smile and can combine this innate behavior with other learned behavior. When performing greeting rituals chimpanzees embrace one another, pat each other's shoulders, and kiss hands. In human ritual, however, innate behavior may be either positively or negatively present, in knowing what is forbidden, e.g., giggling at funerals. Thus ritual can be seen as embracing both behavioral compulsions and prohibitions (just as with Freud's study of obsessional neurotics and hysterics). In one way or the other, ritual, in order to function effectively, *taps* the most basic and primitive contents of the mind, some might say the infrahuman layers of the brain, but always to redirect them toward a higher social purpose (without which the act is not a ritual, but simply instinctive or primitively functional behavior). In this way, for Burkert, ritual necessarily implies a combination of a biological with a social element. Myth, like ritual, is "structured by some basically human action pattern," indeed frequently, just like ritual, by biological programs of action, but, like ritual, myth has a suspended "partial reference to something of collective importance" (57, 23). Myth and ritual thus both arise from a common or similar biological matrix and share a common social function, but they are not necessarily dependent upon one another. Myths and rituals may, however, support one another in a kind of "symbiosis" (57):

> The defect of ritual, in a human society, is the apparent nonsense inherent in its redirection of activity, the "as-if" element; here a tale may supply a plausible context and fill the vacant places. The defect of the traditional tale is its lack of seriousness and stability; here ritual may supply a basis; for the serious character of ritual is guaranteed by the role of anxiety controlled by it, and its stability is secured even by explicit sanctions.

Herms

Burkert applies the lessons of the study of animal behavior (biological ethology) to three Greek religious practices. Of these I will summarize only the first, which best supports Burkert's claim that myths, like rituals, "are founded on basic biological and cultural programs of action" (18).

In antiquity the icon of the Greek god Hermes generally took one of three nonhuman forms. He is sometimes merely a cairn, a heap of stones (*herma* in Greek). Sometimes he is a phallus. From the late sixth century BC he is commonly represented as an orthogonal pillar topped by a human head and otherwise endowed only with a human and erect phallus half-way up the front of the pillar. This is what is normally referred to, in the modern literature, as a "herm." The phallus and the pillar (which is thus doubly phallic in form) were often supposed, even in antiquity, to be fertility symbols. But they are not placed in contexts where one might normally desire fertility. They do not appear in fields, folds, stables, or bedrooms. They are erected, rather, at the doorway, in front of the house, at the crossroads, in the marketplace, at graves, on highways, and at the frontiers. But not all phalli are herms: sometimes a phallus is simply a phallus. Phalli, notably, are drawn or carved on doorways and city walls and other places where one also finds herms. Both seem to serve a common function: their location clearly indicates that they served to mark territory or to avert a threat from outside. In later antiquity the phallus served as a charm to avert the evil eye (a function normally referred to as "apotropaic"). Like the graffiti of modern vandals, these artifacts are effective because they have a certain shock value and catch the eye, but this does not explain their popularity and success as an apotropaic symbol.

"In fact," writes Burkert (40):

> I cannot find any real explanation before ethology observed that there are a species of monkeys [quenons, baboons, and other ground walkers], living in groups, of whom the males act as guards: they sit up at the outposts, facing outside and presenting their erect genital organ. This is an "animal ritual" in the sense noted above: the basic function of sexual activity is suspended for the sake of communication; every individual approaching from the outside will notice that this group does not consist of helpless wives and children, but enjoys the full protection of masculinity.
>
> With man, at least in the more civilized areas of the historical epoch, there is only the artifact left, instead of real action. Still its symbolism, its signal function was understood even by those who called it "apotropaic." People consciously or unconsciously know what this action of display means: a demonstration which transmits a message of potency in its double sense.

Burkert is not in any way attempting to suggest that this symbolism is somehow inherited by humans from their primate ancestors. Rather the animal rituals are said to have "heuristic value" in that they provide instructive models for understanding otherwise puzzling rituals or symbols.

Priapus

Burkert's example helps explain the meaning of a symbol, but not a myth. I know no myths which directly explain how Hermes acquired this particular iconic form. It would, however, be an easy matter to test the insights gained from the study of herms by applying them to myths of Priapus. The icon of Priapus is very similar to the herm, except that his genitals are much exaggerated in size. These figures were placed at the borders of gardens, at doorways, near tombs, and beside roadways. Not surprisingly, Priapus is in myth the son of Hermes and Aphrodite (though Dionysus and Zeus are sometimes also named as fathers). Functionally he is an ancient combination of scarecrow and security warning (I think especially of the lawn signs, found in the better neighborhoods of Los Angeles, which promise an "Armed Response"). The message of the Priapus figures was not always only symbolic. Often the enormous phallus of a Priapus was itself hung with a sign, generally in the form of a poem, warning that the god would assault any who attempted to steal from the orchard, house, or tomb. Several literary versions of these poems survive from antiquity. Martial provides a typical example (*Ep.* 6.49):

> I am not hewn from fragile elm, nor is my member which stands stiff with a rigid shaft made from just any old wood. It is begotten from everlasting cypress, which fears not the passage of a hundred celestial ages nor the decay of advanced years. Fear this, evil doer, whoever you are. If your thieving hand harms the smallest shoots of this here vine, like it or not, this cypress rod will penetrate and plant a fig in you [the slang implies anal intercourse].

Among the myths of Priapus we might examine a number of clearly etiological myths. In one story Priapus was at a revel with Dionysus and his companions. He spied the nymph Lotis (the name means "flower") fast asleep, and began to sneak toward her with the intent to rape her. The ass of Silenus (a companion of Dionysus) started braying and woke her up so that she was able to take flight. Alerted by her clamor, everyone laughed at Priapus's oversized and excited member. In revenge Priapus struck the ass dead. Very similar is the story of Priapus and Hestia (goddess of the hearth). She was fast asleep and he would have molested her, but that Silenus's ass brayed and woke her up and Priapus ran away before he could be apprehended by the companions alerted by the goddess's cries. Another story has it that when Hera had driven Dionysus mad, Dionysus journeyed to Dodona to consult the oracle about a cure. On his way he was confronted by a large swamp. He there met an ass which carried him over the swamp and all the way to Dodona. In gratitude Dionysus gave the ass speech. Later the ass and Priapus fell into an argument "concerning nature" (Hyginus [*poet. ast.* 2.23] says the argument was *de natura*, but the euphemism is explained by Lactantius [*Inst. div.* 1.21.28], who says they argued about whose penis was bigger). The ass won the argument and Priapus, enraged, killed the beast.

All of these myths link Priapus with the ass. The ass is in fact the cult animal of Priapus. At Lampsakos in Asia Minor, the center of the Priapus cult, Priapus was honored by donkey sacrifice. The connection between Priapus and the ass might be explained by their common reputation for ugliness, but especially for their well-known tendency to obvious displays of sexual excitement. One myth explicitly ascribes the ass's death to its proverbial lust. On Greek vases the ass of Dionysus is usually depicted with an erection. In all of these myths, oddly, the guardian function is transferred from Priapus to the ass: he protects travelers (Dionysus), and he guards the household (Hestia) and the garden (Lotis) against the threat of Priapus himself. The braying of the ass somehow acquired the same symbolic power as Priapus's phallus (in the battle between the Olympians and the Giants, the braying of Dionysus's ass is said to have scared the Giants away). The myths are etiologies not only for the donkey sacrifice, but also for the conspicuous sexual excitement of Priapus, since in every case he is frustrated.

It requires little further argument to establish a connection between these myths and both biological action (ritual phallus display) and cultural action (marking territory with phallic symbols). Indeed, they explain the very nature of Priapus in terms of a suspension of his biological pursuit which turns him into an object of display, and even public ridicule. In this way the myths do etiological service in explaining, at least partly, his grotesque and laughable form. The social importance of these myths is also manifest insofar as they relate to cultic activity: they establish a reason for donkey sacrifice and they establish reasons for placing images of Priapus in gardens, by doorways, or on roadsides.

Animal ethology and the analysis of myth

Brilliant and illuminating as Burkert's sketch of the utility of biological ethology for myth analysis may be, this example also helps illustrate some shortcomings of the biological approach. Not least is the problem of comparability. Earlier I complained of the promiscuity of comparatists who indiscriminately bring together the myths and rituals of disparate and unrelated cultures as if they all served a common purpose. But this pales beside the temerity of those who would compare rituals between species (Burkert will go on to compare the pouring of libations to dogs urinating on hydrants, and explain the use of suppliant boughs from the habits of birds). There is a very great risk that animal ritual is much more straightforward than its human counterpart and that the comparison may be too simple and reductive, obscuring more than it illuminates. What makes a ritual for animals, according to Burkert, is the redirection of some biological function for communication. But however surprising or illuminating the information biologists collect on animal rituals, there can be little doubt that human communication is much more complex.

With material so remote, how can we measure its relevance to myth? And since animal rituals are many, what criterion is there to prefer one animal ritual for comparison over another, especially since we are warned against any possible linkage in the form of genetic inheritance? If the comparisons are merely heuristic, we can choose any that point in the direction already indicated by the myth itself. In this case the animal ritual is less of a control on interpretation than illustrative material for an interpretation we have already arrived at. It may be that it serves only to underscore the argument that we are dealing with something very basic and infrahuman.

The specific ape ritual that explains the form of herms has, according to Burkert, no parallels "in the more civilized areas of the historical epoch." If we really have to reach back this far, then the ape ritual gains in importance, and the example's "deep-biological" implications might seem more compelling. Suppose, however, we framed the relevant animal "rituals" differently. These ape rituals are peculiar and specific only to a small group of primates. If we are to look for parallels in the animal kingdom, we might be better served by comparisons with a much broader basis. For example, many social animals, from baboons to chickens, have rituals of domination by which they maintain their position within a social hierarchy. Cocks and even hens will mount their social inferiors in actual or mimed intercourse to establish or maintain their dominance in the pecking order. This seems to me a much more promising avenue for the investigation of ritual as "social communication." The baboon rituals would seem only a special, though perhaps especially interesting example of this type of behavior. If so the message transmitted is not precisely that "this territory is protected by adult males," but rather "don't mess with us or we will bugger you." This is precisely the message that is hung upon Priapus. But it is perhaps less appealing to the biologically minded theorist, because less a redirection of sexual activity than an extension of it.

If, for example, we were to look, for heuristic purposes, at the kind of animal activity which redirects sexual activity for the communication of not just territorial, but what we might call social limits, we would find that it is only part of a system of behavior. In animals, the rituals of domination involving sexual activity are accompanied by rituals of submission. Inferior animals, males as well as females, raise their buttocks, as a sign of submission, at the approach of a dominant male. Perhaps, then, the discussion should not be restricted to phallus display, or phallus display at territorial borders, but be extended to the much larger number of animals which have rituals of genital display.

But once we decide that genital display in general is a relevant category for comparison, we find that there is little need for animal ritual. We know in fact of a large number of genital display ceremonies, real and symbolic, from human cultures, including many which must be considered historical and civilized by any standard. Detlev Fehling notably studied such rituals in Greek antiquity with ample comparanda from other cultures (1974). It seems, perhaps, a bit hasty to ignore these and look for remoter comparisons in the animal kingdom. How are the apes more relevant than the behavior, say, of the Yali tribesmen of Indonesia, who perform their war dance wearing penis-sheaths that stiffen, raise, and exaggerate the size of their members?

If, however, we broaden the basis of comparison in this way, we discover that the animal rituals are not only unnecessary, but misleading. Genital display ceremonies among humans include genital display by women as well as buttock display by both women and men. Here the message is clearly not that the group has the full protection of masculinity. If we were to look for help to the corresponding animal rituals we would have to conclude that these are rituals of submission. But here surely is a clear case where the symbolic communication of animals is too elementary to provide any help in interpreting the human communication. Everyone knows what it means to bare your buttocks at someone (this vernacular body language is alive and well even in our "civilized" society). For humans it has just the opposite meaning from that used in animal communication. Showing buttocks and vaginas are gestures of defiance, not of submission. Apparently, if we must translate these gestures into words, they communicate faith in the impotence of the receiver of the communication, as if one were saying "Here I am. Come and get me if you can. I am not afraid." It can of course take place at borders: "mooning" was famously practiced by soldiers on the Sino-Soviet border in the late 1960s and 1970s. But it need not be: the same years were famous for the fad of drive-by mooning practiced by American teenagers. Social boundaries play at least as much a role as territorial. You bare your buttocks at people who pretend to have power over you: but to deny, not to acknowledge this power.

The human ritual really is discontinuous with sexual activity in a way that the animal rituals are not. This raises another serious theoretical concern. The decision that something is biological, or a primary biological function, and something else a redirection too often seems difficult, if not arbitrary, in the case of animals. In establishing social dominance the animals sometimes have intercourse and communicate their relative social status simultaneously: it is at the same time a biological program of action and a social communication, but without redirection. True, there is "redirection" from the procreative function, if the intercourse is merely mimed and left to gestures of readiness, but this seems no more disconnected with sexual activity than, for example, courting or flirtation. How are we to determine that establishing hierarchies through real or mimed intercourse is not as much a biological program of action as intercourse for the purpose of procreation? And if one can be termed primary and another secondary by some objective criterion, what real difference does that make when both are biologically determined? Baboons indeed seem biologically programmed for the activities involved in these "social rituals." Their physical makeup is even adapted to it. The leading biological ethologist, Konrad Lorenz, writes (1981: 170):

> in several species of baboons and of vervet monkeys, the male carries on his rump structures and colors imitating the genitalia of the estrous female. They are presented during the appeasement gesture to the dominant male. In the gellada baboon . . . a detailed imitation of the rear aspect of the female is shown on the front of the male's chest, and this is also presented during the gesture of submission.

In these animals the behavior displayed in domination and submission seems no less a biological program of action than procreation.

Just how helpful is animal behavior for the study of myth? One could certainly unravel the mystery of the herm without it. I rather suspect that no matter what animal ritual is chosen it will put the emphasis in the wrong place. In the case of Burkert's ape rituals he was tempted to see the ceremony as some sort of act of social self-definition ("we are a community protected by adult males"). But indeed, it is merely a use of body language to threaten an imaginary invader with humiliation and defeat, and an extension of the kind of daily communication that apes practice without regard to matters of social importance. It can, however, certainly be argued that the byproduct of the exercise is social solidarity, and this is certainly interesting in showing that something like rituals are practiced by animals. But human rituals will always provide a better basis for comparison for other human rituals. If they seem unavailable, one is probably looking in the wrong direction. At best, they seem useful for understanding myths and rituals that are inspired by observation of the behavior and properties of animals. At worst, animal rituals function to give the theorist, who wants it, some assurance that a ritual is performed in satisfaction of some very basic human need, indeed, some need even more basic than human.

4.4   BURKERT'S *HOMO NECANS*

Biological vs. cultural evolution?

In Section 4.3 I described the biological approach to ritual and myth in examining the theories of Walter Burkert. Burkert's main contribution as a theorist, however, is less his affirmation of the biological than his distinctively social reading of human biology. His masterpiece, *Homo Necans*, originally published in 1972, argues a "sociobiological" approach, which gives equal stress to both the social and the biological function of myth and ritual.

Homo Necans (= "Man the Killer") argues that men developed their aggression in order to become more efficient hunters. But these developments should not be construed, as many "Social Darwinists" prefer to see it, entirely in terms of an interplay between species and individual in which society only enters as a negative factor. Dawkins (1976), for example, argues that natural selection favors "selfish genes," and that the antisocial members of our species dominate the gene pool, as they dominate the economy. The moral lesson of this disclosure is that the callous exploitation of one man by another is "human nature," and that the vigor and survival of the species are only threatened by any attempt by bleeding-heart liberals and socialists to modify rugged and aggressive individualism.

Burkert's theory is simultaneously a response to both the biological and sociological schools and an attempt to mediate their positions. Natural selection, he says, prefers the social group over the individual, and social selection prefers altruistic over selfish genes. Cooperative group activity lies at the very origin of human evolution and is its precondition. Humans only began to diverge from apes with the organization of individuals into groups of hunters. Individually men were no match for the larger mammals which were the first objects of the hunt. But in groups they were a match for any prey. All those physical and mental features which distinguish humanity from apes are explained by the formation of the first society for the purpose of the hunt: the development of the upright position, of long, slender thighs for running, of prehensile hands for wielding weapons, and of speech for tactical organization.

Cultural and biological evolution worked hand in hand. If hunting in groups required adaptation on the biological side (running on two legs, the development of prehensile hands), it also required adaptation on the cultural side, most conspicuously with the specialization of labor between men and women. Men became the "breadwinners"; women were set free for the task of raising children. This cultural adaptation fed back into the biological as men and women adapted physically, but differently, to their new roles and environments (1983: 17–18):

> Among human beings, hunting is man's work – in contrast to all animal predators – requiring both speed and strength; hence the male's long, slender thigh. By contrast, since women must bear children with ever larger skulls, they develop round, soft forms. Man's extraordinarily protracted youth, his neoteny, which permits the development of the mind through learning and the transmission of a complicated culture, requires long years of security. This is basically provided by the mother at home. The man assumes the role of the family breadwinner – an institution universal to human civilizations but contrary to the behavior of all other mammals.

Cultural and biological evolution worked hand in hand to produce the distinct characteristics of men and women. With the division of labor between the sexes, men, specialized in the hunt, became more aggressive, women less so; men grew stronger and more agile, women softer, gentler, more nurturing. In this way the social actually generated the biological, just as much as biology determined, limited, or predisposed cultural patterns. Or rather, from the point of view of sociobiology, it is no longer very easy to distinguish clearly between biological and social facts. In Burkert's scheme cultural change leads to physical change, which leads to further social and physical changes, in an evolutionary spiral. Social imprinting affects the physical makeup, just as much as the physical makeup determines social behavior.

Cultural troubleshooting with ritual and myth

The division of labor between men and women increased the need for murderous aggression in adult males since the survival of the whole community now depended upon their success in the hunt. At the same time sexual needs "clearly grew out of proportion in order to bind men to women and thus insure that the family would be supported" (Burkert 1983: 20). As a result the sex drive is far stronger in human males than among animals: their penises are disproportionately large, and the mating urge is not limited seasonally, as with most other mammals. (Penis-measurement is something of a fetish for the biological school – but the appeal seems to have more to do with the organ's mythical, than biological, properties: the assumption that there is a direct correlation between the size of the appendage and the size of the libido has never, to my knowledge, been demonstrated.) Both natural and cultural selection also favored those groups in which sexual fidelity was reinforced by cultural practice and controlled by strong social sanctions.

The heightened sex-drive put more biological energy at the service of culture. Since sexual rivalry most threatened to turn the hunter's murderous aggression back in upon the community it was supposed to support, culture invented ways of channeling sexual energy outward from the community toward the hunt. Culture sexualized violence. Both myth and ritual leave many traces of this operation. A particularly apposite illustration of sexualized violence is provided by the plentiful myths of maiden sacrifice, frequently conflated with sexual and marriage imagery. Modern cultural parallels are easily found. But the passage from sex to violence is particularly easy in the world described by *Homo Necans,* where sexuality is just another form of aggression to begin with, primarily "sexual aggression."

Thus the biological and cultural evolution of the human species produced in men necessary, but also dangerously high levels of sexual and physical aggression. If sexuality had to be controlled by culture, even while it was promoted, so, obviously, did "murderous aggression." Without cultural intervention it would not have been easy to establish a clear distinction between aggression that is interspecific (hunting) and aggression that is intraspecific: "it is as easy, or even easier, to kill a man as it is to kill a fleeing beast, so from earliest times men slipped repeatedly into cannibalism" (1983: 18). From the beginning social ideology was riven by two contradictory codes of behavior and two contradictory value systems: aggression and the killer instincts were necessary for the hunt, but threatened to destroy the very social order that made the hunt possible. Aggression therefore had to be encouraged, but so had quiescence, compliance, and all those qualities which lead to peaceable social cohesion.

Cultural evolution required the suppression of "selfish genes." Human society would not have survived if culture had not exerted every means to block aggression when directed toward the detriment of the community while at the same time fostering the aggression that worked to its benefit. Ritual and myth proved the most important tools in society's struggle to control harmful and encourage helpful physical and mental reflexes. In the hunting society, at least, the chief burden of ritual and myth was to draw the line. Ritual, and especially sacrifice, proved effective in demarcating the spaces where violence was allowed and violence forbidden. Indeed, for Burkert animal sacrifice is not only the most ancient and the most universal form of human ritual, it is the ritual par excellence, which serves as an archetype or Urtype for most other forms of ritual.

Sacrifice

Sacrifice does, of course, have other functions. Burkert, with Durkheim, regards social bonding as one of its main functions. Social solidarity can be produced by acting together, by sharing beliefs, or by sharing meals. But the bonding function can be satisfied by any myth or ritual; it has more to do with the simple fact of participation in a ritual, or belief in a myth, than with the symbolic contents of either. A symbolic reading of animal sacrifice shows that its more fundamental purpose is to make a distinction, not so much between sacred and profane, as Durkheim would have it, but between the realms where the community forbids and where the community requires violence.

In its outward form sacrifice is a shared meal. Its root constituent action, says Burkert, is giving. Giving is not something innate. Renouncing egotism for the sake of others is a habit which has to be taught to children. This is "sacrifice" in the non-technical sense. It is also the prerequisite for community life and civilization. Human evolution begins when the individual learns to suppress his selfishness for the benefit of the community. In this sense sacrifice is not pure altruism, but more like enlightened self-interest. One gives to another in the expectation of receiving. One gives to the community and receives the benefits of others giving back. An element of time creeps in. Outstanding mutual obligations and expectations further bind the community.

But sacrifice draws on natural anxiety as well. By Burkert's definition "gift sacrifice is ritualized giving in a context of anxiety." This anxiety is rooted in the instinctual life of the animal, particularly the predatory animal. Having killed the prey, the hunter is anxious about his success in securing it from interlopers stronger than himself and able to appropriate the fruits of his labor. Similarly, when the band of hunters kills a beast, there is great anxiety about the distribution of the meat. If the hunters fell into a quarrel over the spoils, allowing aggression to be turned inward on the community, the social fabric would be torn asunder and the entire community would perish because of the egotism of individuals. In sacrifice, says Burkert, culture draws upon and develops the biological raw material of *homo sapiens* in two ways, through a negative ritual, viz., the prohibition of selfishness, and through the channeling of anxiety related to killing. Sacrifice is a sharing of food in the context of dramatized anxiety.

A pure functionalist might regard animal sacrifice as a means of providing meat from larger domesticated animals in a culture that had no sophisticated means of preserving flesh. The whole community was involved because no individual could consume a whole ox in one sitting. Thus community sacrifice is a convenient arrangement for sharing meat. True, but there is much more to it. It is possible to share meat without making a big production of killing the animal. One could, as in our culture, butcher animals in isolated buildings outside of town, covert and anodyne, using efficient mechanical means, bringing the consumer no closer to the fact of killing than the plastic-wrapped, baloney package on the supermarket shelf. The Greeks, like most ancient and many modern cultures, did not go down this route. On the contrary, they made a spectacle of the killing, before the entire community, in the center of town, on the most holy ground. It was what you might call a "theater of death," since killing was sensationalized in every way.

At or very near the front of an ancient Greek sacrificial procession is a girl who carries a basket on her head. She is required to be a "virgin of faultless parentage" (i.e., noble family, both alive, both citizens, and of faultless reputation). She is called the *kanephoros* or "basketbearer." On her head she carries a basket covered by a cloth which conceals, barley groats (i.e., barley in its natural state, not yet ground for human consumption). And under the barley groats is the knife which will cut the animal's throat. The victim usually follows her more or less directly. There are points of similarity between the girl and the victim. The victim, like the basketbearer, must be a "flawless" animal in earliest maturity, and like the unmarried girl, one that has never "felt the yoke." Also, like the basketbearer, the animal wears its "Sunday best": the victim wears garlands, often also has ribbons tied to its horns, and its horns may be gilded. The participants, who also wear garlands, are also connected to the victim in other ways. In the vast majority of cases, the victim is a higher mammal. Its warm blood and internal organs most resemble human blood and organs. Also the vast majority of victims are domesticated animals like sheep, goats, pigs, and cattle: they are literally a part of the community.

After the animal comes the congregation. Somewhere near the basketbearer is a person carrying a jug of water which is also pure, taken directly from the mouth of a spring. Also close to the front is a musician. In accompaniment to the music the participants sing hymns as they walk. All are united by movement to the same rhythm and it is particularly important that the victim seem to move along of its own accord: being a herd animal it naturally moves along in step as one of the crowd, seduced by the music. The procession walks through the middle of town to the sanctuary of the god or goddess and, as it approaches the shrine and altar of the god, to the extraordinary sounds and movements of the procession are added extraordinary smells from incense burning on the altar, concealing the reek of death and rot near the altar where the decaying heads of previous sacrifices are hung, and the sides of the altar are caked with blood.

The animal is led around the altar and the congregation follows, still singing and moving in rhythm, while the spring water is sprayed about to create a symbolically purified circle. Separated from the community and from ordinary life, this circle demarcates a space in which acts take place which cannot be sanctioned in ordinary community life. All the congregation now stands in the circle facing inward. Then further purification takes place. The participants wash their hands and also symbolically wash the victim by spraying its head with water. This causes the animal to shake its head downward away from the spray, a nod which corresponds to the standard gesture for consent.

Even with the victim's consent the killing does not take place directly. By a series of steps the act is built to a climax: two stages of symbolic killing are followed by the real thing. When the animal stands at the center of the congregation, the basket goes around and each participant takes a handful of barley groats. The priest then calls for a moment of concentrated silence after which he makes a prayer. When he has finished all the participants throw the barley at the animal and the altar. This is the first harmless act of symbolic aggression (in some rites stones were actually used). It implicates the whole community in the act of aggression. The priest now steps forward with the knife still hidden in the basket (but no longer covered in barley), removes the knife, and quickly brings it down toward the head of the animal, but only to cut a few hairs from its forelocks which he throws in the fire. This is called in Greek "the beginning." The victim has been physically violated but no blood has yet been spilt.

In the case of large animals, especially bulls, the final act is more protracted. Someone comes forward with a double ax and whacks the animal's forehead to stun it. A group of men raise the animal up onto their shoulders and the priest plunges the knife into its throat. To highlight the climactic moment and to conceal the death rattle the women in the congregation ululate (a kind of musical scream). Killing at the throat where the blood is under highest pressure adds to the sensationalism, as it jets out in pulses. It is important that no blood touch the ground. The blood is collected in a large basin and then thrown onto the altar. Smaller animals are held up so that the blood falls upon the altar. Now, in sight of all, the animal is cut open so that its entrails are exposed. The heart, often still throbbing, is ripped out and placed on the altar. The mood of anxiety is enhanced by the introduction of an augur who comes to check the animal's liver: if it has an unusual shape this bodes misfortune to the community. The guts are then taken out, lightly roasted over the fire and consumed by the inner circle of participants. The meat is cut from the bones and made ready for cooking. Then follows what Karl Meuli called the "comedy of innocence." The bones are set back in their proper order. The head is raised up and fixed to a post near the altar. This is done to resurrect the animal, minus the meat, as if to deny, or make reparation for, a crime. In one especially ancient and guilt-ridden sacrifice (the Dipoleia), the man who hit the bull with the ax ran away after the sacrifice. In his absence there was a mock trial in which the waterbearers accused the men who sharpened the ax of murder, and these in turn charged the man who handed them the ax, and he charged the man who cut up the ox, and this last charged the knife, which couldn't speak and so was condemned and thrown into the sea. After the slaughter, the meat is boiled or roasted and distributed to all the participants. Feasting begins and there is a sudden change of mood from gloomy to festive.

Why the theater of horror and anxiety? It is a ritual which, through the manipulation of feelings of horror, guilt, and anxiety, functions to separate behavior appropriate inside from behavior outside the community, marking off the world of the hunter from the world of family and friends. The ritual of sacrifice licenses killing only when sanctioned within a fixed context, a circumscribed area, and within a fixed order established by ritual. In the language of myth, killing is allowed, in fact required, where and when the gods demand it. Other rituals, too, can support the function of separating these spheres of action. Hence the importance of initiation rites, especially for adolescent males, who move from the household and the world of women, to the hunting band and the world of men. Ritual therefore attempts to mediate and regulate the central contradiction in the very existence of the hunting community: the necessity of aggression on the one hand, the supreme danger of aggression on the other. Sacrificial rituals are also functionally important insofar as they create a stereotypical pattern whereby the entire community goes through an anxiety-producing situation and emerges triumphant (in partaking of the experience of killing followed by the meal all participants in a sense triumph over death): success is associated with community values and community solidarity.

Burkert's interpretation of sacrifice thus demonstrates his theory that cultural evolution builds upon biological reflexes. According to Burkert early man was both aggressive but also anxious about killing. Sacrifice and other rituals built upon both the aggression and the anxiety, but channeled them in different directions, culturally invigorating the aggression directed outward from the community, and culturally invigorating the anxiety about directing aggression inward into the community.

But it is possible to explain the ritual of sacrifice with a good deal less emphasis upon basic biology. Arguably nothing is lost in the interpretation of Greek sacrificial ritual if we shift the emphasis still further from the biological toward the social. Burkert supposes that a good deal of anxiety about killing is already bred into the human animal. Sacrifice, in his view, is actually designed to help overcome anxiety about killing (1983: 21): "In the shock caused by the sight of flowing blood we clearly experience the remnant of a biological, life-preserving inhibition. But that is precisely what must be overcome, for men, at least, could not afford 'to see no blood,' and they were educated accordingly." But here biological ethology gives no real help. Burkert can cite no evidence of inhibition about killing in the behavior of any species of animal and it is doubtful that man in his most "natural" state has guilt which he must learn to overcome. Burkert does speak of the "anxiety" felt by predators about losing their prey to an interloper, or of hunters losing their prey to the egotism of one of the band, but this has nothing to do with inhibitions about *killing*.

Sacrifice, as described by Burkert, would seem to be orchestrated around four major themes: the symbolic identity of the individual with the victim; the symbolic identity of the individual with the community; the horror of killing (through the creation of a symbolic empathy between the victim and the human participants – in a sense this violent death is your death); and the theme of guilt and remorse – this violent killing is your killing. Greek ritual goes to great lengths to portray sacrificial killing as a culpable act, culpable but necessary in this case, because the gods demand it. It is a theater of horrors inducing pity and fear through a symbolic assimilation of the participants to the victim. But it is also a theater of guilt, demonstrating culpability: through a neurotic obsession with cleanliness and purity; through a systematic diffusion and denial of the responsibility for killing; and through evasive pussyfooting, or avoidance behavior, as foreplay to the act of killing.

It is not easy in all this to see much moral support for the poor hunter who needs to overcome putative biological inhibitions about killing. On the contrary, if the sacrificial ritual parades a guilty conscience, if it insists that everything must be pure and seemingly innocent, it may be precisely in order to instill the unsettling feeling that something is not. Sacrificial ritual does indeed seem to be a tool of cultural evolution by which human society instills inhibitions about killing while still sanctioning killing, but there is no good reason to suppose that this cultural work is founded upon any natural or instinctive anxiety or guilt. The evidence here is not inconsistent with the constructivist position that culture creates the specifically human attribute of conscience, not building upon – but even acting against – the natural tendencies of the biological animal.

Myth and ritual

What makes a ritualist a ritualist is the belief in the existence of a strong general connection between myth and ritual. But the nature of this connection has been variously interpreted. Some maintain that all myths are linked with rites, or vice versa (e.g., Hyman 1962: 25). But other ritualists are content to acknowledge the existence of many counterexamples, such as, for example, myths offering trivial etiologies for the crowing of the cock or the spots of the leopard. Many follow Harrison, too, in maintaining the priority of ritual; in the case of Raglan (1936), indeed, the priority of a single ritual, since he derives all myths everywhere from Frazer's king sacrifice. Yet a few ritualists can be found who would give myth the dominant role (Gaster 1945; Jensen 1963). Others dismiss the question of priority altogether, affirming that neither precedes, causes, or shapes the other, either because they are different aspects of the same thing (Hooke 1933: 3; more forcefully Leach 1954: 13: "myth implies ritual, ritual implies myth, they are one and the same") or because they perform distinct but intricately interdependent functions (Kluckhohn 1942). This was essentially the view expressed by Harrison in *Themis*, that myth and ritual arise *pari passu*, but which was not sustained, and was indeed (as we saw) undermined by her discussion.

Burkert is the first to give a coherent theoretical account for the close relationship between myth and ritual without attempting to derive one from the other, or to deny each their separate and independent spheres. Myth and ritual really do seem to arise *pari passu*, both giving symbolic expression to "basic biological or cultural programs of action" (1979: 18). As such they tend to cluster around the essential needs, common crises, and most anxiety-ridden dilemmas facing the individual and the community, particularly those involving killing, sexuality, transitions, or death. Ritual's function is "to dramatize the order of life, expressing itself in basic modes of behavior" while myth "clarifies the order of life," and very frequently does so by clarifying the dramatized order of ritual (1983: 33). Above all, both create the distinctions necessary for the survival of the community: they direct energies and instill behavior patterns.

For Burkert myth is very much like ritual in that it focuses upon a series of actions. The most important aspect of myth is plot, and the most important aspect of plot is its capacity to represent basic and stereotypical biological action patterns. Burkert's interest in myth's stereotypical pattern of actions gives his theory a strong affinity to the structuralism of Vladimir Propp. To structuralism, therefore, we now turn our attention, postponing further discussion of Burkert's sociobiological interpretation of myth until Section 5.2.

Structuralism

For work a woman, for love a boy, for ecstasy a melon.

Turkish proverb

5.1 SAUSSURE AND STRUCTURAL LINGUISTICS

Relationships and relativity

Viewing "savage" thought from the absolute vantage point of European science and values, nineteenth-century anthropologists like Frazer were blind to the possibility that it might contain some coherence and order. Thought in "savage" societies was treated as a random amalgam of usually false causal associations, though due to the extreme simplicity of life and intellect in savage societies, the same false causal associations were replicated in each and every society. Only at a later stage of development, with material progress, the accumulation of experience, and the invigoration of the rational faculties, do individual cultures begin to sift out, compare, elaborate, and systematize their beliefs. But truly systematic thought was only possible in the final stage of civilization with the triumph of reason. No one probed very deeply into the internal relations of "savage" thought; it seemed pointless so long as scholars supposed it to contain nothing but randomness, confusion, and contradiction. In their view myth was only meaningful or interesting if inserted into an evolutionary framework and contrasted with the one and only perfectly systematic, coherent, and non-contradictory body of beliefs, namely, science.

The twentieth century challenged this view on a number of fronts. From Durkheim onward we find a growing conviction that thought in other societies, including the most primitive, is no less coherent and systematic than that of technologically advanced nations. For Durkheim, Malinowski, and others the beliefs of a given society were meaningful in relation to its practices and institutions and not to any external or absolute criteria. The coherence of myth was derived from its place in the order of a total social system. We could express this shift in dominant values thus:

Nineteenth century	Twentieth century
individual	society
discrete units	system
reason	unconscious/emotion
diachrony/origins/*Urform*	synchrony/contemporary realities
absolute reality	relativity
real world	mind

   These new values extended well beyond interest in myth or primitive culture. They arose from a deep material and cultural upheaval in Western society. The average Westerner's sense of place in society, or sense of belonging to a permanent and dependable social order, was increasingly lost with growing urbanization. In the large cities life was fragmented, social contacts less personal and atomized into professional, leisure, family, and other relations that rarely overlapped. Still worse, in the wake of science, the century brought increasing doubt in religion, in the rectitude of traditional culture and values, and in such concepts as truth, value, and reality . . . ultimately in science itself. Consumer capitalism through fashion and advertising increasingly treated the consumer and society as a whole as a formless clay capable of endless redefinition. Individuals no longer felt themselves securely centered in the social system which they could once take for granted, nor even centered within themselves. The first decades of the twentieth century gave abundant expression, whether in art, literature, philosophy, or science, to its loss of faith in absolute order. Experience was fragmented into autonomous and relative systems. Even people and objects were deprived of their absolute individuality or essence; they were increasingly defined in terms of their multiple, centerless, and often incoherent relationships. The cubist movement in painting (1909–10) played freely with the relationships between parts and wholes, color and shape, representation and represented: its founder Georges Braque declared: "I do not believe in things. I believe only in relationship" (cf. Jakobson 1971: 632). The novel came increasingly to focus on more intimate relationships, not individuals or communities. The heroine of *Howard's End* (1910) speaks of England's new urban culture as a "nomadic civilization which is altering human nature so profoundly, and throws upon personal relationships a stress greater than they have ever borne before" (Forster 1997: 227). "Modern art," and "modernist literature" (directly inspired by both Frazer and Freud) decentered, depersonalized, abstracted, and fragmented the human image; later postmodernism would reduce the "individual" to a "participant" or a "figure" caught in a web of rhetorical forces beyond his control. Ortega y Gasset, one of the first to complain of modernism's dehumanizations (1925), himself attempted to replace absolute reason with a "vital" or "historical" reason in order to accommodate "truth" to a historical, cultural, and individual perspective. In science the most influential expression was Einstein's relativity theory (1905), which rejected the Newtonian absolutes and replaced them with the notion that time and space are relative to particular systems. But perhaps the clearest and most complete articulation of the new paradigm was by a linguist, Ferdinand de Saussure, in a series of introductory lectures delivered in Geneva between 1907 and 1911, later published as the *Course in General Linguistics*.

Saussure

Before Saussure European linguists were mainly interested in tracing the historical roots of words (etymology). The discovery of Indo-European, which engendered the modern science of linguistics, had become the model for serious linguistic study. This traditional study of the evolution of verbal and grammatical forms Saussure labeled *diachronic* linguistics (from Greek, meaning *through time*). In direct opposition to the evolutionary bias of his contemporaries, Saussure claimed that diachronic shifts in language were random, unsystematic, and in themselves meaningless. By contrast, one could study language *synchronically* (*together in time*); the totality of language as it exists at any given moment constitutes a coherent, interrelated system.

Linked to the dichotomy *diachronic/synchronic* there is another very important distinction. Saussure regarded the system of language as an abstract set of rules which was to be distinguished conceptually from the actual uses of language in the isolated utterances of everyday speech. The abstract system of language he designated by the term *langue*. Concrete linguistic utterances he termed *parole*. Of the two, *langue* was the superior aspect of language; *parole* was entirely subordinate to *langue*, since *parole* is simply the materialization and instrumentalization of *langue*. *Langue*, moreover, was a perfectly coherent self-structuring logical system which was no more affected by the individual utterances of *parole* "than the abstract reality of a symphony is compromised by a poor performance." With this distinction Saussure hoped to place his own brand of linguistic studies on a higher plane. Diachronic linguistics was chiefly concerned with *parole*, since shifts in the sound patterns of words were random speech aberrations which somehow caught on despite the conservative safeguards of the system, but they were neither purposive nor meaningful. By contrast a synchronic linguistics would take *langue*, the logical organization of language, for its object and reveal the elements of language which make linguistic communication possible. Moreover, the study of language as a system would reveal the processes that make all forms of human communication possible and hence uncover the very structure of thought itself. Saussure saw his synchronic linguistics as merely the beginning of a new science which would investigate all systems of communication which depended on signs. He called this new science *semiotics*, but until the 1970s most applications of Saussure's thought were known as *structuralism*.

Central to Saussure's linguistic theories is his explanation of the way meanings become attached to words. Before Saussure most linguists took the relationship between words and the things they stand for (i.e., between signs and their referents) as fairly straightforward. Meaning was established in relation to an absolute value. The old school of linguistics adhered to the empiricist notion that the world around us is composed of discrete entities, each with their own fixed place and relations in the universe, and that one simply learned names which corresponded to these unchangeable things – this is a view called *nominalism*. The categories of nouns ("apples," "peaches," "oranges") existed in language because they existed in the real world. This was also true, if less obvious, of verbs ("run," "waddle," "hop") and even abstract nouns ("embezzlement," "justice," "god"). The structure of language (its categories and concepts) stood in direct correspondence to the absolute structure of the world.

If you are asked by a speaker of a foreign language what an "apple" is, you will usually find it sufficient to point to the object. The theory of language acquisition by "ostention" is as old as St. Augustine: "When [my elders] named some object and accordingly moved toward something, I saw this and grasped that the thing was called by the sound they uttered when they meant to point it out" (*Confessions* 1.8). It is a little more difficult when the same foreigner asks you what "embezzlement" is, but in this case a few examples will normally do. Broadly speaking, the nominalist assumes that, though names are different, their meanings correspond: most cultures that have apples have separate words for apples, and most modern societies are constituted in a manner sufficiently like our own as to have a concept of "embezzlement."

One only needs to imagine a foreigner from one of the cultures which does not have a separate word for these things, to see that words and concepts are not tied to any absolute reality. The ancient Greeks, for example, carved up the world in a way that is totally unlike the way modern English speakers carve up the world. The Greek word *melon* can be used to translate "apple," but it denotes any round fruit. It is also a regular metaphor for rosy cheeks. This seems very strange to us, but would have appeared perfectly obvious to a francophone two hundred years ago, who used *pomme* similarly for a variety of round fruits and vegetables, distinguishing *pomme de terre* ("potato") from *pomme de l'air* ("apple"), and referred to cheeks as "little apples," *pommettes*. What is obvious is that simply pointing will not explain "apple" to an ancient Greek, since he would say "apple" next time he saw a peach or referred to cheeks. We are only fooled by the rough equivalences between languages.

We can penetrate a little further into this mystery if we imagine ourselves tutoring an intelligent Martian just beginning her study of English. Pointing at an apple will not do to explain "apple," since the Martian will have no idea where the thing you point at begins or ends, nor any idea of its nature, functions, or qualities. She is just as likely to think that "apple" means the act of stretching the right arm and pointing the index finger. Wittgenstein remarks that "an ostensive definition can be variously interpreted in every case" (1958: 14e, §27). But suppose you overcome these difficulties by resorting to verbal explanations. You will begin by explaining the category of "fruit." After listing all items belonging to this category, you will have to explain contrasting categories, "vegetables" and "weeds," then, moving up higher on the food chain, to explain such categories as "animal" as opposed to "plant," "edible" as opposed to "inedible," "living thing" as opposed to "inanimate," "dead," and so on. The Martian will not stop asking what this and that means until you have exhausted the dictionary, running through every category in the language, comparing and contrasting it to every other. Saussure would argue that it is only when she has acquired the total system that she will know what you meant when you pointed at an apple.

Saussure rejected the dominant formulation of the relationship between language, the mind, and the external world. Words and concepts are *not* directly derived from nature, but are created by language. The world is a confusing and chaotic continuum without beginnings or ends. It is language which parcels it up and reduces it to order. It is language which separates the apple from the tree and the tree from the garden around it. In other words, *it is not the structure of reality that imposes itself upon language, but the structure of language that imposes itself upon reality*.

In order to pry language and thought away from any notion of natural determinism, Saussure stressed the distinction between the word or *sign* and the objective thing to which it refers, the *referent*. But the sign itself can be divided conceptually into two parts: the *signifier*, a sound-image, which points to a mental image, the *signified*. So, for example, the enunciation of the sound "trī" evokes the mental image of a tree. Neither the signifier nor the signified is in any way motivated by the referent. The sounds "apple" or "melon" are in themselves purely arbitrary noises which different languages have pressed into service as signifiers, and, as the example of "apples" shows, one culture's signified may refer to the specific red tree-fruit we know and love, another's signified to any round fruit. The connection between the sign and the referent is therefore for Saussure purely arbitrary and irrelevant to the study of language, while the two parts of the sign, signifier and signified, are in themselves sufficient to account for speech. Saussure evokes the notion of the referent only to dispose of it as being something external to the linguistic system.

This notion represents a radical withdrawal from the objective phenomenal world of traditional empiricist and positivistic science. To appreciate the importance of this move, it is helpful to compare Saussure's position with contemporary empiricist theories of language. Both were concerned with the triad: ideas (mind), words (language), and things (real world/referents). But empiricism focused on the latter two elements at the expense of ideas (mind), while Saussure focused on the former two at the expense of the real world. Once rid of any connection with external reality, language could be thought of as a self-contained, self-structuring system. In effect, the structuralist concept of "language" lies somewhere between the extremes of empiricism and idealism. It locates within a material, observable, empirical entity, namely language, the subjective ideas or cognitive categories which the tradition of European idealism previously placed in purely mental or metaphysical space. Language and linguistic expression behaved like Durkheim's collective consciousness and collective representations, but had none of their rebarbative mysticism. Language can now be perceived as the very stuff of sociality.

For Saussure the structure of language was determined from within language itself, by the relation of its parts. This point is illustrated by the inquisitive Martian who only came to understand the meaning of the word "apple," when she had acquired the total system of the English vocabulary. In this example the value of "apple" was not something positive present in the term itself, but the residual meaning which was left after you explained everything that was not apple. "Apple" means precisely what all the other terms in the language do not mean. It is a place on a complex grid which expands, contracts, or moves as other terms around it expand and contract.

To think of meaning in purely relational terms is to think always in terms of a total structure. Language is a vast network of relations in which the value of each part is completely determined by the structure of the whole. Saussure uses the analogy of a game of chess – a finite, closed system like language but much simpler and easier to grasp. The precise value of any of the pieces at any given moment depends not upon the piece itself, but upon the location of every other piece upon the board. With any move, the value of every piece changes, simply because one piece's change of position transforms the total configuration of the board.

Another metaphor may help to grasp this idea. Suppose that concepts are shapes outlined on a blank page: within the outlines we have only the blankness of the page. The actual contents of each outline are the same – mere blank paper; it is the lines separating one shape from another which give each shape its definition. Now think of this pattern of outlined shapes composed in a fluid medium, in which the position of every line is determined by mutual forces of attraction and repulsion, like a flotilla of elongated magnets. The addition or subtraction of any one line will cause a rearrangement of the shape of the pattern in its entirety, since removal of the magnetic forces keeping each line in place will set off a chain reaction and may result in the total realignment of all the elements in the system. A scientist studying these shapes might decide that: (a) the magnetic strands are organized into a definite pattern (which we would call a system); (b) that this system is rule-governed – one could account for the configuration of the magnetic strands with a mathematical formula; (c) that this formula would hold, even if some of the strands are removed and the surface pattern were redefined; (d) that both the system, as enunciated in the formula, and the surface patterns are meaningfully described as relations between terms, i.e., the interplay of their forces of attraction and repulsion.

Structural linguistics explains the meaning of words in the same way. A concept is not given by nature, but created by the system of language, through a process of opposition and assimilation to other terms. For example, "good" acquires meaning when opposed to "bad," and assimilated to other oppositions which are considered parallel or homologous, like "beautiful," "precious," "delightful," and so on, so that all value terms stand in a relation to the good/bad distinction. In Saussure's words, "the concepts are purely differential and defined not by their positive content but negatively by their relations with the other terms of the system. Their most precise characteristic is in being what the others are not."

This is simple enough when we remain at the level of conscious oppositions and assimilations, but there is more to it than that. The intelligent Martian, in attempting to discover the meaning of "apple," cannot acquire a native understanding of the term simply by memorizing *Webster's Dictionary*. In addition to the conscious relations between the terms, there are many relations which exist only in the semi-conscious or unconscious mind. Here we are dealing with linguistic connotation rather than denotation. No native speaker of English would be too surprised to learn that part of the definition of apple is that it is not a pear, but s/he might be surprised to be told that oppositions such as male/female stood in some relation to the oppositions sun/moon or fire/water. This elaborate cross-referencing is what makes language systematic and entirely interdependent.

By demonstrating the existence of a subconscious level of semantic organization in the human mind the structuralist model exerted an influence far beyond the discipline of linguistics, invading every field of cultural studies, particularly anthropology and literary studies. A simplified view of the structural method in linguistics could reduce it to four basic operations. According to Trubetzkoy (1933), the structural method:

1   shifts the study of *conscious* linguistic phenomena to the study of the *unconscious* infrastructure (viz., the grammatical rules which the speakers of any language carry about in their heads, but which do not enter the conscious mind unless a special study of grammar is undertaken);
2   does not treat *terms* as independent entities, but instead takes as its basis of analysis the *relations* between terms;
3   introduces the concept of *system*;
4   aims at discovering *general laws*, either by induction "or . . . by logical deduction, which would give them an absolute character."

For structuralism language is the universal paradigm and *the* primary semiotic system. All products of culture are merely secondary semiotic systems, but they function, exactly like language, as a vehicle of communication between members of the cultural group, and between one culture and another. These separate cultural systems – myths, kinship, food, political ideology, marriage ritual, cooking, etc. – all constitute partial expressions of the cultural totality, conceived ultimately as a single gigantic *language*. The human mind is and has always been a machine for creating complex, perfectly integrated structures. Nothing is left without a space of its own in some total system of values. Nothing is not related to the rest of a system of thought by a vast network of differences and equivalences. Everything takes its place in a system of meaning according to rules, and these rules can be expressed as relations between any given term and any or all of the other terms in the system.

Why does humanity need to systematize all experience and put it into a symbolic space within a logical category with cross-referencing to other categories? It gives a sense of security, rendering intelligible, orderly, predictable, and even controllable a world that would otherwise be confusing, chaotic, unpredictable, and unmanageable. For this purpose it does not matter whether the categories and cross-references are in any sense real or just imaginary, only that they be in place and that they govern all experience.

5.2 SYNTAGMATIC STRUCTURALISM

Most twentieth-century theorists followed Freud's lead in assuming that myth functions on two levels: behind the apparent or manifest content of a myth there lies a more or less concealed or latent meaning. All major modern theories assume hidden meanings which are received by the societies in which the myths are actively transmitted, though they need not be consciously received, and indeed usually are not. There are, however, important differences among modern notions of the unconscious. Whereas for Freud the subconscious (or unconscious) and conscious mind were frequently at variance, for the structuralist their connection is one of direct expression of unconscious knowledge by the conscious mind: this unconscious knowledge might sooner be described as dormant, rather than repressed. It is dormant because unnecessary. If consciousness were troubled by attention to every detail necessary to its operations, it would break down from overload. But unconscious knowledge often emerges into consciousness as an intuition that something is or is not so, and can frequently be accessed with no resistance from an antagonistic censor.

For the structuralist, linguistics is the primary model for all social sciences. In language the connection between conscious expression and unconscious knowledge is easily grasped. Languages can be learned and spoken by people who have no conscious knowledge of grammar. Yet every native speaker of a language can distinguish between sentences that are grammatical and those which are not ("uneducated speech" is not an exception since most linguists, and all structuralists, would regard it as a different dialect or sociolect from the "official" language). This fact makes it clear that grammatical rules are internalized and used by the speaker, but need not form part of the speaker's consciousness. Through a careful study of speech patterns, the grammarian is able to articulate the rules of grammar which elude the consciousness of the speakers.

In structuralist terminology the actual utterances of native speakers are called "surface structures," while the rules of grammar that enable them to articulate meaningful sentences are "deep structures." We can say, for example, that all sentences in every language must combine a noun phrase with a verb phrase. The number of actual sentences which can be generated by this fundamental rule is infinite. Yet without this rule of combination no sentence can have meaning. In addition to rules of combination the grammarian must also be aware of rules of selection.

Although it combines a noun phrase and a verb phrase, the sentence "Colorless green dreams sleep furiously" is meaningless (except when it exemplifies a "meaningless sentence" in linguistics texts). There are rules for the nouns we select to go with given verbs. Combinatory rules are said to relate to *syntax* or *syntagmatic structure*. Rules of selection are said to relate to *paradigmatic structure*.

Like language, myths have a deep structural organization which can be expressed in terms of syntagmatic and paradigmatic rules. The two structuralist approaches to myth which have come to be called "syntagmatic" and "paradigmatic" structuralism are in reality each concerned with both rules of combination and selection, but differ in their emphasis on one or the other for revealing the deep structures which govern the mythic communication.

Vladimir Propp

The structural study of narrative may be said to begin with the publication of Vladimir Propp's *Morphology of the Folktale* in Russian in 1928. Propp (1895–1970) is generally classified as a formalist, a member of an intellectual movement in Russia active from 1915 until the late 1920s. The formalists were directly inspired by Saussure's linguistics long before structuralism had any effect outside of linguistic circles in the West. One of the principal interests of the Russian formalists and their successors, the Prague structuralists, was discovering the rules or the grammar which underlay literary communication. Propp's book, then, is often read as an attempt to account for the deep structure behind a specific kind of Russian folktale, which he translates as "wondertale." His interest is exclusively in the problem of the classification of folktales and not at all in interpreting them. This is Propp's account of the genesis of his book (1984: 70):

> Before the Revolution, Russian universities cared very little about the literary training of philologists. Folk poetry in particular was completely neglected. To fill the gap, I devoted myself after graduation to the study of Afanas'ev's famous collection. In a series of wondertales about the persecuted stepdaughter I noticed an interesting fact: in *Morozko* [*Frost*] . . . the stepmother sends her stepdaughter into the woods to Morozko. He tries to freeze her to death, but she speaks to him so sweetly and so humbly that he spares her, gives her a reward, and lets her go. The old woman's daughter, however, fails the test and perishes. In another tale the stepdaughter encounters not Morozko but a *lesij* [a wood goblin], in still another, a bear. But surely it is the same tale! Morozko, the *lesij* and the bear test the stepdaughter and reward her each in his own way, but the plot does not change. Was it

possible that no one should ever have noticed this before? Why did Afanas'ev and others think that they were dealing with different tales? It is obvious that Morozko, the *lesij*, and the bear performed the same action. To Afanas'ev those were different tales because of the different characters in them. To me they were identical because the actions of the characters were the same. The idea seemed interesting and I began to examine other wondertales from the point of view of actions performed by the characters. As a result of studying the material (and not through abstract reasoning), I devised a very simple method of analyzing wondertales in accordance with the characters' actions – regardless of their concrete form. To designate these actions I adopted the term *functions*.

Propp's starting point was what he would call a "fact" about the reception of a certain type of tale. The genre concept of "wondertale" arose because wondertales "possess a quite particular structure which is immediately felt and which determines their category, even though we may not be aware of it" (1968: 6). The intuitive classification refers us to an intuited structure or what we may call an unconscious set of rules for recognizing this type of narrative and distinguishing it from others. The relationship between the actual tale and the unconscious criteria by which we recognize the genre is similar to that which exists between a spoken sentence and grammar. The concrete fact of the existence and widespread recognition of this genre concept shows that an unconscious deep structure enables us to recognize certain tales as folktales, just as grammar enables one to recognize certain utterances as declarations, commands, questions, and so on. But as in the case of language grammar, one can recognize genre without being able to account for the criteria of classification. This narrative grammar must be reconstructed from an empirical study of narrative itself.

The division of the folktale into deep-structural and surface-structural levels is a necessary first step. Before Propp folklorists defined the characteristics of narrative genres with reference to surface structures. The most common division was into tales with fantastic content, tales of everyday life, and animal tales. But this category was insufficient since animal tales frequently had fantastic content, or otherwise identical stories were variously classified because of differences which intuitively could be recognized as insignificant: in a Russian version a bear is deceived, but in the West, the devil.

Propp claimed that these details were insignificant and transferable without affecting the tale as a whole. Bears and devils are paradigmatic substitutions allowed by the deep structure of the tale, but do not alter that deep structure in any way. To have an effect on the deep structure a substitution would have to have an impact on the entire narrative beyond the mere fact of substitution. Propp therefore sought to find those parts of a tale whose substitution might change the tale. To be of any use for the analysis, the "constituent units" had to be large enough that their removal or addition would be felt to have a significant impact on the character of the narrative as a whole, yet small enough that other equivalent units might be substituted without a significant impact on the tale.

Propp observed many clear cases in which different contents manifested a similar function in a story, for example:

1   A tsar gives an eagle to a hero. The eagle carries the hero away to another kingdom.
2   An old man gives Súcenko a horse. The horse carries Súcenko to another kingdom.
3   A sorcerer gives Iván a little boat. The boat takes Iván to another kingdom.
4   A princess gives Iván a ring. Young men appearing from out of the ring carry Iván to another kingdom.

All of these actions are unique and different when considered on their own: one is "about Iván;" another "about Súcenko." When considered with respect to the progress of each of the narratives as a whole, however, they are functionally the same, i.e., a donor gives the hero a magic agent and this agent transfers the hero to the vicinity of the object of his search. What is important is not the characters, but the actions, and not the actions in themselves ("giving a horse," "giving a ring"), but the actions considered *in their relation to the total structure of the tale*. Propp calls the constituent units of the deep tale-structure *functions*. A *function* should be defined as an "act of a character, defined from the point of view of its significance for the course or progress of the action of the tale as a whole" (Propp 1958: 20, with 1968: 21 and 1984: 74).

Note that an action is only a "function" when it is viewed from the perspective of the narrative as an abstract system. A function, then, stands in relation to an action, as the deep structure of a narrative stands in relation to its surface structure. The number of actions which could be introduced into a tale is infinite, but functions "serve as stable and constant elements in a tale, independent of how and by whom they are fulfilled" (Propp 1968: 21). There is no direct correspondence between an action and a function. As we have seen, different actions perform the same function, but in addition to qualitative disparity the difference between function and action may also appear as quantitative disparity. The single function *a donor gives the hero a magic agent and this agent transfers the hero to the vicinity of the object of his search* can in theory be broken down into an unlimited number of actions, as it is, for example, in Tolkien's *Lord of the Rings*. Moreover, a single action may perform any number of functions since "[a function] cannot be defined apart from its place in the course of narration" (Propp 1968: 21). Thus the building of a castle by the hero could perform the function of *fulfilling a difficult task*, or *protecting the hero against the villain*, or *celebrating the hero's marriage with the princess*, depending on its position within the tale as a whole.

Armed with these theoretical tools, Propp set about mapping the functions of one hundred Russian wondertales and made two startling discoveries. First, he found that the number of these functions is limited; there were exactly thirty-one. Not all thirty-one functions will appear in every story. Several may be omitted in any tale and some appear only two or three times in his corpus, but all the action of a Russian wonder-tale could be assigned to this limited set of functions. The second, equally surprising discovery, was that all the functions follow exactly the same sequence in all of the stories. Propp's list is as follows:

The preparatory part of the tale

β One of the members of a family absents himself from home. Definition: *absentation*. (1)

γ An interdiction is addressed to the hero. Definition: *interdiction*. (2)

δ The interdiction is violated. Definition: *violation*. (3)

ε The villain makes an attempt at reconnaissance. Definition: *reconnaissance*. (4)

ζ The villain receives information about his victim. Definition: *delivery*. (5)

η The villain attempts to deceive his victim in order to take possession of him or of his belongings. Definition: *trickery*. (6)

θ The victim submits to deception and thereby unwittingly helps his enemy. Definition: *complicity*. (7)

Initiation of the "actual movement of the tale"

A The villain causes harm or injury to a member of a family. Definition: *villainy*. (8)

   or

a One member of a family either lacks something or desires to have something. Definition: *lack*. (8a)

B Misfortune or lack is made known; the hero is approached with a request or command; he is allowed to go or he is dispatched. Definition: *mediation, the connective incident*. (9)

C The seeker agrees to or decides upon counteraction. Definition: *beginning counteraction*. (10)

↑ The hero leaves home. Definition: *departure*. (11)

D   The hero is tested, interrogated, attacked, etc., which prepares the way for his receiving either a magical agent or helper. Definition: *the first function of the donor.* (12)

E   The hero reacts to the actions of the future donor. Definition: *the hero's reaction.* (13)

F   The hero acquires the use of a magical agent. Definition: *provision or receipt of a magical agent.* (14)

G   The hero is transferred, delivered, or led to the whereabouts of an object of search. Definition: *spatial transference between two kingdoms, guidance.* (15)

H   The hero and the villain are joined in direct combat. Definition: *struggle.* (16)

J   The hero is branded. Definition: *branding, marking.* (17). *

I   The villain is defeated. Definition: *victory.* (18)

K   The initial misfortune or lack is liquidated. Definition: *lack liquidated.* (19)

↓   The hero returns. Definition: *return.* (20)

Pr   The hero is pursued. Definition: *pursuit, chase.* (21)

Rs   Rescue of the hero from pursuit. Definition: *rescue.* (22)

O   The hero, unrecognized, arrives home or in another country. Definition: *unrecognized arrival.* (23)

L   A false hero presents unfounded claims. Definition: *unfounded claims.* (24)

M   A difficult task is proposed to the hero. Definition: *difficult task.* (26)

N   The task is resolved. Definition: *solution.* (26)

Q   The hero is recognized. Definition: *recognition.* (27)

Ex   The false hero or villain is exposed. Definition: *exposure.* (28)

T   The hero is given a new appearance. Definition: *transfiguration.* (29)

U   The villain is punished. Definition: *punishment.* (30)

W   The hero is married and ascends the throne. Definition: *wedding.* (31)

*The English translation by Scott unaccountably departs from the alphabetic sequence in labeling functions 17 and 18 (J and I), an oddity retained even in the revised edition (see Propp 1958: 47–8, 1968: 52–3). Propp himself does not use sequential but acrophonic letter labels. The reversed sequence "J I" is retained here because it has, lamentably, become traditional among Anglophone users.

Perseus

Propp did not feel it necessary to explain how these thirty-one functions came to form a genre of oral literature. He hinted at both historical and psychological explanations, but was content with his demonstration of the structuralist assumption that a limited set of generative rules, or a grammar, lay behind all wondertales, and, by implication, that other such sets could be discovered for all forms of narrative. Unlike many of his followers, Propp did not assume that the same thirty-one functions could be pressed into service for all narrative: on the contrary, we instinctively feel the difference between folktale and myth or folktale and the novel – though we may find it hard to articulate rules for the distinction – because of the differences in the grammars that govern these genres. Indeed, if the same thirty-one functions could be seen to apply to other forms of narrative, then Propp would have been wrong to suppose that they form the deep structure of the wondertale and they would prove quite useless as the basis of a system of classification.

It is with some alarm, therefore, that we find Propp later claiming that several myths, those of Perseus, Theseus, or the Argonauts, "are based on the same morphological and compositional system as the wondertale" (1984: 79). The problems that arise from this declaration will be discussed later. For the moment, let us take up the challenge and see how well we can slot Perseus into the Proppian pigeonholes. Apollodorus's version of the Perseus myth is given here with the appropriate functions marked (*Library* 2.4.1–4). We begin with what might (perhaps arbitrarily) be labeled the story of Danae, and will leave it out of consideration, because it may complicate things.

Acrisius asked the oracle about begetting male offspring and the god replied that his daughter would produce a son who would kill him. Fearing this, Acrisius had a bronze chamber constructed underground and imprisoned Danae within it. Some say that Proetus [the brother of Acrisius] seduced Danae and that this was the cause of a feud between Acrisius and Proetus. But others say that Zeus had intercourse with her by turning himself into a shower of gold and flowing through the roof into her lap. When Acrisius later learned that she had given birth to Perseus, he did not believe that she had been impregnated by Zeus, but he put his daughter along with the child into a chest and threw them into the sea. The chest was carried to Seriphos and Dictys picked up and raised the child.

For the sake of demonstrating Propp's claim, let us say the story of Perseus only begins at this point.

Polydectes, the brother of Dictys, fell in love with Danae, but since Perseus had grown to manhood and he was unable to approach her [ε, ζ], he sent out an invitation to his friends and to Perseus among them, pretending that he was gathering contributions toward a bride-gift for Hippodameia, the daughter of Oenomaus [η]. Since Perseus boasted that he would not refuse him even the Gorgon's head [θ], Polydectes asked for horses from the others, but would not accept horses from Perseus; instead he commanded Perseus to bring him the Gorgon's head [a, B]. Under the guidance of Hermes and

Athena he arrived at the home of the daughters of Phorcus, Enyo, Pephredo, and Deino [C, ↑]; these women were the daughters of Ceto and Phorcus, sisters of the Gorgons, and old women from birth. Between themselves the three possessed a single eye and a single tooth, which they shared with one another, taking turns. Perseus grabbed hold of the eye and tooth [D], and when they asked him to give them back, he said he would return them if they guided him on the road leading to the nymphs. The nymphs possessed winged sandals and the *kibisis*, which is said to be a bag. They also possessed the cap of invisibility. So when the daughters of Phorcus led him to the nymphs, he gave them back their tooth and eye [E], and when he was with the nymphs, he got what he wanted and he slung the *kibisis* around his shoulder, put the sandals on his feet, and put the cap on his head [F]. With this cap he could see whomever he wished to see, but he was not visible to others. He also got from Hermes an adamantine sickle [F]. He flew toward Ocean and he came upon the Gorgons as they slept [G]. The Gorgons were Stheno, Euryale, and Medusa. Medusa alone was mortal and this is why Perseus was sent to get *her* head. The Gorgons had heads which were enveloped by the scales of snakes; large tusks, like boars; and bronze hands and golden wings with which they flew. They turned anyone who looked at them into stone. While Athena guided his hand, Perseus stood over them as they slept and turned his gaze away from them, and, while looking into a bronze shield, which reflected the image of the Gorgon [H], he cut off her head [I]. When her head was cut off, the winged horse Pegasus sprang out, as did Chrysaor, the father of Geryon. These Medusa bore from the seed of Poseidon. Now Perseus put the head of the Gorgon into the *kibisis* [K] and started to go back home [↓], but the Gorgons were roused from their sleep and pursued him [Pr], but they were not able to see him because his cap hid him from them [Rs].

He came to Ethiopia [O], where Cepheus was king, and he found Cepheus's daughter, Andromeda, set out as food for a sea monster. This was because Cassiopea, the wife of Cepheus, vied with the Nereids in beauty and boasted that she was superior to all of them. As a result the Nereids were angry and Poseidon, who shared their anger, sent a flood and a monster against the land. But the oracle at Ammon proclaimed that they would be delivered from calamity if Cassiopea's daughter, Andromeda, were exposed as food for the monster. Cepheus acted under pressure from the Ethiopians, and tied his daughter to the rock. Upon seeing her, Perseus fell in love and promised Cepheus to kill the monster, if he would give her to him as his bride when saved [M]. Oaths were given to this effect, Perseus withstood the monster, killed it, and freed Andromeda [N]. But Phineus, the brother of Cepheus, who had first been betrothed to Andromeda [L?], plotted against Perseus. When Perseus learned of the plot [Ex??], he showed him and his co-conspirators the Gorgon and turned them immediately to stone [U?]. When he returned to Seriphos [O], he found that his mother had taken refuge at the altars along with Dictys, because of the violence of

Polydectes [**L?, M?**]. He went to the palace, where Polydectes had summoned his friends and, turning away his gaze, he showed them the head of the Gorgon: upon seeing it each was turned into stone in whatever position he happened to be in [**N?, U**]. He made Dictys king of Seriphos, gave back the sandals, the *kibisis*, and the cap to Hermes, and to Athena he gave the Gorgon's head. Hermes gave the aforesaid back to the nymphs, and Athena inserted the head of the Gorgon into the middle of her shield. . . . Perseus hurried to Argos along with Danae and Andromeda [↓], so as to see Acrisius. Acrisius, when he heard of this and took fright because of the oracle [that he would be killed by Danae's son], left Argos, and went to the land of Pelasgiotis. Teutamides, the King of Larissa, was holding athletic contests in honor of his deceased father. Perseus arrived on the scene [**O**] and, wishing to take part in the contests [**M?**], entered the pentathlon, and throwing the discus at Acrisius's foot, instantly killed him [**U**]. Realizing that the oracle had been fulfilled, he buried Acrisius outside the city. Ashamed to return to Argos to claim his inheritance from a man he had just killed, he went to the son of Proetus, Megapenthes, in Tiryns and organized an exchange and placed Argos in his care. And Megapenthes became King of Argos and Perseus King of Tiryns. He also fortified Midea and Mycenae and he had children by Andromeda [**W**].

Note that functions in Propp's system may be repeated, provided they follow again in the same sequence. A common method of expanding a tale is to embed one tale within another, or simply to repeat a sequence. Recursive sequences have a tendency to come in threes in fairytales, a phenomenon which Propp refers to as "trebling" (1968: 74–5). Thus, in the Ethiopian episode (which we could regard as a story embedded within the tale of the Gorgon quest, which itself is embedded within the tale of Acrisius), we have what appears to be a trebling of the sequence of functions 23–31 (O–W): once with the story of Andromeda where Perseus kills the monster and deals with the "false hero," Andromeda's former suitor, Phineus; a second time with the return of Perseus to Seriphos and the rescue of Danae by turning Polydectes, the suitor of Danae (another "false hero" or villain?), into stone; a third time with Perseus's arrival in Pelasgiotis and the accidental killing of the last "false hero" or villain, his grandfather, Acrisius. We should perhaps also see a trebling of the sequence of functions 12–15 (D–G), with the three groups of donors of magical agents: Hermes and Athena, the daughters of Phorcus, and the nymphs. These rules make the whole exercise much more elastic and imprecise than the rigid rules of sequence first appeared. Another subtle inflection of the sequence rule is provided by the important distinction between *plot* (the logical or causal sequence of the narrative) and *narration* (the actual sequence in which the narrator arranges the presentation of events). Narration, the individual performance of any tale, is, after all, an act of *parole*, while the tale structure, the *langue*, remains constant. In Apollodorus's narration of the Perseus tale, for example, we do not hear of the pretender or "false hero" Phineus until after Andromeda has been saved, thus L seems to come after M. But in terms of the story logic, the betrothal of Andromeda to Phineus (the substance of the claim of the false hero) precedes her exposure to the sea monster, and so in terms of the plot, Propp's rule of sequence is not violated.

The ease with which Propp's functions can be applied to the Perseus myth is impressive, but the myth is not a Russian wondertale, and any strictly theoretical account would have to reckon the correspondence as coincidental and even disturbing. Moreover, the reader is likely to have shared my hesitation in applying function categories to the actions in the Perseus story, particularly in the Ethiopian episode. Someone less disposed to save Propp's theory could justly claim that many of these correspondences were forced. The elasticity allowed by the rules (discussed in the previous paragraph) might even increase the discomfort, since the impressiveness of Propp's claims lies precisely in the uncompromising rigidity of the sequence of thirty-one functions. The less mechanical and the more imaginative the application, the more the theory's credibility relies on the ingenuity and goodwill of the analyst and less on the empirical data. For example, nowhere in *Morphology of the Folktale* does Propp give an adequate definition of his agents. If we begin the story with Acrisius in Argos, is he the hero, false hero, or villain? And if we accept Perseus as the hero, there are still several characters who might vie for the position of villain in the tale: Acrisius, Polydectes, Medusa, and Phineus. Would it then be possible to regard Acrisius, Polydectes, and Phineus as various incarnations of the villain, and Medusa as another donor? – there is nothing particularly villainous about her, except that she is very ugly, like the daughters of Phorcus, and she does after all donate her head, the magical agent which Perseus uses to petrify his real enemies. One could imagine the same tale told with a sympathetic focus on Medusa, innocent victim of Athena's wrath (as indeed it is by Cahill 1995: 70–5, 223–5). If so, then the roles are reversed and the functions will be different. But is it then a different tale ... belonging to a different genre? We might still save Propp's theory, but the assignment of the functions would be totally different, a point which might seem to compromise their utility for a system of classification.

Problems exist not only in the applicability of the functions, or the strictness of the rules of sequence. The exclusivity of the thirty-one functions, Propp's other startling discovery, might also be called into question by our experimental application of his results to Perseus (relying, it will be recalled, on Propp's own claim that the myth fits the structure of his wondertales). There are things that happen in the tale which cannot be assigned to any of his functions. We could excuse the long description of the Gorgon sisters, since this has to do with characterization, and Propp permits actions alone to serve as stable structural elements. (Though even in this case we might ask "Is it really the *same* tale if Perseus cuts the head off a magic pineapple rather than Medusa?") But what of the birth of Chrysaor and Pegasus? Is this just characterization? Or is it perhaps an intrusive element from other tales? What of the returning of the magic agents, Athena's placing the Gorgon on her shield, or the burial of Acrisius? Propp might object that they are nonessential to the story, but if he did, this would add a new and potentially huge element of subjectivity to the method. If only essential actions are worth paying attention to, then it would certainly be possible to reduce the thirty-one functions to a much smaller subset.

Burkert's girls' tragedy

Let us take an example which attempts to apply Propp's method, and not his functions, to myth. In *Structure and History in Greek Mythology and Ritual,* Walter Burkert makes a syntagmatic analysis of a number of myths about the mothers of heroes. For brevity's sake I recount only three of the myths here (drawing also upon the Danae story recounted above) before summarizing Burkert's conclusions.

Callisto, the daughter of Lycaon, had a passion for hunting and left home to join Artemis's troupe of maiden hunters roaming the hills of Arcadia. Zeus fell in love with her and disguised himself as Artemis and raped her. She became pregnant with Arcas. Artemis expelled her from the troupe and, after her son was born, either Artemis or Hera turned her into a bear. The son was exposed but found by shepherds and brought to Lycaon, who chopped him up and made a stew out of him to serve to Zeus. Zeus turned Lycaon into a wolf and put Arcas back together again. Meanwhile Callisto wandered in the form of a bear for fifteen years until her son, out hunting one day, was about to drive a spear through his unrecognized mother. According to Ovid, Zeus took pity on them and transformed them into stars. [The original myth must have been different, however, since Arcas must live on to produce three sons who are the ancestors of the Arcadians.]

Aleus, King of Tegea in Arcadia, received an oracle that his sons would be killed by the son of his daughter, Auge. He therefore made her priestess of Athena, for being priestess involved a vow of chastity. Heracles happened to be passing by at the time the Arcadians were celebrating an all-night feast to the goddess. He joined the feast and got drunk and then raped Auge while she was involved in the celebration of the rites. She tried to conceal her pregnancy and gave birth in Athena's temple, but her father found out and sold Auge into slavery and the child Telephus was exposed on the mountainside. Telephus was suckled by a deer and then discovered by Heracles on a return visit. Heracles recognized him as his son because he was exposed with a ring which had been taken from the finger of the drunken man during the rape. Telephus grew up in a neighboring kingdom, eventually killed his uncles, and fled to Mysia, where he found his mother and became King of Mysia and founder of the city of Pergamum.

Inachus, King of Argos, had a daughter Io who was a priestess of Hera. Zeus fell in love with her and this roused the jealousy of Hera, so Zeus turned her into a heifer to disguise her. Hera, who was not fooled, asked for the heifer and Zeus could not refuse her without betraying himself. Hera then set the monster Argus, who had eyes all over his body, to guard her. Argus bound her to an olive tree and kept watch over her. Zeus sent Hermes to kill Argus and steal her away. Hera then sent a gadfly to torment Io and she fled over the whole earth, maddened by the insect, until she reached Egypt, where she gave birth to a son called Epaphus on the banks of the Nile and recovered her human form. Epaphus was father of Libya who bore Agenor, father of Cadmus and Europa.

Burkert points out that these stories have the same syntagmatic structure. The sequence of action in each of these myths can be generalized into a pattern of five *motifemes* (= functions).

1   leaving home: the girl is separated from childhood and family life
2   the idyll of seclusion: Callisto joins Artemis, Danae is locked in an underground chamber, Auge and Io become priestesses
3   rape: the girl is surprised, violated, and impregnated by a god
4   tribulation: the girl is severely punished and threatened with death
5   rescue: the mother, having given birth to a boy, is saved from death and grief as the boy is about to take over the powers to which he is destined.

Moreover, all of these myths share a common narrative class: all are about the mothers of the founders of cities or the ancestors of tribes: Callisto is mother of Arcas, ancestor of the Arcadians; Danae is mother of Perseus, the founder of Mycenae; Auge is mother of Telephus, the founder of Pergamum; and Io mother of Epaphus, whose sons are the founders of several nations. Enlisting the analysis for his ritualist/ethologist agenda (see Section 4.4), Burkert concludes (1979: 6–7):

The girl's tragedy can be seen to reflect initiation rituals; but these in turn are determined by natural sequences of puberty, defloration, pregnancy, and delivery. If, as observed in certain tribes, the girl has to leave her father's house at first menstruation and only acquires full adult status with the birth of a son, the correspondence to the tale structure is almost perfect.

It must be observed, however, that Burkert's analysis is far less exhaustive than Propp's. There are several events which are important to the myths but have no corresponding motifeme in Burkert's list. In the myth of Auge, for example, as in several others not recounted here, the child is exposed and then suckled by animals. In many myths the girl is metamorphosed into an animal (as in Callisto and Io): Burkert maintains that this is a "modal operator" and so does not count. Propp would have found this evasive in the extreme.

There are a couple of features in Propp's theory which accommodate it to Burkert's ritualist and sociobiological theories. Propp reduces myth to action patterns, and this makes them much easier to assimilate to rituals. Moreover, one of the distinguishing features of ritual for Burkert is that it be composed of an invariable sequence of actions, and this same claim is made by Propp's theory of the wondertale. But here we run into a significant problem in Burkert's application of Propp. The climax of all the "girl's tragedies" that Burkert studies is the giving of birth to a child, and indeed, in all cases, a male child. This being the case, one would have expected him to include in his list a motifeme labeled "bears a male child." But oddly, Burkert avoids this (he merely notes that it happens before motifeme 5). Is it because it does not follow in sequence? Auge and Danae give birth before "tribulation," Io and Callisto after. The great difficulty in making an exhaustive sequential scheme for even four myths as closely related as these shows just how unusual Propp's achievement was. No random selection of a large corpus of tales has ever reproduced it. This is both impressive and unsettling. Of what value are the results of an unrepeatable experiment?

5.3   A CRITIQUE OF SYNTAGMATIC STRUCTURALISM

Urmyths, archetypes, and Urforms

When we read Propp's functions we find, not a set of rules or formulae expressing the manner in which the actions relate to one another, but an abstract story, in fact *the story* of which all actual wondertales are mere transformations. In this respect Propp's functions resemble the comparatist's Urmyths and psychoanalyst's narrative archetypes. We could compare Propp's results to those of works like the Freudian Otto Rank's *The Myth of the Birth of the Hero* (1909), which attempted to view all hero myths as variations on the Oedipus archetype, or the comparatist and ritualist Lord Raglan's *The Hero* (1936), which views all myths as variants of the dying god archetype, or the "universal plot" of the mainly Jungian Joseph Campbell's *The Hero with a Thousand Faces* (1949), which reduces a large number of myths, legends, and dreams from many cultures to the following "monomyth" (1949: 245–6):

> The mythological hero, setting forth from his commonday hut or castle, is lured, carried away, or else voluntarily proceeds, to the threshold of adventure. There he encounters a shadow presence that guards the passage. The hero may defeat or conciliate this power and go alive into the kingdom of the dark (brother-battle, dragon-battle; offering, charm), or be slain by the opponent and descend in death (dismemberment, crucifixion). Beyond the threshold, then, the hero journeys through a world of unfamiliar yet strangely intimate forces, some of which severely threaten him (tests), some of which give magical aid (helpers). When he arrives at the nadir of the mythological round, he undergoes a supreme ordeal and gains his reward. The triumph may be represented as the hero's sexual union with the goddess-mother of the world (sacred marriage), his recognition by the father-creator (father atonement), his own divinization (apotheosis), or again – if the powers have remained unfriendly to him – his theft of the boon he came to gain (bride-theft, fire-theft); intrinsically it is an expansion of consciousness and therewith of being (illumination, transfiguration, freedom). The final work is that of the return. If the powers have blessed the hero, he now sets forth under their protection (emissary); if not, he flees and is pursued (transformation flight, obstacle flight). At the return threshold the transcendental powers must remain behind; the hero re-emerges from the kingdom of dread (return, resurrection). The boon that he brings restores the world (elixir).

But there is an important difference between Propp, the comparatists, and the psychologists. Both comparatists and psychologists sought to explain the relationships between a group of narratives by finding or constructing another narrative from which all the others were supposed to be in some sense derivative. In the case of the comparatists the relationship was genetic: the Urform was the original tale, the one that made sense, and all the others were to a greater or lesser extent degenerate versions of it. The psychologists used narrative archetypes in much the same way: some narratives were closer to the archetypes than others. Propp's conception of the nature of the Urtale is very different.

We have seen the importance of Saussure's structural linguistics to Propp's project. It was not, however, linguistic, but organic, "morphology" which served as Propp's chief theoretical model. The formalists were heir to an elaborate German tradition of morphological poetics which took its ultimate inspiration from Goethe's writings on plant and animal morphology. In 1795, promoting the study of morphology above anatomy and physiology, Goethe described how the three sciences differed in their point of view and method: anatomy and physiology seek to explain biological phenomena through *causal* laws, morphology in terms of *structural* laws (1926: 59). In other words, anatomy and physiology will offer functional or genetic explanations of particular forms, but morphology was oriented to the comparison of abstract structural systems without reference to their origins or purposes. Goethe sought to explain natural organisms through the description of a typological model or *Urtype*, described by Dolezel as "a constructed invariant design in terms of which variable organic structures can be differentiated, compared, contrasted and homologized" (1990: 59). The Urtype was a mechanism for describing and relating structures and as such had only the status of a theoretical construct: it was not to be confused with any particular organism. Consider, for example, Goethe's claim "that all higher organic structures, among them fish, amphibians, birds, mammals, and, at the head of the last category, man, are formed according to one prototype [*Urbild*] which in its constant parts fluctuates only within certain limits and which is formed and transformed daily through reproduction" (Dolezel 1990: 59). But Goethe's model of a vertebrate is not to be mistaken for a description of the actual ancestor of all fish, amphibians, birds, and mammals. Nor is the "story" we read when reading Propp's list of functions to be confused with any actual story.

This is the chief point of difference with comparatism: the comparatist Urmyth is an actual *historical* entity which is identified as the *cause* of all derivative myths. Similarly, a psychological archetype, for both Freud and Jung, has a historical referent as well as a "material" existence as a trace or imprint on the mind. Propp's tale, by contrast, is a purely theoretical construct. Not only does it differ from the comparatist's and psychoanalyst's Urform as construction to reality, but it also differs in the dynamic of its relation to all variants: for the comparatists and psychoanalysts all variants derived their meaning and authority from proximity to the Urform, but for the formalists the Urform could only derive meaning and authority from the variants of the tale, all of which were of equal consequence.

Propp criticized from a structural perspective

Propp is best viewed as a liminal figure in the history of theoretical speculation about myth and folktale. *Morphology of the Folktale* is generally

taken as the first important application of structuralist ideas to narrative.
Yet Dolezel has aptly called it the "swan song of the organic model" of
narrative (1990: 146). The phrase points to Propp's still considerable
distance from later structuralism. There is, indeed, much in Propp which
anticipates Lévi-Strauss, particularly the notion of an invariable form behind
a group of narratives, the conception of the manifest contents of any tale
as a transformation of the formal invariant, and the conviction that the
parts of a tale are related by a systemic logic. But the differences are
still more striking. Although in my account of Propp I used the terms
"surface structures" and "deep structures" in order to bring out the distinctly structuralist aspects of Propp's approach, these are not Propp's terms,
and they are misleading to the extent that they conceal the prestructuralist
conceptual models at work in his theory. Despite substantial agreement,
there is a fundamental difference between formalism and structuralism
in the way each defines the relationship between the invariant and variable properties of a tale. As Lévi-Strauss explained it, Propp, like other
formalists, opposes "form" to "content" (1973: ch. 8). Form is abstract,
content concrete. Moreover, form is the privileged value in this dualism.
It was a double inheritance from Saussure and from comparatism which
induced Propp to conceive of abstract form as something intelligible, meaningful, systematic, and timeless, while concrete contents were deemed
arbitrary, meaningless, random precipitates of a degenerative temporal process. Structuralists, on the contrary, distinguish between surface structure
and deep structure, a distinction which, in theory at least, contained no
such antinomies. One is the direct expression of the other. Both are equally
"structure" and both are real. "Structure," for Lévi-Strauss, "has no distinct content; it *is* the content captured in its logical organization, which
is conceived as a property of what is real" (1973: 139).

  Propp's concept of structure is therefore much narrower than Lévi-
Strauss's. For Lévi-Strauss there is nothing in a tale that escapes the structural organization, but Propp's opposition of form to content allows him
to dispose of large parts of the tale as mere contents. The logical organization of a tale is confined by Propp almost exclusively to action patterns
and to the linear sequence of events.

  By focusing on the action Propp excludes a great deal. This is justifiable
in a study of plot types, perhaps, since we tend to identify plot with action
pattern. But Propp claims to do more than this. He is producing a morphology, "a description of the tale according to its component parts and
the relationship of these components to each other and to the whole" (1968:
19). Unlike his predecessors, who usually regarded characters as the
primary constants in folktales and used the principal characters as a
criterion for classification, Propp assumes that action is what is constant

and the characters variable (1968: 20; I have changed the translator's "personage" to "character" for the sake of terminological consistency):

> Just as [in myths] the characteristics and functions of deities are transferred from one to another, and, finally, are even carried over to Christian saints, the functions of certain characters in the tale are likewise transferred to other characters. Running ahead, one may say that the number of functions is extremely small, whereas the number of characters is extremely large. This explains the twofold quality of a tale: its amazing multiformity, picturesqueness, and color, and on the other hand, its no less striking uniformity, its repetition.

The reason that Propp privileges action in this way is not simply a quantitative disparity between the parts. He believes that the sequence of actions alone is governed by a synchronic system, while other ingredients of the tale are nothing but the historical remnants of obsolete social and mythological systems, whose survival is fortuitous. "In the study of folktales it is only important to ask *what* the characters are doing; *who* does something, or *how* he does it, are questions of merely marginal importance" (1970: 29 – only the French translation captures the vigor of Propp's declaration). Though function may be defined as the "act of a character," the stress is clearly on the *act*, not the *character*.

Propp's stress on action to the exclusion of all else is most apparent in the style of his presentation. To each of the sentences describing the functions in his list, Propp notably attaches, in the way of a more scientific-looking "definition," a subjectless verbal noun, such as "Departure," or "Marking," in order to stress the elemental and self-sufficient nature of the actions. Propp's desire to promote action over character is even so powerful that it causes him to muddle his own theoretical distinctions. In the passage just cited, where Propp argues the importance of action, by referring to the great disproportion between the limited number of actions and the vast number of characters, Propp says: "Running ahead, one may say that the number of functions is extremely small, whereas the number of characters is extremely large." He has apparently lost sight of the distinction between abstract and concrete levels which is fundamental to his method, because by comparing functions to characters he is confusing categories. The comparison should not be between the "number of functions," which is extremely small, and the "number of characters," which is extremely large, but either at the concrete level of content between the number of "actions" and the number of "characters," or at the abstract level of form between the number of "functions" and the number of "function-performers" (namely "heroes," "villains," "donors," "false-heroes,"etc.). If we compare the number of possible actions to the number of characters in a wondertale, we find, despite Propp, that they are both equally unlimited. But if we compare the number of functions in a wondertale with the number of function-performers, we find the opposite of what Propp claims to be true: the number of functions is in fact far greater, thirty-one, than the number of "function-performers," which is only seven. This fact sadly undermines the point Propp is trying to make, and disembodied action seems not to deserve the overriding importance Propp ascribes to it.

Propp's method, in effect, dismisses as unstable, random, and unsystematizable a very large part of any narrative: characters, accessories, places; their qualities, relations, feelings, attitudes, intentions, and motivations. For these aspects of a tale Propp claims that there can be no rational, only a historical account. It is as if Propp, intending to produce a grammar for the English language, decided that only the use of verbs was rule-governed, while all other parts of speech were randomly attached to verbs in order to make speech seem more colorful.

Propp's exclusive concentration on the linear sequence of events is a still more serious shortcoming. As stated earlier, a proper grammar should provide rules of selection (paradigmatic) as well as rules of combination (syntagmatic). But Propp is interested only in the syntagmatic, and even here he produces only one basic rule, that the functions should follow one another in a preset order. This rule *seems* to be validated by Propp's results: the rule of sequence is based, he insists, on the empirical evidence of the tales, and one need only refer to the tales for confirmation. Unfortunately there is a certain circularity in the process. One might even venture to say that it is not his method which enabled the discovery of the thirty-one functions, but rather his method which *created* them. Since a function "cannot be defined apart from its place in the process of narration," it is perhaps a little less than amazing to discover that the functions all fall into their proper places, since they do so, admittedly, because their places were established by the very act of definition. To take an extremely reductive example, it is a little like someone claiming that they have established the three universal "functions" of all narrative which, defined from their place in the process of narration, can be labeled (1) the "beginning," (2) the "middle," and (3) the "end," and, what is even more remarkable, this sequence is *invariable* in every tale! Certainly, at least, functions such as "beginning counteraction," and "the hero's reaction" will follow what goes before as surely as would a function labeled "that which happens next." In a moment we will see in more detail how the sequencing is ordained by the very description of Propp's functions.

Propp shows that there is a certain logic to a wondertale. But he does not help us to discover what that logic is. He explains neither the internal necessity by which one function always follows another nor the logic which unites the variety of events falling under each of his function headings. While his method provides rules by which one can recognize the deep-structural identity of two different tales, it provides no rules to account for the differences in surface structure. It is a grammar which does not explain how one generates transformations.

You might object that I am faulting Propp for failing to do something he never attempted: he only wanted to establish a system of classification for folktales. But it is precisely because he ignores paradigmatic rules that his scheme fails to do even that! Propp's *Morphology* provides no means of distinguishing the wondertale from other folktale genres apart from the fact that wondertales have thirty-one functions and seven function-performers. Yet this might have seemed sufficient if Propp himself did not unwittingly advertise its inadequacy (1984: 79): "There are myths based on the same morphological and compositional system as the wondertale. Such are, for example, classical myths of the Argonauts, Perseus and Andromeda, Theseus, and many others. At times they correspond, down to minute details, to the compositional system studied in *Morphology of the Folktale*." We have already had occasion to wonder at this statement, but not to exhaust its implications. It is clear that when Propp calls some tales "myth" and others "wondertale," it is not just a *façon de parler*, it is because he recognizes and prefers *some other criterion for classification to the one he himself created*! He knows that myths are not wondertales, but he cannot say why. By his own classificatory criterion the myths have the distinguishing features of the wondertale.

But what about the internal classification? Can we use the functions for breaking wondertales into different groups? Without paradigmatic rules the functions are so rigid that it is hard to see how this would work. Propp divides each function into genus and species. The genus is the function label or "definition" from the chart. But the genus description exists at such a high level of abstraction as to prove useless for classification, e.g., "departure" (function 11). Could we have "departure" and "non-departure" wondertales? The drawer with the first label would be full, that with the second empty. Fortunately Propp also gives a list of species under each function, which list the kind of actions which perform the function. The first five of the seventeen species of "villainy," for example, are listed as:

1   The villain abducts a person.
2   The villain seizes or takes away a magical agent.
3   The villain pillages or spoils the crops.
4   The villain seizes the daylight.
5   The villain plunders in other forms.

But here is a great paradox for a classificatory scheme. At the abstract level of the function, there is only one action. At the species level, the descriptions of the kinds of villainy are so specific as to be virtually identical with the narrative of an actual tale. Here all the actions that confront us in the corpus come back to haunt us. At the abstract level of form there is only one tale. At the next lowest level, there are nearly all the tales of the corpus. "The problem is only shifted elsewhere," says Lévi-Strauss (1973: 159):

> We know what *the story* is. But since observation presents us not with one archetypal story, but with a multitude of particular stories, we do not know any longer how to classify them. Before formalism we were indeed unaware of what these stories had in common. After it we were deprived of every means of understanding how they differ. We have gone from the concrete to the abstract, but we cannot come back down from the abstract to the concrete.

It is as if in presenting you with a method for classifying sentences, I were to give you the deep structure of an assertive sentence as NOUN PHRASE + VERB PHRASE, in that sequential order, and then underneath this genus I were to list as subclasses rubrics like: "The cat ate the mat." "The rat wears a hat," etc., etc., ad infinitum.

Propp seems aware of this difficulty, because he does not appeal to the function subspecies as a classificatory aid, but turns his attention instead to a serendipitous feature of the wondertale's set of functions. There is one near-incompatibility between functions which allows for a further breakdown of wondertales into four categories. Tales rarely include both the combat sequence (H J) and the task sequence (M N) in the same section of the tale. Where both occur they are in logically independent movements of the tale (in conformity with the sequence rule, the task always follows the combat motif). Hence the importance of what Propp calls the four "moves:"

$$
\text{ABC} \uparrow \text{ D E F G}
\begin{array}{c}
\text{H J I K} \downarrow \text{Pr–Rs O L} \\
\rule{6em}{0.4pt} \\
\text{L M J N K} \downarrow \text{Pr–Rs}
\end{array}
\text{Q Ex T U W}
$$

Thus four subcategories of tale can be formed: (1) combat tales (first + upper + last); (2) task tales (first + lower + last); (3) combat and task tales (first + upper + lower + last); (4) tales with neither combat nor task (first + last). Further division can also be made according to whether function A (villainy) or function a (lack) begins the movement of the tale, since these two functions are incompatible (hence numbered 8 and 8a).

But there is another disturbing contradiction here. Propp offers his scheme as a method of classification. The method is based on the presupposition that tales are formed from a system of functions which are defined by their relations with other functions and with the tale as a whole. To be part of a system each function is necessarily related to all the others by the logic of the narrative. Yet here we find that there are functions which exclude each other, and, moreover, that an internal system of classification is only possible because of these incompatibilities. Would it not be more in conformity with Propp's own methodological claims to suppose that we have a conflation of different tale types? To externalize the internal incompatibilities?

Yet even with these incompatibilities we do not get much further with the classification system. Each category still contains vast legions of tales. At this point Propp suggests a final breakdown according to the species of functions A and a: "Further classification can also be made according to the varieties of these elements. Thus at the head of each class will come the tales about the kidnapping of a person, then tales about the stealing of a talisman, etc., on through all the varieties of element A" (1968: 102). The content of the tale, initially rejected as a basis for classification, is now brought in through the back door to save the experiment from the consequences of its own methodological failure.

Rethinking Propp

The impact of Propp's pioneering study of the invariant elements in the plot of the Russian wondertale was not felt in the West for more than thirty years, when in the 1960s its "discovery" had a considerable influence upon structural poetics and the fledgling discipline of narratology. But whatever the virtues of the *Morphology of the Folktale,* Propp was an indifferent theorist. If his results were inspiring, he did not succeed in giving a coherent account of them.

Propp's place in the development of contemporary theory is often based on something of a misconception. Propp's method has come, erroneously, to be known as *syntagmatic structuralism.* In his later writings Propp even seems to embrace the label. But this mistakes both the formalist quality of his work, and overlooks much that is not even typically formalist in its inspiration and execution: Propp does not take his primary inspiration from Saussure or linguistics, but, as we saw, from a much older tradition of German morphological poetics. Propp's analysis does not produce a proper grammar, but an Urtype. (One has difficulty imagining what a language grammar written on this model would look like – What is an

Ursentence?) It is questionable even whether we have anything like a sufficiently abstract form. If we read the series of functions in order, we get what looks too much like another tale, a new member of the corpus, albeit a skeletal and colorless one. Not only the subspecies, but even the functions themselves are too close to the surface structures of the tales to give expression to the relations which govern their composition. For either a formalist or a structuralist the objective is not to produce anything that looks like another tale, but to produce a set of rules governing the genera- tion of a folktale, or at least a description of the relations linking its parts.

Without, therefore, wishing to fault Propp for failing to achieve something which arguably he never attempted, it might nevertheless be helpful to follow some cues offered by Lévi-Strauss's review of Propp's book (1973: Ch. 8), and show how a structuralist might rework Propp. To begin with, Propp's presupposition that a function must be strictly defined by its place in the story allows for little flexibility. In the list of Propp's functions, for example, one can see no reason other than position for distinguishing certain actions as performing different functions. The sequence O L M N T (unrecognized arrival, unfounded claims, difficult task, solution, transfiguration) appears to be a variation on ↑ A H I J (depar- ture, villainy, struggle, victory, marking), and might be treated as such, though this would destroy the sequencing rule. If the analysis must save Propp's hypothesis, then functions A and L can be kept separate. But Propp gives no reason why the rigid sequence of functions should operate as a rule of syntax and it remains uneconomical. Would it not be more eco- nomical to regard the combat sequence H J I (struggle, marking, victory) and the task sequence M N T (difficult task, solution, transfiguration) as transformations of the same set of functions? (But if we did this, then even Propp's fourfold classification system goes to ruin.)

Following the same line of reasoning we find redundancy in a number of functions:

B ("the hero is approached with a request") = M ("a difficult task is proposed to the hero")
K ("the initial misfortune or lack is liquidated") = N ("the task is resolved")
J ("the hero is branded") = T ("the hero is given a new appearance")
↑ ("departure") ≈ O ("the hero, unrecognized, arrives home or in another country") ≈ ↓ ("return")

Redundancy also appears in the designation of function performers: there is no real criterion for distinguishing the "false hero" from the "villain." Why not just call him another villain? Propp himself seems to regard them as functionally equivalent in function Ex ("the false hero or villain is exposed"). If they *are* functionally equivalent, L ("a false hero presents unfounded claims") is just another form of A ("villainy") and η ("the villain attempts to deceive his victim"), and the exposure of the false hero (Ex) may be a form of defeating the villain (I).

In addition to the transformational variations which we gain by tossing out the rigid notion of sequence, there are gains to be made by treating the temporal relations as logical relations. We find several pairs of relations of logical implication:

γ (interdiction)	implies	δ (violation)
η (trickery)	implies	θ (complicity, i.e., = "being tricked")
α (lack)	implies	K (lack liquidated)
↑ (departure)	implies	↓ (return)
H (struggle)	implies	I (victory)
J (marking) or O (unrecognized arrival)	imply	Q (recognition)
Pr (pursuit)	implies	Rs (rescue)
M (difficult task)	implies	N (solution)

Most, if not all, the functions could be assigned to logical pairs in this way. But Propp does no more than note the existence of these pairs. Had he pursued this any further, he might have been able to formulate some paradigmatic rules for the narrative. For example, in some pairs the logical implication is also characterized by opposite or contradictory relations: δ "violation" is the opposite of C insofar as C is merely "obeying the injunction" we find in B. At the same time violation is the reverse of γ "interdiction," and "interdiction" is the negative transformation of the injunction implied in B ("the hero is approached with a request or command") or M ("a difficult task is proposed to the hero"). All of these functions might have been regarded as simple logical transformations of one another. In the same way the opposite of a "departure or quest" (↑) might be described as a "return" or "pursuit" (↓ or Pr), and "departing on a quest" has a logical relationship with "finding the villain" (G), at least when, as in the Perseus tale, the object of the quest is the villain. Similarly "quest" (↑) might be seen as the reverse of "pursuit" (Pr), which is the opposite of rescue (Rs). A simple relation of opposition also exists between recognition (Q) and lack of recognition (O), each of which reverses disguise (J or T) and exposure (Ex). Once we begin to look at logical connections in this way, we begin to see that the choice of a particular function within the syntagmatic chain is constrained or excluded by previous choices. That is to say, we begin to discover the paradigmatic rules governing the syntax.

5.4 PARADIGMATIC STRUCTURALISM

Roman Jakobson and the structure of the phoneme

In the 1930s Roman Jakobson (1896–1982) made some discoveries in the field of phonetics which completely altered the structuralist concept of system. Phonemes, the individual sound-components of words, are the smallest material units of language. If Saussure was right about language being a total system, then it should be possible to discover a logical system governing the phonemes of any language. Saussure himself claimed that "phonic elements are above all oppositive, relative and negative entities" (1972: 164, 466), but never succeeded in showing how this was so, and indeed the whole tendency of his treatment of phonemes contradicted this statement.

The logical outline of Saussure's theory proved an insuperable obstacle to discovering any place for phonemes in the system of language. In particular, Saussure was hampered by the rigidity with which he deployed the distinctions between langue and parole, synchronic and diachronic, paradigmatic and syntagmatic, and signifier and signified. Signifiers, material speech sounds, could only be produced or received in temporal succession, and, like time, had a linear quality: "acoustic signifiers have only the line of time at their disposal; their elements appear one after another; they form a chain" (1972: 103). In other words, signifiers have a special relationship with the syntagmatic and the diachronic and are the stuff of parole. Signifieds, on the other hand, are purely conceptual, and derive their value from the system of language which is simultaneously present to the mind. Signifieds, therefore, have a special relationship to the paradigmatic and the synchronic orders and are the stuff of langue. We have already seen that both Saussure and Propp found system and meaning only in the synchronic, while they supposed the diachronic random and meaningless (although Propp, unlike Saussure, linked the synchronic with the syntagmatic).

Saussure's treatment of phonemes illustrates the way signifiers, the syntagmatic, and the diachronic tend to be dismissed as parole. In Saussure's view phonemes are the most purely material components of the signifier. In themselves they have no logic and are of no interest. Logic and system only appear in their linear accumulation. When one *combines* phonemes, one begins to see that there are laws governing their juxtaposition. For example, the phoneme /b/ in itself belongs to no system of logic, but one can combine it with some phonemes, and not with others: *bla* is a perfectly acceptable syllable in English, *sba* is not. System and logic only appear in the combination of sounds (and even there the rules of selection seem minimal and arbitrary until the combination of sounds is long enough to form morphemes).

Jakobson was not content with this treatment of phonemes. It epitomized the failure of Saussure's description of language to live up to his own structural principles, because of Saussure's habit of privileging the signified, the paradigmatic, synchrony, and langue as belonging to the logical and systemic aspects of language, while treating their opposites, the signifier, syntagm, diachrony, and parole, as relatively random, material, and meaningless. Saussure advertised the structuralist project in linguistics as a "total systemic logic," but under the packaging the description applied strictly to only half of the contents, to the other half, less well or not at all. When Jakobson succeeded in describing phonemes in terms of the strictly relational logical organization which structuralism promised (1971: esp. 294–300), he did so precisely by rejecting Saussure's rigid dichotomization of language. In doing so he revealed fundamental problems in Saussure's description of language. Though explicitly aimed at phonemes, the most elementary level of language structure, Jakobson's critique has important implications for understanding the most complex linguistic structures, namely narratives.

The main obstacle to discovering the logical organization of phonemes was that they did not have the obvious relations with one another we find in larger units of speech. If one takes the word "big," it is easy to see that it stands in significant opposition to the word "small." Even words like "apple," which have no strict opposite, contrast significantly with other words, in this case "tomato," "plum," etc. It is possible to see some sense in the statement that the meaning of "apple" is determined by considering what these other words are not. But phonemes have no signifieds, they are only signs that combine to make other signs, namely words, and so they cannot be contrasted in this way. What is the opposite of /b/? So far Saussure's tendency to assign strict systematic logic, "oppositive, relative, and negative" meaning, to signifieds rather than signifiers seems to be vindicated.

But Jakobson questioned the notion that signifiers express order only in linear combination and through time. He treated the phoneme in the way Saussure treated signifieds, as an order, based on significant oppositions simultaneously present in the phoneme itself. Though the phoneme is an "atomic" unit of language in the sense that no smaller material unit exists, nevertheless Jakobson discovered that, like an atom, the phoneme could be further divided conceptually into parts. The parts of the phoneme are related to the movable parts of the human vocal organ which one can either use or not use in the production of sound. For example, one can allow free passage of sound through the mouth or one can constrict

STRUCTURALISM

The phonemic pattern of English broken down into inherent distinctive features

	o	a	e	u	ə	i	l	ŋ	ʃ	ĵ	k	ʒ	ʒ	g	m	f	p	v	b	n	s	θ	t	z	ð	d	h	#
1. Vocalic/Non-vocalic	+	+	+	+	+	+	+	−	−	−	−	−	−	−	−	−	−	−	−	−	−	−	−	−	−	−	−	−
2. Consonantal/Non-consonantal	−	−	−	−	−	−	+	+	+	+	+	+	+	+	+	+	+	+	+	+	+	+	+	+	+	+	−	−
3. Compact/Diffuse	+	+	+	−	−	−		+	+	+	+	+	+	+	−	−	−	−	−	−	−	−	−	−	−	−		
4. Grave/Acute	+	+	−	+	+	−									+	+	+	+	+	−	−	−	−	−	−	−		
5. Flat/Plain	+	−		+	−																							
6. Nasal/Oral								+	−	−	−	−	−	−	+	−	−	−	−	+	−	−	−	−	−	−		
7. Tense/Lax									+	+	+	−	−	−		+	+	−	−		+	+	+	−	−	−	+	−
8. Continuant/Interrupted									+	−	−	+	−	−		+	−	+	−		+	+	−	+	+	−		
9. Strident/Mellow									+	−	+	−									+	−	+	−				

Key to phonemic transcription: /o/ - pot, /a/ - pat; /e/ - pet, /u/ - put, /ə/ - putt, /i/ - pit, /l/ - lull, /ŋ/ - lung, /ʃ/ - ship, /ĵ/ - chip, /k/ - kip, /ʒ/ - azure, /ʒ/ - juice, /g/ - goose, /m/ - mill, /f/ - fill, /p/ - pill, /v/ - vim, /b/ - bill, /n/ - nil, /s/ - sill, /θ/ - thill, /t/ - till, /z/ - zip, /ð/ - this, /d/ - dill, /h/ - hill, /#/ - ill. The prosodic opposition, stressed vs. unstressed, splits each of the vowel phonemes into two.

FIGURE 9 "Phonematic Pattern of English Broken Down into Inherent Distinctive Features" from R. Jakobson, *Selected Writings*, vol. 8, *Major Works, 1976–1980*, ed. S. Rudy (Berlin: Mouton de Gruyter, 1988, p. 643)

it (vocalic/nonvocalic), or by opening and closing the uvula one can allow sound to resonate in the nasal cavity or not allow sound to resonate (nasal/oral), and so on. In the same way certain movements implied other movements opposed to them: peripheral constriction of sound in the mouth was opposed to medial constriction of sound in the mouth (grave/acute). Jakobson identified twelve binary pairs of options which accounted for the production of all possible phonemes. Empirical evidence showed that phonetic systems were structured by these binary pairs. For example, the use of any of these sound components in any language necessarily implied the coexistence within the phonetic system of its opposite feature. Thus, if a language used the grave feature, the acute feature was also present in the system. Humans have a very poorly developed capacity to detect sound stimuli in an absolute fashion. Auditory perception responds to relations, and the relations of speech sounds were structured by the binary opposition of what Jakobson called *distinctive features*. Figure 9 shows the system of distinctive features behind the set of phonemes used in standard British English.

Rather than simple notes, the discovery of the distinctive features allowed one to think of phonemes as musical "chords" or "bundles of features." Some of these chords are more closely related than others. /P/, for example, is opposed to /f/, /v/, or /b/ by only a single feature. /P/ and /t/ stand in a significant relationship with one another through the grave/acute opposition. The same is true of /b/ and /d/ or /m/ or /n/. The distinctive features allow us to see previously hidden logical relationships between phonemes. We can express these in algorithms such as *m:p :: n:t* (focusing on the nasal/oral opposition) or *p:b :: t:d* (focusing on the tense/lax opposition).

For our purposes the importance of Jakobson's theory of distinctive features is the way it reveals and solves serious shortcomings in Saussure's concept of system. The relation of signifiers to the syntagmatic axis of language and to diachrony, mentioned above, is called into question by Jakobson's demonstration that even within the smallest component of the signifier there exist paradigmatic relations and a synchronous system. A more immediate problem is the simple impracticability of Saussure's model of language. He presents us with an abstract system directly governing the terms within the system, but between individual terms and systemic totality there is no middle ground. To understand the meaning of a single word, one needs to grasp its place within the totality of the system. Some role was played by oppositions, but Saussure leaves the impression that oppositions operate indifferently in all directions and thus ultimately implicate the entire system in any derivation of relational meaning. Such a view of language is open to serious objections.

Theoretically, it is impossible to see how meaning can be produced from a formula like *the meaning of X = all the other terms in a language − X*. If a term has no positive content, but depends for its meaning on its opposition to all other terms simultaneously, one will end up jumping from term to term, without any hope of understanding any of them, but somehow, after reaping an entire field of nullities, Saussure thinks that our bag will suddenly become replete with relational meaning. It is as if you had a dictionary in which each entry X simply invited you to *See Entry Y*, and Y in turn says *See Under Z*, and so on, until the last entry refers you to X again. There seems little hope of enlightenment at the end of the quest. Jacques Derrida (1976) exploited this paradox and suggested that meaning in language is indeed "endlessly deferred," in effect, impossible. The more empirically-minded will conclude that the source of the failure is not in language, but in the account.

The view that the components of language have meaning only in relation to the entire system also makes it impossible to understand how anyone acquires language in the first place. If one cannot learn a language gradually, bit by bit, it must be acquired all at once or not at all. But this all-or-nothing approach to language does not square with our experience of language acquisition: children and adults do acquire language step by step and manage to communicate effectively long before attaining complete mastery of the total system.

The first problem is solved quite simply by Jakobson's demonstration that the total system of language is organized into smaller, more local, systems, and that these more local systems can function without reference to the linguistic totality. Thus, there is no "endless deferral of meaning." The value of a given term is immediately related to a manageable bundle of other terms. Language is acquired bundle by bundle. Understanding, of course, increases as one advances toward mastery of the system. But it is intuitively obvious that "peach" and "plum" are more important distinctions for one struggling to grasp "apple," than are terms like "persnicketiness."

The problem of language acquisition is solved by the demonstration that the structures intermediary between term and totality are all arranged hierarchically, so that each lower-level system constitutes a term in each higher-level system. Jakobson showed not only that children acquire phonemes step by step following the same sequence of acquisitions, no matter what their language, but, by means of the distinctive features, he was able to explain the logic behind these universal patterns (1971: 491):

> Ordinarily child language begins . . . with what psychopathologists have termed the "labial stage." In this phase speakers are capable only of one type of utterance, which is usually transcribed as /pa/. From the articulatory point of view the two constituents of this utterance represent polar configurations of the vocal tract: in /p/ the tract is closed at its very end while in /a/ it is opened as widely as possible at the front and narrowed toward the back, thus assuming the horn-shape of a megaphone. The combination of two extremes is also apparent on the acoustic level: the labial stop presents a momentary burst of sound without any great concentration of energy in a particular frequency band, whereas in the vowel /a/ there is no strict time limitation, and the energy is concentrated in a relatively narrow region of maximum aural sensitivity. In the first constituent there is an extreme limitation in the time domain but no ostensible limitation in the frequency domain, whereas the second constituent shows no ostensible limitation in the time domain but a maximum limitation in the frequency domain. Consequently, the diffuse stop with its maximal reduction in the energy output offers the closest approach to silence, while the open vowel represents the highest energy output of which the human vocal apparatus is capable. This polarity between the minimum and the maximum of energy appears primarily as a CONTRAST between two successive units – the optimal consonant and the optimal vowel.

In the next stage the child acquires its first consonantal opposition, that between nasal and oral, followed by grave/acute, making it possible to distinguish /p/ from /m/, /p/ from /t/, and /m/ from /n/. It is no accident that the baby words for mother and father in almost all languages make use of these distinctions. The earliest sound distinctions are coordinated with the earliest semantic distinctions: "papa" and "mama." Each new binary opposition increases the child's phonetic range exponentially. Though there is some truth in the claim that our appreciation of /p/ increases in subtlety

STRUCTURALISM 217

when the entire system is in place, it is enough that its binary opposite be present to make it a functional distinction.

Lévi-Strauss and structural anthropology

Lévi-Strauss (1908–94) met Jakobson while he was at New York's New School for Social Research in 1941–5. This acquaintance proved the single most formative element in the development of Lévi-Strauss's structural theory. From Jakobson he took his sense of the importance of binary oppositions, hierarchical organization, the characterization of primary structural units as "chords" or "bundles of elements," and the belief that structuralism could reveal universal truths about human culture and the human brain, not only at the level of structure, as Saussure argued and as Jakobson had shown in developing a universal phonetics, but even at the level of specific contents, as revealed, for example, by the quasi-universals of baby-talk.

Before going on to look at myths, it may be instructive to consider how cultural systems in general can behave like language. The subject of kinship is deliciously paradoxical. Kinship appears to be a fact of nature: mothers, fathers, sisters, and brothers are simple givens, not cultural artifacts to be shaped and organized like narratives. True, sisters and brothers are products of nature, but it is not biological sisters and brothers which constitute a kinship system, it is what we make of them. The meaning of "sister" and "brother" is established not by the natural contents of the terms themselves, *but by the relations between members of the family group*. Nature merely provides a raw material which culture works into a meaningful system.

In his essay "The Structural Method in Linguistics and Anthropology" (1958 Ch. 2), Lévi-Strauss considers a peculiar problem: in most primitive societies a special relationship exists between a boy and his maternal uncle. The problem is that these relationships may be of two antithetical types (1958: 49): "In one case the maternal uncle represents family authority; he is feared and obeyed, and possesses certain rights over his nephew. In the other case, the nephew enjoys privileges of familiarity in relation to his uncle and can treat him more or less as his victim." Earlier anthropologists noted that the nature of the relationship between the boy and his maternal uncle is always the inverse of the relationship between the boy and his father: if the relationship with the uncle is distant and hostile, the relationship with the father is close and friendly; if the relationship with the uncle is close and friendly, that with the father is distant and hostile. Lévi-Strauss points out that the problem is more broadly based: he gives a number of examples to show that in every society the relationship between husband and wife is antithetical to that between brother and sister, i.e., if the relationship between a man and his wife is warm and friendly, then the relationship between brother and sister is distant and hostile, and if the husband and wife are distant, then brother and sister are close. These two sets of relationships, joined in antithetical pairs, in fact form part of a system which determines one friendly and one hostile relation in each generation.

	Affinal group	*Consanguineous group*
Different generation	maternal uncle/nephew	father/son
Same generation	husband/wife	brother/sister

One can express these relationships with the formula:

maternal uncle/nephew : brother/sister :: father/son : husband/wife.

The formula states that for each pair, if the intergenerational relationship is positive, then the intragenerational relationship will be negative, and vice versa, and if the affinal relationship is positive, then the consanguineous relationship will be negative, and vice versa. Each pair of terms is opposed in the same way.

```
BROTHER − SISTER + HUSBAND
      +            /
        BROTHER − SISTER + HUSBAND
              +            /
                BROTHER − SISTER + HUSBAND
                      OR
BROTHER + SISTER − HUSBAND
      \            +
        BROTHER + SISTER − HUSBAND
              \            +
                BROTHER + SISTER − HUSBAND
```

The reason for this structure is the exchange of women. In all groups women are an item of exchange and they are exchanged by men. The maternal uncle is an important part of the system because a man gives his sister or daughter to another man, and the second man's son will be obliged to do the same. The friendly/hostile opposition is kept in place by incest and fidelity taboos, designed to keep this system of exchange between groups active. In order to understand this we have to conceive of the possibility of unilineal descent, i.e., incestuous procreation within one group. It is *theoretically* conceivable that you have a society with only warm relations between parents and children and siblings. In theory (?) this would encourage incest and bring an end of the communication between affinal groups through the exchange of women. You could also have a society where all relations are hostile. This would also end all communication. The structural solution to this dilemma is to create alternating relations of warmth and hostility between generations and between groups. If an uncle is distant with his sister, he will be close to her son; if a wife is distant with her husband, she will be close to her brother. A system of divisive and cohesive forces link the two family groups together and prevent them from becoming isolated from one another. One could think of it as like a pump, "which perpetually 'pumps' women out of their consanguineous families in order to redistribute them in so many other domestic [i.e., affinal] groups, which turn into consanguineous families in their turn" and whose function it is "to ensure the permanency of the social group by interweaving, as in a textile, consanguineous and affinal ties" (Lévi-Strauss 1958: 342; the "pump" metaphor is suggested by Jacobson and Schoepf's English translation of Lévi-Strauss's less colourful "extract"). But most importantly, one must think of it as a form of social communication, an ongoing "dialogue" between two groups, who have taken the raw material of nature and reshaped it into a language, precisely for the purpose of binding their families into a social unit.

The structural study of myth

Lévi-Strauss's theory of myth is summarized in "The Structural Study of Myth," an essay first published in 1955 (in Sebeok 1965: 81–106; expanded in Lévi-Strauss 1958: Ch. 11). He begins by calling attention to the basic contradiction which exercised all theories of myth: it appears that almost anything can happen in myth, its contents seem to defy the laws of logic and the norms of experience, yet nevertheless, despite the arbitrary appearance, myths of the same stamp and often with the same details reappear throughout the world. A similar problem faced linguists: like the comparatist and psychological (especially Jungian) schools of mythology, they looked at surface structures and tried to find the internal necessity which connected a sound and a meaning (e.g., liquid consonants [r, l] correspond to a flux in nature: *r*iver, *f*low, *f*lu). No progress was possible until it was determined that verbal signs were arbitrary. The condition for creating meaning lies not in the material nature of signs, but in the manner of their combination.

Myth relates to language in two ways: it is like language; it is also part of language. Language reveals a hierarchy of levels: phonemes, the smallest sound units, combine to create morphemes (words or meaningful parts of words), which in turn combine to form semantemes as the unit components of the sentence. But linguistic analysis could be continued beyond the sentence level to include narratives. Lévi-Strauss posits the existence of "gross constituent units" of mythic narratives, or *mythemes*. The established sequence of linguistic hierarchy (phoneme ⇒ morpheme ⇒ semanteme) has its own logic: the phoneme is constituted by groups of distinctive features; a phoneme grouped with other phonemes constitutes a morpheme; a morpheme grouped with other morphemes forms a semanteme; a semanteme grouped with other semantemes forms a sentence. The mytheme should, accordingly, be composed of groups of sentences. Furthermore, Lévi-Strauss argues, the logic of the linguistic series requires that the value of each mytheme must be constituted relationally, just as phonemes, morphemes, and semantemes are relational. Each mytheme, therefore, can be described as a "bundle of relations," and it is only when these bundles are combined with other bundles that they acquire significance. It is clear that Lévi-Strauss has Jakobson's analysis of the phoneme in mind.

There is one other respect in which myth functions like language. It partakes of both temporal dimensions of language, the diachronic and the synchronic. The telling of a myth is an act of *parole*. Like any utterance it is governed by nonreversible time, as the description of one event follows another in linear sequence. But myth is also like *langue*, an abstract system which is simultaneously present to the mind, and so has an aspect of timelessness, or reversible time. Indeed, myth has an unusually close connection with *langue* and the synchronic. This is evident in some of the special qualities of myth which set it off from other forms of narrative. Myths are often set at the very beginning of time, outside of historical time. Moreover, the value of myth derives from its quality of permanence which binds past, present, and future together, and so its very contents express this ideal of reversible time. In this it most resembles political ideology: history is written to retroject present-day values, to endow them with a distinguished pedigree, and to suggest their permanence for all time to come. Perhaps the most compelling evidence of myth's special relation to time can be evinced by a comparison between myth and poetry. Of all forms of narrative, myth is least affected by the medium and style of its delivery; a myth is easily translatable. In this it stands opposite to poetry, where virtually everything is lost in the translation. There are two ways of expressing this: (1) myth stands at a kind of zero degree of enunciation or *parole* and tends toward pure system, whereas poetry stands at an absolute degree of *parole*; (2) myth has a special relation with signifieds, poetry with signifiers, or to put it otherwise, myth is more oriented toward meanings than expressions. This contrast between myth and poetry gives expression to the by-now familiar alignments of the divisions of language, which Lévi-Strauss inherits from Saussure.

Myth	Poetry
langue	*parole*
signified	signifier
synchronic	diachronic
paradigmatic	syntagmatic

Like the phoneme, myth, seen from one perspective, was governed by *parole*, the diachronic and the syntagmatic, but, like Jakobson and his phonemes, Lévi-Strauss was more interested in seeing it from another, where it appeared as *langue*, synchronic and paradigmatic.

Once this theoretical apparatus is in place, the procedure for identifying mythemes looks deceptively simple. Take an individual myth. Break down the story into the shortest possible sentences. Write each sentence on an index card bearing a number corresponding to its place in the unfolding of the story. This is basically the same procedure as that taken by Propp in defining his functions. But Lévi-Strauss does not privilege verbs in the same way. Each sentence is a relation between a *character* and an *action*, and not the kind of disembodied action envisioned by Propp. Indeed some cards, as we will see, contain only nouns: characters, proper names, objects.

These index cards still do not constitute mythemes, but only the constituent units of mythemes. This is apparent first from the analogy of the phoneme. Just as in the case of phonemes, where it was not the juxtaposition of phonemes which produced meaningful distinction, but the multitude of relations engaged by their distinctive features, so the significant units of myth are not single index cards but bundles of index cards. Secondly, the specific relations between a character and an action found on the file cards cannot be mythemes because they function in temporal succession and do not show that aspect of reversible time which characterizes myth. The bundle of index cards forming a mytheme are to be found not on the syntagmatic but the paradigmatic axis. Their relations will be conceptual relations, not relations of physical collocation. To find the units that fit the theoretical prescription, Lévi-Strauss invites you to participate in a thought experiment (1958: 234):

> Imagine the archaeologist of the future falling to earth from another planet, after all life on Earth has disappeared, and excavating the site of one of our libraries. These archaeologists will be entirely ignorant of our writing but they will try to decipher it. After they have discovered that the alphabet as

we print it is read from left to right and from top to bottom, there will still be a category of volumes which will remain undecipherable in this way. These will be orchestra scores, preserved in the music section. Our archaeologists will no doubt attempt to read the scores starting at the top of the page and reading all in succession. Then they will notice that certain groups of notes repeat themselves at intervals either in an identical or a partial fashion, and that certain melodic contours, apparently separated from one another, offer analogies between themselves. Perhaps they will ask themselves then whether these contours, sooner than being read in succession, should not be treated like elements of a whole which have to be read simultaneously. At that point they will have discovered the principle of what we call harmony. An orchestra score makes no sense except when read diachronically along an axis (page after page, and from left to right), but at the same time, synchronically along another axis, from top to bottom. In other words, all the notes placed on the same vertical line form a large constitutive unity, a bundle of relations.

Lévi-Strauss then demonstrates the theory using the myth of Oedipus, starting from the story of Cadmus and the foundation of Thebes and extending to the quarrel between Oedipus's sons, the civil war resulting in their deaths, and the story of Antigone. Sequential events are to be read from left to right. The "harmonies," or mythemes, are arranged in four columns.

I	II	III	IV
Cadmus looks for his sister Europa		Cadmus kills the serpent	
	the Spartoi kill each other		Labdacus (father of Laius) = "lame" (?)
	Oedipus kills his father Laius		Laius (father of Oedipus) = "left-sided" (?)
		Oedipus kills the Sphinx	Oedipus = "swollen-foot" (?)
Oedipus marries his mother, Jocasta			
	Eteocles kills his brother, Polynices		
Antigone buries her brother, Polynices, despite the king's prohibition			

Reading down the columns one can find a common theme. Column I expresses "an overrating of blood relationships." Column II, by contrast, expresses "an underrating of blood relationships." Column III is slightly more elusive. Cadmus kills the serpent from whose teeth, when Cadmus sows them onto the ground, spring the original inhabitants of Thebes. The Sphinx is a creature which was born from the ground and it kills the inhabitants of Thebes. Killing these monsters are taken as analogous acts, their common theme being "a denial of autochthony," i.e., a denial of the belief that the original inhabitants of Thebes were born from the earth. Column IV presents not actions, but significant names, all of podiatric interest. To interpret these names Lévi-Strauss reaches far beyond Theban legend to find analogues in the native myths of North America: "In mythology it is a universal characteristic of men born from the Earth that at the moment they emerge from the depth they either cannot walk or they walk clumsily. This is the case of the chthonian beings in the mythology of the Pueblo . . . [and of] the Kwakiutl." The series of names indicating foot problems is then taken to express "an affirmation of auto-chthony." The deep-structural meaning of the myth can then be summed up by an algorithm expressing the relations between the four mythemes, a homology between two pairs of binary oppositions:

the overrating of blood relationships : the underrating of blood relationships ::
the denial of autochthony : the affirmation of autochthony

What does this meaning mean? According to Lévi-Strauss:

The myth has to do with the inability for a culture which holds the belief that mankind is autochthonous, to find a satisfactory transition between this theory and the knowledge that human beings are actually born from the union of man and woman. Although the problem obviously cannot be solved, the Oedipus myth provides a kind of logical tool which relates the original problem – born from one or born from two? – to the derivative problem – born from different or born from same?

There is some suggestion here that "the overrating of blood relationships" is an expression of "being born from same," because overrating implies incest (as between Oedipus and Jocasta), and hence being born from the same family, not different families. Unfortunately Lévi-Strauss is far from explicit in this demonstration. Indeed, the demonstration model has many problems which he did not care to deal with. One has to do with the precise function of this mythic algorithm. According to Lévi-Strauss the function of myth is to resolve cultural contradictions, especially those which set culture against nature, or cultural ideologies against the empirically known facts of nature (as the theory of autochthony is set against the facts of life). It does not really solve these contradictions, but by establishing pseudo*logical* resolutions, it serves to alleviate concern. Like music, it beguiles and soothes the savage breast when it is exercised by the contradictions of its collective ideology. In this respect it may be compared to the neurotic rituals, discussed by Freud, which provided fantastic resolutions to deep anxieties (see above, Section 3.1). Lévi-Strauss's explanation of the logical mechanism in the Oedipus myth is unfortunately one of the most unsatisfactory features of his demonstration: "The inability to connect two kinds of relationships is overcome (or rather replaced) by the assertion that the contradictory relationships are identical inasmuch as they are both self-contradictory in a similar way." This would appear to compound the problem rather than resolve it.

A far better explanation of the logic, and one more consistent with Lévi-Strauss's structuralist theories, is offered by John Peradotto (1977: 91–2). He points out that the two pairs of terms are not, in fact, "both self-contradictory in a similar way." Columns III and IV are what Aristotelian logic calls "contradictories." Contradictories allow no middle term: either one is autochthonous or one is not. But Columns I and II are "contraries." They do allow a middle term. The solution to the problem of overrating and underrating is quite simply giving something its proper rating:

III Denial of autochthony $\left.\begin{array}{c} \end{array}\right\}$ $\Longrightarrow$ $\left\{\begin{array}{l} \text{I Overrating blood relationships} \\ \textit{Proper rating of blood relationships} \\ \text{II Underrating blood relationships} \end{array}\right.$

IV Assertion of autochthony

In this way the problem of autochthony finds a pseudo-solution. By equating the contradictory to the contrary, the myth in effect offers the soothing reassurance that since $A = B$, and since B can be solved, therefore A can be resolved. If this is true, then myth acts like a thimblerigger's patter, beguiling the anxious savage, while trading his contradictories for contraries, and sending him home shortchanged but satisfied.

Superior features of Lévi-Strauss's structuralism

Before going on to consider these ideas more closely, let us pause briefly to compare Lévi-Strauss's method with that of his rivals. Lévi-Strauss's method is much more comprehensive than any of the previous myth analysts so far examined. He insists that nothing is to be left out of the interpretation. It is true that many of the events in the Theban cycle of myth have been left out of the analysis. But this is due to concision. Lévi-Strauss offers Oedipus only as a "demonstration model." It would be a simple matter to reinsert various events under the four columns of the analysis. Oedipus's curse upon his sons, Creon's refusal to bury his nephew Polynices, the burial, instead, of his niece Antigone, alive, in a cave – all these might find a place as examples of "underrating blood relations." "Affirmations of autochthony" might be found in the fact that Oedipus is taken from his parents and left exposed on the earth, or that Cadmus and his wife Harmonia are transformed into chthonic dragons, or that Antigone serves as a crutch for the infirm and aged Oedipus of podiatric fame. Lévi-Strauss himself mentions in passing that Jocasta's self-destruction can be placed under "denial of autochthony," though he does not say why. At a guess, dying by hanging from a noose in midair may be regarded as the structured opposite of springing to life from the ground. Here too, we could presumably include the suicides of Antigone, Haemon, and Eurydice. Lévi-Strauss also interprets Oedipus's self-blinding as an affirmation of autochthony in so far as wounding his head is a variation on wounding his feet (opposition "high/low").

The comprehensiveness of Lévi-Strauss's method of analysis is most evident when compared with that of Propp. He accounts for a great deal of information that Propp would have ignored: the relationships between characters, their physical characteristics, their names, and so on. In general, paradigmatic structuralism is far less selective in the material which it admits into the interpretation. In Burkert's "girl's tragedy," for example, many of the actions in the tale are omitted even when they occur in all the stories (such as the giving of birth to a male child which in some myths occurs before "tribulation," in others after), or regular functions such as the metamorphosis of the god or of the rape victim (which are dismissed as modalities of character), while the functions that he does include often depend on specific mythic variants (Ovid's version of Callisto and Arcas has no rescue by the son, but murder by the son and catasterism). By contrast, Lévi-Strauss admits all versions of a myth and claims that, since myth represents a zero degree of *parole*, all versions will reveal the same deep-structure (1958: 240):

> A striking example is offered by the fact that our interpretation may take into account, and is certainly applicable to, the Freudian use of the Oedipus myth. Although the Freudian problem has ceased to be that of autochthony *versus* bisexual reproduction, it is still the problem of understanding how *one* can be born from *two:* how it is that we do not have only one procreator, but a mother plus a father? Therefore, not only Sophocles, but Freud himself, should be included among the recorded versions of the Oedipus myth on a par with earlier or seemingly more "authentic" versions.

Lévi-Strauss goes even further to suggest that all related myths will have related structures, so that in principle one does not need to draw a sharp and arbitrary line where one decides that the myth of Oedipus ends and another myth begins. Other methodologies would start or stop their analysis of Oedipus at a point in the Theban cycle dictated by convenience, but Lévi-Strauss alleges that his structuralist interpretations will work no matter where the line is drawn.

5.5 MEDIATION

The function of myth, according to Lévi-Strauss, is to provide a solution to a cultural contradiction. The solution is never logical, strictly speaking, but it imitates logic. If the problem were capable of a purely logical solution, there would be no need to have recourse to myth. But myth can do what logic cannot, and so it serves as a kind of cultural trouble-shooter. Rather than thinking of it as a kind of placebo which creates the mere impression of a solution to a problem, it may be regarded as a mechanism for relieving anxiety.

Many find the intellectualism of Lévi-Strauss's theory odd and irreconciliable with their ideas about the primitive context of myth. It is difficult, for example to imagine the hairy and indigent savage tossing and turning in his bed, struggling to reconcile, in the depths of his soul, the theory of autochthony with his empirical observations on human reproduction. We are much more ready to think of him troubled by castration fear or worries about how to fill his belly. Lévi-Strauss would say that our reluctance to allow the savage such intellectual concerns is an inheritance from those Victorian myths which depict the savage as living almost entirely within his emotions and only using his brain to recognize something good to eat. Savages, he argues, use their intellects no less than the civilized, and for the same purposes, namely to give order to the world around them, for emotional security as well as the better manipulation of their resources. Savage minds are in no way qualitatively inferior and differ only by the contents of the variables used in making their equations: not logical abstractions, but the concrete images, myths, and symbols, which experience shows to be "good to think with." But even on this definition the work of myths is not purely intellectual. Ideas that appear purely theoretical on the surface may nonetheless carry a deep emotional investment. Indeed, a good deal of theoretical speculation seems ultimately to have as much or more to do with managing emotions than it does with any disinterested exercise of the rational faculty.

Mediators

Not all mythic problem-solving involves the explicit equation of contradictories with contraries that we found in the Oedipus myth. Many
mythic structures simply equate an extreme opposition with a milder one
(a contrary is just a special case of milder contradiction). We can think of
the equation of big contradictions with small contradictions as a form of
logical fine-chopping, which in theory might be extended until the poles
of the original opposition seem to merge into one. The narrower oppositions can be said to "mediate" the big contradictions. Another form of
mediation is effected by symbols, characters, or actions in which the terms
of the contradiction merge. These are called *mediators*.

In his essay on the "Structural Study of Myth" Lévi-Strauss gives a number of examples of types of characters or objects which serve as mythic
mediators. There are certain kinds of "liminal" characters, for example, the
"tricksters" of North American indigenous myths, who mediate between
life and death. The trickster is almost always a raven or a coyote. Why
is this? It is because they are carrion eaters. Consider the oppositions listed
in the following chart.

Initial oppositions	First triad	Second triad
life		
	agriculture	
		herbivores
		carrion eaters
	hunting	
		predators
	war	
death		

The initial opposition life/death allows no middle term. But the opposition can be assimilated to economic activities which support life by means
of killing, and to this extent lie somewhere between the extremes of the
initial opposition. Agriculture supports life by producing plant life and
partakes of death only in the sense that harvesting kills the crops. It can
be opposed to hunting, which sustains life through killing a life one has
not produced, and an animal life more obviously alive with a life like our
own. A further opposition can be added by the opposition hunting/war.
War is like hunting in that it involves a chase and killing, but it sustains
life only indirectly, while it takes a human life and so produces a more serious form of death. To this triad of economic activities, one can compare

the economic activities of animals. Herbivores harvest plants and so practice a kind of agriculture, though they do not themselves bring the plants to life. Predators are like hunters in that they kill what they eat, but also a little like warriors in that they can kill men. Midway between these extremes stand carrion eaters, which are like predators in that they eat flesh, but like herbivores in that they do not kill what they eat.

This attempt to mediate the opposition of life/death is expressed not only in native North American myth, but also in its language and ritual. In ritual, for example, scalps possess a certain magical power because they are also middle terms in the same system of thought: they are products of war, but they are harvested like grain. In the Tewa language the words for coyote, scalp, and mist derive from the same root, *pose*. This may be because all are connected in thought as mediators between aligned oppositions: the carrion eater between herbivores and predators; the scalp between agriculture and war; and mist between sky and earth. All are connected with the opposition of life to death.

Lévi-Strauss gives several examples of mediators which appear in many unrelated cultures. (It is instructive to compare these with Freud's universal symbols discussed in Section 3.2.) Clothing is a mediator between culture and nature: naked we are all children of nature; clothed we are fully products of culture; by clothing we manifest all cultural differences: status, rank, nationality, gender, profession, etc. Shoes mediate between us and the earth, between high and low, and as vehicles of locomotion, between here and there. Garbage is another mediator between culture and nature. It is something we throw out of civilized space into natural space. Similarly rats, lice, and other vermin mediate between culture and nature in many societies, since they are unwanted products of nature, but they breed in the midst of the human community, and most prolifically where the population is most dense.

There are mediators between heaven and earth: mist, ashes (which rise from the fire), soot which rises from the hearth and climbs the chimney. Since they mediate between natural highs and lows, they can also mediate between cultural highs and lows, high status and low status, for example. Both in Native American and in European thought, ashes, clothing, and garbage mediate between low status and high status. This, says Lévi-Strauss, is why old shoes, soot, and chimney-sweeps are supposed to bring good luck in European folklore. In Europe one used to kiss chimney-sweeps for good luck. The Greeks mark a cross with candle soot above the door every Easter. At midnight on New Year's Eve Italians throw old furniture and clothing into the streets. Old shoes appear on charm-bracelets, are tied to the bumper of the wedding car, and until recently it was a widespread European custom to throw a shoe or boot after the coach of newlyweds as they departed. This custom seems in fact to go back to classical antiquity. On an Attic red-figure pot (name-vase of the Painter of the Athens Wedding) sandals arc thrown after a wedding party (Boardman 1989: Fig. 295). Ancient Greek iconography uses sandals as fertility symbols, closely associated with weddings, erotic scenes, and Aphrodite. In this case the sandals mediate not only between high and low, but between sterility and fertility, life and death. The magic of such charms and rituals, according to Lévi-Strauss, has less to do with their sexual symbolism, as Freud maintained, than with their power to mediate between fundamental oppositions.

Cinderella

In his essay on "Structure and Form" (1958: Ch. 8), Lévi-Strauss locates the principal difference between myths and folktales in the strength and quality of the oppositions they mediate. Myths serve a more central and serious cultural function, hence deal with more important cultural anxieties and are subject to stricter demands for logical coherence, to concerns about religious orthodoxy, and to pressure to support cultural values and institutions. Folktales develop in a popular milieu which often sets itself in opposition to the cultural establishment, so that myth and folktale may stand in ideological opposition to one another. But folktale is subject to fewer cultural pressures, since it is, by definition, less important. Folktale oppositions are therefore weaker than in myth, and are usually different in kind from mythic oppositions. In myth the oppositions are sooner cosmological, metaphysical, and natural, while the oppositions in folktale tend to be local, social, and moral. Ultimately this distinction relates to the opposition of nature to culture, which is fundamental to Lévi-Strauss's conception of myth: we could say that *myth : folktale :: nature : culture.*

The tale of Cinderella gives a good example of how tales can function to alleviate real, everyday concerns. Most people will know the tale from the Disney cartoon version. I take this summary from Pace (1982: 251), who also provides the point of departure for the following analysis.

> The death of her father consigns the beautiful Cinderella to the role of scullery maid, while her wicked stepmother and two ugly stepsisters enjoy the riches of the house. When these ungenerous step-relatives leave to attend the royal ball, Cinderella is left behind. Her fairy godmother, however, intervenes, and produces a series of magical transformations: rags into a sumptuous dress, boots into glass slippers, pumpkin into a coach, mice into coachmen, etc. Cinderella is sent off to the ball with all the trappings of wealth, but with

the admonition that she must return before midnight. At the ball, the prince falls in love with Cinderella, but at the stroke of midnight she flees the palace, leaving behind the glass slipper her fairy godmother had created for her. The prince, determined to marry this mysterious beauty, searches the kingdom for the woman who can fit into the tiny slipper. The stepsisters attempt to put it on and fight among themselves, but only Cinderella can wear it. The story ends with the marriage of Cinderella and the humiliation of her stepmother and stepsisters.

The tale is structured around the personal transformation of Cinderella, and this in turn is effected by a series of object transformations. The personal transformation of Cinderella is expressed as a diachronic opposition between low status at the beginning of the tale and high status at the end of it. But throughout the tale there are also synchronic oppositions which stress the importance of this transformation, and these synchronic oppositions are expressed in terms of the personal relationships between the heroine and all the other characters in the story. The most obvious opposition in this tale is between Cinderella and her stepfamily. We could express the opposition between Cinderella's and her stepfamily's personal charms with the following chart:

Cinderella	Stepfamily
beautiful	ugly
industrious	lazy
humble	arrogant
passive	aggressive
-----------------	-----------------
low-status	high-status
dirty	clean
hated by all	mutually loved

The list of opposed qualities falls into two groups, depending on whether the qualities are natural or cultural.

	Nature	Culture
Cinderella	High	Low
Stepfamily	Low	High

It is easy to see that nature/culture distinctions account for the qualities of all the characters in the story. Opposed to Cinderella's natural family on one side is her stepfamily, family only by virtue of civic law and hence a cultural family. On the other side Cinderella's stepfamily is balanced by a family by virtue of religious law, family in the eyes of God, represented by Cinderella's godmother. Let us call it a supernatural family, since "godmother" suggests a position mediate between divine and human. Indeed, the story itself insists upon this supernatural position by identifying her as a "*fairy*-godmother." The contrast between cultural and supernatural families is enabled by the disappearance of the middle term, Cinderella's natural family, of whose absence we are constantly reminded, because the death of Cinderella's mother and father are what delivered her into the clutches of her evil stepfamily to begin with. Opposed to the cultural and supernatural families there is the prince, who comes from yet another family. We are encouraged to infer that his natural qualities are like Cinderella's: he is good, handsome, etc., but he stands at a cultural high which is opposed to Cinderella's cultural low. At the end of the tale this cultural opposition will be dissolved when Cinderella and the prince unite to form a new natural family.

It will be noted that there is a strict symmetry in the male/female opposition which expresses itself at the syntagmatic level. The story begins with the death of Cinderella's father which causes Cinderella to acquire low status; she acquires high status by gaining a new male relation, the prince, her future husband. These events form the beginning and end of the tale. This framing opposition is strictly balanced by the interior opposition on the female side, where the acquisition of an evil stepmother (on the death of her mother) leads to low status (actuated after the death of her father), but the evil stepmother is counterbalanced by the good fairy godmother, who helps her gain high status.

Culture	Nature	Supernature
Stepfamily	Family	Godfamily
Female (triple)	Male 1	Female
	Male 2	

The actual mediation between low and high status is effected by objects which mediate between culture and nature: Cinderella's rags become a beautiful gown; the vermin and garbage around her (mice, rats, pumpkins, etc.) become symbols of high status (footmen, horses, coach). The choice of the pumpkin is perhaps due to the fact that it is a garden vegetable and hence a part of culture, but in Europe, at least, it is treated as only semi-edible, and in this respect close to weeds, which are unwanted products of nature. Pumpkins are used as pig fodder and eaten by the very poor. In some parts of Europe it was customary for women to reject proposals of marriage by sending their suitors pumpkins, apparently to signify that the suitors were of insufficient social standing (the custom survived in the Ukraine until the last century, and even now дáти гарбузá, "give a pumpkin," is a popular idiom for "refuse a proposal of marriage"). The coach (the wedding vehicle) stands in significant opposition to the pumpkin (culture : nature :: high : low :: marriage : celibacy).

The final transformation, however, is effected by a glass slipper, originally an old shoe transformed by the godmother. To understand the structural role of the glass slipper one must make reference to the folk ritual of throwing old shoes at the coach of the departing bride and groom at European weddings. Cinderella's departure from the ball is an inversion of this ritual. In the wedding ritual the coach carries the united couple; in *Cinderella* the coach carries Cinderella alone, forcibly separating her from the prince. In the wedding ritual the shoe is thrown by others at the coach of the departing couple; in *Cinderella* a departing member of the couple leaves the shoe behind. Yet in the end the marriage ritual is restored when the groom and the shoe catch up with Cinderella. A comparatist or ritualist might be tempted to suppose that Cinderella was an etiological myth for the marriage rite, but it is clear that the tale simply expresses the same unconscious ideas as the rite. We could say that the tale does its work of mediation in part by accessing the same social codes as the marriage ritual.

For the listener, the mediation between culture and nature is effected by Cinderella herself. The name "Cinderella" comes from "cinder," and all the corresponding names in European languages refer to cinders or ash (cf. French *Cendrillon*, Italian *Cenerentola*, German *Aschputtel*, Russian *Zolushka*), and ashes mediate between low and high places, as we have seen. For Cinderella herself the rise from low to high is effected by her opposite, a slipper of glass, a substance opposed to soot as translucence is opposed to murk. Like soot, too, glass is a product of fire, but one which melts down under the flame, rather than rising with it. Between Cinderella and the slipper stands an opposition between light and dark, homologous to high and low. The slipper (light) was left behind by the girl (dark) at the liminal moment (midnight) between day and night, light and dark. There are other medial characteristics about Cinderella: she is an orphan, hence at the very margins of culture, but soon to find her place at its center as princess; she is also a nubile virgin, hence at a midpoint between sterility and fertility, girlhood and womanhood, her father's house and her husband's house. Moreover, she cleans but is dirty; she is affectionate but hated: she embodies the contradiction which arises in the lack of reciprocity between culture and nature.

At the root of this tale is the age-old social anxiety about class distinctions. The upper classes justify their privilege by saying they are better, hence deserve more. According to them, class divisions are rooted in nature. Yet it is a manifest fact – the lower classes are quick to point out – that "evil flourishes like the green bay tree." The story of Cinderella represents a kind of collective popular wish that it were really true that social privilege resulted from natural merit and that a strict correspondence existed between the qualities endowed by nature and culture. At the end of the story, of course, this is what actually occurs: Cinderella becomes a princess and the stepfamily is humiliated. In folktale, the element of wish-fulfillment is more direct and obvious because under considerably less constraint. But note that the wish is fulfilled less by direct possession by the imagination of the object of desire, than by a logical operation which would seem to secure its object forever by incorporating the utopic vision within the order of things.

Cinderella : Charila :: folktale : myth

A comparison can help clarify the distinction made earlier between myth and folktale, between the former's cosmological and natural oppositions and the latter's social and moral oppositions, and between the way myth and folktale give vent to cultural desires. In folktale wish-fulfillment seems relatively direct and obvious; in myth it is repressed and deeply submerged, but at the same time its logical operations seem more exuberant and grandiose. Plutarch describes a myth and associated rite which were told and practiced at Delphi where he was a priest in the early second century AD (*Moralia* 293B–F):

> As a consequence of drought, famine afflicted the people of Delphi. The citizens came with their wives and children as suppliants before the king's door. He gave some barley and pulse to the more illustrious citizens as there was not enough for everyone. An as yet small orphan girl approached him and, when she persisted, he struck her with his sandal and threw his sandal in her face. Though she was poor and abandoned, she was not ignoble by nature, so she went away, took off her waistband and hanged herself. As the famine continued and disease also erupted in the community, the prophetess gave an oracle to the king that he must propitiate Charila, the maiden who had killed herself. So they discovered, with some difficulty, that this was the name of the girl whom the king had struck and they performed a sort of sacrifice and rite of purification combined, which they still perform today every eight years. The king sits in state and hands out barley and pulse to everyone, citizen and stranger alike. A childlike effigy of Charila is brought before him and, when all have gotten their share, the king strikes the effigy with his sandal. Then the leader of the Thyiads picks up the effigy and carries it to a gully, and there they tie a rope around its neck and bury it in the place they buried Charila when she hanged herself.

In this story the oppositions are more pronounced than in *Cinderella*. The powerful king confronts the helpless orphan; the contrast is marked on several scales: social (high status/low status), economic (rich/poor), relational ("father of the community"/child without parents), and biological (adult male/female child). Charila, like Cinderella, is a mediating figure, but in this case, Charila does not stand between high and low status, but between poles that encompass and far exceed this opposition: she stands between life and death. The ritual commemorates an event which took place at a time of famine when the community's survival was in question. As an orphan, a child of the dead, and a maiden too young to bear life, Charila was well-suited to mediate between life and death. As one living on the margins of community life she was well-suited to mediate between the community and the world outside. The ritual expresses this mediation in a movement from the palace at the heart of the community to the wild places beyond. There is even a high/low opposition between the myth and the ritual: in the former, the maiden hangs herself, presumably from a tree, whereas in the ritual her effigy, with a rope around its neck, is lowered into a chasm and buried. The myth is clearly an etiology for a scapegoat ritual. But the myth's efficacy in large part derives from the way its structure perverts the rituals of marriage and sacrifice. The king's throwing of a shoe in her face is presumably meant to transfer the threat of death from the community to the girl, just as throwing a sandal at a wedding is meant to transfer fertility to the bride. And as opposed to departing in procession with her husband, Charila departs alone, and she loosens her waistband, not to consummate marriage – the expression "loosen her waistband" is a standard euphemism in Greek for the consummation of marriage – but to end life. Charila is also the opposite of the "basket-bearer" who leads an ordinary sacrifice (cf. section 4.4). The basketbearer must be a nubile maiden of aristocratic family whose parents, by cultic requirement, must both be alive, but Charila is a beggar, orphan, and mere girl. Moreover the basketbearer carries the barley which is distributed to the participants at the sacrifice and then thrown at the animal before it is killed. In this myth and ritual, the king usurps the basketbearer's role, Charila that of the victim. The threatened community withheld the barley from Charila, but threw a shoe at her to make her the sacrifice.

5.6   TOTAL STRUCTURE

Lévi-Strauss and the paradigmatic

The distinction generally made between syntagmatic structuralism (in the style of Propp) and paradigmatic structuralism (in the style of Lévi-Strauss), while widely current, and in some ways helpful, is also misleading. As we saw in Section 5.3, structuralism requires a total account of all aspects of a mythic narrative. Unlike Propp's formalism, true structuralism does not permit itself to dispose of all intractable elements of a narrative with the convenient claim that they are neither essential nor rule-governed. On the contrary, true structuralism is a totalizing theory: analysis is incomplete until every aspect of a narrative has been explained. To the extent, then, that the distinction between "syntagmatic" and "paradigmatic" structuralism implies that it must be one or the other, but not both, the terms are misleading. It is nevertheless true that the two chief pioneers of the structural analysis of narrative did privilege one axis over the other. Propp ignored the paradigmatic altogether. Lévi-Strauss merely treats the syntagmatic chain as a means to the end of establishing the paradigmatic relations. More than merely privileging "harmonies" over "melodies," Lévi-Strauss would have us believe that the melodies are there only to supply the intervals of the harmonic chords. This is already clear in his description of the structural method in "The Structural Study of Myth" (see above, Section 5.4), where no attempt was made to explain the linear progress of the myth of Oedipus. But it is most explicit in *The Raw and the Cooked* (1964: 313):

> Considered on its own, every syntagmatic sequence must be judged meaningless: either because no meaning is immediately apparent, or because we think we see a meaning, but do not know if it is the right one. In order to overcome this difficulty, there are but two procedures. One consists in dividing the syntagmatic sequence into segments that can be laid on top of one another, which you can then show to constitute variations on one and the same theme [as in the treatment of Oedipus]. The other procedure, which is complementary to the first, consists in placing a syntagmatic sequence in its totality – in other words, a complete myth – over other myths or segments of myths. In each case, therefore, it is a matter of replacing a syntagmatic sequence with a paradigmatic sequence; the difference is that in the first case the paradigmatic entity is extracted from the syntagmatic chain, and in the second it is the sequence that is the whole chain that is incorporated into it. But whether the whole is made up of parts of the sequence, or whether the sequence itself is included as a part, the principle remains the same. Two syntagmatic sequences, or fragments of the same sequence, which, considered in isolation, contain no sure meaning, together acquire one simply from the fact that they stand in opposition. And because the meaning emerges at the precise moment when they are brought together, it is clear that it did not exist previously in some hidden but present state like an inert residue in each myth or fragment of myth when isolated. The meaning is entirely in the dynamic relation which simultaneously underlies several myths or parts of the same myth, and as a result of which these myths, or parts of myths, acquire a rational existence and take shape together as opposable pairs of one and the same set of transformations.

In depositing rational order and meaning solely in the paradigmatic axis, Lévi-Strauss shows himself a better student of Saussure than of Jakobson. Since the division between paradigmatic and syntagmatic rests upon the distinction between synchrony and diachrony, Lévi-Strauss, like Saussure, takes great pains to extenuate the importance of time and temporal sequence in mythic narrative. Myths are described as timeless and this timelessness allegedly endows myth with its unique power and beauty. Indeed, apart from the demonstration model of the Oedipus myth, Lévi-Strauss avoided myths from historical, voluble, "hot" cultures, and focused almost exclusively upon simple, static, "cold" cultures, since he believed that myths in historical cultures were corrupted by a temporal consciousness which compromised myth's essential timelessness. Before the "finale" of his four-volume set of *Mythologiques* (1964–71), Lévi-Strauss even speaks of myth's power to "abolish time" with a kind of mystical rapture (1971: 542):

> Thus it may be that the most thankless of quests has gained its reward, namely, that of having located – without looking for or actually reaching it – the site of that long-promised land where calm besets the threefold impatience provoked by a "later" that we wait for, a "now" that slips away, and a voracious yesteryear that draws to itself, decomposes and collapses the future into the debris of a present already confused with the past. If this is so, our enquiry will not only have been a search for time lost. The category of time revealed by the study of myth is, in the final analysis, none other than that of which myths themselves have always dreamed: something better than time regained, time abolished, time as experienced by someone who, though born in the twentieth century, as he aged would (albeit unwittingly) be filled by the growing feeling that he had, in youth, the good fortune to live in the nineteenth century in the company of his elders who were part of it, just as they themselves had had the good fortune to be still living in the eighteenth century, through having been intimately acquainted with people belonging to that century – but they were not aware of the fact either; so that if we all joined forces to weld together the links in the chain – each period devoting itself to keeping the preceding one alive for the benefit of the next – time would truly be abolished. And if all mankind had known this from the beginning, we could have formed a conspiracy against time; the love of books and museums and the taste for antiques and curios attest, in a sometimes paltry way, that such an aspiration persists at the heart of contemporary civilization, naturally desperate, and inevitably vain, to stop time and make it move in the other direction.
>
> The interest we think we take in the past is, in fact, only an interest in the present; by binding the present firmly to the past, we believe we are making it more durable, and are pinning it down to prevent it breaking away and itself becoming part of the past. It is as if, when put into contact with

the present, the past would, by a miraculous osmosis, itself become present, and the present would thereby be protected from its fate, which is to become part of the past. That is surely what the myths strive to do for their subject matter; but the amazing thing is that they actually do it, by virtue of what they are.

Taken to its logical conclusion, the analysis of myths rises to a point where history cancels itself out.

"Timelessness" is what myths themselves signify. The abolition of time and history is what raises life and perceptions from the chaos of the phenomenal world to a sphere of pure logical relations, a world of Platonic forms, full of peace, stability, and meaning. Indeed, Lévi-Strauss was only interested in the myths of traditional and pre-"historical" cultures, "cold cultures" like those of the Amazonian Indians (as opposed to "hot" rapidly developing historical cultures like that of Greek antiquity). We will have an opportunity to contemplate Lévi-Strauss's metaphysical leap in Section 5.7. For the moment, I am only concerned to show that it is unnecessary to privilege the paradigmatic over the syntagmatic and the synchronic over the diachronic and to show that structuralism, in fact, works better when these binary oppositions are relaxed and when structuralist "values" such as meaning and order are distributed more evenly throughout the structure as a whole.

The myth of Athenian succession: Syntagmatic analysis

In his discussion of the myth of Oedipus Lévi-Strauss declares, in passing, that the Athenian myth of Cecrops is part of the same cycle and should, upon analysis, reveal the same anxiety about autochthony and being born of one or two. Peradotto offers an interesting analysis (1977) of this myth, upon which we can expand a little. Peradotto's analysis is concerned to vindicate the importance of time in myth on two levels: on the level of narrative, to show that the syntagmatic is part of the logical order of the myth; and on the level of culture, to show that myths from historical cultures are no less structured than those from static cultures. The myth of the early Athenian kings seems ideally suited to the project, since it is infused with history at both of these levels. It is structured as a genealogy, so that the myth itself insists on the importance of temporal succession. It also belongs to a complex culture which experienced rapid historical change throughout the period from which we derive our sources for the myth.

The story of the succession of the first eight Attic kings can be summarized as follows:

1 Cecrops springs from the earth, is the first King of Athens, has three daughters and a son who dies young without issue.
2 The kingdom passes to Cranaus, who springs from the earth, has three daughters and no sons, and is driven out by his son-in-law Amphictyon.
3 Amphictyon, who has also sprung from the earth, has no issue and is expelled by Erichthonius.
4 Erichthonius, both sprung from the earth and the child of a sexual union, has one son, Pandion, by Praxithea.
5 Pandion has two sons and two daughters by Zeuxippe.
6 Pandion's son, Erechtheus, has three sons and four daughters by Praxithea II.
7 Erechtheus's son, Cecrops II, has one son by Metiadusa.
8 Cecrops II's heir, Pandion II, has four sons by Pylia.

Initially the syntagmatic chain shows an increasing sterility in the autochthonous line (1–3: Cecrops, Cranaus, and Amphictyon, who all spring from the earth and have progressively fewer children). A more serious matter for the kingdom is the lack of peaceful hereditary succession: Cecrops's son dies without issue and the next two rulers have no sons. Later, this trend is reversed when the kings begin to be products of sexual union (4–8). There is a steady increase in fertility in the male line (except in the case of Cecrops II) and continuous succession to the throne of father to son. The myth, therefore, does appear to show the same anxiety we find in the analysis of the myth of Oedipus: a contradiction between the tradition of autochthony and empirical knowledge that humans are born from sexual union.

The myth of Athenian succession: Paradigmatic analysis

Erichthonius is at the midpoint and turning point of the story. The figure who reverses the trend from sterility to fertility and autochthony to sexual union also has a special character, which is only appreciable through paradigmatic analysis. Consider the story of Erichthonius's birth as told by Apollodorus (3.14.6):

Athena came to Hephaestus wishing to have some armour fashioned. Hephaestus, who had been abandoned by Aphrodite, fell into a sudden passion for Athena, and began to pursue her; but she fled. When with a great deal of effort he closed on her (he was lame, remember), he made an attempt at intercourse. But she was chaste and a virgin, and would not submit. He ejaculated on her thigh. In disgust, she wiped the semen away with wool and threw it on the ground. She fled away, and as the semen fell onto the earth, Erichthonius was born. Him Athena raised unknown to the other gods, wishing to make him immortal. And having put him in a chest, she committed it to Pandrosus, daughter of Cecrops, forbidding her to open it. But the sisters of Pandrosus opened up the chest in their curiosity, and beheld a snake coiled about the infant. As some would have it, they were killed by the snake; others say that Athena's anger drove them insane, and they threw themselves from the Acropolis. Erichthonius was raised by Athena herself in the sacred precinct.

Erichthonius succeeds where other kings fail because he is the perfect mediator. Namely he mediates the contradiction between autochthony and birth from two parents by being at one and the same time autochthonous *and* a product of a sexual relation. In addition, Peradotto brilliantly identifies (1977: 94):

> a measure of elegant logical "overkill" bound on making the solution really air-tight: Hephaestus bears the telltale lameness of the autochthonous, but more important for our original dilemma, he is born from *one,* as Athena is born from *one,* in the one case, male from unaided female, in the other, female from unaided male [a tradition at least as old as Hesiod's *Theogony* (924–9) makes the virgin birth of Hephaestus an act of vengeance by Hera for Zeus's unaided birth of Athena], and it is out of their explicit *difference,* their remaining apart (*eris*) that *Eri*-chthonius is paradoxically born. The cleansing wool (*erion*) is there to dramatize the original disjunction (*eris*) all the more.

As Peradotto shows, not just the genealogy of the hero, but the very name *Erichthonius* is determined by the mediating function assigned to him by the myth. The word *eris* in Greek means "strife," or "struggle," which divides individuals or a community. Hyginus adds that Poseidon was responsible for setting Hephaestus on Athena, because he was angry at being defeated in the contest for possession of Athens (to be described below). He mentions this in explanation of the name of Erichthonius (*Fabulae* 166): "they called him 'Erichthonius' because a dispute [or fight] is called *eris* in Greek, and the earth is called *chthon*." The name "Struggle-Earth" is therefore doubly determined in the mythic account: referring both to the dispute between Athena and Poseidon over Athens, and to the attempted rape of Athena by Hephaestus and the consequent impregnation of the earth. We can perhaps find another verbal connection condensed in the name *Erichthonius*: the wool (in Greek *erion*) is responsible for the paradoxical success in turning a situation of disjunctive strife (*eris*) into an act of sexual union (*eros*). If this is allowed, then the name contains all three elements of the cultural dilemma: auto*chthony*, and the knowledge that human beings are born of two (*eros*), not one apart (*eris*). The name of Cecrops's only son, Erysichthon, may be a variation on Erichthonius.

Turning now to the myth's paradigmatic structure, we find it expresses the same concerns about being born of one or two. Cecrops was born from the ground and his lower body had the shape of a snake. In Greek and many other mythic traditions snakes are chthonic beasts par excellence: they move easily from below to above the earth and in joining the lower and upper worlds they also mediate between life and death, especially through their habit of sloughing off their skin, which the Greeks regarded as a kind of self-regeneration (heroes, mortals who had attained a kind of semi-immortality, were symbolized as snakes). Cecrops is thus both a symbol of autochthony, and a symbol of regeneration. He is also said to have been the inventor of marriage. An ancient source tells us that this was the cultural advance which elevated Athens from savagery to civilization (Schol. Aristophanes, *Wealth* 773). Later authors explain that Cecrops was said to be "of two forms," not because he was half-man and half-snake, but because he first taught people that they had fathers as well as mothers (Clearchus of Soli ap. Athenaeus 13.555d): "Previously sexual intercourse took place haphazardly, and all men had unrestricted access to all women. Therefore he seemed to some to be thought to be of two natures, as none of the earlier men knew their fathers because of the large number of men [who had intercourse with their mothers]." This later rationalizing explanation of Cecrops's double nature reveals that the ambiguity of his character refers both to birth from one and birth from two: the snake body indicates an autochthonous nature; the human body the product of a sexual union.

Cecrops was said to have invented marriage to suppress the power of women. The conflict between the sexes arose because of Athena and Poseidon's struggle for possession of Attica. First Poseidon appeared and struck the Acropolis with his trident, causing a sea to appear or, in some versions, a well of salt water from which issued the roar of the sea. Athena appeared and called upon Cecrops to be a witness as she planted an olive tree on the Acropolis to stake her claim. Apollodorus (3.14.1) tells us that "when a dispute (*eris*) arose between them concerning the possession of the land, Zeus appointed arbiters, not as some said, Cecrops and Cranaus, nor Erysichthon, but the twelve gods." Cecrops gave evidence for Athena and the land was adjudicated to her. Poseidon, in anger, flooded the Thriasian plain with sea water. It is clear that the myth brings sea water into binary opposition with the olive. As the myth implies, sea water is sterile: Poseidon's vengeance makes barren the most fertile plain in Attica (the center of later olive cultivation), turning it into what Homer calls the "unharvestable sea." By contrast, the olive became Attica's agricultural staple. Sea water is corrosive and parches. Olive oil is preservative and lubricant. Olive is to sea as wetness to dryness, fertility to sterility, and as life is to death.

Between Athena's struggle with Hephaestus and her struggle with Poseidon there is a causal link: an ancient source tells us that the vengeful Poseidon first suggested to Hephaestus that he ask for Athena in marriage as a reward for freeing Hera from the throne with the golden chains: Hephaestus's assault on Athena was interpreted as an attempt by Hephaestus to claim his prize (see Gantz 1993: 75–8). The structural connection between Athena's dispute with Poseidon and the struggle with Hephaestus emerges from a version of the myth preserved by Varro (ap. Augustine, *City of God* 18.9). In this version an olive tree and a flood suddenly appeared in different parts of Attica. Cecrops inquired of the Delphic oracle the meaning of these portents and was told that the people of Attica had to choose whether they would adopt Athena or Poseidon as their chief deity. A general assembly was held to put the question to the vote. At the time women still enjoyed full citizen rights. All the men voted for Poseidon, all the women for Athena. Since the female population outnumbered the male by a single head, Athena won. Poseidon flooded the country, and to appease his wrath the Athenians decided to deprive women of the vote and to forbid children to bear their mother's names. The tale replicates the general thematic of *eros* and *eris*, sex and struggle.

This account puts the contest between Athena and Poseidon into direct relation with the control of women and offspring through marriage. Before marriage existed, children only knew their mothers. After the invention of marriage, children knew that they had fathers as well and they identified themselves by their father's rather than their mother's name. Thus this second strife leads to cultural fertility, just as the first strife, which gave the Thriasian plain to olive cultivation, led to natural fertility: male citizens were henceforth able to perpetuate themselves through their offspring.

The rest of the tale of early Attic kings replicates these structures. Cecrops had a son Erysichthon, who went to Delos to fetch the image of Eleithyia, the goddess of childbirth, but died before returning home, leaving no offspring. Cecrops also had three daughters who all have significant names, Aglaurus (= Glistening), Herse (= Dew) and Pandrosus (= All-Dewy), evoking the glossy wetness of olive oil, and through it fertility. Aglaurus had by Ares a daughter named Alcippe. At a spring by the side of the Acropolis a son of Poseidon, Halirrhothius (= Sound of the Surge of the Sea), raped Alcippe but was caught and killed by her father Ares.

Poseidon prosecuted Ares for the murder and the case was tried before the twelve gods. This episode seems a replay of the stories of Hephaestus and Athena and Poseidon and Athena rolled into one. It is also one of the foundation myths of the Court of the Areopagus, whose doublet, significantly, is that of Orestes, who murdered his mother to avenge his father. Athena's role in that trial was the inverse of the part played by the women of Athens in adjudicating the country to her. They cast their vote for the female deity and won by a margin of a single vote; Athena voted for the primacy of the male and her single vote acquitted Orestes.

Despite their fertile, "dewy names" all the daughters of Cecrops also represent sterility, as symbolized by their untimely deaths by turning into dry rock, or falling upon it. Hermes (= Pile of Stones) fell in love with Cecrops's second daughter, Herse. Athena made her sister Aglaurus jealous, so that, when Hermes visited, Aglaurus barred his way and declared she would not move. "Agreed," said Hermes, and turned her into stone with the touch of his *caduceus* (a staff with two coupling snakes upon it). The two remaining sisters died when Athena placed Erichthonius in a chest and put it in their care with strict instructions that they never look inside. They did, and discovered a creature half-child and half-snake. In panic they killed themselves by jumping from the Acropolis onto a place called the "Long Rocks."

The names of the next generation mark their opposition to the promised fertility of the Cecropids. From Cecrops the kingdom passed to Cranaus (= Rocky), who was born from the ground and had three daughters: Cranae (= Rocky), Cranaechme (= Spearpoint-Rock) and Atthis (= Athenian Woman). Atthis died a maiden.

But even stone and rock can mediate between sterility and fertility. It was during the time of Cranaus that the flood of Deucalion took place. This flood did not affect Attica, and in one version Deucalion came to Attica to escape the waters. Deucalion and Pyrrha repopulated the earth by throwing stones behind them, causing people to spring up out of the earth. Deucalion and Pyrrha, insofar as they are ambiguously the parents of these autochthons, are figures that mediate between birth from one and birth from two. The ambiguity in their reproductive role is also expressed by variants in the myth of their son Amphictyon, who is said by some to be the natural child of Deucalion and Pyrrha, and by others to be one of their autochthonous offspring. Amphictyon (= Neighbour) became Cranaus's son-in-law, though the marriage brought him no grandchildren and only an ambivalent succession, since Amphictyon himself usurped the kingdom.

Though at first telling the myth may seem episodic and devoid of narrative logic, we can uncover the harmonies after the fashion of Lévi-Strauss by lining up the episodes in columns as follows:

I	II	III	IV
Cecrops born from the earth and is half-snake.	Cecrops is half-human, invents marriage and first taught people that they have fathers as well as mothers.	Sea water.	Olive.
		Strife between men and women.	Children bear fathers' names.
			Erysichthon goes to fetch image of goddess of childbirth.
		Erysichthon dies without issue.	
	Hermes and Herse.	Aglaurus bars Hermes and turns to stone.	
	Halirrhothius rapes Alcippe.	Ares kills Halirrhothius.	
		House of Cecrops without succession.	
Cranaus is born from the earth.		House of Cranaus without succession.	
Deucalion and Pyrrha make people spring from the earth.		Deucalion's flood.	
Amphictyon is born from the earth.	Amphictyon also born from Deucalion and Pyrrha.		
Hephaestus is lame and walks with snaky movements.	Hephaestus "rapes" Athena.	Athena rejects Hephaestus (who was even rejected by Aphrodite).	Hephaestus's seed impregnates earth.
Erichthonius is born from the earth, is part snake.	Erichthonius is born from the union of Athena and Hephaestus; is part human.		House of Erichthonius does have succession.
Names with *chthon*.		Rocky names suggesting sterility. The "Dewy" sisters die on the Long Rocks.	Dewy names suggest fertility.

Column I deals with autochthony and birth from a single parent; Column II with sexual reproduction; Column III with death and sterility; Column IV with fertility. Columns III and IV relate to the opposition of death to life, and so are closely related to the preoccupation with sexual reproduction exhibited by Columns I and II. The paradigmatic harmonies might be summed up with the formula:

birth from one (autochthony) : birth from two (sex) :: sterility (death) : fertility (life).

In this instance we do not have a contradictory mediated by a contrary. Neither pair of terms allows a mediating term, logically speaking. But mythically we do have a mediating term between autochthony and sexual reproduction in the figure of Erichthonius. Death and life are also mythically mediated by a constant and inextricable coalescence of the opposites. Chief among these is the opposition of love and strife, *eros* and *eris*, a pair which is closely aligned with the contradictories of our paradigmatic chains and a pair, moreover, which reminds us of the positive and negative forces which perpetuate Lévi-Strauss's elementary system of relationship. What mediates between life and death, single parentage and double parentage, is the social regulation of sexual reproduction, i.e., marriage, a relationship between opposites, male and female, which is also conceived as a constant alternation of love and strife, and which allows the male to perpetuate his lineage, through the strict control of female reproductivity. Through marriage a mortal man gains a share in the life of his descendants, and especially his male descendants, who continue his line and perpetuate his family name. Through the institution of marriage and the family, culture finds a midterm between the natural polarities of life and death.

Separating the syntagmatic and the paradigmatic

Perhaps we should pause at this point and ask a question which will exercise us more thoroughly in the next section. Lévi-Strauss treats the syntagmatic order as something simply given by the surface structure of any given myth. But is this so? When Lévi-Strauss writes the actions of the syntagmatic sequence onto his index cards in preparation for paradigmatic analysis, is this first action really innocent of the second? Of all the characters and events in the Theban cycle, how did he arrive at those eleven which fill his columns? No version of the myth is told or even likely to be told in the way it appears as we read from left to right across his columns. None of these "sentences" really is a minimal unit of the tale which would appear in any account. Would a tale-teller recount the "Seven against

Thebes" with the simple formula "Eteocles killed his brother Polynices"? Lévi-Strauss is summarizing, not telling, and what appears in the summary is at least in large part predetermined by what will fit into the columns. Lévi-Strauss appears to present index cards covered with raw data; in reality he is stacking the deck. But it is not so much that he has substituted a paradigmatic for a syntagmatic series; rather his syntagmatic series is always already paradigmatic. It is only the way we lay out the cards or the direction we read them that establishes a distinction.

If the parts of a tale were simply given by the syntagmatic sequence, then the meaning of a tale would be nothing more than the sum of its parts. But in reality, whether for the listener, reader or analyst, the exact shape and significance of the parts are determined by their relation to the whole. This means that as we listen we form hypotheses about the meaning of what it is we are listening to, and as we learn more, we revise and form new hypotheses, but it is not till we have absorbed the whole tale that we can turn around and identify its significant actions. What seemed a simple and mechanical task in Lévi-Strauss's procedural instructions – excerpting the syntagms from their temporal sequence – is in fact highly problematic. The syntagms do not come equipped with perforated edges; the paradigms are not colour-coded. The syntagmatic structure is derived from the paradigmatic as much as the paradigmatic from the syntagmatic. Neither order is simply given by the tale, but both are a matter of checking hypotheses, by trial and error, until one grid lines up with the other.

5.7 TOTALIZING STRUCTURE

Elementary semantic structures

We noted above (Section 5.4) that Saussure's concept of system created a vicious paradox in which individual terms could be understood only through the system and the system only through its terms. Jakobson solved the problem in his work on phonetics by positing intermediate structures between the system and its terms. But Jakobson's model was not directly applied to the semantics of narrative until A. J. Greimas's *Sémantique structurale* (1966) and *Du Sens* (1970). Greimas's "elementary semantic structure" is a four-term homology which, not coincidentally, bears a close resemblance to the four-term algorithm of Lévi-Strauss's mythemes. This "atom" of meaning is a structure in which two contraries are matched with their contradictories by a formula which can be rendered $A:B :: -A:-B$. In *Du Sens*, Greimas applies his elementary semantic structures directly to narrative. A story as a whole has meaning above and beyond the sum of meanings in its individual parts because the form of a tale embodies one of these elementary structures. Moreover, the elementary structure is expressed on both the syntagmatic and the paradigmatic axes of a narrative: in the syntagmatic structure as an opposition between an initial state and a final state; in the paradigmatic structure as a thematic situation or problem which is inverted or resolved at the end of the narrative (1970: 187):

> To have a meaning a story must form a signifying whole. It therefore con-
> stitutes an elementary semantic structure. . . . the temporal dimension in which
> [stories] take place is divided into a *before* and an *after*. To this *before* and
> *after* there corresponds a "reversal of situation" which, in terms of implicit
> structure, is nothing other than an inversion of the signs of the content. Thus
> there is a correlation between the two levels [i.e., temporal or syntagmatic
> and thematic or paradigmatic] :

$$\frac{\text{before}}{\text{after}} \cong \frac{\text{inverted content}}{\text{given content}}$$

If we follow the logical implications of Greimas's scheme, we will find that the syntagmatic and paradigmatic order are imbricated upon one another so thoroughly as to call into question the priority of one over the other, whether with respect to meaning or temporal organization. In mapping one order upon another Greimas makes an important departure from Lévi-Strauss's conception of myth as a structure of meaning outside of time. For Lévi-Strauss the syntagmatic sequence was only meaningful insofar as it could be divided up and slotted into the paradigmatic chain; meaning was extracted from the harmonies and not from the melodies. Greimas is more strictly structural. For him the syntagmatic and the paradigmatic organization amount to the same thing looked at from different perspectives: an initial situation which contrasts with a final situation, analyzable both in terms of temporal sequence and thematic content. The result is that the relation to time of both the paradigmatic and the syntagmatic structure is the same, but inverse. On the one hand, the paradigmatic structure is temporally organized insofar as it contrasts an *initial* with a *final* thematic situation. On the other hand, the determination of the precise form of the initial and final state in the syntagmatic structure is free from time to the extent that the initial state is subject in the reader's or listener's mind to constant revision and reassessment, while the final state is a matter of continual anticipation and constantly reformulated conjecture. Hence the syntagmatic structure is not simply given by the tale any more than the paradigmatic structure. Moreover the syntagmatic structure is no more or less subject to time than the paradigmatic, but both are subject to a circular temporality, such that the precise configuration of the *initial* state is only really given once the *final* state has been reached, and the *final* state only once the *initial* state has been fixed. In other words, from the point of view of time, the syntagmatic and paradigmatic organization are both subject to and independent of time in much the same way.

Vernant's Pandora: The grammar of actions

The French classicist Jean-Pierre Vernant (1914–) is responsible for several of the most successful structuralist interpretations of myth. Unlike Lévi-Strauss, whose chief interest is in the relatively stable traditional societies of native North and South America, Vernant is a student of the voluble *historical* culture of archaic and classical Greece. Highly sensitive to the different nature of his material, Vernant pays closer attention to the temporal and historical elements in narrative. As a result, he shares with Greimas the same reserve about Lévi-Strauss's manner of conceptualizing the relationship between the syntagmatic and paradigmatic axes of mythic narrative. He recommends a three-stage approach to the analysis of myth which combines syntagmatic, paradigmatic, and ideological analysis (1974: 244–6). In the *first* stage he recommends one stick close to the text in question and focus upon the narrative's temporal sequence and causal relations. The goal is not to examine the articulation of the plot but the logic or "grammar" governing the permutation of its actions. At a *second* stage of the analysis one may depart from the specific text to examine other versions of the same myth or even different myths with comparable contents. Here the aim is to locate the homologies and oppositions deployed by the myth (whether they involve places, times, objects, agents, actions, or the contrast between initial and final situations). In doing so one should pay close attention to the links between the framework established by the grammar of the tale and its concrete semantic contents. The *third* stage is a cultural or ideological analysis aimed at placing the myth within its social context. What are the categories of thought, what the systems of opposition and classification which allowed this particular myth to be produced in this particular form? How did the society which generated the myth carve up its reality and encode it in its language and cultural artifacts?

The procedure is beautifully illustrated by Vernant's analysis of the myth of Pandora in Hesiod. (The following account follows Vernant 1974: 177–94 in outline, but I have modified considerably the exposition of "the grammar of actions" in order to sharpen and foreground their logical structure and to make some points about the relation between syntagmatic and paradigmatic analysis.) Hesiod tells the tale in two different works, the *Theogony* and *Works and Days*. The versions are closely related and make implicit reference to one another. Hesiod, *Theogony* 535–616:

> At the time when the gods and mortal men were coming to a settlement at Mekone, [Prometheus] eagerly divided a large ox into portions and placed it before Zeus, attempting to trick him. For men he laid out flesh and entrails rich with fat which he had placed in the oxhide and hidden inside the ox's stomach. For Zeus he laid out the ox's white bones which had been carefully arranged for a stratagem of deception and hidden in white fat. The father of gods and men then addressed him, saying "Son of Iapetus, most distinguished among all the lords, my dear fellow, how unfairly you have divided the portions." In this way Zeus, whose schemes never fail, reproached him. Prometheus, of subtle cunning, answered with a slight smile and a mind busy with the art of deception: "Zeus, most glorious and greatest of the immortal gods, take whichever of these suits your fancy." This he said with treacherous intent. Zeus, whose schemes never fail, fully detected and was not unaware of the deceit. And he contemplated evil for mortal men in his heart, which the future brought to pass. He nevertheless took up the white fat with both hands, but his mind seethed with rage, and anger filled his heart, when he saw the white oxbones set for a stratagem of deception. And ever since then the race of men on earth make white bones burn on the smoking altars for the immortal gods. Greatly vexed cloud-gathering Zeus addressed him: "Son of Iapetus, clever beyond all others, my dear fellow, your mind is still full of the art of deception." In this way Zeus, whose schemes never fail, spoke in anger.
>   From that moment he kept brooding on this deceit, and he did not give the power of undying fire to the ash trees for mortal men, who inhabit the earth. But the good son of Iapetus tricked him by stealing the gleam of far-beaming, undying fire in a hollow fennel stalk. And it stung high-thundering Zeus to the depths of his spirit and enraged his very heart, when he saw the far-beaming gleam of fire amongst men. At once he devised an evil for men in exchange for fire. The famous supple-limbed god [Hephaestus] fashioned from earth the likeness of a chaste maiden after the design of Kronos's son. The gray-eyed goddess Athena dressed and adorned her with a white garment and with her hands drew a colorful veil down around her head, a wonder to look at. And Pallas Athena wrapped lovely garlands of herbs blooming with flowers. And when he had fashioned this beautiful evil in exchange for good, he led her, beautified with the finery of the gray-eyed daughter [Athena] of the mighty sire, out into the presence of the other gods and of men. Wonder took hold of the immortal gods and mortal men when they gazed on this deep deceit. From her came the female sex. They [women] live with their husband as a great affliction for mortals, unadapted

to wretched poverty, but only to abundance. As the bees in their roofed hives feed the drones who conspire in evil deeds, and the former bustle about every day all day until the setting of the sun and build the white honeycomb, while the latter wait inside the covered cells to gather another's labor to their bellies, just so high-thundering Zeus made women, conspirators in pernicious deeds, to be an evil for mortal men.

And he provided another evil in exchange for good. He who avoids the destructive acts of women and does not wish to marry, will come to a grievous old age bereft of support. While he lives he is not short of means, but when he dies distant relations will divide up his livelihood. But for him whose lot it is to marry, if he has a good wife endowed with good sense, good will match evil continually all his life; whereas the man who gets the troublesome kind, lives with unrelenting sorrow in his breast, mind and heart, and the evil is incurable.

In *Works and Days*, after explaining to his brother Perses the virtue of honest hard work, Hesiod explains how the need for hard work originated (42–105):

For the gods have hidden from men their livelihood. Otherwise you would easily work enough in even a single day to provide for yourself and be at your ease for an entire year. You would quickly place the steering oar above the smoke [to preserve it while unused] and the labors of oxen and steadfast mules would cease. But Zeus hid [men's livelihood] when angry at heart because Prometheus, of subtle cunning, deceived him. As a result he schemed grim troubles for men. He hid fire. From cunning Zeus the good son of Iapetus [Prometheus] stole it for men in a hollow fennel stalk unseen by Zeus who delights in lightning. In anger cloud-gathering Zeus addressed him: "Son of Iapetus, clever beyond all others, you are pleased that you have stolen fire and beguiled my wits, but this will prove a great calamity for you yourself and for men in the future. I will give them an evil in exchange for good, such that they will all delight in their hearts as they embrace their evil." This the father of gods and men said and he laughed out loud. He commanded famous Hephaestus at once to mix earth with water, to put in it a human voice and strength, and to liken in appearance the beautiful, lovely form of the maiden to an immortal goddess. Then he commanded Athena to teach her crafts, to weave the embroidered loom, and Aphrodite to pour golden charm around her head and painful longing, and debilitating erotic fixation. He bid Hermes, the messenger who killed Argus, to put into her the mind of a bitch and a thievish disposition.

This he commanded, and they obeyed Lord Zeus, son of Kronos. Immediately the famous supple-limbed god molded from earth the likeness of a chaste maiden after the design of Kronos's son. The gray-eyed goddess Athena dressed and adorned her. The Graces and Lady Persuasion placed golden necklaces about her neck, and the lovely-haired Seasons crowned

her with spring flowers. The messenger who killed Argus put lies, wheed-
ling words and a thievish disposition in her breast at the bidding of deep-
resounding Zeus. The herald of the gods also put voice into her and called
the woman Pandora, since all [*pan*] who inhabit Olympus gave her as a gift
[*doron*], a calamity for grain-eating men. Then when he completed this deep
inescapable deceit, the father sent the famous killer of Argus, leading the
gift, to Epimetheus. And Epimetheus did not call to mind that Prometheus
warned him never to receive a gift from Olympian Zeus, but to send it back,
lest it prove to be some evil for men. Only after he received it, when he had
the evil, did he realize.

Formerly the races of men lived on the earth without evil, hard work,
and grievous ailments, which brought men death. For mortals age quickly
amidst hardships. But they escaped after woman removed the great lid from
the jar with her hands: she contrived grim troubles for humankind. Hope
alone remained there inside in her secure home under the lips of the jar
and did not fly out, because she [woman] put back the lid of the jar by the
design of cloud-gathering, aegis-bearing Zeus. But countless troubles wander
among humans: the earth is full of evil and full the sea. Illnesses visit humans
uninvited by day and by night silently carrying evil for mortals, since cunning Zeus deprived them of voice. And so there is no way whatsoever to
escape the will of Zeus.

Vernant's first level of analysis is based on the precise wording of the
original texts. Hesiod's account presents us with a series of actions which
represent a battle of wits fought out by the two protagonists, Prometheus,
the champion of men, backed by his brother, Epimetheus, and Zeus, king
of the gods, backed by the other Olympians. The actions can be summarized as follows:

I *Syntagmatic structure: Narrative sequence*

   A Hesiod's *Theogony* 535–616:
     1 Prometheus *tricks* Zeus *into accepting* the inedible parts of the sacrifice.
     2 Zeus *pretends to accept* "but he was not unaware of the deceit."
     3 Zeus *withholds* ("did not give") the celestial fire from men.
     4 Prometheus *steals* fire and gives it to men.

   B Hesiod's *Works and Days* 42–105:

     1 The gods *hide* from men their means of livelihood.
     2 Zeus *hides* fire from men.
     3 Prometheus *hides* fire in a fennel stalk.
     4 Prometheus *steals* fire from the gods.
     5 Zeus *tricks* Epimetheus *into accepting* Pandora.
     6 Epimetheus *accepts.*

Each action has not only a linear or sequential relationship with all the others but also a conceptual relationship. All are permutations of acts of giving and taking. The battle of wits is conducted as an exchange of gifts between Zeus and the gods on the one hand and Prometheus, Epimetheus, and humankind on the other. But this is no straightforward exchange. Throughout, the narratives insist on one quality Zeus and Prometheus have in common, their cunning intelligence (Greek *metis*), an "art" or "craft" of trickery and deception. By it their manner of gift-giving is distinguishable from ordinary gift-giving. Ordinary gift-giving is open and acknowledged and would have little purpose without the recognition and appreciation which this openness allows. But the exchange between Zeus and Prometheus is a perverse form of gift-giving in which both the intent and the true nature of the objects of exchange are concealed. Each action of the myth's syntagmatic structure expresses in the mode of cunning intelligence – let us call it "the mode of concealment" – one of the four possibilities of gift exchange. In normal gift exchange one can either give or not give, take or not take. To each of these actions there correspond special forms of giving and not giving, taking and not taking, in the mode of concealment. We can tabulate the following *Grammar of Actions*.

A Giving

	giving	not giving
openness	offer	withhold
concealment	trick into accepting	hide

B Taking

	taking	not taking
openness	accept	refuse
concealment	steal	pretend to accept

By insisting upon a grammar of actions Vernant makes a significant break with Lévi-Strauss's paradigmatic method. For Lévi-Strauss the syntagmatic axis of the myth was something clearly separable from the paradigmatic, while the latter alone seemed systematic and meaningful: syntagmatic stood to paradigmatic much the same way as Saussure's "material" signifiers to his "conceptual" signified. But Jakobson was able to show that a phoneme, though the smallest element of the signifier and the smallest element of the syntagmatic chain, was so far from being neatly separable from the paradigmatic order that it was itself already an expression of a complex paradigmatic order. In the same way Vernant invites us to see that the smallest units of the narrative syntax are already manifestations of a system of paradigmatic relations. The actions of the grammar belong to both orders simultaneously.

If we were to express Vernant's grammar of actions in terms of Greimas's elementary structures of signification and redraw our charts as "semiotic squares," we would find that each mode, that of openness and that of concealment, expresses the Greimasian algorithm $A{:}B :: {-}A{:}{-}B$.

Semantic square in the mode of openness

offer ---------- c o n t r a r y -------- **accept**

refuse ---------- c o n t r a r y ------- **withhold**

Thus, in the mode of open gift-giving, *to offer* is opposed to *to accept*, but the contradictory of *to offer* is *to not offer*, i.e., *to withhold*. Similarly, the contradictory of *to accept* is *to refuse* (i.e., *to not accept*): one either accepts or does not.

There are in fact two distinct logical domains accessed by the myth's grammar of actions. The one we have just looked at (which joins pairs diagonally across the square) is a sort of absolute logic of contradiction: one either offers or does not offer – one either does a thing or one does not. But this is somewhat different from the logic which links the horizontal pairs. Here we oppose two distinct actions like offering and accepting. These terms are not opposed by a logic of positive and negative, do or don't, but by the groundrules of a particular cultural institution, namely, that of gift exchange. It is not necessarily true that one either offers or accepts. One could share, for example, or ride a bicycle or eat cake, actions which have nothing to do with exchange relations. But the actions in the Hesiodic tale are special forms of non-participation in a gift-exchange relationship. They do not ignore the rules of the game but invert them.

In the mode of concealment, the internal logic of the square is only intelligible with relation to the mode of openness which it perverts. This perversion is a form of negated gift exchange, a negative logic which stands to the mode of openness as the algebraic equation *-A:-B :: --A:--B* stands to the Greimasian *A:B :: -A:-B*. A concealed form of *offering* is *to trick someone into accepting*; a concealed form of *accepting* is *to steal*; *to withhold* something in covert fashion is *to hide* it; and *to refuse* something deviously is *to pretend to accept* while not really accepting as such. Therefore, a strictly symmetrical logic binds the mode of concealment.

Semantic square in the mode of concealment

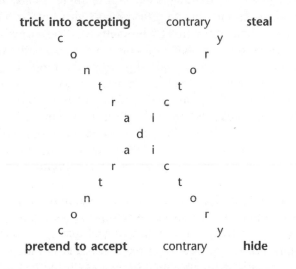

When we look at the syntagmatic structure of the myth of Prometheus, we see that it shows a duel of wits between men and gods conducted by means of gift-giving. If we take both tales together as one, we might see that the actions are true to the qualities of the actors. Prometheus and Zeus are both characterized by their cunning intelligence and they act in the mode of concealment: Prometheus *tricks into accepting, hides,* and *steals*; Zeus *pretends to accept, hides,* and *tricks into accepting*. The other gods obey Zeus's commands and participate in his schemes. But Epimetheus fails to obey Prometheus. Moreover, he fails to play the game of gift-giving-and-taking by the rules of cunning intelligence. He simply *accepts* the gift of Pandora, naively acting in the mode of openness. The tale tells how humanity fell from a trouble-free existence to a life of toil. Its main function is to delineate what is divine and what human. On the basis of this analysis we could say that cunning intelligence is divine, but humanity partakes of both modes of intelligence, the cunning of Prometheus (foresight) and the guileless naivety of Epimetheus (aftersight). Humanity falls from grace when it loses a battle of wits, because of inferior cunning and foresight.

If we compare the two versions, however, we notice that each narrative has the same structure. In each a battle of wits is lost, because one of the protagonists lapses into the mode of openness. We notice that in *Works and Days* Hesiod states that Zeus hid fire as he hid grain, but in the *Theogony* (563), Zeus "did not give" fire, i.e., he withheld it, acting in the mode of openness. If we follow the language of the *Theogony*, the story will break down into two symmetrical confrontations. In one, Zeus attempts to withhold something which Prometheus steals. In the other, Prometheus warns Epimetheus to refuse Zeus's gifts but Zeus outwits him. An attempt to withhold, outwitted by Prometheus, is balanced by an attempt to refuse, outwitted by Zeus. Each version represents a battle of wits which is lost when one of the combatants slips from the mode of concealment into the mode of openness. Each confrontation ends in man's receipt of a divine "gift": fire and woman. The shifting of the treatment of fire by Zeus (whether "withholding" or "hiding") from one narration to the other preserves the syntagmatic parallelism between one story and the other.

Superficially the story signifies, as Hesiod puts it, that man cannot compete with the gods; though he partakes of the divine intelligence represented by Prometheus, he also partakes of the qualities of Epimetheus. At a deeper level it indicates that there is something devious about the way gods deal with men, their generosity is perversely mixed with hidden malice, their gifts a deceptive mixture of evil and good. From a purely theoretical perspective, the beauty of the analysis lies in the demonstration that the paradigmatic structure, just as much as the syntagmatic structure, can be expressed as a function of time, as a shift from an initial state or thematic situation in the mode of concealment (here truly a *contenu inversé*) to a final state or resolution of the conflict in the mode of openness.

Vernant's Pandora: Semantic Analysis

The meaning structure of the Pandora myth is not exhausted when we have discovered the logic governing its actions (through the syntagmatic analysis). Vernant offers still two further levels of analysis. At the second level, the *semantic analysis*, we are more strictly concerned with paradigmatic structures, though less in terms of the actions in the myth, than the objects and persons which play a part in this gift exchange. Nevertheless, the paradigmatic structure is not independent of the syntagmatic structure, but, as we saw above, it can be viewed as something which folds out of the contrast between an initial situation and a final situation. In this case the myth describes humanity's fall from grace, contrasting an initial situation, where men lived together with the gods and enjoyed a life of comfort and ease, with a final situation, where men live apart from the gods and live in hardship, receiving only mixed blessings.

The transition from the initial to the final situation is effected by the loss of a number of benefits, to each of which is opposed a subsequent gain of ambivalent worth. In the struggle between Zeus and Prometheus, Zeus hid "undying fire" from men, and in exchange men received a different fire, a "Promethean fire"; Zeus hid from men "their livelihood," that is to say, in the Golden Age, food appeared spontaneously from the ground, but Zeus kept it hidden in the earth, and it was not till Prometheus taught men the practice of agriculture that they were able to tease food out of the ground once again at the cost of a great deal of labor: "Otherwise you would easily work enough in even a single day to provide for yourself and be at your ease for an entire year." In the Golden Age, too, men were autochthonous, babies sprang from the earth, but Zeus ended this by molding earth into the shape of a woman. With Pandora there also came as dowry the jar full of disease and old age, where previously, as Hesiod tells us in the *Works and Days* (112–16): "men lived like gods without a care, without toil or woe, and there was no wretched old age, but with no diminution of the strength of their feet and hands they delighted in feasting, free from all evil, and they died as if falling asleep." If we add to this list the sacrifice at Mekone with which the myth begins, and which constitutes both the "initial situation" and the catalyst which precipitates the fall, then we can see in this list all of the objects which formed the playing pieces of the battle of gifts uncovered in the syntagmatic structure.

Each gift belongs to a distinctly human domain. Technology (fire), agriculture, marriage, and sacrifice are the blessings of culture which set human life apart from the squalid existence of beasts. But if the bestial represents a negative aspect of nature, the life of the gods (and of men in the Golden Age) represents the positive. The myth of Prometheus shows how culture is a mixed blessing which divides humanity from the carefree existence of gods, but raises humanity above the wretched life of brutes.

Golden age	Present age
commensality with the gods	sacrifice by men to gods
divine fire	Promethean fire
spontaneous appearance of food	agriculture
spontaneous birth	marriage with women
no disease, no old age	jar releases disease and old age, but retains hope
---	---
Unmixed good	Good mixed with evil

Vernant's paradigmatic or "semantic" analysis shows that each of these five pieces, the sacrifice, fire, agriculture, Pandora, and the jar, form through their similarities and oppositions a "bundle of relations," analogous to the elementary semantic structure uncovered in the syntagmatic analysis. Vernant organizes his investigation by focusing on the contrasts and similarities between Pandora and the other objects of exchange. Pandora is like the sacrificial animal. Her seductive exterior corresponds to the seductive package of inedible parts which Prometheus offered to Zeus. These were camouflaged under a wrap of appetizing white fat. Pandora has the appearance of a goddess and a virgin, and, like a bride, is clothed in a white robe with an embroidered veil.

Her evil interior is the inverse of the package Prometheus gave to man. Prometheus wrapped these in a double envelope surrounded by the hide and the stomach (bad outside), while the edible meats are concealed within (good inside). Pandora's attractive exterior conceals the mind of a bitch, the character of a thief, and a voice designed for deception. In her character as an insatiable stomach which consumes the livelihood of men, she resembles the stomach used by Prometheus to wrap the sacrificial meat: but these stomachs also contrast with one another since in the one case, a lovely exterior hides a greedy stomach which takes away man's food, while in the case of the sacrifice, the unappetizing stomach hides the meat which nourishes men. Both Pandora and man's portion of the sacrifice have a tripartite nature: Pandora's nature has aspects which are divine (appearance, crafts), human (voice) and bestial ("mind of a bitch"). Prometheus's action in wrapping edibles in a stomach condemns the human race to continually having to fill that paunch in order to sustain life: thus the stomach conceals humanity's allotment in the distribution between men and gods. Earlier, in the *Theogony* (26), the Muses address Hesiod, saying "Shepherds of the wilderness, wretched things of shame, mere bellies" and in the *Odyssey* (7.216) Odysseus tells the Phaeacians that "there is nothing more doglike than a stomach." We are reminded that Hermes put a doglike mind into Pandora. The stomach to the archaic Greek is a shameful, odious, and maleficent thing.

But Greek thought cross-referenced women, dogs, and stomachs in yet another way: the Greek word *gaster* means not only "stomach," but "womb." Dogs were proverbial for their shamelessness and for their appetites, not only alimentary, but sexual. In the *Odyssey* (11.425–7) the embittered shade of Agamemnon, betrayed and murdered by the "dogfaced" Clytemnestra, declares that "there is nothing more doglike than a woman"; later, the maidservants of Odysseus who sleep with the suitors are called "doglike" (20.18). These homologies come together in the *Works and Days* (586), when Hesiod asserts that at the time of the Dog Star (Canis Major) women are most lascivious and insatiable in their erotic appetites. Pandora's mind of a bitch implies lasciviousness as well as voraciousness.

Pandora is also the counterpart of Promethean fire at several semantic levels. As a trick, the bringing of fire has the same structure as the distribution of the sacrifice and the bringing of Pandora. Hidden in a fennel stalk, the stolen fire has the appearance of a green plant: interior and exterior are opposites (hot/cold; dry/wet). On the other hand Promethean fire, unlike the deathless fire of the gods, must be fed to be kept alive. The fire must also be seeded. In Greek epic and lyric, coals or embers are referred to as "the seed of fire." In the same way, the farmer must seed the earth and man the womb. Like fire, woman burns a man and withers him with labor and worries; according to Hesiod's *Works and Days* 702–5: "A man wins nothing better than a good wife, and, again, nothing worse than a bad one, a glutton, who roasts her husband like a torch, though he be strong, and consigns him to savage old age [before his time]." An ancient commentator on this passage (Palladas of Alexandria) makes the structural connection: "Zeus, as ransom for fire, made us a gift of another fire, women. . . . Fire at least can burn out, but woman is an inextinguishable fire, full of ardor which constantly reignites. . . . She burns man with worries and consumes him, exchanging his youth for premature old age." In exchange for dying fire, which was stolen to replace perpetual fire, Zeus gave men another inextinguishable fire that would consume them. Moreover, in exchange for the theft of fire, Zeus gave a fire that is also a thief. Pandora has the "disposition of a thief." "He who trusts a woman," rants Hesiod elsewhere in the *Works and Days* (375), "trusts a thief."

Pandora also corresponds to man's livelihood – the grain which Zeus conceals along with celestial fire. Just as Prometheus hid meat in the ox's stomach, and the seed of fire in the fennel stalk, man must hide his seed in the womb of woman if he wishes to have children, and so Pandora is like the earth, which must be planted with seed, if he is to have grain. Pandora is, in fact, a name given to the earth in Greek myth and cult, and Greek art shows Pandora rising from the earth like grain (see Figure 10).

FIGURE 10   Attic red-figure volute krater, *c.*450 BC. Ashmolean Museum, Oxford G275 (V525)

To Hesiod and like-minded Greek misogynists, marriage is a kind of exhausting agricultural chore in which woman is the furrow and man the plower. Here there is a further relationship between agriculture and woman: though woman consumes, she also produces.

Finally, Pandora is like the jar which the gods give her to bring man as her dowry. Like Pandora, the jar is a gift which conceals an evil interior which brings hardship to men. Yet the interior of the jar contains not only evil, but hope. Since the Bronze Age large jars of the type designated in the myth (*pithos*) were buried in the ground to serve as refrigerated storage bins for the preservation of agricultural produce, and especially grain. Thus men place seed and food in it, as men place grain in the earth at planting time, and as men place food in stomachs. But the form of the jar is also stomach-like and womb-like: a jar has a hidden belly (*gastra* in Greek) with only the neck and lips visible emerging from the ground: in it men place the seed grain, which is the *hope* for the next year's crop, just as men place their seed in the womb in hope of offspring. As we saw in discussing the myth of the early Attic kings in the last section (5.6), marriage is a way of perpetuating the family line, and therefore conceived as a kind of cultural immortality, a second best to the natural immortality of the gods. In this way a man places his hope for this ambivalent immortality in children. Through the cultural institution of marriage man can rise to a midpoint between the natural mortality of beasts and the natural immortality of the gods.

The paradigmatic or semantic analysis of the Prometheus myth can be summed up as follows:

Woman	*Sacrifice*	*Agriculture*	*Fire*	*Jar*
white robe and appearance of goddess, conceal mind of bitch: i.e., good outside, bad inside	envelope of white fat on bones: i.e., good outside, bad inside	grain concealed in earth	fire (hot/dry) concealed in fennel stalk (cold/wet)	lid of jar conceals evils
gaster (stomach/ womb) inside: mixed blessing because man must feed stomach and seed womb, but women also bear children	hide and ox stomach (*gaster*) on meat: i.e., bad outside, good inside	earth must be worked and seeded, but produces	Promethean fire must be seeded and fed	hope, a mixed blessing, stays in belly of jar
burns man with worries and consumes him, brings premature old age: woman is a fire with character of a thief		labor brings premature old age and death	stolen fire	jar emits disease, and old age

The paradigmatic structure, like the syntagmatic structure, shows how humans differ from gods: the syntagmatic structure reveals a qualitative difference in their respective intelligence; the paradigmatic structure shows that the human lot differs qualitatively from that of the gods, as good inextricably mixed with evil differs from unmitigated good. With the gifts of the gods, however, the cultural institutions of sacrifice, marriage, agriculture, and fire (technology), the human lot is at least far elevated above that of beasts. These mixed blessings, like humanity's mixed intelligence, place humanity at a midpoint between beasts and gods.

Vernant's Pandora: Ideological analysis

There remains Vernant's third level of cultural or ideological analysis, which we need signal only briefly here, since we will pick it up again at the beginning of Chapter 6. Vernant concludes by noting that sacrifice, marriage, and agriculture are all inextricably linked with one another in Greek cult, ritual, myth, and institutional practice, where they serve, as in the Pandora myth, to define the distinctive traits of the human condition. The sacrificial meal implies ritual cuisine, hence fire: that given to the gods is burned on the altar, that eaten by men is roasted or boiled. Sacrifice in turn implies agriculture: generally speaking, only domesticated animals are sacrificed and domesticated animals are to wild animals as cultivated plants are to wild plants. In Greek sacrifice, moreover, the slaughter of the animal is preceded by offerings of grain and wine. The links between agriculture and marriage are frequently stressed in myth and ritual: in the Thesmophoria, for example, the principal festival of Demeter, the goddess of agriculture, only married women were allowed to participate, and the main sacrifice was to promote the fertility of the crops.

Perhaps the most interesting expression of cultural ideology to be found in the Pandora myth is its view of women. Women stand in stark contrast to men in their moral inferiority. Pandora is the source of the mixing of all blessings. In her tripartite nature, as in her narrative function, she mediates between the bestial and divine, and expresses, thereby, the human condition. She has divine appearance, bestial nature, and human voice and strength. But even though she speaks the language of men, she uses it only to tell lies and deceive, so that communication is not only impossible but dangerous. The ambivalence of the Greek view of women is also an expression of ambivalence about the human condition, in which all the institutions of culture and all the bounty of the gods are goods laced with evil. This ambivalence is further attested in the ambivalence toward Hope, which remains in the stomach of the jar. If humans had the foresight and intelligence of the gods, they would not need hope, nor would they need it if they were without intelligence and unaware of their own mortality, like beasts. It is because they are caught between Foresight (Prometheus) and Aftersight (Epimetheus) that Hope keeps leading them on in vain.

6

Ideology

Verbal-ideological decentering will occur only when a national culture loses its sealed-off and self-sufficient character, when it becomes conscious of itself as only one among *other* cultures and languages. It is this knowledge that will sap the roots of a mythological feeling for language, based as it is on an absolute fusion of ideological meaning with language; there will arise an acute feeling for language boundaries (social, national and semantic), and only then will language reveal its essential *human* character; from behind its words, forms, styles, nationally characteristic and socially typical faces begin to emerge, the images of speaking human beings.

M. M. Bakhtin, *The Dialogic Imagination* [Discourse in the Novel], 370

6.1 STRUCTURE AND IDEOLOGY

Woman as Ideologeme

A large number of myths dealing with women or goddesses express cultural concerns about female sexuality and the reproductive power of women. In structuralist parlance they typically mediate "natural" extremes of life and death, and the "natural" extremes of sexual comportment that lead to fertility and sterility, through the cultural institution of marriage (as in the myths of Athenian succession discussed in Section 5.6).

One hardly needs a sophisticated method of analysis to discover the moral message purveyed by such myths: they typically portray sexual abstinence and sexual promiscuity as perilous excess ending in disaster and death. From a purely functional perspective the myths reinforce one of the basic institutions of Greek society, the family, the smallest unit of political power in the Greek state, which was dominated and represented by the adult male citizen. And it is fairly obvious that the family is threatened by extinction through the sexual abstinence or promiscuity of either sex. The real gain of a sustained structural analysis of related myths and their cultural contexts is the model it provides for the way a cultural ideology is constituted.

No viable culture relies upon punishment and police functions alone to regulate the behavior of its citizens. Such external regulation is only exceptionally necessary. Far more important is the internal regulation by the society's system of beliefs and values which both shape the mind of the individual and create his or her needs and desires. Structuralism offers a fairly detailed model for understanding just how important values, such as chastity, were sustained and reinforced by the weight of the total system of thought which constituted ancient Greek ideology.

According to Vernant, the analysis of the myth of Pandora can only finally be confirmed, or made fully intelligible, by examining the myth's social and historical context. Vernant's analysis of the Prometheus myth (in Section 5.7) uncovered an intricate system by which the Greek mind cross-referenced a number of disparate objects (food, fire, woman, a jar) and institutions (sacrifice, technology, marriage, agriculture). The conceptual links between these objects and institutions would not have been "legible" to the ancient consumers of the myth if they were limited only to the structure of the Pandora myth. The assumption is that myths communicate because they belong to a higher level of language, which is acquired in the same way as ordinary speech, through the process of acculturation. A structuralist might extend the linguistic series leading from phoneme to mytheme (Section 5.4) by stating that bundles of myths constitute an ideologeme, and bundles of ideologemes constitute a cultural mentality or ideology. If the Pandora myth can express the social significance of "woman" with reference to food, fire, or jars, it is because it can access a preexistent, perfectly structured, oppositive, and relative semiotic system in which the concepts of sacrifice, agriculture, technology, and marriage are already organized into relations of homology. One only needs to find other expressions which observe the same structure to confirm the "grammatical rule."

The "ideological analysis" (third level of analysis) in Vernant's interpretation of the Pandora myth is found in his introduction to Marcel Detienne's *Gardens of Adonis* (1972), an analysis broadly extended by Detienne (1935–), who brilliantly unveils a number of "codes" in the total system of Greek thought: nutritional, botanical, zoological, astronomical, and many others, which all converge in the expression of a uniform set of values. At first blush these codes would seem to have little to do with marriage or women. But this is not so.

Cooking, agriculture, marriage

The nutritional code has its most complete expression in the structure of the sacrificial feast. Sacrifice separates men from beasts despite their common nature: both are mortal and both have the same need to replenish themselves by the daily consumption of nourishment which is also perishable; but in the case of men it is cultivated cereal or cooked meat of domesticated animals, and, in the case of animals, wild plants, and raw meat of wild animals. The homologous pairs of oppositions cultivated/cooked and wild/raw is an ideologeme common to many myth-producing cultures (Lévi-Strauss examined it among South American indians, notably in *The Raw and the Cooked*). The ideologeme allows most cultural activities to be regarded as a form of "cooking." Also, since beasts eat raw, and men eat cooked, a culture can choose to extend the logic and suppose that the gods eat overcooked. But since the gods are also natural, this provokes a double-dimensionality in the system of logic, which often results in charts with triangles. Food and incense are burnt on the altars of the gods. By the same logic, sacrifice is governed by paradigmatic rules which prefer "culturally pre-cooked" victims, namely domesticated animals, and altars are sprinkled with cultivated cereal before the slaughter of the animal. In this way sacrifice also distinguishes men from gods at the very same time that it establishes contact between them. Men receive the dead and perishable meat, but the gods receive the smoke from the bones and from incense, which, because they are imperishable, are as unsuited for consumption by humans, as they are suited for consumption by the immortals.

Because aromatic spices, myrrh, and incense tend toward imperishability, they are ideally suited to mediate between earth and sky. But there are other good reasons for their role as mediators: according to the Greek experts myrrh and aromatic spices grew in Arabia, the hottest and driest part of earth. They (wrongly) believed that spices were collected when most potent at the time of the Dog Star, in July, when the sun is closest to the earth, and when the heat of the sun shrivels plants and beasts. Though myrrh grows on the earth, it partakes also of the fiery nature of the heavens, through this intense solar cooking. This kind of cooking is in fact directly related to the imperishability of myrrh and spices, because cooking eliminates moisture and moisture causes rot. And just as moisture causes rot and bad smells, cooking produces good smells, and the sweetest scents are from substances which can sustain the highest degree of cooking.

The association of moisture with corruption is linked with a vast network of other beliefs: that the inhabitants of hot climates live longer, for example, and especially the black-skinned Ethiopians, who live next to the source of the sun and were reputed to eat gold, the most imperishable of substances; that animals stink because of their phlegmatic humors but leopards are fragrant because of their fiery nature; that, for the same reason, Alexander the Great smelled much better than the average Macedonian; and that the gods leave a fragrance wherever they pass.

Agriculture is also described as a kind of cooking. By plowing one allows the upturned earth to "cook" in the sun before planting. Cultivated plants thus partake of cooked nourishment which renders them soft and sweet. But not all plants are suitable for cultivation: wild plants favour cold and wet environments. Only plants predisposed to this kind of internal cooking can be cultivated. Grain is the most cooked of all edible plants (spices are only semi-edible). Grain grows in "cooked earth;" it cooks in the summer sun; it is roasted, ground, and then cooked again on the fire. Thus sacrificial practice reveals a whole system of homologous oppositions:

IMPERISHABLE (life)	god	burnt	myrrh, incense	hot	fragrant	dry
	man	cooked	grain			
PERISHABLE (death)	beast	raw	wild plants	cold	putrid	moist

One sees right away the importance which agriculture holds for the Greek mind in defining humanity in relation to beasts and gods. One also begins to see why fire has such an important role as a mediator: not only does it make possible sacrifice, the mediation between gods and men, and not only does it distinguish man from beast, in that it permits him to cook his food and to eat grain, but it mediates between cold and hot, putrid and fragrant, moist and dry, and a whole series of homologous oppositions which define man in relation to beasts and gods. But where, then, does marriage fit into this system? In the Pandora myth, marriage was likened to sacrificial cooking, to fire, and to agriculture. All assure humanity of a continued existence: sacrifice, agriculture, and fire insofar as they permit the individual to sustain his life through the consumption of food, and marriage insofar as it permits the individual to perpetuate himself after death in the form of offspring. Marriage is, as Plato declares, "the way by which the human race, by nature's ordinance, shares in immortality" (*Laws* 721b). Marriage raises humanity halfway up to the immortality of the gods, producing a kind of immortality within mortality. In the natural wild state sexual encounters are haphazard and promiscuous, as

they are with the beasts: children born from such savage unions have a
mother but no father (cf. the myth of Cecrops in Section 5.6). No marriage means no means of extending the paternal family lineage. There may
be natural reproduction, but no social reproduction.

Just as sacrifice implies agriculture and fire, so does marriage. As Vernant
puts it, "for the Greeks marriage constituted a form of agricultural labour
by which the female is the furrow of earth, the male the farmer. If the
wife does not make herself cultivable earth, then she cannot bring forth
the desired fruits, legitimate children in which the father can recognize
the seed he has sown" (1972: xii). Like plowing earth, marriage is a form
of cultural "cooking."

The link between marriage and agriculture is explicitly drawn in the
Athenian marriage ritual. The marriage contract was formed when a
father, in the presence of his future son-in-law, repeated the formulaic words
"I give you this girl for the tillage of legitimate children." On the day of
the marriage we are told that Athenian brides carried a vessel for roast-
ing barley. At the wedding ceremony a child wearing a crown of thorny
plants mixed with acorns said "I have fled the bad and found the better,"
and distributed loaves of bread carried in a winnowing fan to all the invited
guests. Afterwards the bride and groom were showered with myrrh and
unguents. In the evening a torchlight procession accompanied the wagon
which carried the bride to the groom's house. In the procession a child
carried a sieve (used for separating fine from coarse meal). The bride was
then led to the hearth of the husband's house, where she was showered
with nuts and figs. Bride and groom then retired to the bedchamber, above
the door of which was hung a pestle (used for grinding grain).

The various symbols seem disparate and arbitrary, until related to the
system of thought we have been examining. All the symbols mediate
between the natural and the civilized state. The Greeks referred proverbially to the former as the "life of thorns," and to the latter as "the life
of ground grain."

BAD				BETTER
	crown of thorns	barleyroaster		
life of thorns	acorns	sieve	bread	life of ground grain
	nuts	winnowing fan		
	figs	pestle	child	
BEFORE CULTURE				CULTURE

Through this symbolism we can see that married stands to unmarried as
cooked to raw, and cultivated to wild.

Demeter, Artemis, Aphrodite

Demeter is the goddess of grain as well as of marriage. It is for Demeter that wives celebrate their principal festival, the Thesmophoria. In opposition to Demeter stand two goddesses, Artemis and Aphrodite. Both goddesses embody a form of savagery which puts the institution of marriage at risk: Artemis represents the disposition and comportment of the virgin and Aphrodite that of the prostitute. "Fleeing contact with men, far from civilization, the virgin shares a savage life in company with Artemis, the virgin huntress and mistress of wild beasts and uncultivated forests; it is this state which is symbolized in the marriage ceremony by the crown of thorns and acorns" (Vernant 1972: xiii). (Acorns, which are just barely digestible, were reputed to be the food of Arcadians, most backward of all Greeks, and of cavemen.) "To enter into the civilized state, the life of ground grain, symbolized by the barleyroaster, sieve, winnowing fan and pestle . . . the virgin must renounce that state of savagery which previously kept her apart from men" (Vernant 1972: xiii). The Greek words for "wife" make this state analogous to that of a wild ox or horse broken to bear the yoke or bit. An ancient writer says that thank-offerings were given to Demeter at the Thesmophoria because "her gift of Demetrian fruits [i.e., grain] *tamed* the human race" (Schol. Lucian, Rabe 273f.). "Under the yoke of marriage, [the virgin] domesticates herself in the full sense of the term, by participating henceforth in one of the family units which form the city, she integrates herself into community life" (Vernant 1972: xiii).

Opposed to the realm of Artemis, but equally threatening to the institution of marriage, and also opposed to Demeter, is the form represented by Aphrodite. In Vernant's words (1972: xiii):

> The prostitute also finds herself outside of marriage, but inversely. Her savagery is not hatred and wild rejection of men, but an excessive attraction and unbridled licence. She delivers herself to the embrace of every passing male, and offers each the dangerous and seductive illusion of a life of spices and perfumes, which occupies a position relative to the life of ground grain which is symmetrical but opposite to the life of thorns.

Opposed to the crown of thorns at the beginning of the wedding ceremony are the perfumes showered on the bride and groom before the procession to the groom's house and in anticipation of their introduction to the realm of Aphrodite. But throughout the ceremony the stress is upon the mean between the complete rejection of sex and exclusive exultation in sex. Both are culturally sterile, since the first produces no children, and the second produces illegitimate, fatherless children which the city cannot "ingest." The realm of Demeter stands between those of Artemis and Aphrodite, since it is a realm of licensed sexuality and controlled abstinence, but it stands opposite to both, insofar as it produces "cultural" offspring.

CULTURE	Demeter		fertility (life)
NATURE	Artemis	Aphrodite	sterility (death)
	cold	hot	
	universal repulsion	universal attraction	
	thorns	spices	
	raw acorns	inedible incense	
	sterility	uncontrollable fecundity	

This ideologeme gives meaning to nearly all myths which set any two of these goddesses in opposition to the other, and a great many myths which deal with extremes in the sexual comportment of women or men. For the remainder of this section we will examine a few of the more striking expressions of this ideologeme uncovered by Detienne in *The Gardens of Adonis*. They will suffice to give an impression of how the conceptual framework of this ideologeme is relentlessly replicated in myth and ritual, despite endless variation. They seem but a few strands of a vast and seamless web, whose fearful symmetries and haunting consistencies drum home a single ineluctable and incontrovertible message.

Myrrha and Adonis

In the erotic regime of marriage, myrrh and aromatic spices may play a part: myrrh, as a constituent of perfumes and unguents, helps mediate horizontally between the sexes, as it mediates vertically, in the form of incense, between human and divine. But, though they may play a role in marriage, the use of unguents is not essential. Indeed, the excessive use of unguents, like excessive indulgence in sensual pleasure, risks diverting the marriage from its proper end, which is the production of legitimate children, and risks introducing a form of sterility, which is every bit as harmful to marriage as the complete rejection of sexual union.

The myth of Myrrha, an etiology for the power of myrrh, is a cautionary tale in which the heroine straddles both extremes on either side of marriage. Myrrha (Greek for "myrrh") was the daughter of Kinyras, King of Cyprus. She offended Aphrodite by refusing to pay her homage, and because she refused to marry, though she was sought by a vast number of suitors. Aphrodite took her revenge by making Myrrha fall in love with her own father. Tormented by shame and guilt, she would have committed suicide, had her faithful nurse not discovered her secret and offered to help the girl satisfy her passion. She seized her chance while Kinyras's wife, Queen Kenchreis [the name plays on *kenchroi*, millet seeds, i.e., grain/ legitimate wife], was away for twelve days observing the Thesmophoria of Demeter. The nurse approached Kinyras, informed him that a young woman, one of his subjects, was passionately in love with him, but ashamed, and wished to visit him at night, in the dark, without disclosing her identity. For several nights Kinyras had incestuous relations with his daughter, until curiosity got the better of him, and, lighting a lamp, he discovered with whom he had been sleeping. In rage he grabbed his sword and pursued Myrrha, but the gods took pity on her anguish and changed her into a myrrh tree, which continually drips with her tears.

Marriage is the (suppressed) middle term between the two states of Myrrha. She begins as a fastidious virgin rejecting all men and ends as a woman of unbridled sexuality: for her complete denial of Aphrodite, the goddess takes revenge by uniting her with the one man from whom society would most keep her apart. The "tear" of the myrrh tree is of course its sap, which is harvested like a fruit to produce myrrh, which is employed in the most potent unguents, perfumes, and in incense.

The fruit of the incestuous union of Kinyras and Myrrha is Adonis, and, insofar as he is the product of the myrrh tree, he represents the powers of attraction and mediation of unguents and incense. According to myth, he was prodigiously beautiful. While still very young he was collected by Aphrodite, who jealously put him in a box, so that none of the other gods or goddesses could see him. She entrusted the box for safekeeping to Persephone. But Persephone opened the box and fell in love with Adonis and refused to give him back to Aphrodite. They appealed to Zeus, who decided that Adonis should spend a third of each year with each of the two goddesses and a third of the year with whomever he wished. Adonis therefore spent two-thirds of each year with Aphrodite. One day Adonis went hunting and was himself chased by a boar (sent, according to Euripides, by Artemis in revenge for Aphrodite's killing of Hippolytus). Adonis, terrified by the charging beast, ran and took refuge in a patch of lettuce, or according to another version, was hidden in lettuce by Aphrodite. But Adonis was killed nonetheless, and Aphrodite laid out his corpse on lettuce leaves.

The story of Adonis and the story of Myrrha are linked by a series of oppositions, which give eloquent confirmation to Lévi-Strauss's claim that connected myths will express the same structure:

Myrrha	Adonis
refuses marriage when she comes of age (untimely overattachment to Artemis)	gives himself to sensual pleasure while still a child (untimely overattachment to Aphrodite)
power of Aphrodite joins the two humans whom society most separates by marriage taboo (opposites joined in love by Aphrodite)	seductive power of Adonis joins Queen of Underworld with Heavenly Aphrodite (joins Aphrodite and her opposite in love for him)
Myrrha is destroyed by the act by which a woman normally achieves full civic status, i.e., conception of a child (failure to fulfill promise of womanhood)	Adonis is destroyed in the act which normally serves as the test of manhood (killing a boar) and fails to fulfil promise
killed by Aphrodite	killed by Artemis
Myrrha turned into myrrh tree	Adonis killed in lettuce patch
Myrrha, wishing to keep herself at one extreme, with regard to marriage, finds herself on the other (hoping for sterility, she finds perverse love, which bears fruit)	Adonis, though sexually overactive, fails to have offspring (enjoying perverse love, remains sterile)

Contrasting the initial and final situation, we find the syntax opposes the hypervirginity of Myrrha with her hypereroticism, and the hyper-eroticism of Adonis with sterility and death. Freud, of course, would say that the goring of Adonis by the boar is a symbol of castration (see Section 3.3). Effectively, the same result can be produced by structural analysis. The death of Adonis in a lettuce patch is not arbitrary, but closely determined by the convergence of botanical science with attitudes to sex and marriage. According to Greek science and popular thought the effects of lettuce are just the opposite of the effects of myrrh: eating lettuce was widely believed to cause sexual impotence. This was because of its high water content and susceptibility to rot. So, far from mediating between man and immortality, lettuce was considered "the food of corpses" (Eubulus PCG F 13.5). According to Pliny, lettuce was popularly called "impotence plant" and "eunucheion" (Nat. Hist. 19.127). Like Myrrha and Adonis, myrrh and lettuce occupy opposite ends of the botanical scale: while myrrh is internally cooked, hot, dry, aphrodisiac, and imper-ishable, lettuce is uncookable, cold, moist, anaphrodisiac, and highly perishable.

Phaon and Mintha

Structurally very similar to the story of Adonis is the story of Phaon. Phaon was an old man who had spent his life operating a ferry service on the island of Lesbos. One day Aphrodite, disguised as an impoverished old woman, asked to be ferried across the strait, and he complied, demanding no fare in return. As a reward for his selflessness she gave him a bottle of myrrh. Anointing himself with it, he was transformed into an irresistibly beautiful young man. All the women of Mytilene fell in love with him, including the poetess Sappho, and many, like Sappho, threw themselves off the cliff at Leukas in despair. One day he was caught in the act of adultery and killed by the jealous husband. It seems that Aphrodite herself fell in love with Phaon and hid him "in fair lettuce-beds." It is not clear, however, whether the lettuce was to hide Phaon so Aphrodite could keep him to herself, or if it was to preserve him from his assailant. A variant has Aphrodite hide Phaon in "a field of unripe barley" (Athen. 2.68d), where the symbolic emphasis presumably falls upon the "unripe" state of the grain.

Phaon shares the same movement from erotic hyperactivity to impotence, which we find in Adonis. In this case his sexual activity is not only sterile but destructive, since he breaks up marriages and is responsible for the deaths of wives throughout Mytilene:

Phaon	Adonis	Myrrha
too old for love, but postmaturely brought to the prime of manhood	too young for love, but prematurely brought to impotence and death without attaining manhood	ripe for marriage
irresistible because of myrrh	irresistible because born from Myrrha, i.e., he is myrrh	resists all suitors
Aphrodite falls in love with Phaon	Aphrodite falls in love with Adonis	Aphrodite makes her fall in love with father
killed by jealous husband	killed by wild boar (and in some versions Ares, who is a jealous husband)	father (an adulterous husband) attempts to kill her
hidden in lettuce patch	hidden in lettuce patch	turns into myrrh tree

Lettuce stands opposite to myrrh as the virgin to the prostitute and Artemis to Aphrodite. But all stand in implicit opposition to grain, as the province of Demeter and the legitimate wife.

The convergence between botany and the sociology of women would be incomplete without a place for the concubine. In Greece the concubine had an ambivalent status. In states like Athens in which citizenship was carefully controlled, marriage was only allowed between citizens. Consequently, many stable relationships, otherwise indistinguishable from marriage, were not legally marriage, because the wife (or husband) was not a citizen. But if relations of concubinage resembled marriage, they could produce no legitimate citizen offspring (in states like Athens, after 450 BC, only children of citizen parents on both sides were recognized as citizens). Thus a concubine is like a wife, but sterile, as she cannot produce legitimate offspring, and yet her particular brand of sterility is not easily assimilated either to the virgin or the prostitute.

This position is occupied by Mintha, the mythical personification of mint. The nymph Mintha lived in the Underworld as Hades' concubine. But when Hades brought Persephone down to be his wife, the abandoned mistress began to make threats which angered Persephone and her mother Demeter. Mintha said she was more beautiful than her rival and that she would soon win Hades back as her lover and have Persephone thrown out of the palace. According to one version Persephone then tore her to pieces, but Hades turned her into sweet-smelling mint. Another version has Demeter stomp on her with her sandals until she is reduced to dust, but Mintha grows back out of the earth in the form of the "insignificant herb" that bears her name. A third version has it that Demeter, while still in mourning for Persephone, happened to cast her eyes upon wild mint and was so seized by hatred for the plant that she condemned it to sterility by decreeing that it should never bear fruit. Mint, in fact, does not bear seeds but reproduces by sending runners up out of the ground from the roots. Indeed, the botanical and sociological codes converge here entirely: Persephone and Demeter are to Mintha as grain is to mint, since grain bears fruit, while mint does not; but Persephone is also to Mintha as legitimate wife to concubine, and legitimate wives bear legitimate children, but concubines only illegitimate.

In the Greek pharmacopoeia mint's position is every bit as ambivalent as the concubine's. It is an aromatic plant and an aphrodisiac: in small quantities it excites the body. But in large quantities it has contraceptive powers, and can even be used to procure abortions; when taken by males it dilutes sperm and causes impotence or a general loss of virility. So while it excites sexual desire it also turns it from its procreative function. For this reason it is classified both as an aromatic and as a cold and wet vegetable. The ambiguous botanical status of mint is homologous to the double state of Mintha's mythic metamorphosis into a sweet-smelling but insignificant and sterile plant. For just as mint is aphrodisiac but in large quantities causes abortion and impotence, so the concubine is good for erotic play, but remains unproductive.

The botanical code expressed by the myths of Myrrha, Adonis, Phaon, and Mintha is thus consistently homologous to the sociological code used to classify women. We could express the ideologeme graphically as follows:

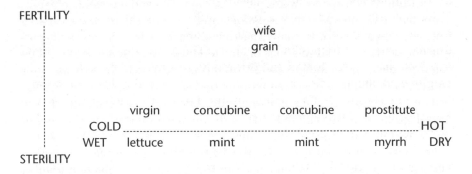

FERTILITY

                                    wife
                                    grain

                virgin   concubine   concubine   prostitute
        COLD .... HOT
        WET   lettuce   mint   mint   myrrh   DRY
STERILITY

Thesmophoria and Adonia

The principal annual women's festivals were the Thesmophoria, celebrated for Demeter, and the Adonia, celebrated for Aphrodite in commemoration of the death of Adonis. According to Detienne, the Thesmophoria was celebrated exclusively by legitimately married citizen women: admission was refused not only to men, but to women who were virgins, prostitutes, or concubines. It took place in autumn just before the sowing of the grain and the coming of the winter rains. In Athens the women camped in the sanctuary of Demeter for three days (in some cities the festival lasted as many as ten). On the first day women called "bailers" descended into a chasm to collect the rotting remains of piglets which had been ritually thrown to their death some time before. The rotten pig flesh, called *thesmoi*, was mixed with phallic cookies and the seed grain which was to be sown at the end of the month. On the second day the women fasted, in imitation of Demeter's mourning for Persephone. While fasting they lie on beds formed from a plant called "agnus castus," literally translated in English as the "chaste"-tree. On the third day there was a sacrifice and a feast in honor of a goddess called "The Beautiful Birth." In preparation for the festival the women were required to refrain from sexual activity, though there was a good deal of ritual obscenity included in the rites.

Of special interest here are the qualities which suit the chaste-tree to the rites of Demeter. It grows in the wetlands of the Mediterranean and owes its name to its well-known anaphrodisiac properties; it was mixed into drinks to calm the sexual appetite (it contains a sedative, vitexine). It also gives off a slightly offensive odor. Stench is in fact a major motif of the Thesmophoria, with its rotten piglets and fasting ("to smell of fasting" meant to have bad breath). There is also some evidence that wives prepared for the Thesmophoria by eating quantities of raw garlic, which made sexual abstinence somewhat easier.

According to Detienne the Adonia was celebrated, not by wives, but by prostitutes and concubines. Male lovers were also invited. Unlike the Thesmophoria, the Adonia was not an official celebration, organized by the state, but privately arranged by the women themselves, and celebrated in small groups of friends and neighbors. The festival lasted several days and took place in the hottest and driest days of summer, at the time of the Dog Star. Although the celebration commemorated the death of Adonis, just as the Thesmophoria commemorated Demeter's grief for the loss of Persephone, the festival was given to drinking and feasting in a mood of merriment and seduction. This happened on rooftops, where vast quantities of incense were burned in honor of Aphrodite. In addition the women grew gardens, called "gardens of Adonis." In broken pots they planted wheat, barley, lettuce, and fennel. In the blazing heat of July the plants germinate and shoot up quickly, before their root systems have a chance to develop, and after a few days of prematurely vigorous/growth they wither and die. On the eighth day the women took the desiccated gardens and threw them into the sea or into springs. The Adonia was not just very different from the Thesmophoria, but opposite in almost every way.

	Adonia	Thesmophoria
Divine powers	Adonis and his mistress Aphrodite	Demeter and her daughter Persephone
Time of year	hottest and driest season of the year, when the sun withers all plants	beginning of the rainy season in fall, just before the sowing of the grain
Civil status	private festivals	official festival
Sociological status of women	prostitutes and concubines	legitimate wives
Status of men	invited by the women	excluded
Sexual comportment	seduction	total abstinence
Location	rooftops	lying on the ground, descending into chasms and pits
Botany	incense and myrrh	chaste-tree
Odours	overuse of perfumes	stench
Food	feasting and drinking	fasting
Activity	growing gardens which wither prematurely (sterility rite)	mixing rotten pig corpses with seed grain (fertility rite)

Frazer interpreted the ritual of the gardens of Adonis as a magic fertility rite. But on Detienne's reading, it is just the opposite. Moreover, its magic functions not to alter nature, but to stabilize culture. Structural analysis allows us to see that the garden-growing ritual replicates the meaning of the myth of Adonis: excessive or unseasonal abandonment to sensual pleasures causes sterility, premature loss of vitality, and death. The plants used in the gardens are chosen for their botanical properties, but these, as we have seen, are already patterned after social categories of thought about women – indeed, the place of plants and women is mutually determined and overdetermined by the numerous homologous codes of a perfectly integrated and totalizing system of thought. The gardens of Adonis configure the botanical code in microsystem. Lettuce represents the cold, wet, wild, and raw vegetables, with all their connotations of impotence, rot, death, bestiality, and savagery. Opposed to lettuce is one of the few aromatic plants actually cultivated in Greece, fennel. According to the ancient pharmacopoeia fennel warms and dries out the body, but it is also "excellent for the genitals" and provokes an abundance of sperm (Pliny, *Nat.Hist.* 20.257). The microsystem represented by the gardens of Adonis thus shows the same opposition between aromatics and humid vegetables (fennel to lettuce) as we found in the myths of Adonis and Phaon (myrrh to lettuce). The entire garden ritual emphasizes the transition from sudden premature growth to sudden premature death, and from the hot and dry (withered plants, fennel) to the cold and wet (thrown into springs, lettuce).

But the gardens also represent the middle terms, grain and barley, which are the fruits of Demeter. The ritual is a perversion of the normal procedure for producing grain. The grains of Demeter are planted in autumn when there is equilibrium between hot and cold, dry and wet; by contrast, the grains of Adonis are grown at the hottest, driest, and most inopportune season for planting. The grains of Demeter grow from the cool and wet season to the hot and dry, but the grains of Adonis are first desiccated and then thrown into water. The grains of Demeter are sown deep in the earth; those of Adonis are put in shallow potsherds high on the rooftops. The grains of Demeter are brought to fruition by eight months' hard labor by men. The grains of Adonis wilt and die during eight days of play and merriment by women. Unlike real agriculture, this rite is a fruitless and aimless game, a futility rite, as fruitless and aimless as erotic play with the prostitutes and courtesans that perform it. The broken pots on the roof, in contrast to the pithos jars that preserve the seed grain in the earth, symbolize the women's wasted wombs (like the broken pots in which the Danaids, who murdered their husbands, are condemned to collect water in Hades). In all these ways the gardens of Adonis emphasize the symbolic opposition of the prostitute and courtesan to the legitimate wife and their capacity to undermine the serious obligation of marriage, namely, the production of offspring: in the rite the grain suffers the same fate as the fennel and the lettuce. Overdry and overwet are the extremes which wither or rot the grain, just as Aphrodite and Artemis represent the states of excessive sexual indulgence and excessive abstinence which waste the marriage.

The homologies discovered in our structural analysis of the myth of Prometheus and Pandora are confirmed by a wider analysis of the social context of the myth: we find the same way of carving up and organizing the world not only in other Greek myths and rituals, but in a broad network of social thought and practice. Vernant's third step (ideological analysis) thus confirms the second (semantic or paradigmatic analysis). In particular, the assimilation of marriage to agriculture and fire is consistent and pervasive throughout myth, ritual, language, literature, and science. By contrast, prostitution and concubinage are as consistently marked as a kind of anti-marriage and anti-agriculture. They are, like the gardens of Adonis, an illusory game, not a serious or useful occupation, and threaten to drain a man of his virility and lead to premature senility, sterility, and death without issue.

Not only is the place of women in society determined through the vast network of meaning that makes up the cultural system as a whole, it is rigidly overdetermined. Every place in the conceptual system is ultimately cross-referenced by every other, indeed ultimately determined by every other. Structuralism's model of ideology is a totalizing system, from which there is no escape, and no position from which one can opt out or even criticize the system. It is a steel trap gripping the minds of men and women, without their knowledge, but naturally with full consent, since even prostitutes joyfully celebrate their uselessness and social inferiority.

6.2 POSTSTRUCTURALISMS, POSTMODERNISM, AND IDEOLOGY

In this section we turn our attention to a number of critical trends, which, particularly in their convergence with one another, have extended the concept of myth well beyond that of primitive or traditional tale. The new broader concept of myth embraces the characteristic expression of our own contemporary mass culture. In doing so, it opens contemporary culture up to the methods of myth analysis examined in earlier chapters, but also introduces important theoretical refinements to these methods and brings new insights into the nature of myth, even myth in the more traditional sense of the term.

For two or three decades several strains of radical social criticism have dominated the humanities and social sciences in Western university campuses: feminist criticism, queer theory, black studies (in the USA), postcolonial criticism (in Britain), and several other varieties of social criticism dedicated to unmasking the social structures which perpetuate the oppression of historically marginalized groups. The generally acknowledged goal of such cultural criticism is the equalization of rights and opportunities, or put more succinctly (and sensationally), "liberation." These groups do not constitute schools of thought with independent methodologies or hermeneutic theories, but are, rather, interest groups united, not by procedure, but by a common area of concern and shared objectives. All of these groups tend to be theoretically eclectic, drawing heavily upon structuralism, psychoanalysis, and the other approaches studied in earlier chapters. The largest debt of all, however, is owed to a variety of critical theories which have appeared in the wake of structuralism. Of these we may single out two trends. One "poststructuralist" theoretical group, in which I will lump such disparate figures as Jacques Derrida and Michel Foucault, generally allies itself with the values of "postmodernity." A second group is much more closely informed by Marxist theory. The distinction between postmodern and Marxist is not, however, an easy one, since even Derrida and Foucault were heavily influenced by Marxism, while, conversely, a great many Marxists have allied themselves in various ways with postmodernism (whence some refer to themselves as "postmarxists"). The most significant result of the critical convergence of structuralism, Marxism, and liberation-oriented cultural studies has been a general coalescence of the concept of myth with the concept of ideology.

In this critical discourse "myth" is not necessarily a traditional tale, nor the product of a primitive mentality, nor the expression of a contrasting culture: no longer conceived as an attribute of the Other, myth by this new definition is very much the stuff of our own modern Western/global society. Admittedly, even with Frazer, Freud, and Burkert, the mythmaker had been insinuating himself ever-closer to the heart of our own civilization. It was only a matter of time before the science of mythology abandoned the us-and-them framework which first engendered it. The credit for taking the crucial step should probably go to the French Marxist and structuralist critic Roland Barthes (1915–80). In a volume of essays entitled *Mythologies* (1957), Barthes combined structural anthropology and Marxism to investigate the mass culture of his contemporary France. He reconceived myth as a speech act (or *parole*, which can include any signifying act, whether writing, painting, photography, gestures, or actions) with second-order reference to something of social importance. Note that "second-order" is not "secondary," or, as with Burkert, "partial"; mythical meaning is in

this sense often "primary." Translated into the language of structural linguistics, second-order means that the "sign" of the speech act serves as
the "signifier" of the myth. (Thus, in the "first order," linguistic signifier
+ linguistic signified = *linguistic sign/mythological signifier*; and, in the second order, *linguistic sign/mythological signifier* + mythological signified =
mythological sign.) It is this typical act of imbricating a mythical message
upon a seemingly innocent sign which, in Barthes's view, makes bourgeois
capitalist ideology particularly sinister. Myth's parasitic relation to the sign
allows bourgeois ideology to pass the cultural off as the natural, or the
historically contingent off as the essential and permanent. It does this because
the double nature of the *linguistic sign/mythological signifier* provides the
myth with an "alibi." Take, for example, the picture of a black soldier in
French uniform looking up and saluting the flag on the cover of *Paris-
Match*. As a sign, the final term of the "linguistic system," this is un-
objectionable and innocent, the black soldier doubtless really existed and
doubtless really saluted with as much fervor as could be expected of a
common soldier posing for the national press. But as a second-order signifier,
first term of the "mythological system," the message is anything but innocent. "Naive or not I see very well what it signifies: that France is a great
empire, that all of its sons, without distinction of colour, faithfully serve
under its flag, and that there is no better reply to those who denounce its
supposed colonialism, than the zeal shown by this black in the service of
his supposed oppressors" (1957: 201). But because of the ambivalence of
the sign/signifier, the myth parades as a simple and indisputable fact, for
ideology rests its case upon the first-order sign, and denies any complicity
with the second-order signifier.

   In this example mythology is indistinguishable from a particular ideological function, mystification, and a particular operation claimed to be
especially characteristic of bourgeois ideology, namely naturalization
(concealing the constructed nature of the "myth" by making the myth sit
invisibly upon the seemingly unassuming and matter-of-factual linguistic
sign). But since Barthes, Marxist and general cultural studies have merged
the concept of ideology in *all* its various forms and functions with the
concept of myth, so that the two terms are virtually interchangeable. This,
in turn, has had a powerful impact upon the study of myth in its more
traditional sense. Already, as we have seen, Vernant and Detienne's
third level of the analysis of myth (ideological) effectively equates the
myth-system with cultural mentality (Sections 5.7 and 6.1). More recently
Lincoln defined myth as "ideology in narrative form" (Chapter 1). It is
this broader concept of myth which stands behind my own definition in
Chapter 1 as anything which is told, received, and transmitted in the conviction of its social importance. By these definitions, the question of whether

or not something is true or false is largely irrelevant to the question of whether or not it is myth. Truth was never a sufficient condition for something being believed or repeated. It is much more relevant to consider the motive behind its transmission and reception. If it spreads because it is *thought* true, valid, important, or interesting for a given social group, then it is a myth. Admittedly, just about anything can become myth (though of course not everything is).

After structuralism

From the 1970s the various theoretical trends which dominated the humanities and social sciences in Western universities were generally labeled "poststructuralist." The label is an implicit acknowledgment of their ambivalent relation to structuralism of both indebtedness and disaffection (even those who continued in more or less the same path as the structuralists began to call themselves "semioticians"). Feminist and other "liberation" critics were fascinated with structuralism's ability to map the intricate networks of values which make up an ideological system. As Detienne shows (Section 6.1), a vast number of sensations, concepts, and activities, from the way one perceives smells, or understands the properties of plants, to the way one conducts a private party – all worked to fix the place of ancient women and keep them in it. Structuralism offered a kind of blueprint for ideology, revealing how the consciousness, perceptions, and desires of working people, women, blacks, colonials, etc., were "constructed." Many in particular found symbolic solace in the structuralist notion of the "arbitrariness" of the sign. "If there is 'health' in language," said Barthes, "it is founded upon the arbitrariness of the sign; what is disgusting in myth is its recourse to a false Nature," i.e., healthy language should perform like Brecht, baring its devices and never permitting the illusion that it mirrors nature (1957: 212). To feminists or blacks, for example, the arbitrariness of the sign symbolized the absence of any essential or fixed cause for their historically inferior social role. It suggested that if people could be constructed they could also be deconstructed and reconstructed.

But structuralism was also highly problematic. To groups dedicated to changing history structuralism was rigidly ahistorical. More seriously, to groups dedicated to liberation, structuralism seemed rigidly deterministic. Structuralism's model of culture constituted an inescapable "prison-house of language" (Jameson 1972). Vernant and Detienne's analysis (Sections 5.7 and 6.1) shows us an ideological system so totalizing, so homogeneous, and so perfectly integrated that it leaves no free space within the system from which one could launch an independent critical thought, let alone mount a challenge to the system. With no allowance for diversity within the system there was neither room for ethical choice nor any leverage for generating historical change. Historical change could only come from outside the system, randomly and mechanically, in the form of asteroids, plagues, or barbarian invasions.

Determinism and ahistoricity adhere to the very foundation of structuralism in Saussure's theory of language (and remain, despite efforts of theorists like Vernant and Detienne to historicize the method; Section 5.6). Saussure's exclusive focus upon language as an abstract and timeless system was effectively bought at the cost of denying the importance of actual utterances made by real people referring to specific things in concrete social situations and at precise moments in history. Particularly revealing is Saussure's treatment of the referent, i.e., the material or conceptual objects to which speech refers. It has no place in his linguistic system. Saussure's system does not link words to things, but links sounds (signifiers) to concepts (signified). But while expelling the referent from the front door, Saussure is forced to admit it surreptitiously through the back. He packs the referent, which remains a theoretical necessity despite Saussure, into the signified, as if the real world, outside language, could be reduced to a shadow-presence adhering to the underside of the sign itself. This leads Saussure into serious contradictions, most obvious, as Benveniste demonstrated (1966: 49–55), in his discussion of the "arbitrariness" of the sign. At one moment he speaks of the arbitrariness in the connection between signifier and signified, but elsewhere he insists that they are as necessary to one another and as inseparable as the two sides of a piece of paper. The logic of Saussure's theory as well as his examples required that he place the arbitrariness between the sign and the referent: there is no motivation for giving this sound to this or that thing; but arbitrariness between signifier and signified is an absurdity. At the cost of self-contradiction Saussure excluded the real world in order to make language a pure, autonomous and perfectly abstract conceptual system. As the Marxist critic Terry Eagleton (1943–) puts it, the very "founding gesture of structuralism had been to bracket off [reality]" (1983: 109):

> In order to reveal the nature of language, Saussure . . . had first of all to repress or forget what it talked about: the referent, or real object which the sign denoted, was put in suspension so that the structure of the sign itself could be better examined. . . . [Structuralism] spring[s] from the ironic act of shutting out the material world in order the better to illuminate our consciousness of it. For anyone who believes that consciousness is in an important sense *practical*, inseparably bound up with the ways we act in and on reality, any such move is bound to be self-defeating. It is rather like killing a person in order to examine more conveniently the circulation of the blood.

Cut off from the material world in this way Saussure's system of language could have no meaningful relationship with either society or history. Indeed, Saussure effectively denies them any independent or meaningful existence apart from language: for him society is nothing more than "the speaking masses," while history is nothing more than a record of random and meaningless change. Both propositions are nicely illustrated by Saussure's discussion of change in language. As logic and order exist only within the synchronic system, while diachronic linguistics were without system, purpose, or reason, change in language is ascribed to *une force aveugle* (1972: 122–8, 140). Language, and consequently social thought, is beyond human control: "not only would no individual be able to effect the tiniest modification of the choice that language has made, but the masses acting in concert could not exercise sovereignty over a single word; they are bound by language just as it is" (1972: 104). This, he argued, is because (paraphrasing 106–8):

1   The sign is arbitrary. As there is no rational link between the signifier and the signified, there can be no rational critique of the sign, no reason to change it.
2   Language has a multitude of signs. It cannot be easily reformed as could, for example, an alphabet.
3   Language is too complex a system. It is beyond the grasp of most users of language. Change would require the intervention of specialists, but this has never happened.
4   The masses resist all efforts at linguistic innovation. Unlike other codes, language is constantly used by everyone. This cardinal fact is alone enough to demonstrate the impossibility of a revolution [*sic*]. Of all social institutions, language offers the smallest purchase to any initiative. It is of a piece with the life of the masses and, since they are naturally inert, they appear above all as a conservative force.

The second and third reasons amount to no more than saying that language as a whole is too big to change, but this, if it is true, does not explain why we cannot change any of its parts, and most emphatically does not explain why "the masses acting in concert could not exercise sovereignty over a single word." And yet it follows from Saussure's concept of total relativity within the system that any change in a part of language necessarily entails changes within the entire system. Far more influential, however, is the first reason he gives. Even if we follow Saussure in placing the arbitrariness of the sign between signifier and signified, the belief that this arbitrariness places the sign beyond the reach of reasoned critique is utterly inconsistent with the general thrust of Saussure's theory, which assures us that the meaning structure of a sign is determined and overdetermined by the linguistic system as a total logical order. If we find a sign offensive it is not in its arbitrary relation of an acoustic image with a mental concept; it is in the relations of difference and equivalence within the system which produce the specific value assigned by the system to a given term. In English, for example, the term "mankind" is being displaced by "humankind," "spokesman" by "spokesperson," etc. These changes occurred in response to the protest and public pressure mounted by women's groups. The "arbitrariness" of the sign did not frustrate or invalidate a critique implicating both signifier and signified. On the contrary, the presence of "man" within the signifier was deemed to concede male privilege to the signified.

Saussure's fourth reason is most telling: he asserts as a universal truth that the masses are "naturally inert." And as language, unlike maritime signals, is always everyone's affair, we are asked to believe that any attempt by an individual speaker to deviate or innovate in language will immediately be squashed by the collective will of all other speakers acting in concert. This obviously counterfactual claim (new phrases are coined every day) reveals the flaw in Saussure's concept of language as an absolutely homogeneous and autonomous system. It is, in fact, neither homogeneous nor autonomous. Between the abstract totality of *langue* and the isolated utterance of *parole*, between the system and the individual (as also between the system and its terms; cf. Section 5.4), there stand an infinitude of middle terms. The phenomenon of language change appears truly bewildering if we look at language as a homogeneous entity which confronts the arbitrary catachreses of isolated speakers and weeds them out with the united fervor of the collective will. However, the process of linguistic change becomes readily intelligible once we recognize that the linguistic group is infinitely subdivisible, that any social group in close contact will almost certainly develop a subcode whose terms diverge from the main code when condensed and transformed by the knowledge of shared interests and shared experience, that, in effect, the linguistic code comprises a vast number of subcodes of varying size based on the shared experiences and interests of social, professional, religious, and other cultural groups, and that these groups are arranged in an ever-changing hierarchy of influence. Resistance to change in the code as a whole is undermined by the receptivity of smaller groups to the creation of subcodes (sociolects) which reflect more local communities of interests. In practice, "deviant" speech forms part of the linguistic subsystem of groups who may be acutely aware of the reality of the diachronic values, past and future, contained by their terms. Far from being "blind" and "unsystematic," changes like "spokesman" > "spokesperson" were deliberate, motivated, teleological, and directly related to a system of social values.

Saussure's privileging of system, synchrony, and sign over utterance, history, and referent was so extreme that, as we have seen, even structural linguists like Jakobson and Benveniste had to correct his concept of structure just to make the theory self-consistent and serviceable. Nonetheless it was Saussure's model, more than any other, which formed the main target of the critical reaction. The earliest and most promising "fix" was by V. N. Volosinov's *Marxism and the Philosophy of Language,* written in Russian in 1929, but only "discovered," with its first translation, in 1973. Volosinov's linguistic theories effectively invert Saussure: they are centered on diachrony, parole, and social interaction, declaring that "language as a stable system of normatively identical forms is merely a scientific abstraction"; "language is a continuous generative process implemented in the social-verbal interaction of speakers"; "linguistic creativity cannot be understood apart from the ideological meanings and values that fill it"; and "the structure of the utterance is a purely sociological structure" (1986: 98). Far more influential, however, were the critical theories of Derrida and Foucault. In particular Derrida's "deconstruction" set one group of extreme tendencies in Saussure's theory against another, and pushed Saussure's faulty logic to opposite (and equally absurd) conclusions.

Poststructuralism and postmodernism

As noted above, disillusionment with the structuralist project sparked two very different, and frequently opposite, reactions. One strain of poststructuralism denounced structuralism as the culmination of the Western humanist tradition. This strain, originally highly vocal in its social criticism, rejected all traditional Western values and embraced attitudes and values generally identified as "postmodern," but has grown progressively mute as the culture of "postmodernity" establishes itself around it.

In general these poststructuralists simply defanged structuralism's bleak vision of culture by extending the logic that seemed to place it beyond human control. They argued that so far from anything being totalizing, there was nothing in control of the social system, in fact both system and terms were metaphysical illusions: history, society, ideology, and even the individual human were nothing but fragments of a discourse which was itself a fragment of a confused and incoherent chaos of fragmented, incoherent, and self-contradictory discourses. With millenarian fervor, "man" (meaning human individuals), "history," and "ideology" were all in turn declared to be dead, or simply to have never existed. "Meaning," too, could be tossed out the window: deconstruction was particularly fascinated by Saussure's claim that the meaning of a sign was a product of total systemic logic, namely, that it meant what all the other signs in the system did not mean. Derrida declared that meaning was thus endlessly "deferred" since one signifier simply pointed to all the others without ever accumulating a signified (see Section 5.4). This deferral of meaning rendered ideology impotent; the prison-house of language was not just full of holes, it was nothing but. All this, in retrospect, seems little more than academic comfort food designed for the generation of 1960s radicals who were now happily tenured at elite universities, and otherwise getting too old and too busy for protest marches. It was cold comfort, however, since it offered no consolation beyond the assurance that, if you could not do anything to change society, no one else could either (leaving aside the big question whether "you" and "society" exist in the first place). Almost the only thing that these poststructuralists left intact was talk (fragmented, autonomous, and purposeless language and discourse) – it was well suited to ivy-league undergraduate curricula: noisily anarchic, and profoundly innocuous, since the revolution had neither subject nor object; it spoke of an oppression without either oppressor or oppressed.

This kind of poststructuralism was most innocuous when it spoke of liberation. For if oppression could come from within the system itself, so could liberation. Deconstruction made a fetish of Saussure's "arbitrariness of the signifier." The deferral of the signified seemed to make it float freely, never to be tied down to a meaning or slotted into the system. Paul de Man's *Allegories of Reading* (1979) makes frequent reference to "the liberating theory of the signifier," "the arbitrary power play of the signifier," and the "liberation of the signifier from the signified." Liberation was now an effect of inward meditation: like some strange form of Zen, it required only the mental intoxication of theory to realize that it was always with us, as an automatic and ongoing consequence of a natural tendency of language to be self-willed, whimsical, and senseless. Discourse ruled, but its rule was structureless, fragmented, and meaningless. The masses acting in concert could no more change discourse than they could *langue*, its totalizing, structured, homogeneous, and meaning-saturated predecessor.

Marxism

Another strain of poststructuralism allied itself with some of the goals of traditional Western humanism, in particular the "enlightenment project" and the struggle for social equality. It set itself against what it saw as the globalized Western culture of postmodernity. The dominant theoretical orientation came directly or indirectly from Marxism.

If they showed little interest in social class, feminists, queer theorists, black liberationists, postcolonial critics, and many other cultural critics shared Marxist concern with the distribution of power and the goal of liberation. Moreover, as all had their institutional basis in the humanities divisions of Western universities, they shared Marxism's concern for understanding the function of language, art, and literature within a total social context. Moreover, many Western Marxists shared their conviction that cultural criticism was a legitimate and important form of activism: Barthes argued that analyzing modern cultural myths "is the only effective way for an intellectual to take political action" (1953: 108). Feminists and black liberationists had also largely abandoned direct political action by the 1970s, partly in recognition that the most serious obstacles to equality were not political but ideological. Women, for example, had had the vote for over two generations (in Canada since 1918 and in Britain since 1918–28), and had, since World War II, made considerable inroads into the workforce. Yet, despite this, women had not only failed to gain effective control of the political process, but frequently proved to be the most staunchly conservative, even reactionary, part of the electorate. The same predicament had earlier been faced by Western Marxists laboring under the double disillusionment of a Soviet-style Marxism, which proved even more oppressive to common people than the czarist regime it replaced, and the failure of Western European workers to seize control of power in the years following World War I, despite the fact that the material conditions for revolution existed there (as they did not in the Soviet Union). Antonio Gramsci, the leader of the Italian Communist Party, while imprisoned by the Fascists in the 1930s, identified "ideology" as the central problem for modern Marxism: the existence of the objective material conditions for change (or as in the Soviet Union, actual political change) meant nothing so long as the subjective mental conditioning of the masses remained the same. Abandoning the strict materialism of Engels and Lenin, the dominant strain of current Marxist cultural theory recognizes that social ideologies are important, perhaps the most important sites of social struggle, and as such can be changed by human agency for the benefit of humanity. In other words, Marxism offered just what structuralism seemed to deny the struggle for social justice.

The relationship between the two strains of poststructuralism has grown increasingly uneasy. The first treats the second as naive idealists and dismiss their theoretical concepts as metaphysical illusions. The second treats the first as capitulationist and worse. So far from ideology being dead, they claim that the postmodernism embraced by their rivals is itself perhaps the clearest theoretical expression of the ideology of postindustrial or consumer capitalism. The description of society offered by structuralism more nearly corresponds to the social reality of the late twentieth century: totalizing, autonomous, dehumanizing, abstract, and increasingly based upon self-referential and referentless signs. The vision offered by postmodernism connives in naturalizing, perpetuating, and libidinizing these totalizing structures.

The culture of postindustrial capitalism

Throughout this book we have identified reasons why Western culture has grown progressively more decentered and relativistic. But the general drift toward cultural relativism was precipitated suddenly, if predictably, by a fundamental change in Western economies. Since about 1960 Western economies have been dominated not by industrial capitalism (the manufacture of goods) but by commodity exchange. Typically the very rich make their money not by owning and operating factories, but by participation in the exchange of goods. The emphasis in this new economy is not so much on things as on representations. To begin with, the utility of objects is much less important than the way they are advertised, marketed, and packaged. Vastly more effort is put into creating the right symbolic significance for products, wrapping them in "mythical" glamors, and manufacturing desire, than into developing the intrinsic merits, if any, of the widgets in question. The mass media and the bulk of the resources of postindustrial consumer capitalism are directed to representations whose connection with reality grows increasingly tenuous.

This trend toward an abstract economy of signs has only accelerated since the 1990s, with the division of the global economy between manufacture in the Third World and marketing in the West. Increasingly, the economy in the West is driven by big-name products which are manufactured in Asia at small cost, and then sold in the West at a considerably greater cost, with the bulk of the profits going to the firms who control the logo (Nike or Gap), though they manufacture nothing but a lifestyle mythology which attaches to the logo as signified to signifier. The case is well put by Naomi Klein (2000: 21):

> Overnight "Brands, not products!" became the rallying cry for a marketing renaissance led by a new breed of companies that saw themselves as "meaning brokers" instead of product producers. What was changing was the idea of what – in both advertising and branding – was being sold. The old paradigm had it that all marketing was selling a product. In the new model, however, the product takes a back seat to the real product, the brand, and the selling of the brand acquired an extra component that can only be

described as spiritual. Advertising is about hawking product. Branding, in its truest and most advanced incarnations, is about corporate transcendence. . . . On Marlboro Friday [April 2, 1993] a line was drawn in the sand between the lowly price slashers and the high-concept brand builders. The brand builders conquered and a new consensus was born: the products that will flourish in the future will be the ones presented not as "commodities" but as concepts: the brand as experience, as lifestyle.

Since the new economy is an economy driven by representations, and since the economic is the ultimate determinant of social reality – and in this case the base may be said to "generate its superstructures with a new kind of dynamic" (Jameson 1991: xxi) – representations (signs! myths!) have become the reality which they self-reflexively represent. They rehearse in this way the role of the ultimate reality of consumer capitalism, which is, of course, money, itself a mere representation of exchange value. And even money, which has admittedly been around for a long time, is growing more abstract as it grows more important: once precious metals, then paper (still promising emptily to "pay the bearer [gold] upon demand"), now money is itself "represented" by plastic or by mere blips on a computer screen. The goods being purchased are also frequently abstract and invisible, most notably on the financial markets, where there is normally no interest in the actual goods being purchased, since these are themselves only symbols in an exchange in which money is used to purchase itself, much like the signifiers which chase each other in an endless quest for signifieds in the ultimately self-referential economy of the postmodern–poststructuralist sign. You buy porkbellies or Brent Crude for August delivery, but the transaction is pure representation; the last thing you want to see is a truck dumping porkbellies on your doorstep. Investors do not buy material goods but signs, "floating signifiers," of fluctuating value, to be traded for other signs, and their fluctuations seem ever more arbitrary and disconnected to the actual referent of the transaction, whether stocks, commodities, or currencies.

In the same spirit, financial markets respond ever less to real situations than to symbolic ones. Investors know that they are speculating not on the real value of goods but on the market value, which is determined less by supply and demand than by the behavior of other investors. The day-to-day fluctuations of the markets are often driven by events which have at best only symbolic or mythical connections with economic realities. Investors are known to buy or sell on quite arbitrary signals. Daily news events, which in themselves could have no real economic impact, will nonetheless impact the market, since there investor reaction is everything. When ex-president Nixon died, American investors sold. It was not that any of them believed that Nixon's life sustained the economy (he had been removed from the presidency for very bad behavior two decades earlier). Investors were reacting to the fear that other investors would react to a ritual signal to sell. Such ritualized investor behavior is easily misperceived as impersonal "market forces," and indeed, with computerized trading, the system no longer needs to pass through human consciousness. The economy seems a postmodern self-regulating and autonomous sign system which works its arbitrary and irrational destiny through humans or despite them.

Market economists do not as a rule recognize the autonomy of the sign. Still committed to a materialist ideology, they speak of "fundamentals" which will curb the autonomous swings of the financial markets, like some hidden god dispensing an ultimate economic justice; or they speak of sudden swings in the market as mere "profit-taking," as if this was not the whole point of the exercise. But fundamentals (the supposed "real" economic conditions) only "correct" the market precisely when, in self-fulfilling prophecy, the economic forecasters provoke the next market swing. In other words, the "real market conditions" only assert their control if converted to a representation in this confused self-deconstructing world where sign becomes reality and reality becomes sign.

Myths and symbols constitute the reality of political and social life every bit as much as the economic: politics has become more theatrical: and more stage-managed than ever. The real politician or the real political agendas are irretrievably buried under the gloss of image-makers, publicity agents, and spin doctors. Indeed, even if the real political agendas emerge from behind the smoke and mirrors, they seem to matter less than such purely artificial and openly manufactured glamors as "leadership." On the very day I write this the radio announces that Arnold Schwarzenegger, "the Terminator," is taking on the biggest "role" of his life, after ousting Gray Davis as Governor of California, who suffered from an acknowledged "image-problem." The voters of California, untroubled by the movie star's lack of experience or policy, elected Schwarzenegger because he looked like a tough-guy, the main election issue being whether his alleged molestation of a host of female employees was consistent with this representational value. Screen politics may seem particularly endemic to California, which is the heartland of the mass media, and, not coincidentally, the home of Clem Whitaker, the man who invented campaign-management services (in 1933) and first used marketing techniques to sell politicians. But California is only the extreme manifestation of a much wider phenomenon. Ronald Reagan was exported to become the most popular president in American history and, also not coincidentally, "the first postmodern politician . . . who understood the power of free-floating symbolism, rooted in nothing at all" (Anderson 1990: 165). Politicians, like policies, like products, are increasingly valued as floating signifiers, screens on which the image-makers project and constantly adjust a set of significations. There is little to distinguish the marketing of "democratic" government from hair gel.

Culture is also no exception. "In postmodern culture, 'culture' has become a product in its own right" (Jameson 1991: x). In the age of consumer capitalism, cultural forms which were once separated from or opposed to economic life appear fully integrated in the form of the commodity. Indeed, consumer capitalism swallows and incorporates its own critics. Feminism has been used to sell cigarettes, and Che Guevara's image is a copyrighted logo for a soda company. The cultural values of pluralism and diversity, once the theoretical icons of liberation movements on the Left, are now a marketing tool for an unprecedented trade in new values, identities, and lifestyles. Postmodernists can well imagine that the revolution will come from the sign-system itself, and that when it comes it will be meaningless. The marketing process reduces these values to superficial glamors. A vast industry offers ready-made self-representations to quench the thirst for personal identity and distinction which mass culture itself created by alienating, uprooting, and destroying traditional identities. In the USA, the ultimate secular state, people regularly fight their sense of spiritual bankruptcy by buying religion, often weird cults cynically cobbled together with a superficial knowledge of myth and ritual, for hungry consumers, who will provide two days'-worth of true-belief, and an initiation fee of $500 for a weekend initiation (hotel included). In our uprooted world, belief comes easily and shallowly, like the "reality effects" of a cleverly constructed discourse. One's real self, for those who still believe in it, becomes harder to identify and define as traditional national, regional, religious, class, and family ties are increasingly dissolved by the confused, fragmented, centerless, and constantly fluctuating discourse of the mass media. In Japan, there are agencies where lonely bachelors can go to hire a family who will come over and eat Sunday dinner, playing the role of mother, father, wife, or children, and then wash the dishes and withdraw before you get tired. Identity is itself a commodity in consumer capitalism, equivalent and exchangeable with any other. In the great marketplace of the pluralistic modern society you can consume any identity you wish; they are all just labels, market effects; personal identity is meaningless packaging, ultimately a product of marketing discourse.

In *The Illusions of Postmodernism* Eagleton argues that the postmodern poststructuralists are "politically oppositional but economically complicit" (1996: 132). In this respect postmodernism closely resembles structuralism: "pressing a sort of technological determinism all the way through to the mind itself, treating individuals as the mere empty locus of impersonal codes, it imitated the way modern society actually treats them but pretends it does not, thus endorsing its logic while unmasking its ideals" (131). This contradiction in postmodernism, and structuralism before it, is in turn based on a contradiction in advanced capitalist society. On the one hand, there is a need for its liberal humanist ideology to believe in certain absolute values, such as the autonomy and self-identity of individuals: upon them depend such things as the law courts and the electoral system. On the other hand, the economic system is based upon the construction of consumers through a stream of ephemeral and discontinuous media representations: postindustrial capitalism treats individuals as the fleeting effects of its discursive practices. Says Eagleton (132–3):

> Postmodernism is radical in so far as it challenges a system which still needs absolute values, metaphysical foundations and self-identical subjects; against these it mobilizes multiplicity, non-identity, transgression, anti-foundationalism, cultural relativism. The result at its best, is a resourceful subversion of the dominant value-system, at least at the level of theory. . . . But postmodernism usually fails to recognize that what goes at the level of ideology does not always go at the level of the market. If the system has need of the autonomous subject in the law court or polling booth, it has little enough use for it in the media or shopping mall. In these sectors, plurality, desire, fragmentation and the rest are as native to the way we live as coal was to Newcastle before Margaret Thatcher got her hands on it. Many a business executive is in this sense a spontaneous postmodernist. Capitalism is the most pluralistic order history has ever known, restlessly transgressing boundaries and dismantling oppositions, pitching together diverse life-forms and continually overflowing the measure.

6.3   DECRYPTING IDEOLOGY

In this section I undertake to describe the root assumptions of an ideological analysis of myth. This is not an easy task, for despite a general convergence of the concept of myth with ideology, neither Marxism nor poststructuralism has a particular interest in myth beyond extending its traditional meaning to the stereotypes or "common-sense truths" of contemporary mass culture. No Marxist or poststructuralist account offers a theoretical exposition of the ideological function of myth in the traditional sense of the term. Indeed, it is questionable whether the past thirty-five years have brought any new methods for analyzing texts: since structuralism the trend has been to shy away from grand theories, unifying visions, or universal claims (even to a degree among Marxists). The kind of all-embracing, system-building theory that we have studied so far in this book seems to fall away, perhaps significantly, with the collapse of Western imperialism. The rejection of all "master narratives" is a shibboleth of the poststructural age.

The general suspicion of "grand theories" has given way to a theoretical pluralism. This pluralism expresses itself in the eclectic use and adaptation of earlier theories of interpretation, especially psychoanalysis and structuralism; and in the multitude of theoretical perspectives available in any branch of poststructural criticism. The general mood has been negative and critical (if fruitfully so) and set more toward sapping the ideological foundations of earlier theories than toward new construction. For this reason it is impossible to select one or two theorists or works as fundamental, dominant, or even representative expressions of the current practice of ideological criticism. In previous chapters I attempted to characterize a general approach by focusing upon a particular representative. Here I am limited to characterizing typical assumptions and methods of ideological analysis by extracting and assembling ideas from a large number of recent and contemporary theorists. There are a great many Marxist and poststructuralist analyses of the ideological function of products of modern culture, especially literature, art, music, drama, and film. Much of this discussion is broadly adaptable to the analysis of archaic forms of myth, but much is not.

Social structure

Marxist and Marxist-influenced criticism typically find that a literary narrative is structurally related to the total structure of a society. Within this total structure, the economic structure, including the relationship of the social classes, is for classic Marxism the most important part. Some "postmarxists" treat this as an ideologically motivated hierarchy to be deconstructed. On the other hand, cultural critics, including most modern Marxists, generally reject the traditional Marxist notion (really more due to Engels and Lenin) that ideology is more or less passively shaped by the economic base, or "infrastructure." The acceptance of a "semi-autonomy" for the cultural sphere permits a concept of literature, art, etc., as less determined and passive: art (in the inclusive sense of the term) not only expresses social relationships but is an active agent of their reproduction or alteration. Art influences, positively or negatively, the way we perceive social structures, and ultimately affects our desire to maintain or to change them. Many theorists would see all art as inherently conservative, others as inherently revolutionary. (The latter view often presupposes, as with Adorno, an elitist distinction between "authentic" art and mass culture.) But it is easier to assume that some art acts in a conservative way to integrate and perpetuate a certain social order, and some in a revolutionary way to agitate for change. Indeed, critics often find both tendencies in a single work at any given moment, or varying through time: frequently the revolutionary art of one era becomes the conservative art of the next, or vice versa.

The recognition of the possibility of dissenting cultural forms marks an important departure from the structuralist concept of ideology. Rejecting structuralism's view of ideology as homogeneous and monolithic, most contemporary theorists prefer to view ideology as fragmented and conflicted. Ideology is fragmented because society has divided interests. It is conflicted because ideology is a primary site of social struggle. It is more common therefore to speak of social ideologies in the plural. For most postmodern theorists this pluralism and diversity eliminate the possibility of any human group exerting effective control upon the social system as a whole; for Marxist and other liberation-oriented poststructuralists, this fragmentation is needed precisely in order to think the possibility of any social group exerting control. The monolithic and totalizing ideology theorized by structuralism admitted neither the possibility of dissent nor the possibility of rationally motivated change.

Some theorize not only plural ideologies, but different levels at which they work. Simplest and perhaps most important is the distinction between general ideology and subgroup ideologies. There is a general cultural level at which the function of ideology is to bind the interests of the whole society and create common values and common perceptions. But beneath the general ideology there are also other ideologies which promote the interests of the more important social subdivisions. The largest and most important of these social subdivisions are usually class, race (or ethnicity), religion, and gender. Since everyone belongs to a multiplicity of categories, as well as to the general culture, these subgroup ideologies are rarely expressed by any individual in anything like a pure form. Generally speaking, every individual is the site of many competing and frequently opposed ideologies.

Ideologies working at different levels normally work at cross-purposes. The subgroup ideologies of subordinate classes are most likely to oppose aspects of the general ideology. The function of subgroup ideology is to promote the solidarity and social interests of the subgroup. Since the interests of social classes are to a very large extent opposed, the values promoted by their subgroup ideologies will also be opposed. Therefore, from the perspective of the society as a whole, it is the nature of subgroup ideology to be divisive. The general social ideology works to counteract the divisiveness of subgroup ideologies. It has to find or create a common ground between the subgroup ideologies, or at least the more important subgroup ideologies and, as much as possible, the general ideology has to bridge over, obscure, or efface the divisions between the ideologies of the dominant social subgroups.

This in particular is the task of myth, art, music, literature and, indeed, theoretical and scientific discourse. Just where a particular work positions itself with relation to general and subgroup ideologies is variable. Those which are most conspicuously aligned with a particular subgroup agenda will have messages which come through with a clarity and redundancy which will make most people reject them as shallow, simplistic, or propagandistic. The greatest currency and highest esteem are likely to be reserved for those cultural products capable not only of bridging the divisions in the general ideology, but of remaining open to differential readings from different and even opposed ideological perspectives. Complex, polysemous texts thrive best in fragmented and unstable cultures. (It is little wonder that contemporary criticism makes such a virtue of the "open" text.)

Ultimately the quest to produce a general cultural ideology is a quest to bridge the unbridgeable, and so general cultural ideologies reveal the strains generated by the contradictions at base. Moreover, even the general ideology is a product of intellectual and physical labor, and is likely to be skewed toward the interests of the dominant subgroups who control the means of cultural production. This bias need have little to do with either the author or the consumer. Generally speaking, the more complex the process of production, the less control either is likely to exercise over the ideological content. Both may be of less importance than the general values promoted by the form and manner of artistic production (the genre, its sponsors, and the medium of production).

Reading ideology

"Contradiction" is a key term for ideological analysis. In heavy usage in Marxist (Hegelian) dialectic, it may simply stand for any opposition in which the terms are definable in relation to their opposites (Engels uses it for oppositions like "heredity" and "adaptation" in the natural sciences). More commonly it is used of oppositions in social structure and in social thought, both of which are important for analyzing ideology. The term "contradictions in reality" may be used to refer to opposed historical or social forces, such as the opposition of capitalists and proletariat, or contrary tendencies in the social structures designed to contain those forces. "Ideological contradictions" are contradictions in social values, language, discourse, or practice. Ideological contradictions may appear as real, logical contradictions (i.e., the simultaneous assertion that A and -A are both true), or simply as ambiguities, ambivalences, inconsistencies, indeterminacies, or silences in what is said, thought, assumed, or practiced. The ultimate task of ideological analysis is to establish the relationship between the ideological contradictions in myth, art, literature, etc., and real contradictions. The relationship is not simple. As Eagleton put it (1991: 135):

> It might then be thought that ideological contradictions somehow "reflect" or "correspond to" ["real"] contradictions in society itself. But the situation is in fact more complex than this suggests. Let us assume that there is a "real" contradiction in capitalist society between bourgeois freedom and its oppressive effects. The ideological discourse of bourgeois liberty might also be said to be contradictory; but this is not exactly because it reproduces the "real" contradiction in question. Rather, the ideology will tend to represent what is positive about such liberty, while masking, repressing or displacing its odious corollaries; and this masking or repressing work, as with the neurotic symptom, is likely to interfere from the inside with what gets genuinely articulated. One might claim, then, that the ambiguous, self-contradictory nature of the ideology springs precisely from its *not* authentically reproducing the real contradiction; indeed were it really to do so, we might hesitate about whether to term this discourse "ideological" at all.

A simple logical contradiction is therefore only the most conspicuous index that rational discourse has bumped up against the limits of power and failed. Throughout this book we have noticed a number of ideological contradictions and suggested how these might ultimately be rooted in real contradictions: such, for example, were the contrasting European visions of primitive races as noble savages and beasts (Section 2.1); Müller's contradictory description of the Aryas as a poet of language and a bland observer and recorder of celestial phenomena (Section 2.2); Frazer's savage elites who are dedicated to science, truth, and progress and who are at the same time liars who impede social development by deceiving the masses in order to maintain their political ascendancy (Section 2.4). Closely related to such contradictions, ambivalences often reveal an attempt to accommodate opposed ideological perspectives or to bridge antagonistic values: the ambivalence of Freud, toward both superego and the id, might be read as shaped by class struggle, particularly in light of his own applications of the psychic dynamic to politics and social relations (Section 3.4). Most challenging of all for the ideological critic is to detect the simple effacement of real contradictions altogether. According to Pierre Macherey (1966), the object of an ideological analysis of literary texts is to discover the significant silences. One might compare the way Saussure's structuralism simply effaces and then displaces the referent or dismisses diachronicity as beyond rational discourse (Section 6.2).

The classic example of an ideological critique is Karl Marx's analysis, in *Capital* (1867) and in *Theory of Surplus Value* (1861–3), of the classic British economists' theory of value. In particular, Marx declared the contradictions of Adam Smith's *Inquiry into the Nature and Causes of the Wealth of Nations* (1776) to be "of significance because they contain problems which it is true he does not solve, but which he reveals by contradicting himself" (1999: 151). Smith's is a classic bourgeois description of the market as an autonomous system which, if allowed to run by its own laws, that is to say so long as exchange was free and equal, would work for the ultimate benefit of all. The system includes laws which keep prices, despite occasional fluctuations, close to what Smith calls "natural" values or "natural" prices. The "natural value" or "natural price" of a commodity was one which gave a fair return on capital and rent as well as labor. At the same time Smith correctly determined that the exchange value of a commodity was measurable only by the amount of labor required to produce the commodity. Smith tried to reconcile these two competing views by maintaining that, while labor alone produced exchange value in a primitive economy, the laws governing exchange value were different under capitalism, where he felt the need to affirm that capital and rent also had a role in producing exchange value. And yet Marx repeatedly shows that, despite himself, Smith's notion of value in the primitive economy invades his discussion of the capitalist economy, or conversely, that his attempt to modify the labor theory of value for capitalist production generated further logical knots elsewhere in his theory. Smith's error was in thinking that labor time was no longer the immanent measure of exchange value under capitalism, when in fact he should have concluded that the quantity of labor no longer equalled the value of labor under capitalism (i.e., the wage paid to workers was lower than the exchange value their work created).

The overt contradictions in Smith's theory allow him to keep silent about a more fundamental contradiction within liberal bourgeois ideology. The conspicuous silence in Smith has to do with the real relations expressed by the commodity form, which at base are the unequal relations between capital and labor. Smith's refusal to allow the labor theory of value to continue into the modern economy is an exercise in logical acrobatics which enables Smith to maintain the illusion that exchange in the market is free and equal, even when the exchange is between the worker offering his labor and the capitalist paying wages. But in fact, says Marx, because market conditions are precisely not free and equal, workers are forced to sell labor power at a price less than it is worth: the difference goes directly to the capitalist as profit. Only labor, not capital nor rent, is a source of exchange value. The capitalist or rentier takes a share of the exchange value of goods, but does not determine them. Their share comes directly at the expense of the workers.

The contradictions in Smith's theory therefore arise from a deeper ideological contradiction, namely that between the free and equal exchange liberal capitalism insists upon, and the unfree and subordinate condition in which it must place workers. On the one hand Smith's theory gives expression to the labor theory of value, despite his belief that it is not operable in a capitalist economy. On the other hand, Smith's theory omits all discussion of the real social and economic relations between capital and labor. He focuses instead upon the commodity and conditions of exchange. He hides these purely historical and contingent relations behind a self-regulating and beneficent Nature, which governs the market with an "invisible hand," and is concerned to give all "producers" – landowner, capitalist, and laborer alike, their fair and equitable return.

The silences, distortions, and contradictions in Smith's theory do not derive from Smith alone. They are ideological blind spots shared by his class and culture. In studying the economy he begins naturally with appearances, what we might call the "surface structures," the commodity and the system of exchange, not with the class relations of which these appearances are the expression. This merely replicates a function attributable to the commodity itself. As Marx puts it (1906: 83):

> A commodity is . . . a mysterious thing, simply because in it the social character of men's labour appears to them as an objective character stamped upon the product of that labour; because the relation of the producers to the sum total of their own labour is presented to them as a social relation, existing not between themselves, but between the products of their labour. In order, therefore, to find an analogy, we must have recourse to the mist-enveloped regions of the religious world. In that world the productions of the human brain appear as independent beings endowed with life, and entering into relation both with one another and the human race. So it is in the world of commodities with the products of men's hands.

New uses for old methods

Ideological analysis provides a goal, but few procedural instructions. Perhaps this reticence is due to the fact that the manoeuvres of ideology are too many or too evasive to catalogue. More probably it is because schematization and systematization are simply contrary to the negative and analytical spirit of the poststructuralist era. From this avoidance, however, comes one of the main strengths of poststructural criticism: its methodological eclecticism. The interpreter is free to pick and choose from the tools of past theories while reserving a healthy skepticism for their grand, all-encompassing worldviews. Psychoanalysis and structuralism have proven particularly adaptable to the ends of ideological analysis.

Many find a procedural model in Freud. Macherey himself proposes a "symptomatic" reading of literary texts in imitation of Freudian psychoanalysis. The dynamic of repression closely resembles the function of ideology, especially when it works simultaneously to resolve and to conceal at the level of superstructure the conflicts and divisions at the level of infrastructure. The analogy emerges most clearly in Freud's description of the symptoms of neurosis or perversity as ambiguous and contradictory resolutions of the struggle between opposed regions of the mind (1940–68.11: 374):

> A [neurotic] symptom takes shape as a much-distorted product of unconscious libidinal wish-fulfillment, as a cleverly selected ambiguity with two completely contradictory meanings. In this alone we can recognize a difference between dream-formation and symptom-formation; for in dream-formation the preconscious intends merely to preserve sleep and to allow nothing to penetrate through to consciousness which could disturb it; it does not make a point of confronting the unconscious wish impulse with a sharp countermand "No, on the contrary." It can be more tolerant because the condition of a sleeping person is less dangerous. The condition of sleep suffices in itself to prevent the wish from becoming reality.

Just as the dreams and delusions of a neurotic are effective because they leave their relation to the patient's true desires hidden in the psychic unconscious, so ideology is effective because its relation to power remains buried in what might be described as a "political unconscious" (cf. Jameson 1981). Moreover, ideology is legible in much the same way that neurotic symptoms are legible. Even when repression is total, when the manifest content is silence, ideology, like the symptoms of neurosis, can be read in the displaced tensions created by contradictory forces, because ideology's reassuring narratives speak compulsively *around* the very contradictions which they conceal in silence.

A symptomatic reading of a text resembles the psychoanalyst's method of "reading" the discourse of his patient. The language of the patient reveals and conceals at the same time: he describes himself, but describes himself in the way he would like to see himself and would like others to see him. The psychoanalyst must reach behind the patient's words to reveal the real self that the words conceal. The psychoanalyst, as Benveniste puts it (1966: 78):

> has to be attentive to the contents of the patient's discourse, not least and above all to the gaps in his discourse. The content informs the psychoanalyst about the way the patient represents the situation to himself, and about the way he positions himself towards it, but the psychoanalyst looks through this content for another, namely the unconscious motives unleashed by the hidden complex. Beyond the linguistic symbolism he perceives a specific symbolism which the patient unknowingly constructs as much from what he omits as from what he says. From the story in which the patient presents himself the analyst extracts another which will explain his motives. He thus takes his discourse as the deception of another language which has its own rules, symbols and syntax, and which gives access to the deep structure of the psyche.

In precisely this way Freud was able to read an attempt to reconcile ambivalent feelings about marriage into the words of the woman who dreamt about attending the theater, even though her words made no reference to marriage (Section 3.1). An ideological analysis similarly reads against the grain of a text to find the unconscious motive behind its omissions, distortions, circumlocutions, and contradictions, with the difference that the complex underlying the representations is not a psychic conflict but a social one. The real content in either case, at least theoretically, is never entirely absent, but inferable as the hidden cause for all the distortions, elisions, displacements, condensations, and symbolizations. One has only to place the hidden cause, not in the contradiction of unconscious and conscious mind, but in a contradiction in social reality.

Structuralist procedures also have much in common with ideological analysis and are easily adaptable to its ends. Like structuralism, ideological analysis views the conceptual world as a social construct. Like structuralism, ideological criticism views language as a privileged site for ideological struggle, since it forms the actual material basis for consciousness. Moreover, the function of ideology is closely analogous to the function of myth in Lévi-Strauss's structuralism. Myth offers a pseudo-solution to the latter's great oppositions in much the same way that ideology offers a way of reconciling and uniting the contradictions which arise from the economic base or the opposed values and perspectives of its class divisions. Structuralist theory also suggests that it may be this very capacity of a myth or artwork to resolve contradictions that accounts, in part, for its interest and social appeal. Ideological analysis thus often draws directly upon a structuralist conception of ideology, organized into chains of meaning, and arranged into hierarchies, often governed by key, "transcendental signifiers," which function as the value terms of a certain political order. Even structuralism's key opposition of culture to nature has some analogue in theories of ideology, like Barthes's, which focus upon ideology's tendency to naturalize the cultural. The structuralist procedure of detecting significant binary oppositions and the relations between them and homologous binary oppositions often provides a fruitful method for uncovering the deep ideological contradictions upon which a myth or some other artifact plays.

But ideological analysis parts with structuralism in ways which must also temper any adaptation of its methods. Most significantly, ideological analysis regards language and semiotic systems as practical, not abstract, as social, not autonomous, and as conflicted, not homogeneous. This means that in ideological analysis the emphasis shifts from the system of *langue*, to *parole*, or rather the *langue/parole* opposition is superseded by the concept of "discourse," which combines some of the organized, supraindividual, and systematic qualities of *langue*, with the active, material, and practical qualities of *parole*. All of these new qualities are of course related. People do things with language, not all of which are "ideological," but nonetheless speakers promote a certain view of the world, and groups of people, who have interests in common, come through their verbal social interactions to develop a connected and reasonably coherent way of expressing their views; that is to say they develop a discourse around certain topics. Depending on how big, how influential, and how vocal these groups are, their discourses will be heard more often, and they will respond to and be shaped by the discourse of other social groups, especially those who are big, influential, and vocal. Insofar as speech and discourses have practical aims, individuals and groups will find themselves urging arguments, perspectives, and values, which will be opposed by others. Insofar as different groups in a given society share the same language, each group will mark, or, as Volosinov puts it, "accent," their common words in a different way. Speech, in other words, becomes a site of social conflict and struggle, and the traces of social struggle can be found, not only in whole discourses, but even in the conflicting, even contradictory meanings, of individual words, especially such political buzzwords as, in our society, e.g., "freedom" and "democracy." Moreover, the historical volubility in the meaning of a sign is directly related to changes in the hierarchy of dominance of different social groups. As Volosinov puts it (1986: 23):

> The very same thing that makes the ideological sign vital and mutable is also, however, that which makes it a refracting and distorting medium. The ruling class strives to impart a supraclass, eternal character to the ideological sign,

to extinguish or drive inward the struggle between social value judgments which occurs in it, to make the sign uniaccentual.

The practical consequence is that the oppositions pursued by ideological analysis may be opposed meanings of a single word or symbol, rather than the separate but opposed terms of structural analysis. These opposed meanings, as Vernant also insisted (Section 5.7), must be pursued well beyond the text or any group of texts, to the social discourse of opposed groups, and to their concrete life-experience and material interests.

History

We noted that the current theories of ideology and models of ideological analysis are based on societies and cultural artifacts of the modern era. If poststructuralism has taken little interest in myth (in the traditional sense), it is doubtless because the models of analysis were developed for complex and highly voluble societies, like our own. Many myths, however, derive, or are thought to derive, from simple "cold cultures" which maintain the same social structure indefinitely, until absorbed by a more advanced culture. Classic structuralism is perhaps more likely to capture the ideology of Bororo myths than any of the theories and procedures for ideological analysis discussed in this chapter. Just how "hot" or historically active a culture needs to be for this kind of ideological analysis is a matter for debate. It would be an ideological delusion to suppose that ideology works in precisely the same way in all eras and all societies. Certainly, myths do not have the same function or character everywhere and at all times.

There is even a (much exaggerated) basis to the claim that ideology, at least in its classic function of social legitimation, is dead. There is generally little discussion of the changing character of ideology. Habermas, exceptionally, has identified different historical stages in ideology's function of social legitimation. As summarized by Geuss (1981: 67–8), they are:

(a) an archaic stage in which agents use particular myths to give a narrative account of their social world and institutions;
(b) a "traditional" stage in which agents use unified mythic, religious, or metaphysical world-pictures or views about reality as a whole to legitimize their social institutions. Although these world-pictures are not just sequences of narratives, but are "argumentatively structured," they are not themselves ever called into question and need not ever prove their own validity as sources of legitimation;

(c)   a "modern" stage characterized by the appearance of "ideologies" in the narrow sense. These ideologies claim to be "scientific," i.e., to be able to give a full argumentative account of themselves and legitimate the social order by appeal to universal norms and principles, universalizable interests, and interpretations of the "good life."

(d)   (purportedly) "postideological" forms of social legitimation which claim to justify the social order by exclusive reference to its technical efficiency and which reject any appeal to moral principles, norms or ideals of the "good life" as "ideological" in the pejorative sense.

This last stage is most apparent in the claims by contemporary governments that they have no choice in the globalized world but to follow policy dictated by industry or else face dire economic consequences. Right-wing governments are especially prone to justifying policy through cost or convenience. In Canada, for example, the Alberta government resisted the federal government's decision to sign the Kyoto Protocol, upon which the survival of life on earth arguably hangs, purely on the grounds that it was too expensive to implement.

Myth, as the term is traditionally understood, belongs to the first and second of Habermas's stages of social legitimation, and, in principle, to societies that are less complex and less "hot," and which enjoy a generally greater probability of success in managing their differences with a cohesive general ideology. Myth in this sense is likely to be more constrained by the general ideology than art and literature in modern society, which, as we saw, might be more openly oppositional. (This may also be partly by definition, as we saw in Section 5.5, since tales which take a narrower subgroup perspective are likely to be classed as folktales or fables.) But traditional myths are also normally subject to greater institutional pressure for conformity than the art or literature of the modern period. The latter can be more narrowly targeted to specific social subgroups, and, as physical objects, are more likely to survive with a narrower base of transmission than required by the primarily oral tales of traditional societies.

6.4   AN IDEOLOGICAL ANALYSIS
OF THE MYTH OF HERACLES

"Freedom" in Archaic and Classical Greece

Myth is one of the most important media for ideological work. Most ancient myths survive because they operate at the highest ideological level: they participate in the creation of a unifying general ideology. In doing so they must address the society as a whole, and cannot exclusively adopt the position of a single subgroup. In appealing to the interests of opposed groups, a myth will incorporate within its structure the contradictions that arise from the opposed interests of the larger subgroups. In myth these contradictions may appear in many forms: among them are logical contradictions in the narrative, ambiguities and ambivalences in the motives or ethical character of the actions, and the proliferation within the narrative of redundant and mutually exclusive motives. We will find that all of these appear in the myth of Heracles.

The most important ideological medium is language, and it is often the case that a myth elaborates the ideological charge inherent in certain value terms. (I stress the word "elaborates," which is not to be taken as passive "reflection," but as an active refinement and "clarification" of the world some social group or subgroup would like to see reflected in language.) We can begin our analysis of Heracles by examining the connotations of the word "freedom" in Archaic and Classical Greece (*c.*700–323 BC). A highly charged term in almost any language, freedom *(eleutheria)* was enormously important to the general ideological discourse of Greece, especially in the slaveholding and democratic cities of the Classical period. At the general level it was freedom which divided the citizen classes from the slaves. The general ideology therefore held that freedom makes a man truly human; forced labor makes a man little better than a beast. Freedom allows a man to develop virtues like reason, self-control, courage, generosity, high-mindedness. Slaves exercise no mental or spiritual faculties at all and so are irrational, undisciplined, wild, cowardly, selfish, pusillanimous. In fact, some ancient theorists, like Aristotle, went so far as to claim that good and bad character are not the result of freedom and slavery, but the cause of it, reasoning that a society governed by people with reason, discipline, courage, and so on, will never be conquered and enslaved. Those who are slaves by culture are so precisely because they were slaves by nature. Such an ideology makes it seem natural and right that those who are free *should* govern those who are not. It is to everyone's benefit, especially the slaves'.

So far there is an inversion of reality, a confusion of culture for nature, but no internal contradiction as such. This is because slaves have no power and no say and their viewpoint, subsequently, has little impact upon the general cultural ideology. The contradiction comes from the attempt by the citizen subclasses to utilize this general notion of "freedom" to promote their own subclass interests. The citizen class in Archaic and Classical Greece was composed of powerful aristocrats and a much larger nonaristocratic class composed of peasants, merchants, tradespeople, and wage-laborers. To a purely aristocratic ideology a man who must work for monetary gain is little better than a slave: merchant, wage-laborer, and slave all work under compulsion and differ only by degree. So, they reason, there is no difference in kind, but only degree, between the lust for gain that drives the merchant, the pangs of hunger that drive the laborer, and the fear of the whip that drives the slave. "Free" in the aristocratic sociolect meant having the leisure for education, physical training, and the pursuit of various forms of status-competition. Though in the common language the word *eleutheros*, "free," designated anyone who was not a slave, the term is often used by aristocrats to refer to those who do not have to work for a living. The word *aneleutheros*, "unfree," is applied still more often to working-class citizens, even though they are legally "free" citizens, and the word *eleutherios*, literally "like a free man," was particularly cultivated by members of the elite to refer exclusively to one who could attain their own leisure-class ideals, much like its Latin counterpart, the word *liberalis*, whose basic flavor still survives in the term "liberal arts," or "liberal education."

Aristocrats pictured their social and economic activities as something utterly different in kind from those undertaken by merchants, craftsmen, peasants, and slaves. They conceived of their activity as a form of self-cultivation, undertaken for honor and not for material benefit, even when these activities really conferred money, or what ultimately could be converted to the same coin, status, and power. Moreover, Greek aristocrats liked to think that what they did, they did, not subject to any form of compulsion, but always as a matter of free choice. To the eyes of the working classes aristocratic activity and "freedom" could be, and indeed was, sooner viewed as a sort of social parasitism, even a destructive parasitism. Aristocratic activities, gala parties, sports and games, were regarded as wasteful indulgence, potlatches, and wanton orgies of conspicuous consumption. They were indeed extravagances which to a man who works and knows the value of money threatened to reduce a man to poverty and servitude. The merchant, tradesman, or farmer was more likely to connect honor with the virtues of industry, patience, and enterprise, by which the more successful of their class acquired wealth and social freedom. What to the aristocrat is the expression of freedom, to the merchant appears an expression of moral degeneracy. The two rival ideologies defined their perspectives in polar opposition: to one, work for material gain is a form of slavery, to the other, the means of acquiring and preserving freedom; to one, sports and games are the expression of freedom, to the other, a wasteful means of losing it. Each might view the pursuits of the other as pointless and distasteful.

Though both classes agree in opposing their freedom to the constraints of slavery, they differ in viewing other kinds of labor as equally constrained, if in a different way and to a lesser degree. For a myth to be acceptable to both classes, it must remain fairly ambivalent about how it defines freedom or how it values different forms of labor. At the same time, however, it is argued that myth, literature, or art will normally reveal a preference for one class perspective over another. This preference cannot be very obtrusive, or it will be rejected by the groups whose interest it opposes, and thereby will be likely to be deselected by the tradition. If it is unobtrusive, it will be most effective, in urging a partisan ideological perspective upon the society at large.

Heracles

It is interesting to note that so shrewd a student of social ideologies as Nicole Loraux denied that the Heracles myth was susceptible to political interpretation. Heracles is above politics, she claimed, because the myth was so popular that "no city was able to appropriate him definitively"; the site of what she calls the "process of reevaluation" of the myth was not "the political field, with its multiple identifications and inevitable distortions, but rather within the logic that presides over the Greek concept of the powerful hero" (1990: 23). One sees the influence of structuralism in this turn away from social context to internal logic. The Marxist critic Peter Rose faults Loraux for speaking as if only states generated ideologies, as if the internationalism of myth takes it out of the reach of political interests (just as historical stagnation for Lévi-Strauss took myth out of time, with the result that in both cases one is allowed to bracket off the enunciation context altogether and look for a rigorous and systematic "logic" immanent in the myth). Loraux conspicuously excludes class ideologies from her concept of politics. Rose does not himself offer a counter-interpretation, except to say that "Heracles celebrates inherited excellence – the claim of ruling class males to have by birth an innate superiority ultimately derived from divine ancestry" (1993: 219–20). But this interpretation brings the myth entirely within aristocratic ideology and reveals none of the ambiguities and contradictions that ought to appear in the myth, given that Heracles, far from being merely an aristocratic hero, was the most popular mythical hero of antiquity.

The Heracles myth, as we have it, was mostly assembled during the Archaic and Classical periods. These periods were marked by the transition from a social system dominated by a landed aristocracy to a form of democracy dominated by a largely urban class of merchants, tradesmen, and laborers. Like other aristocracies, the Greek aristocracy was an exclusive competition group. They had a very strong sense of class solidarity, but they did not aspire to be a society of equals. On the contrary, aristocrats worked very hard to establish themselves at the upper end of a fiercely contested pecking-order. The position of an aristocratic family depended on its past and present performance in specified forms of ritual competition with other aristocratic families. In the earliest period it was through military rituals: leading one's retainers and serfs out to raid another aristocrat's cattle or crops, or in extreme cases to destroy their cities. But once the subject classes began to acquire power through industry and trade, and once the lower classes managed to impose more efficient military science based on cooperative group tactics, the aristocracy had to give up such internecine feuds. More peaceful means of prestige competition emerged to structure the aristocracy's internal hierarchy. The most important of these was athletic games. The great Panhellenic games were instituted in the eighth to sixth century BC (the traditional dates for the institution of the Olympic games is 776 BC, for the Pythian and Isthmian games 582 BC, and for the Nemean 573 BC). This was a time of an enormous expansion in trade and industry which created the economic conditions for the rise of the Greek polis. There is an interesting parallel here with developments in the late medieval period. With the rise of mercantilism in fourteenth-century Europe, Barbara Tuchman notes that "tournaments proliferated as the nobles' primary occupation [war] dwindled" (1978: 65).

Like jousting, Olympic events, from chariot racing to wrestling, were for a long time pretty exclusively aristocratic, since no one else had the resources or the leisure for the equipment and training. There is a good reflection of the aristocrat's view of sports and trade in the Phaecian game in Book 8 of the *Odyssey*. Odysseus has been washed up on the island, and is still an anonymous castaway, but though he is received as an aristocrat by the royal family, his real status is in doubt. He is invited by the prince Laodamas to participate in some sporting competitions, since "through all a man's lifetime, there is nothing that brings him greater glory than what he achieves by speed of foot and by strength of arms" (147–8). But Odysseus declines, since he is too depressed about his troubles. At this point, an uppity young lord, Euryalus, starts heaping ridicule upon Odysseus (159–64): "Yes truly, stranger, you do not look like a man much practiced in any known sports. You look more like the kind of man who plies about in some big ship, leading a crew of merchant sailors, always anxious over the cargo out, watchful over the cargo home in expectation of greedy gains; there is nothing of the athlete in you."

Aristocratic ideology likens sports to trade (or farming), insofar as they are a kind of labor, but with the all-important difference, that sports are a specifically aristocratic form of labor, labor freely undertaken for the sake of glory, not for gain (or by necessity). If commerce is beneath contempt, agricultural labor is still lower (we saw some of the attitudes to agricultural labor expressed by Hesiod in Section 5.7). Different forms of class labor might be represented on a descending scale of value and liberty, as follows:

Class	aristocracy	merchants/tradesmen	farm laborers
Activity	sports	trade	agriculture
Object	glory	money	food
Motive	free choice	greed	necessity

Heracles' aristocratic labors

Given this social context, one can easily see Rose's point. Heracles appears very much the aristocratic hero, especially in his close association with athletic competitions in both myth and cult. Mark Golden enumerates the principal connections (I paraphrase from Golden 1986: 151–2). Heracles is credited with having instituted many Panhellenic games, among them the most prestigious, the Olympic and Nemean games. He is depicted in art as a pankratiast and wrestler. He is said to have invented the pankration. We know the names of his teachers in chariot racing and wrestling. Boxing and horse and chariot racing are shown on his shield. His statues were erected in gymnasia and wrestling grounds; sport facilities were attached to his shrines, and so were athletic competitions. He was emulated by individual athletes: the famous wrestler Milo of Croton is reputed to have worn a lion skin and brandished a club when he led an army against Sybaris in 510. Athletes who won both the wrestling and pankration competitions on the same day at Olympia called themselves "successors of Heracles." His name was adopted by the professional associations of athletes, who called themselves "those involved with Heracles" or "synod of Heracles." The insights of Golden's essay (rehabilitated in 1998: 146–57) are the inspiration (and often the substance) of the following analysis.

Ambivalence

True to this aristocratic image of Heracles, even the deeds which have little or no connection with sports are categorized, if not described, as if they were sporting events. Heracles's deeds are called *athloi*. The Greek word means "contests." *Athloi* is normally used of the panhellenic contests which played such an important role in aristocratic status-competition. *Athlos* specifically refers to contests for prizes, prizes which in theory at least were mere symbols of glory, and of no intrinsic value. Diodorus reports that Heracles introduced the first games at Olympia for "only a crown since he himself had conferred benefits on the race of men without receiving any pay" (4.14.1–2).

It is thus easy to read the myth of Heracles as a paradigm for the pursuit of pure glory through deeds of exceptional strength and endurance, and, as such, a paradigm for any athlete. For this reason, many of his deeds are assimilated in myth to athletic competitions: he wrestles the Nemean lion, Antaeus, Thanatos, Polygonus, Telegonus, Menoetes; Eryx he defeats in three falls in succession, the number needed for an Olympic victory. At Delphi he even wrestles Apollo for his tripod. Epinician poetry regularly draws an analogy between winning the panhellenic games and conquering death. The myth of Heracles does more than any other to sustain the illusion that the successful athlete in some way surpasses the condition of ordinary mortality. Heracles' deeds not only bring him undying fame, but literally confer immortality. Artistic representations of his ascent to Olympus adopt the *schema* of the homecoming of an athletic victor. Heracles is usually seen crowned, in a winged chariot, driven by Athena, or by Nike, the personification of victory itself, up to the house of his father Zeus and the assembled gods who eagerly await him. Diodorus describes Heracles' immortality as the "contest prize" *(epathlon)* of his labors. He is the god of victory, the proverbial champion *(kallinikos)*.

All this makes Heracles appear very aristocratic. And it is not surprising to find that Heracles, in addition to being famed for his glorious exploits, is famed for his freedom. In cult he is known as the "liberator." Prodicus made his decision to undertake his labors a paradigm of free will, giving it the character of an informed choice by a noble spirit of the hard road of virtue in preference to the way of luxury and ease. In Plato's *Gorgias* Callikles is able to speak of Heracles breaking free even from the bonds of convention (484b).

And yet the myth of Heracles is very different from other hero myths. Despite the aristocratic glamor lent to Heracles' deeds or the ethical coloring of free choice, the myth offers us another very different view of Heracles' deeds and the conditions of their performance. Greek literature regularly speaks of Heracles' "travails" *(ponoi)* and Latin literature of *Herculis labores*, whence our expression the "Labors of Heracles," which connotes a very different form of activity from *athloi*, but this translation is not altogether arbitrary. Heracles has a special relationship with labor. It was his travails *(ponoi)* which won him undying virtue *(athanatos arete)*, as he himself says in Sophocles' *Philoctetes* (1419–20), and he consoles Philoctetes by saying his travails will bring him fame too. From this it is apparent that Heracles is thinking not just of his "labors" but of something that goes well beyond glorious combats. Indeed, Loraux notes that *ponos* in Sophocles' *Trachiniae* refers not just to Heracles' exploits (21, 170, 825), but to his sufferings (680, 985) and also to his servitude (70, 356), i.e., the passive suffering and effort expended under necessity. And for this kind of *ponos* Heracles was just as famous as for his exploits. In antiquity he was proverbially associated with "laboring uselessly" (*allos ponein*), and "laboring for others" (*allois ponein*). *Ponos* can embrace all heroic exploits as well as suffering and drudgery. But less ambivalent language is also used. Aristotle refers to Heracles as a "serf" (*Eth. Eud.* 1245b39); *Trachiniae's* Dianeira characterizes him as a lackey, always "at someone's service" (*latreuonta toi*) and Aeschylus refers to him as a "slave" (*Ag.* 1040–41). There is even an ancient etymology of Heracles' name from the word *era*, meaning "service." The conditions under which Heracles performed his deeds is a matter of some consequence. As Austin and Vidal-Naquet say, for the ancients work in itself had no intrinsic value (1977: 15):

> What mattered as much or more were the conditions under which work was carried out. In the modern world a man's labour has become distinct from his person: it is a saleable commodity which he can sell to others without this implying, in theory, any subjection on his part. In the Greek world, by contrast, this distinction was unknown: to work for someone else meant to subject oneself to one's employer and [quoting Aristotle, *Rhetoric* 1376a32] "the condition of the free man is that he does not live for the benefit of another."

There is more in the Heracles myth than just a portrait of an aristocratic superhero. Even the myth of the Athenian hero Theseus fits the aristocratic model much more comfortably. According to Plutarch, after Aethra tells Theseus to go to Athens to find his father, he decides to walk in order to offer proof of his noble birth by performing equally noble exploits; he is said to pursue the Marathon bull, because he is "eager for action"; he goes to Crete with the Athenian victims, not because the lot falls upon him, but because he rises to the challenge to undertake a great exploit and liberate his people (Plut. *Theseus* 7, 14, 17). Heracles, by contrast, is a paradoxical figure. He wins his glory mainly by exploits which he undertakes under various forms of compulsion. Moreover, though some of Heracles' labors may seem to be modeled after athletic contests, others are definitely not. Among them we find the most degrading forms of agricultural labor, including shoveling dung from Augeas's stables. And finally, the characterization of the labors as in themselves pointless, despite the final reward of immortality, is hard to reconcile with the aristocratic model of Heracles' labors as undertaken purely for the glory of the achievement.

The myth constantly accesses and confuses the ideological categories of labor as well as the kinds of constraint under which the different varieties of labor are performed and the ends to which they are directed. Even at the start of the narrative the motives for undertaking the labors are heavily overdetermined, a curious mix of servitude, penance, and thirst for glory: The labors are imposed upon Heracles in penance for the murder of his children, but they are also performed as part of Heracles' servitude to Eurystheus, and at the same time the Pythia offers immortality as a reward for their successful completion. This confusion stretches right through the saga of Heracles: again and again he labors as an athlete, as a penitent, as a slave or bondsman, as a wage-laborer, "for love" (or rather for or out of "gratitude" = Greek *charis*), and usually in several capacities and for several motives at one and the same time.

Penance

Several labors are undertaken with a self-imposed compulsion, or at least imposed with Heracles' acquiescence. In penance for killing Linus, his music teacher, Heracles goes to Cithaeron, where he kills his first lion while tending the herds. In penance for killing his children, he is constrained to serve Eurystheus (in the canonical version), and performs his twelve labors. In penance for killing his guest-friend Iphitus, he sells himself to Omphale and deals with various local ogres. In some versions his selling himself into slavery is also in penance for his attempt to steal the Delphic tripod, or in penance for Iphitus and the tripod-debacle together.

Slavery

Slavery is insisted upon by the labors imposed by Eurystheus, which are sometimes humiliating, especially shoveling dung in the Augean stables, or gratifying Omphale's kinky sexuality. In this latter episode he is debased to the point of wearing women's clothing and doing women's work, while Omphale struts about with Heracles' club and lion skin. The effeminization of Heracles here is complete when, in one account, he and Omphale make love in a cave, wearing each other's clothes, while Pan gropes his way into the cave and sexually assaults Heracles in the dark, thinking him Omphale. The condition of slavery is also insisted upon in the episode of the Cerynian hind. When Artemis confronts him with stealing her hind, he pleads "necessity" and gets off. He insists, in other words, that his labor was entirely unfree. But notice the ambivalence. These are all self-imposed necessities. The affair with Omphale is also confused with merchandizing for profit, insofar as Heracles sells something, namely himself, and also with paying a debt, since he owes Eurytus the blood-price for his son Iphitus.

There are two other occasions on which Heracles is forced into servitude of the worst sort, namely to do backbreaking agricultural labor. One is the episode of Syleus, an ogre who intercepted passersby and forced them to work in his vineyard, and then, in some versions, killed them. He forced Heracles to work for him, but Heracles tore up his vineyard and killed him. The other episode is that of Lityerses, who, like Syleus, forced passersby to engage in a plowing contest, and after defeating them, killed them. But Heracles won, and killed him instead. Notice the ambivalence here. The plowing is both slave labor and a contest like an athletic game.

Wage labor

Heracles' bondage directly contradicts the notion that Heracles undertook his "contests" for glory, but it also frequently happens in the myth that Heracles undertakes his labors, not for glory, or expiation, but for material rewards. When Eurystheus commands him to clean the Augean stables, he contracts with Augeas to do the work for a tenth of the cattle. When he passes by Troy in his ninth labor, he contracts with Laomedon to free his daughter from a sea monster in return for some mares. When he goes to Oechalia he enters an archery contest, not for glory, or a merely symbolic prize, but for a material reward. He is said to go specifically because he wants Iole, Eurytus's daughter, for his wife. When he goes to Calydon he has a wrestling match with Achelous, but the purpose is to possess Dianeira, who is more than a token, since he went to Calydon expressly to marry her. The profit-motive in these episodes contradicts the image of Heracles struggling only for glory.

For love and from obligation (Charis and Philia)

Since Heracles is a culture hero, we would expect him to act for charity or love of his fellow humans, like Prometheus, when he founds cultural institutions, or defeats monsters. Diodorus (4.1.6) celebrates Heracles for "having conferred the greatest benefactions upon the human race." Such, for example, is the liberation of Thebes from Erginus, which Diodorus tells us Heracles did "returning to his homeland the gratitude *(charitas)* he owed it" (4.10.4). The same motive is ascribed to incidental deeds, such as the cleansing of Crete of wild animals (undertaken, according to Diodorus, in the course of his tenth labor, "wishing to show his gratitude *[charisasthai]* to the Cretans" for honoring him; 4.17.3). But, in general, Heracles is rarely motivated either by social ties *(philia)* or by gratitude for past favors *(charis)*. Indeed, these categories are conspicuous for their absence. So, for example, we know the names of Heracles' teachers in many different arts. Students are normally thought to owe their teachers a debt of *charis*. Instead, Heracles ends up killing a surprising number of them, and usually by the instrumentality of their own benefice. The lyre teacher, Linus, is killed, when Heracles hits him with his own lyre; Eurytus, the archery teacher, is killed by Heracles' bow; Chiron taught Heracles hunting and medicine only to be shot by one of Heracles' arrows while he was fighting centaurs, and though shooting Chiron was an accident, Chiron incurred a wound which could not be cured even by the medicine he taught Heracles. Similarly, Heracles usually fails to pay back the proper respect to hosts and guests. Pholus the centaur proves himself the perfect host to Heracles, but Heracles repays him by willfully breaking open a pithos of wine, despite Pholus's protests, and starting a drunken riot which leads to the death of Pholus by one of Heracles' arrows. Similarly, though he is the guest of Eurytus, he starts a fight, steals Eurytus's horses, and later ends up sacking Eurytus's kingdom and killing all his sons. He twice kills the sons or relatives of his hosts while they are serving him, for trivial offenses, like accidentally splashing him with water while offering him a basin to wash his hands (Athen 410f–411a; Schol. AR 1.1212.). Heracles' reputation for being a bad guest lived on in comedy and even tragedy. His role in the story of Alcestis is a unique example of a positive repayment of gratitude to his hosts, but in Euripides' play, despite it, he is still an unseemly guest. He fares no better as a host. He kills his guest Iphitus, the son of Eurytus, when he comes to look for the missing mares, even though Iphitus, in some versions, staunchly defended Heracles against accusation of theft. If Heracles does not repay kindnesses *(charis)* well, he is no better at performing acts governed by the broader and less defined obligation of the relationship of family or friendship *(philia)*. None of Heracles' marriages ends happily; all his wives, along with their children, are discarded, or passed on to someone else, if they are not killed by Heracles. Ironically, his own death comes through the agency of a "love gift."

Heracles and frustration

We noted earlier that "To labor like Heracles" became proverbial in antiquity for laboring uselessly. Is this not odd, given that the myth, at least on the surface, rewards Heracles' efforts with the greatest possible prizes, namely immortality, deification, eternal youth (symbolized by his marriage with Hebe whose name in Greek means "youth")? And yet, it is true that the motif of frustrated labor recurs throughout the myth. One can of course see the element of frustration as complementary to the quest for glory. Making Heracles a kind of pagan Job, who is rewarded in the end for his patience (in fact, Greek philosophers from the Pythagoreans to the Stoics received Heracles as a symbol, if not the "patron saint," of patient endurance). The more seemingly hopeless, the more heroic the effort. Without doubt, it is this tension that gives the story much of its narrative efficacy. But nonetheless, the theme of frustration does not *simply* complement a narrative about immense rewards for extraordinary virtue.

Frustration is there from the beginning. Even Zeus is frustrated in his desire to make his son king. Even Hera is frustrated in her effort to destroy him. We have seen that anyone who attempts to enter into a civilized relationship with Heracles is frustrated. But, most of all, it is Heracles' labor that is frustrated. The very monsters he confronts often symbolize frustration: hydras that grow twice as many heads when you decapitate them; animals with impenetrable skin; ogres like Antaeus and Alcyoneus, who jump up with doubly renewed vigor each time they are knocked to the ground.

But the theme of frustrated labor is most evident in the labor that Heracles undertakes for gain. Every time Heracles works for wages, the wages are withheld, and the value of wage-labor is undermined. In his fifth labor Eurystheus commands him to clean the Augean stables. But Heracles also contracts with Augeas to clean them for a portion of the cattle. When he succeeds, Augeas refuses to pay. And not only is he cheated of his wage by Augeas, but Eurystheus refuses to count the labor because Heracles did it for wages. So Heracles is doubly cheated. The motif is redoubled in the course of his ninth labor when, at Troy, he undertakes to rescue King Laomedon's daughter, Hesione, from a sea monster in exchange for an immortal horse. But when he kills the monster, neither honor nor gratitude can make Laomedon fulfill his bargain. In this case Heracles is cheated by a double cheater, since Laomedon had previously refused to pay Apollo and Poseidon their wages for building the walls of Troy. This episode has a close counterpart in the case of Iole. Heracles participates in an archery

contest to win her hand, but when he wins the contest, Eurytus refuses
to give him Iole. In every case Heracles is cheated of his bargain.

One can look at just about all the motives for Heracles' labors and find
this theme of frustrated or wasted effort, whether Heracles is formally motivated by profit, wages, penance, servile necessity, gratitude, or debt. For
example, his most conspicuous commercial transaction is slave dealing, but
it brings him no profit, as it is himself that he sells into slavery, and in
any case the proceeds go directly to Eurytus as blood-price for the murder of Iphitus. When Heracles liberates his homeland Thebes, he receives,
as a token of gratitude, the king's daughter, Megara, with whom he brings
up children, but ends up losing everything when he kills her and her children and is expelled from Thebes.

Heracles' life is a life of useless struggle, except in one important
respect, and this is where we find the decisively aristocratic spin in the
tale. The aristocratic work he does pays off: insofar as he worked "for
glory," he gets in the end his just reward in the form of everlasting fame
and real immortality. Even his losses are made up, though only according to the aristocratic code: he revisits those who cheated or dishonored
him and recovers his honor by avenging all those who treated him with
contempt: he sacks the cities of Laomedon, Augeas, and Eurytus (not to
mention others who slighted him, like Neleus and Hippokoon). His labors
are only frustrated insofar as all the rewards, apart from honor and glory,
fail to materialize, and all losses, apart from honor and glory, generally
prove irrecoverable, or are recovered (like Iole) at a greater cost than they
are worth.

The aristocratic spin

Heracles embodies a social contradiction in that he labors in the modes
and for the motives of all social classes: not just as aristocratic hero, but
as merchant, laborer, bondsman, and slave. This social confusion is cou-
pled with narrative ambiguities, insofar as most of Heracles' toils are undertaken for several, normally incompatible motives at once. Indeed these
ambiguities lead to outright logical contradiction when we see Heracles
laboring at one and the same time out of free will and under constraint.
The Heracles myth does not therefore simply reflect aristocratic ideals,
but the ideological fragmentation of a society in which different forms of
economic activity define the man, and in which the value of different types
of economic activity are hotly contested. Heracles is the mythical laborer
par excellence, and as such he addresses the activities, concerns, and aspirations of all classes. His Protean character allows him to represent all work,

work in the abstract, whether for rewards or for freedom. Heracles was the "warder-off of evil" *(alexikakos)*, the archetypal liberator, and this aspect of the god doubtless had some appeal even in the realm of work. For this reason Burkert can explain "the influential spiritual force" of the figure of Heracles by calling him "a model for the common man who may hope that after a life of drudgery, and through that very life, he too may enter into the company of the gods" (1985: 211). But Heracles' appeal is not only afterworldly, since the confusions in his tale allow some small glamor of heroic effort to attach to even the most squalid toil.

Yet for all the universality of appeal in the myth's treatment of labor, the aristocratic perspective remains dominant, if largely hidden within the tangle of ambivalence, ambiguities, and contradictions. The myth treats the work of a slave, a day-laborer, a tradesman, and a merchant as all alike. They bring only frustration. Above all the myth stresses the way such labour is dependent upon others, who can cheat, and upon circumstances that can change. This kind of work is put in conspicuous opposition to the performance of great deeds which depend only upon the prowess of the individual, and, once achieved, stand outside time, and cannot fail to bring immortal glory. The successful deeds are those most persistently assimilated to the typical aristocratic pursuit of sporting competition where performance is voluntary, solitary, and independent, pitting the individual and his personal resources against formidable odds. In this way the character, style, and values associated with aristocratic labor are shown to be supreme, uniquely valuable, and uniquely effective.

In a structural sense, Heracles might be said to mediate between the polarities of the contradictory views in Greek society about just where one draws the line between free and unfree. But if Heracles is a mediator because he moves freely between sociological categories, he is also a seductive enticement to other social classes to accept, even unwittingly, an aristocratic view of labor. The aristocratic perspective is urged not only by the outcome of the events as they unfold in the myth but by the very categories of the motives and modes of labor which the myth assumes. The myth presents, as if an exhaustive "grammar of actions," a set of motives and modes which are products of an unmistakably aristocratic logic. The various forms of labor which come into play in the myth are determined by two intersecting oppositions: one of motive, whether action is undertaken for gain or for glory and goodwill; and one of modality, whether action is freely chosen or imposed by some necessity. It should be clear from the chart below that the myth's logical ("paradigmatic") structure urges the same evaluation of labor we find argued by the outcome of the myth's actions ("syntagmatic structure"): namely, that labor for gain is unfree and labor for glory and goodwill is free.

The motives

Gain

	unfree	free
work for self	profit *(kerdos)*	glory *(kleos)*
work for others	wages *(misthos)*	gratitude *(charis)*

No gain

	unfree	free
work for self	debt *(chreos)*	penance *(poine)*
work for others	slavery *(doulia)*	obligation *(philia)*

The modes

Mode of necessity

	gain	no gain
work for self	profit *(kerdos)*	debt *(chreos)*
work for others	wages *(misthos)*	slavery *(doulia)*

Mode of freedom

	gain	no gain
work for self	glory *(kleos)*	penance *(poine)*
work for others	gratitude *(charis)*	obligation *(philia)*

One cannot accept the motives without accepting the modes. Once internalized, this seemingly exhaustive selection of the motives and modes of labor serves to imprint or urge subgroup values and perspectives upon the minds of an audience to which these values and perspectives may be alien or even contrary to their best interests.

Epilogue

Throughout this book, in addition to explaining theories of myth and exemplifying methods of analysis, I have tried to situate important enunciations of each major approach to myth in two ways. I have tried to situate them in their historical and social contexts, and I have tried to situate them in relation to one another in the development of the critical discourse on myth. Each of these contexts, arguably, made a very different contribution to the science of mythology. The historical and social contexts allowed the science of mythology to come into being, and to be, for a very long time, an object of consuming public interest. But these contexts are also responsible for serious ideological distortions. In general other people's myths become interesting and important when they are incorporated into one's own mythology. The theories of myth had a paradoxical tendency to imitate the objects of their study and become myths in their own right.

But this is not the whole story. Later theorists reacted against the ideological depositions of their predecessors, and in doing so they created a critical and scientific dialogue, which, if it did not demystify the ideological contents of earlier theories, at least diluted these ideological contents with a stronger draught of reason. Even if this dialectic has produced no certain incontrovertible truth, the science of mythology, through its internal critical dialogue, has brought measurable progress and enlightenment. One has only to take a synoptic view of the positions described in this book. Our great-grandfathers were confident in their own cultural superiority, in the belief that their beliefs alone constituted real knowledge, and in the certainty that their ways were God's ways. If few now believe this, this is thanks to the discourse on culture, of which the discourse on myth was a very large part. The strong oppositions our great-grandfathers made between science and mythology, truths and myths, themselves and others, was pure wish-fulfillment. This was ideology. The danger now is that we reject any distinction between science and myth in a postmodern orgy of self-effacement and homogenizing relativism. This is also ideology.

If the science of mythology has progressed by dialogue, a large part of this progress could be described as a dialectic between science and myth itself, since it is primarily the most obvious myths about myths which critical discourse has discarded. The most conspicuous result of this historical dialogue has been a greater awareness and understanding of the part played by ideology in any social discourse. This growth in self-awareness was possible because science is not just wish-fulfillment, it is also rational discourse. Rational discourse can sometimes succeed in detecting and disposing of some of its own ideological distortions and, by doing so, can expand the limits of its own possibility. The history of the science of mythology would seem to offer an exemplary proof that theoretical discourse can demystify itself, provided it remains free and rational and does not succumb, at the very moment of discovering its internal myths, to the myth that there is and can be nothing but myth.

A Little Further Reading

The following is far from being a comprehensive guide to all books on myth or theories of myth. Any in-depth study should begin with a reading of the primary works and authors discussed in this book. Happily almost all of them are brilliant writers as well as theorists. This section does not include the works discussed in earlier chapters. Rather it points to general works touching upon authors, theories, or social and historical trends treated in this book. Occasionally it also makes references to specialized works which provide further background to specific points raised in the analysis of the specific myths I examine here. Recent books and books in English take precedence. I do not include websites: they are many, often ephemeral, and will easily be found by the experienced web-searcher.

GENERAL

There are several mythological encyclopedias, all limited to Greco-Roman myth. Gantz (1993) is the first place to look for the versions of Greek myths as they existed down to the fifth century BC, though it usually contains ample discussion of later sources and variants. The nine-volume *Lexicon Iconographicum Mythologiae Classicae* (Zurich and Munich 1974–2000) is a complete catalog and discussion of the evidence of art for Greek, Roman and Etruscan myth, with a general survey, usually, of textual evidence, and further bibliography (entries are written in English, German, French, or Italian). Preller (1894–1923, in German), though dated, is the best comprehensive encyclopedia for Greco-Roman myth, including both iconographic and literary sources. Carpenter (1991) is a valuable guide to using the iconographic material. For the textual evidence Roscher (1884–1937, in German) is still valuable, if outdated and often given to quaint, frequently solar, interpretations. Graves (1960) can be surprisingly helpful, but reveals many of the excesses of comparatism and is addicted to outlandish etymologizing. Comparable myths from other cultures can often be found by a skilful use of the index to Frazer (1907–15) or the footnotes and appendices to Frazer (1921). Hansen (2002) is a valuable guide to comparative study of many well-known Classical myths. Aarne and Thompson (1961) collects references to sources for myth and folktale with recognized typical motifs.

Of general books on theories of myth, Edmunds (1990) is outstanding, offering the most important collection of theoretical essays since Sebeok (1965). It is especially useful for current comparative, psychoanalytic, and ritual approaches. The most complete survey from an anthropological perspective is Harris (1968; revised and updated 2001). Lincoln (1999) is a fascinating look at the role of racial ideologies in forming several modern schools of myth interpretation. Quicker, more topical surveys of theoretical approaches to myth can be found in Segal (1999), with a decided preference for ritualism and Jung, and Dowden (1992), with a decided preference for ritualism and much helpful discussion on Greek views of myth. Graf (1993) has an excellent two-chapter survey of modern approaches and several very interesting and learned chapters on the function of myth in Greek culture. For a lively and more thoroughly contextualized study of the uses of myth at ground level and in daily life in Greece one must consult Buxton (1994).

COMPARATIVE METHOD

Detienne (1986) examines the background to the invention of the concept of "mythology" in nineteenth-century Europe. Lincoln (1999) throws new light on the conditions surrounding William Jones's linguistic researches (chapters 4 and 11). He is particularly strong on the precursors of the comparative method, the influence of inter-European rivalry, especially German nationalism, upon the formulation of the comparative method, and the role of antisemitism in modern theory. Bologna (1988; in Italian) examines the background to the rise of comparative mythology. Stocking (1987) is a fascinating account of the rise of anthropology in Great Britain. Dorson (1965) gives a thorough treatment of the craze for solar interpretation. Trautmann (1997) is an excellent account of the race politics of Müller's mythology. See Cannadine (2001) for changes in British administrative policy in the later half of the nineteenth century. Peel (1971) contextualizes Spencer's thought. Ackerman 1987 is a thorough and perceptive study of Frazer. Fraser (1990) studies the background, genesis, and argument of *The Golden Bough*. Burrow (1966), Stocking (1968), and Fabian (1983) discuss the ideological implications of Victorian evolutionary theory. Duvignaud (1973; in French) examines the homology between the savage and the proletarian in early anthropological thought. For the anticlerical leaning of the English intelligentsia, see Trevelyan (1967: 578–84), and especially page 580 for the climate at Oxford and Cambridge. For the modern reception of Frazer's theories, see, most recently, Mettinger (2001). For comparative studies of the Kingship in Heaven motif see Littleton (1970), Kirk (1974: 113–21), Burkert (1987), Mondi (1990), Penglase (1994), and West (1997: 276–305). For the Derveni Papyrus, see Burkert (1987) and most recently Janko (2001).

PSYCHOANALYSIS

The classic psychoanalytic analyses of Greek myth are Rank (1964 [1909]), Slater (1968), and Caldwell (1989). Caldwell (1990) is an excellent discussion of current psychoanalytic approaches to myth. Gay (1988) is a brilliant and highly readable account of Freud's life and the development of his thought. Wollheim (1971) offers a good short and schematic introduction to Freud's theories, although Freud's own "General Introduction to Psychoanalysis" is an incomparably lucid and natural starting-place for anyone desiring a general overview of his thought (Freud 1953–74, vol. 15 [1915–17]). Recommended introductions to Jungian psychology are Jung (1964) and Jung and Kerényi (1963). The many works of Joseph Campbell also present, in an engaging and popular style, a basically Jungian, though eclectic, approach to myth (he was the mythological advisor to the movie *Star Wars*). A Freudian analysis of the Oedipus legend appears in Devereux (1973) (cf. Buxton 1980). Edmunds (1985) collects the comparable versions of the myth. For feet, limping, and castration symbolism see Sas (1964; in German). Benveniste (1966: ch. 7) discusses Freud's primitive language theories. Gay (1988: 501–22) is very good for Freud on women. For the continuing controversy, see Young-Bruehl (1990) and McClintock (1995). Spain (1992) gives a glimpse of the current state of psychoanalytic theory in anthropology. For the later reception of *Totem and Taboo*, see Fox (1967) and Freeman (1969).

RITUALISM

This is still the most common approach to ancient myth. Apart from Harrison and Burkert, the classic enunciations are by Kluckhohn (1942), Raglan (1965), Girard (1977), and, most recently, Versnell (1990). Ritual theory is criticized by Bascom (1957), Fontenrose (1966), and, with particular reference to the origin of drama, by Friedrich (1983, 1996). The Cambridge Ritualists are studied by Ackerman (1991) and the essays collected in Calder (1991). There are two excellent, and very different recent biographies of Jane Harrison, by Beard (2000) (more speculative) and Robinson (2002). Burkert's "sociobiology" is particularly well expressed in Burkert (1996).

STRUCTURALISM

There are many good accounts of structuralism, particularly in relation to narrative and myth. Most helpful are Culler (1975, 1981), Hawkes (1977), and Segal (1996). Saussure's relationship to empiricism is well expressed by Harland (1987: 17–19), which is otherwise an extremely helpful account of structuralism and poststructuralism. On Propp and later "narratological" structuralists, see Chatman (1978) and Martin (1986). For the relationship of Propp to the German tradition of organic morphology, see Dolezel (1990: 53–146). Lévi-Strauss (1973: ch. 8) offers a thorough and penetrating criticism of Propp (to which my own discussion in Chapter 5, Section 3 is much indebted). On Lévi-Strauss, Leach (1974) is often helpful. For the notion of nominalism, ostension, and "object-language" as understood by logical positivism (Chapter 5, Section 1), see Russell (1948: 62–77). The analysis of the Cinderella myth borrows some ideas from Pace (1982). For the throwing of sandals at ancient weddings (and other wedding rituals), see Karusu (1970) and Oakley and Sinos (1993). Pumpkin-giving in the Ukraine is described by Makarenko (1957: 328). For the analogy of marriage to agriculture in ancient Greek thought, see Dubois (1993). On the ancient connection between women and pithos jars, see Hanson (1990: 324–30).

IDEOLOGY

The most penetrating criticisms of structuralism are Jameson (1972) and the briefer and livelier discussion in Eagleton (1983: 91–126). Winkler (1990: 188–209) offers a feminist and in some ways ideological critique of Detienne's *Jardins d'Adonis*. On the manifold meanings of the concept of ideology see Eagleton (1991) and Hawkes (1996). On postmodern theory and culture, see the brilliant analyses of Jameson (1991) and Eagleton (1996), and the very lively and accessible (descriptive, not theoretical) studies by Anderson (1990) (general culture) and Klein (2000) (brand-name economics). The classic Marxist–semiotic analyses of the economy and culture of postindustrial capitalism are by Debord (1967) and Baudrillard (1975, 1981). For Marxism and literary and cultural criticism, see Macherey (1966), Eagleton (1976), Williams (1977), Jameson (1981), Bennett (1990), and Haslett (2000). On Heracles and labor, consult also Golden (1998: 141–75), Loraux (1982, 1990), and Nagy (1990: 116–145).

Bibliography

Aarne, A. and Thompson, S. 1961. *The Types of the Folktale*. Helsinki. [Original by Aarne 1910, enlarged by Thompson].

Ackerman, R. 1987. *J. G. Frazer: His Life and Work*. Cambridge.

Ackerman, R. 1991. *The Myth and Ritual School: J. G. Frazer and the Cambridge Ritualists*. New York.

Anderson, W. T. 1990. *Reality Isn't What it Used to Be*. New York.

Austin, M. M. and Vidal-Naquet, P. 1977. *Economic and Social History of Ancient Greece: An Introduction*. London.

Barthes, R. 1953. "Maîtres et esclaves," *Lettre nouvelles*, March, 108.

Barthes, R. 1957. *Mythologiques*. Paris. Partially trans. A. Lavers, *Mythologies*, New York, 1972, and R. Howard, *The Eiffel Tower and Other Mythologies*, New York, 1979.

Bascom, W. 1957. "The Myth–Ritual Theory," *Journal of American Folklore* 70: 103–14.

Bascom, W. 1965. "The Forms of Folklore: Prose Narratives," *Journal of American Folklore* 78: 3–20.

Baudrillard, J. 1975. *The Mirror of Production*. St. Louis, MO. [French original 1973.]

Baudrillard, J. 1981. *For a Critique of the Political Economy of the Sign*. St. Louis. [French original 1972.]

Beard, M. 2000. *The Invention of Jane Harrison*. Cambridge, MA.

Bennett, T. 1990. *Outside Literature*. London.

Benveniste, E. 1966. *Problèmes de linguistique générale*. Vol. 1. Paris. Trans. M. E. Meek, *Problems in General Linguistics*, Coral Gables, FL, 1971.

Boardman, J. 1989. *Athenian Red Figure Vases: The Classical Period*. London.

Bologna, M. P. 1988. *Ricerca etimologica e ricostruzione culturale: Alle origini della mitologia comparata*. Pisa.

Burkert, W. 1979. *Structure and History in Greek Mythology and Ritual*. Berkeley, CA.

Burkert, W. 1983. *Homo Necans: The Anthropology of Ancient Greek Sacrificial Ritual and Myth*. Berkeley, CA. [German original 1972.]

Burkert, W. 1985. *Greek Religion*. Translated by J. Raffan. Cambridge, MA. [German original 1977.]

Burkert, W. 1987. "Oriental and Greek Mythology: The Meeting of Parallels," in J. Bremmer, ed., *Interpretations of Greek Mythology*, London, 10–40.

Burkert, W. 1996. *The Creation of the Sacred: Tracks of Biology in Early Religions*. Cambridge, MA.

Burrow, J. W. 1966. *Evolution and Society. A Study in Victorian Social Theory*. Cambridge.

Buxton, R. 1980. "Blindness and Limits: Sophokles and the Logic of Myth," *Journal of Hellenic Studies* 100: 22–37.

Buxton, R. 1994. *Imaginary Greece. The Contexts of Mythology*. Cambridge.

Cahill, J. 1995. *Her Kind: Stories of Women from Greek Mythology*. Peterborough, Ont.

Calder, W. M., ed. 1991. *The Cambridge Ritualists Reconsidered*. Illinois Classical Studies, Suppl. 2. Atlanta, GA.

Caldwell, R. 1989. *The Origin of the Gods*. Oxford.

Caldwell, R. 1990. "The Psychoanalytic Interpretation of Greek Myth," in L. Edmunds, ed., *Approaches to Greek Myth*, Baltimore, MD, 344–89.

Campbell, J. 1949. *The Hero with a Thousand Faces*. Princeton, NJ.

Cannadine, D. 2001. *Ornamentalism: How the British Saw their Empire*. Oxford.

Carpenter, T. H. 1991. *Art and Myth in Ancient Greece*. London.

Chatman, S. 1978. *Story and Discourse*. Ithaca, NY.

Cox, G. W. 1870. *The Mythology of the Aryan Nations* I. London.

Culler, J. 1975. *Structuralist Poetics*. London.

Culler, J. 1981. *The Pursuit of Signs*. Ithaca, NY.

Darwin, C. 1968. *The Origin of the Species*. Ed. J. W. Burrow. Harmondsworth. [Original 1859.]

Dawkins, R. 1976. *The Selfish Gene*. Oxford.

Day, G. 2001. *Class*. London.

Debord, G. 1967. *Society of the Spectacle*. Detroit. [French original 1967.]

Derrida, J. 1976. *Of Grammatology*. Baltimore. Trans. G. C. Spivak. [French original 1967.]

Detienne, M. 1972. *Les Jardins d'Adonis*. Paris. Trans. J. Lloyd, *Gardens of Adonis*, Princeton, NJ, 1994.

Detienne, M. 1986. *The Creation of Mythology*. Chicago. [French original 1981.]

Devereux, G. 1973. "The Self-Blinding of Oidipous in Sophokles: Oidpous Tyrannos," *Journal of Hellenic Studies* 93: 36–49.

Dolezel, L. 1990. *Occidental Poetics*. Lincoln, NE.

Dorson, R. 1965. "The Eclipse of Solar Mythology," in T. A. Sebeok, ed., *Myth: A Symposium*, Bloomington, IN, 25–63.

Dowden, K. 1992. *The Uses of Greek Mythology*. London.

Downie, R. A. 1970. *Frazer and the Golden Bough*. London.

Dubois, P. 1993. *Sowing the Body: Psychoanalysis and Ancient Representations of Women*. Chicago.

Duncan, D. 1908. *The Life and Letters of Herbert Spencer*. 2 vols. New York.

Durán, D. 1967. *Historia de las Indias de Nueva España*. 2 vols. Mexico City.

Durkheim, E. 1897. *Le suicide*. Paris. Trans. J. Spaulding and G. Simpson, *Suicide*, New York, 1962.

Durkheim, E. 1938. *The Rules of the Sociological Method.* Trans. S. A. Soloway and J. H. Mueller, Chicago. [French original 1894.]

Durkheim, E. 1986. *De la division du travail social.* Paris. [Original 1893.] Trans. G. Simpson, *Division of Labor in Society,* New York, 1933.

Durkheim, E. 1991. *Les formes élémentaires de la vie religieuse.* Paris. [Original 1912.]

Duvignaud, J. 1973. *Le langage perdu. Essai sur la différence anthropologique.* Paris.

Eagleton, T. 1976. *Criticism and Ideology.* London.

Eagleton, T. 1983. *Literary Theory.* Minneapolis, MN.

Eagleton, T. 1991. *Ideology.* London.

Eagleton, T. 1996. *The Illusions of Postmodernism.* Oxford.

Edmunds, L. 1985. *Oedipus: The Ancient Legend and Its Later Analogues.* Baltimore, MD.

Edmunds, L. 1990. *Approaches to Greek Myth.* Baltimore, MD.

Fabian, J. 1983. *Time and the Other: How Anthropology Makes its Object.* New York.

Fehling, D. 1974. *Ethologische Überlegungen auf dem Gebiet der Altertumskunde.* Munich.

Fontenrose, J. 1959. *Python: A Study of the Delphic Myth and its Origins.* Berkeley, CA.

Fontenrose, J. 1966. *The Ritual Theory of Myth.* Berkeley, CA.

Forster, E. M. 1997. *Howards End.* Boston. [Original 1910.]

Fox, R. 1967. "Totem and Taboo Reconsidered," in E. R. Leach, ed., *The Structural Study of Myth and Totemism,* London, 163–75.

Fraser, R. 1990. *The Making of the Golden Bough.* London.

Frazer, J. G. 1910. *Totemism and Exogamy.* 4 vols. London.

Frazer, J. G. 1907–15. *The Golden Bough,* 3rd ed. 12 vols. London. [Original edition in 2 vols., 1890. Second edition in 3 vols., 1900.]

Frazer, J. G. 1918. *Folklore in the Old Testament.* 3 vols. London.

Frazer, J. G. 1921. *Apollodorus: The Library* II. Cambridge, MA.

Frazer. J. G. 1922. *The Golden Bough.* Abridged ed. London. [Abridgment of 12-vol. 3rd ed., 1907–15.]

Frazer, J. G. 1994. *The Golden Bough.* Abridged ed. R. Fraser. Oxford.

Freeman, D. 1969. "Totem and Taboo: A Reappraisal," in W. Muensterberger, ed., *Man and His Culture: Psychoanalytic Anthropology after "Totem and Taboo".* London.

Freud, S. 1940–68. *Gesammelte Werke, Chronologisch Geordnet.* Ed. A. Freud et al. 18 vols.

Freud, S. 1953–74. *Standard Edition of the Complete Psychological Works of Sigmund Freud.* Ed. J. Strachey et al. 24 vols.

Freud, S. 1985. *Übersicht der Übertragungsneurosen: Ein bisher unbekanntes Manuskript.* Edited by Grubrich-Simitis. Frankfurt. Trans. A. and P. T. Hoffer, *A Phylogenetic Fantasy,* Cambridge, MA., 1987.

Friedrich, R. 1983. "Drama and Ritual," in J. Redmond, ed., *Drama and Religion (Themes in Drama* 5), Cambridge, 159–223.

Friedrich, R. 1996. "Everything to Do with Dionysos? Ritualism, the Dionysiac, and the Tragic," in M. S. Silk, ed., *Tragedy and the Tragic: Greek Theatre and Beyond*, Oxford, 257–83.

Gantz, T. 1993. *Early Greek Myth*. Baltimore and London.

Gaster, T. H. 1945. "Divine Kingship in the Ancient Near East: A Review Article," *Review of Religion* 9: 267–81.

Gaster, T. H. 1959. *The New Golden Bough: A New Abridgement of the Classic Work by Sir James George Frazer*. New York.

Gay, P. 1988. *Freud: A Life for Our Time*. New York.

Geuss, R. 1981. *The Idea of a Critical Theory*. Cambridge.

Girard, R. 1977. *Violence and the Sacred*. Baltimore, MD. [French original 1972.]

Gluckman, M. 1965. *Politics, Law and Ritual in Tribal Society*. Chicago.

Goethe, J. W. 1926. *Goethes Morphologische Schriften*. Jena. Ed. W. Troll.

Golden, M. 1986. "Sport and Wage-Labour in the Heracles Myth," *Arete* 3: 145–58.

Golden, M. 1998. *Sport and Society in Ancient Greece*. Cambridge.

Graf, F. 1993. *Greek Mythology: An Introduction*. Baltimore, MD. [German original 1987.]

Graves, R. 1960. *The Greek Myths*. Harmondsworth. [Revised ed., original 1955.]

Greimas, A. J. 1966. *Sémantique structurale*. Paris.

Greimas, A. J. 1970. *Du Sens*. Paris.

Griffiths, J. G. 1960. *The Conflict of Horus and Seth*. Liverpool.

Hackmann, O. 1904. *Die Polyphemsage in der Volksüberlieferung*. Helsingfors.

Hansen, W. 2002. *Ariadne's Thread: A Guide to International Tales Found in Classical Literature*. Ithaca, NY.

Hanson, A. E. 1990. "The Medical Writer's Woman," in D. Halperin, J. J. Winkler, and F. I. Zeitlin, eds., *Before Sexuality*, Princeton, NJ, 309–38.

Harland, R. 1987. *Superstructuralism*. London and New York.

Harris, M. 1968. *The Rise of Anthropological Theory*. New York.

Harrison, J. 1963a. *Mythology*. New York. [Original 1924.]

Harrison, J. 1963b. *Themis: A Study of the Social Origins of Greek Religion*, 2nd ed. Cambridge. [Reprint of 1927 edition; 1st ed. 1912.]

Haslett, M. 2000. *Marxist Literary and Cultural Theories*. New York.

Hawkes, D. 1996. *Ideology*. London.

Hawkes, T. 1977. *Structuralism and Semiotics*. Berkeley, CA.

Hooke, S. H., ed. 1933. *Myth and Ritual: Essays on the Myth and Ritual of the Hebrews in Relation to the Culture Pattern of the Ancient East*. London.

Hyman, S. E. 1962. "Leaping for Goodly Themis," *The New Leader* 45.22: 24–5.

Jakobson, R. 1971. *Selected Works*, 2nd ed., vol. 1, *Phonological Studies*. The Hague.

Jameson, F. 1972. *The Prison-House of Language*. Ithaca, NY.

Jameson, F. 1981. *The Political Unconscious: Narrative as a Socially Symbolic Act*. Ithaca, NY.

Jameson, F. 1991. *Postmodernism or The Cultural Logic of Late Capitalism*. Durham, NC.

Janet, P. 1911. *L'État mental des hystériques*, 2nd ed. Paris. [First ed. 1892.]

Janko, R. 2001. "The Derveni Papyrus (Diagoras of Melos, Apopyrgizontes Logoi?) A New Translation," *Classical Philology* 96: 1–32.

Jensen, A. E. 1963. *Myth and Cult among Primitive Peoples.* Chicago.

Jones, W. 1807. *Works of Sir William Jones.* Vol. 3. London.

Jung, C. G., ed. 1964. *Man and his Symbols.* New York.

Jung, C. G. and Kerényi, C. 1963. *Essays on a Science of Mythology.* Princeton, NJ.

Karusu, S. 1970. "Die «Schutzflehende» Barberini," *Antike Kunst* 13: 34–47.

Kirk, G. S. 1970. *Myth, its Meaning and Functions in Ancient and Other Cultures.* Berkeley, CA and Cambridge.

Kirk, G. S. 1974. *The Nature of Greek Myths.* Harmondsworth.

Klein, N. 2000. *No Logo.* London.

Kluckhohn, C. 1942. "Myths and Rituals: a General Theory," *Harvard Theological Review* 35: 45–79.

Leach, E. R. 1954. *The Political Systems of Highland Burma.* London.

Leach, E. R. 1974. *Claude Lévi-Strauss.* New York.

Leach, E. R. 1982. Critical Introduction to M. I. Streblin-Kamenskii, *Myth.* Ann Arbor, MI, 1–20.

Lévi-Strauss, C. 1958. *Anthropologie structurale.* Paris. Trans. C. Jacobson and B. G. Schoepf, *Structural Anthropology*, Harmondsworth, 1972.

Lévi-Strauss, C. 1964. *Le cru et le cuit.* Paris. Trans. J. and D. Weightman, *The Raw and the Cooked*, New York, 1969.

Lévi-Strauss, C. 1971. *L'homme nu.* Paris. Trans. J. and D. Weightman, *The Naked Man*, New York, 1981.

Lévi-Strauss, C. 1973. *Anthropologie structurale deux.* Paris. Trans. M. Layton, *Structural Anthropology 2*, Harmondsworth, 1978.

Lincoln, B. 1999. *Theorizing Myth: Narrative, Ideology, and Scholarship.* Chicago and London.

Littleton, C. S. 1970. "Is the 'Kingship in Heaven' Theme Indo-European?" In G. Cardona, H. M. Hoenigswald, and A. Senn, eds., *Indo-European and Indo-Europeans*, Philadelphia, 383–404.

Loraux, N. 1982. "Ponos: Sur quelques difficultés de la peine comme nom du travail," *Annali del Seminario di Studi del Mondo Classico* 4: 211–37.

Loraux, N. 1990. "Herakles: The Super-Male and the Feminine," in D. M. Halperin, J. J. Winkler, and F. I. Zeitlin, eds., *Before Sexuality: The Construction of Erotic Experience in the Ancient Greek World*, Princeton, NJ, 21–52.

Lorenz, K. Z. 1981. *The Foundations of Ethology.* New York and Vienna. [Revised and expanded version of the 1978 German original.]

Lubbock, J. 1865. *Pre-Historic Times, as Illustrated by Ancient Remains and the Manners and Customs of Modern Savages.* London.

Macherey, P. 1966. *Pour une théorie de la production littéraire.* Paris. Trans. G. Wall, *A Theory of Literary Production*, London, 1978.

Makarenko, A. S. 1957. Педагогическая поэма. in Макаренко, А.С. Сочинения в семи томах. Том первый. Moscow.

Malinowski, B. 1954. *Magic, Science, and Religion and Other Essays.* Garden City, NY.

Mannheim, K. 1936. *Ideology and Utopia.* London.

Marcuse, H. 1955. *Eros and Civilization*. New York.

Marett, R. R. 1909. *Threshold of Religion*. London.

Martin, W. 1986. *Recent Theories of Narrative*. Ithaca, NY.

Marx, K. 1906. *Capital*. New York. [English trans. by S. Moore and E. Aveling of German 4th ed., ed. F. Engels, 1890.]

Marx, K. 1999. *Theories of Surplus Value*. New York. [German original written 1861–3.]

McClintock, A. 1995. *Imperial Leather: Race, Gender, and Sexuality in the Colonial Context*. New York.

Mettinger, T. N. D. 2001. *The Riddle of the Resurrection: Dying and Rising Gods in the Ancient Near East*. Stockholm.

Mitscherlich, A. 1963. *Auf dem Weg zur vaterlosen Gesellschaft*. Munich. Trans. as *Society without the Father*, New York, 1970.

Mondi, R. 1990. "Greek Mythic Though in the Light of the Near East," in L. Edmunds, ed., *Approaches to Greek Myth*, Baltimore, MD, 142–98.

Morris, D. 1967. *The Naked Ape*. New York.

Müller, F. M. 1847. "On the Relation of the Bengali to the Arian and Aboriginal Languages of India," *Report of the British Association for the Advancement of Science, 1848*: 319–50.

Müller, F. M. 1867. *Chips from a German Workshop* II. New York.

Müller, F. M. 1869. *Lectures on the Science of Language, delivered at the Royal Institution of Great Britain in February, March, April and May, 1863*, 2nd ser. New York.

Müller, F. M. 1881. *Selected Esays on Language, Mythology, and Religion* I. London.

Müller, F. M. 1885. "Solar Myths," *Nineteenth Century* 18: 900–22.

Müller, F. M. 1892. *Address Delivered at the Opening of the Ninth International Congress of Orientalists held in London, September 5, 1892*. Oxford.

Nagy, G. 1990. *Pindar's Homer: The Lyric Possession of an Epic Past*. Baltimore, MD.

Oakley, J. H. and Sinos, R. H. 1993. *The Wedding in Ancient Athens*. Madison, WI.

Ortega y Gasset, J. 1925. *La deshumanización del arte e ideas sobre la novela*. Madrid.

Pace, D. 1982. "Lévi-Strauss and the Analysis of Folktales," in A. Dundes, ed., *Cinderella: A Folklore Casebook*, New York and London, 245–58.

Peel, J. D. Y. 1971. *Herbert Spencer: the Evolution of a Sociologist*. London.

Penglase, C. 1994. *Greek Myths and Mesopotamia: Parallels and Influence in the Homeric Hymns and Hesiod*. London.

Peradotto, J. 1977. "Oedipus and Erichthonius: Some Observations on Paradigmatic and Syntagmatic Order," *Arethusa* 10: 85–101.

Preller, L. 1894–1923. *Griechische Mythologie*. Fourth edition, revised by C. Robert. Berlin.

Pritchard, J. B. 1969. *Ancient Near Eastern Tests Relating to the Old Testament*, 3rd ed. Princeton, NJ.

Propp, V. 1958. *Morphology of the Folktale*. Bloomington, IN. Trans. L. Scott. [Russian original 1928.]

Propp, V. 1968. *Morphology of the Folktale*. Austin, TX. Trans. L. Scott, rev. and ed. L. A. Wagner.

Propp, V. 1970. *Morphologie du conte*. Trans. M. Derrida et al. Paris.

Propp, V. 1984. *Theory and History of Folklore*. Minneapolis, MN.

Raglan, L. 1936. *The Hero: A Study in Tradition, Myth and Drama*. London.

Raglan, L. 1965. "Myth and Ritual," in T. A. Sebeok, ed., *Myth: A Symposium*, Bloomington, IN, 122–35.

Rank, O. 1964. *The Myth of the Birth of the Hero*. New York. Trans. P. Freund. [German original 1909.]

Robinson, A. 2002. *The Life and Works of Jane Ellen Harrison*. Oxford.

Roscher, W. H. ed. 1884–1937. *Ausführliches Lexikon der griechischen und römischen Mythologie*. Leipzig.

Rose, P. 1993. "The Case for Not Ignoring Marx," in N. S. Rabinowitz and A. Richlin, eds., *Feminist Theory and the Classics*, New York, 211–37.

Rousseau, J. J. 1968. *Essais sur les origines des langues*. Ed. C. Porset. Paris. [Original 1783.]

Russell, B. 1948. *An Inquiry into Meaning and Truth*. London.

Sas, S. 1964. *Der Hinkende als Symbol*. Zurich.

Saussure, F. de 1972. *Cours de linguistique générale*. Ed. C. Bally, A. Sechehaye, A. Reidlinger, and T. de Mauro. Paris. First published in 1915. Trans. A. Baskin, *Course in General Linguistics*, London, 1959.

Sebeok, T. A., ed. 1965. *Myth: A Symposium*. Bloomington, IN. [First published 1955.]

Segal, R. A. 1996. *Structuralism in Myth*. London.

Segal, R. A. 1999. *Theorizing About Myth*. Amherst, MA.

Simpson, W. K. 1973. *The Literature of Ancient Egypt*. New Haven, CT.

Slater, P. E. 1968. *The Glory of Hera: Greek Mythology and the Greek Family*. Boston.

Smith, W. R. 1887. "Ctesias and the Semiramis Legend," *English Historical Review* 2: 303–17.

Smith, W. R. 1894. *Lectures on the Religion of the Semites*, 1st ser.: *The Fundamental Institutions*, 2nd ed. London.

Spain, D. H. 1992. *Psychoanalytic Anthropology after Freud*. New York.

Spencer, H. 1862. *First Principles*. London.

Sperber, H. 1912. "Über den Einfluß sexueller Momente auf Entstehung und Entwicklung der Sprache," *Imago* I: 405–53.

Stocking, G. 1968. *Race, Culture, and Evolution*. New York.

Stocking, G. 1987. *Victorian Anthropology*. London and New York.

Thompson, S. 1965. "Myth and Folktales," in T. A. Sebeok, ed., *Myth: A Symposium*, Bloomington, IN, 169–80. [First published 1955.]

Tiger, L. 1970. *Men in Groups*. New York.

Tiger, L. 1999. *The Decline of Males*. New York.

Todorov, T. 1984. *The Conquest of America*. New York. Trans. R. Howard. [French original 1982.]

Trautmann, T. R. 1997. *Aryans and British India*. Berkeley, CA.

Trevelyan, G. M. 1967. *English Social History*. Harmondsworth.

Trubetzkoy, T. 1933. "La Phonologie actuelle," in H. Delacrois et al. eds., *Psychologie du langage*, Paris, 227–46.

Trubetzkoy, T. 1939. "Gedanken über das Indogermanenproblem," *Acta Linguistica* 1: 81–9. Reprinted in A. Scherer, ed., 1968, *Die Urheimat der Indogermanen*. Wege der Forschung 166, Darmstadt, 214–23.

Tuchman, B. 1978. *A Distant Mirror: The Calamitous Fourteenth Century*. New York.

Tylor, E. B. 1958. *Primitive Culture*. New York. [Original 1871.]

Vernant, J.-P. 1972. "Introduction" in M. Detienne, *Les Jardins d'Adonis*, Paris, i–xlvii. Trans. J. Lloyd, *Gardens of Adonis*, Princetion, NJ, 1994.

Vernant, J.-P. 1974. *Mythe & société en Grèce ancienne*. Paris. Trans. J. Lloyd, *Myth and Society in Ancient Greece*, Brighton, 1980.

Versnell, H. S. 1990. "What's Sauce for the Goose Is Sauce for the Gander: Myth and Ritual, Old and New," in L. Edmunds, ed., *Approaches to Greek Myth*, Baltimore, MD, 23–90.

Volosinov, V. N. 1986. *Marxism and the Philosophy of Language*. Cambridge, MA. [Re-edition of 1973 English translation, Russian original 1929.]

West, M. L. 1997. *The East Face of Helicon: West Asiatic Elements in Greek Poetry and Myth*. Oxford.

Williams, R. 1977. *Marxism and Literature*. Oxford.

Winkler, J. J. 1990. *The Constraints of Desire: The Anthropology of Sex and Gender in Ancient Greece*. New York and London.

Wittgenstein, L. 1979. *Remarks on Frazer's Golden Bough*. Atlantic Highlands, NJ. Ed. R. Rhees.

Wittgenstein, L. 1958. *Philosophical Investigations*. New York. Third edition by G. E. M. Anscombe and R. Rhees. Trans. G. E. M. Anscombe.

Wollheim, R. 1971. *Freud*. New York.

Young-Bruehl, E. 1990. *Freud on Women*. London.

Index

Abel, K. 124–5
aborigines (i.e., Australian first nations) 38, 45, 51, 138, 149
abreaction 83–4
Achelous 310
Ackerman, R. 55
Acrisius 101–2, 109, 195, 197–9
Adonia 273–6
Adonis 40, 119, 269–71, 273–6
Adorno, T. 291
Aeschylus 308
Africa 4–5, 30–2, 34–5, 37, 99, 115, 155, 196–8, 200, 265
Agamemnon 257
Aglaurus 241–3
agriculture 37, 40, 56, 119–20, 144, 227–8, 231, 240–1, 255–60, 263–8, 273–6, 305–6, 308, 310
Alcestis 311
Alcyoneus 312
Alexander the Great 265
ambivalence 92, 96, 101, 107, 111–20, 242, 255, 259–60, 272, 278–9, 294, 298, 302, 304, 306–14
ambiguity 96, 125–6, 240, 242, 294, 297, 302, 304, 313–14
America (i.e., North and South) 11, 32, 37, 52, 138, 140, 223, 227–8, 237, 247, 264 see also Canada; conquistadores; "Indians"; United States
anatomy 31, 172–3, 203
Andromeda 81, 101, 103, 196–8
Antaeus 307, 312
anthropology 3, 5–7, 11–13, 30–2, 36, 45–51, 54, 94, 113–21, 123, 134–5, 141–2, 153, 181, 188, 217–19, 277 see also comparatism; ethnography
Antigone 222, 225
Anu 70–3, 77
Aphrodite/Venus 119, 167, 229, 238, 249, 267–71, 273–4, 276

Apollo 24, 146, 312
Apollodorus 57, 68–70, 98, 100, 195–8, 238–40
apotropaion/apotropaic symbol 98, 166–8
arbitrariness 186, 204, 213, 219, 266, 279–82, 284, 287–8, 307
archaeology 30–2, 119, 122, 148, 153
archetype 174, 202–3, 208, 314 see also Urform/Urtype
Ares 119, 241–3
Argonauts 195, 207
aristocracy 19, 21, 25, 27, 29, 121, 176, 234, 302–6, 308–9, 313–14
Aristotle 159, 224, 302, 308
art/arts 93, 109, 117, 127, 146, 150, 153–4, 159, 182, 247, 277, 285, 291–4, 298–301, 304, 307, 311
Artemis/Diana 37–40, 42–3, 199–200, 267–71, 276, 309
Aryan/Aryas 15, 20–9, 31, 40–2, 126, 294 see also Indo-European; racism
Asia Minor 70–8, 119, 168, 200
Athena 68–9, 74–5, 77, 98, 101–2, 196–200, 238–43, 248–9, 307
athlete/athletics 305–10
Attis 38, 40, 119
Auge 199–201
Augeas 308–10, 312–13
Augustine 184
Austin, M. M. 308
Australia 30–2, 52, 138, 141, 149 see also Aborigines
Austria 80–1, 87, 90, 121, 140
autochthony 223–6, 238–44, 255–6
autoeroticism 91–2, 120
avoidance 114–17, 127, 179 see also omission
Aya 71–3

Baer, K. E. von 46–7
Bakhtin, M. M. 262
Balder 40–1